FIRST OVER THERE

FIRST OVER THERE

MATTHEW J. DAVENPORT

THE ATTACK ON CANTIGNY, AMERICA'S FIRST BATTLE OF WORLD WAR I

THOMAS DUNNE BOOKS
ST. MARTIN'S PRESS 〰 NEW YORK

THOMAS DUNNE BOOKS.
An imprint of St. Martin's Press.

FIRST OVER THERE. Copyright © 2015 by Matthew J. Davenport. All rights reserved.
Printed in the United States of America. For information, address St. Martin's Press,
175 Fifth Avenue, New York, N.Y. 10010.

All maps copyright © Cameron Jones, except for original artillery map, p. 109, courtesy
of the National Archives, Robert R. McCormick Research Center.

www.thomasdunnebooks.com
www.stmartins.com

The Library of Congress Cataloging-in-Publication Data is available upon request.

ISBN 978-1-250-05644-3 (hardcover)
ISBN 978-1-4668-6027-8 (e-book)

St. Martin's Press books may be purchased for educational, business, or promotional use. For information on bulk
purchases, please contact the Macmillan Corporate and Premium Sales Department at 1-800-221-7945,
extension 5442, or write to specialmarkets@macmillan.com.

First Edition: May 2015

10 9 8 7 6 5 4 3 2 1

To the Doughboys, who rest eternally "Over There"

Contents

Author's Note

The war that began in Europe in 1914 was known at the time as the "Great War," the "World War," or simply "the war." Among Allied troops, German soldiers on the other side of the front were called "Jerry," "Huns," "Fritz," or—mostly by the French—"boche." British troops were nicknamed "Tommies," and French soldiers, many of whom wore thick mustaches or beards, were nicknamed "poilu" ("hairy one[s]").

When America entered the war, its forces deployed to France were collectively known as the American Expeditionary Forces, or "AEF." Its uniformed troops—including soldiers and Marines—were called "Yanks," "Sammies," and most commonly "doughboys." Doughboys in France were said to be "over there." Though the precise origin of "doughboy" remains uncertain, the nickname was employed extensively in rallying posters, songs, and literature. Among Allied nations, "doughboy" was used flatteringly, and "over there" became a patriotic rallying slogan. The reader will also notice that "men" appears often to collectively refer to troops or soldiers, reflecting the all-male Army of 1917–1918.

The source for every quotation in this book is cited in the Notes, except for successive quotes in the same paragraph from the same source. In the interest of clarity, spelling and punctuation errors have been corrected in the original quotations to avoid adding the intrusive "[*sic*]," and all spelling corrections are specifically listed in the Notes.

US Army Ranks and Unit Structure, 1917–1918

During World War I, US Army ranks and units were organized as follows:

SOLDIER
SQUAD: 9 to 17 soldiers, usually led by a corporal or sergeant
PLATOON: 4 to 5 squads, 60 soldiers, usually led by a lieutenant
COMPANY: 4 platoons, 250 soldiers, usually commanded by a captain
BATTALION: 4 companies, 1,030 soldiers, usually commanded by a major or lieutenant colonel
REGIMENT: 3 battalions, plus a machine-gun company, approximately 3,700 soldiers, commanded by a colonel
BRIGADE: 2 infantry regiments, plus a machine-gun battalion, approximately 8,400 soldiers, commanded by a brigadier general
DIVISION: 2 brigades, plus a field artillery brigade, an engineers regiment, a machine-gun battalion, and a signal corps company, totaling approximately 28,000 soldiers, commanded by a major general
CORPS: 2 to 6 divisions
ARMY: 3 to 5 corps

No one with a heart in his breast, no American, no lover of humanity, can stand in the presence of these graves without the most profound emotion. These men who lie here are men of a unique breed. Their like has not been seen since the far days of the crusades. Never before have men crossed the seas to a foreign land to fight for a cause which they did not pretend was peculiarly their own, but knew was the cause of humanity and of mankind.

—PRESIDENT WOODROW WILSON,
speaking on Memorial Day,
May 30, 1919, at the first of many US
cemeteries in France dedicated to America's
fallen in the World War.

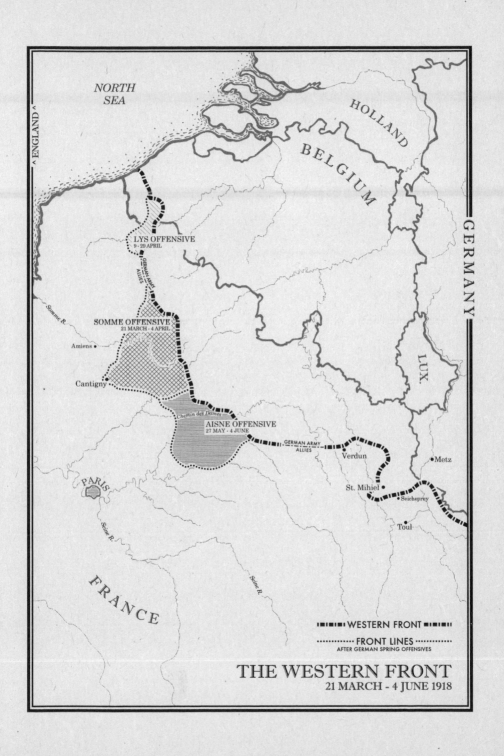

NORTH SEA

ENGLAND

HOLLAND

BELGIUM

GERMANY

LUX.

LYS OFFENSIVE
9 - 29 APRIL

GERMAN ARMY
ALLIES

Somme R.

SOMME OFFENSIVE
21 MARCH - 4 APRIL

Amiens

Cantigny

Chemin des Dames

AISNE OFFENSIVE
27 MAY - 4 JUNE

GERMAN ARMY
ALLIES

Verdun

Metz

St. Mihiel

Seicheprey

PARIS

Toul

Seine R.

Seine R.

FRANCE

◼▮◼ WESTERN FRONT ◼▮◼
·········· FRONT LINES ··········
AFTER GERMAN SPRING OFFENSIVES

THE WESTERN FRONT
21 MARCH - 4 JUNE 1918

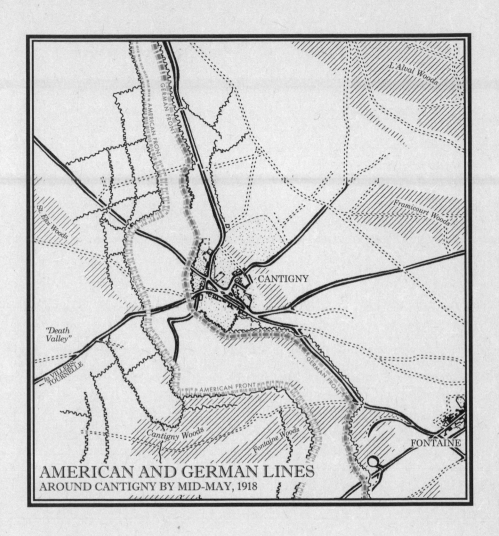

L'Alval Woods

Framicourt Woods

St. Éloi Woods

CANTIGNY

"Death Valley"

to VILLERS TOURNELLE

AMERICAN FRONT

GERMAN FRONT

Cantigny Woods

Fontaine Woods

FONTAINE

AMERICAN AND GERMAN LINES
AROUND CANTIGNY BY MID-MAY, 1918

FIRST OVER THERE

PRELUDE.

A Speech

The fourth winter of the World War lingered throughout northern France on Tuesday, April 16, 1918, reluctant to give way to spring. Mercury hovered in the low forties at midmorning under an overcast, almost colorless sky, shaping what one officer described as "a cold, bleak April day." The persistent cold was especially discomforting to the division commander, Major General Bullard, who suffered from neuritis that shot debilitating pain through his right arm and left him shivering with chills even on warm days.

Standing before the three-story chateau serving as his temporary Division Headquarters, Bullard eyed the long approach road for the distinctive four-star command car of his boss, the "Big Chief," Gen. John "Black Jack" Pershing. Ever the field commander, Bullard stood informally in dusty, spurred riding boots and khaki soft-sided cap, the two-star rank on his shoulders concealed by his bulky wolfskin coat. At his side, a handful of staff officers stood braced in anticipation, polished in Sam Browne belts under buttoned-up, sleek olive overcoats. General Pershing was on his way to address the division's officers, and Bullard, knowing the Big Chief's impatience for sickly commanders, concealed his physical agony and forced a display of complete health.

A West Pointer from Alabama, fifty-seven-year-old Robert Lee Bullard was slim and refined. He stood five feet ten inches tall, and his clear blue eyes peered warmly from a pale face of delicate features, with short, frosted wisps of brown hair poking out from under his cap. His reading glasses appeared instantly when there was a map to be studied or memorandum to be reviewed, underscoring an erudition that more closely resembled a professor than an Army commander. But a highly informal and energetic command style belied his patrician appearance, and he drove his troops hard.

Bullard commanded the 28,000 soldiers of the US Army's 1st Division, celebrated the previous summer as the first "doughboys" to land in France after America's entry into the war. By fall, they had earned the distinction of being the first in the trenches, the first to fire a shot at the Germans, and the first to suffer combat casualties. In the bitter cold of January, as other fresh divisions of the AEF (American Expeditionary Forces) were trickling into France for training, Bullard led his troops into the front lines of an active sector, gaining for them indispensable experience under fire and fixing a fighting institutional tone.

Despite the neuritis that stung his shoulder and arm and hampered him with insufferable cold spells, Bullard remained an unbroken presence in the field by his men through the stretch of winter conditions so harsh many called it the "Valley Forge of the War." In the privacy of his headquarters, staff officers occasionally spotted him wrapped in blankets in front of a roaring fire, but before his soldiers he forced a stoic façade betrayed only by a strained expression and a clench-fisted right arm slung in the grip of his left hand. Bullard believed the best officer was "ready to do and to bear all that his men do and bear," and in living this—and through his folksy, courteous leadership style—he quickly earned the affection of his men.

Three weeks earlier, a massive German offensive forced Allied lines back forty miles, the most alarming movement yet on a Western Front marked by three and a half years of strategic rigor mortis. In the face of this great crisis, General Pershing offered French General Ferdinand Foch—the Supreme Allied Commander—"all that we have." Of the five American divisions in France, Pershing ordered his favored 1st—which he openly regarded as the brightest star in the AEF's expanding constellation—to the front to help stem the German tide. Thirteen months after America entered the war and ten months after landing in France, Bullard's troops were finally headed into battle.

That morning, General Bullard and his staff awoke in their stately chateau situated on the edge of the town of Chaumont-en-Vexin serving as the division's temporary headquarters on the way to the front lines. On a landscape still unreached by the fighting, green pastures were crossed by age-old stone walls, hedgerows, and patches of forest. Inside the chateau was a scene common in wartime France—elegant furniture and polished hardwoods invaded by clacking typewriters, scaled wall maps, and buzzing field phones.

General Pershing was scheduled to arrive at 10:30 a.m. to "speak a few words of confidence and encouragement" to all the officers of the division before they led their men off the next day for the three-day journey to the front and into the war. Out back in the chateau's grass courtyard, an audience of more than 900 officers stood gathered. They huddled in familiar groups—frosty-haired field commanders, newly minted lieutenants, disheveled artillery battery commanders, and polished staff officers. With disparate sections and smaller subunits typically spread over miles of countryside in large sectors, rarely before had these leaders all assembled together, and never without the men under their charge or their ever-present French Army advisors. This gathering was a singular event, and theirs was a peerless group. As the collective leadership of America's first fighting force to enter battle against the German Army, these officers personified the tip of the spear—the first face of US military power on a global stage.

Out in front of the chateau, with the crunch of tires on gravel, two cars pulled up, led by General Pershing's distinctive olive-green Locomobile limousine with its American flag and four-star placards bordering the front windshield. Two staff officers emerged from the second car, and from Pershing's car stepped the AEF supply officer, Col. Charles Dawes, along with the Big Chief himself.

Poised and handsome with broad shoulders and chiseled features, John J. Pershing was the ideal physical expression of America's military presence in Europe. At fifty-seven years old, he was the picture of health and self-possession. His doctors said he had "the heart and arteries of a man of thirty-five and the eye lens crystal of a boy of eighteen." He stood five feet nine inches tall, but his ramrod-straight posture and commanding bearing often left those in his presence with the impression he was six feet tall or taller. A French magazine described him as "slender as a sub-lieutenant," and a correspondent effused that he was "tall, powerful of frame, without an ounce of fat anywhere on his body, and hard as bronze." He was, as the doughboy and future historian S.L.A. Marshall would later write, "tailor-made for monuments."

General Pershing walked up to the 1st Division headquarters wearing polished knee-high leather boots; a long, sleek, uniform dress coat; leather gloves; and a rigid peaked cap pulled squarely forward so the brim dipped almost to cover his eyes. General Bullard, in stark contrast, in his tilted side cap and wolfskin coat (a non-regulation gift from his men) must have rankled his fastidious and impeccably uniformed boss. After a flurry of salutes, Bullard ushered Pershing and his retinue up the limestone steps and through the chateau toward the courtyard.

Although both were general officers with careers that began just one year apart at West Point, their differences could hardly have been more pronounced—a contrast that began as far back as their childhood. A four-year-old John Pershing had seen Confederates overrun his Missouri town, where his father was a home-guard officer who used his general store to supply Union soldiers. Robert Bullard's earliest military inspiration was seeing his brother-in-law return to his Alabama home from the same war in Confederate grays, and after young Robert's home county was renamed Lee County for the revered general, he personally asked if he could be baptized "Robert Lee" instead of his own given name, "William Robert." In a manner that marked their regional differences, Pershing spoke with a calm voice and discernible Midwestern accent, while Bullard—who complained he "couldn't pronounce the 'g' on the end of a word if his life depended on it"—spoke in a high pitch with a deep Southern twang.

Lacking connections that would have afforded him a position commanding one of the few Regular Army units that fought in the Spanish-American War and the Philippines, Bullard had spent much of his career effectively forming and holding together volunteer regiments of citizen soldiers, experience that instilled in him a personal, informal leadership style. He had little patience for highfalutin military ceremony and no regard for formality, being more concerned with building good fighters than good marchers. His biographer notes that the men he led in combat in the Philippines "respected [his] poise, aggressiveness, and concern for their welfare . . . and his disregard for military ceremony"—sentiments that would be echoed by men under his command in the World War.

For his part, Pershing lived in spotless living quarters and was never seen publicly with a thread out of place. Obsessive over proper military appearance, regimented uniformity had gained ascendancy in him over all other virtues. He had an abiding dislike for disorder, insisted on perfection, and was, in the atmosphere of Army life, official and distant. Pershing was fond of formal ceremony and held himself publicly aloof from his men at almost all times. Bullard considered him "too impersonal" and "too given over to pure business and duty," traits that "inspired confidence but not affection."

It was only in private moments that Pershing's warmer, sensitive side, buried beneath many layers of reserve, revealed itself. "He spoke of the soldiers as a father speaks of his sons," one war correspondent noted. But to most officers who served with him and to the millions who served under him, Pershing's personality was as impenetrable as any one of the bronze or stone monuments that would materialize in his likeness in the years to come.

For all their professional and personal differences, both generals invested their fullest measure of effort into their respective roles in America's part in the war, and their commitment to the Allied cause was total. Most significantly, John Pershing had unflagging confidence in Robert Bullard. He had personally handpicked Bullard as the division commander five months earlier, and his later selection of the 1st Division to enter battle against the Germans before all others was the highest proof of his faith. Pershing believed in the men and he believed in Bullard, and imparting his confidence was the purpose of his visit.

The officers assembled behind the headquarters were listening to some preparatory remarks from the division operations officer—a tall, lanky, thirty-seven-year-old lieutenant colonel from Pennsylvania named George C. Marshall Jr. Destined to become the Army's senior five-star general in World War II, Marshall was one of many young 1st Division officers filling the courtyard who embodied the very future of American military leadership. Twenty-nine-year-old Capt. Clarence Huebner, a company commander from Kansas, would go on to lead the 1st Division ashore at Omaha Beach on D-Day as a major general in the next world war. Thirty-year-old Maj. Theodore Roosevelt Jr., a battalion commander and son of the former president, would also lead men on D-Day, where he would earn the Medal of Honor as the first general officer ashore at Utah Beach. And Lt. John Church, a twenty-five-year-old platoon leader who one year earlier had quit his classes at NYU to volunteer, would cross the Rhine as a brigadier general in the next war, and would lead the 24th Infantry Division in brave fighting as a major general in the Korean War.

At perhaps no other moment in American military history was the future so brightly on display. In the present war and wars to follow, the 1st Division officers present would produce seven division commanders, four corps commanders, and three Army chiefs of staff. It was as if the entire future of the US Army was assembled in the small French courtyard, and General Pershing was coming not only to send them off to their first battle, but into a future of war and challenges that lay far beyond his own horizon-filling vision. The leaders there, Pershing would later write, "formed a rare group. These splendid looking men, hardened by the strenuous work of the fall and by two months in winter trenches, fairly radiated the spirit of courage and gave promise that America's efforts would prove her sons the equals of their forefathers."

The officers were called to attention when General Pershing stepped out the back of the chateau and into the courtyard. All except the most senior officers had only ever seen the man in passing, typically while they were braced at attention in salute. One lieutenant noted that, prior to this, his only "personal connection with the general" had been "reveille at 3 a.m. on a December morn, a long march, ten miles or more, on a very cold day over roads slippery with ice; a long, shivering wait in the streets . . . presenting arms while the general's party passed" followed by "another long march back to the billets." At the shouted command of "At ease," they formed a large semicircle around their Big Chief a dozen deep, and strained to see him in this unusually intimate setting.

For all his public appearances and ceremonial duties as the head of American forces in Europe, Pershing was averse to giving speeches. The thought of giving any kind of formal talk, he once remarked, "makes me shiver." The previous summer, at the July 4 parade in Paris honoring the newly arrived Americans, Pershing had designated a staff colonel to speak in his stead, whose words at the occasion—"Lafayette, we are here"—would be long ascribed to Pershing. When a speech was necessary, he preferred speaking extemporaneously, and in that manner he "found no difficulty." Although he doubtless pondered his remarks on the ninety-minute car ride from his headquarters, he would later say his words to the officers that morning were "spoken under the inspiration of the moment."

"I did not want you to enter into real participation in this war without my having said a word to you as a body," Pershing began, pointing with his gloved hand. "I believe you are well prepared to take your place along with the seasoned troops of our Allies." Training was complete, he explained, but "war itself is the real school where the art of war is learned," and the fighting principles they had been taught would soon be applied "in the actual experience of war." Imploring the young leaders not to strain to recall text from training manuals while in battle, he imparted plainly: "You will be called upon to meet conditions that have never been presented to you before."

It was on the soldiers under their command, "upon their stamina, upon their character and upon their will to win," that the officers were to rely.

Pershing beseeched them to keep their men's interests foremost, to keep their morale "at the highest pitch," to "keep in close touch with them" and be an example for them "in everything that personifies the true soldier, in dress, in military bearing, in general conduct, and especially an example on the battlefield." Most important, he urged them to prepare their soldiers mentally to bear thoughts of their own mortality, "that when the occasion demands it they must make the supreme sacrifice."

Pershing used no flowery diction and employed no powerful metaphors, but through the pin-drop silence of the frosty air, his words carried an affirmation of high purpose. One officer said it was just "a few simple words" to show the Big Chief's "confidence in them and what they would do to uphold the traditions of their country." Brig. Gen. Charles Summerall, the division artillery commander, noted Pershing's "personality and his lofty sentiments were an inspiration." One of the brigade commanders, Brig. Gen. John Hines, was reminded of a football coach getting his team up for a game, and the official Division History would later engrave it as "Pershing's Farewell to the First."

Behind Pershing stood Bullard, cradling his stiff right arm in his left hand and wearing what one officer described as a "solemn, determined look." Of the speech, Bullard observed "it was not oratory," describing it as "earnest but not . . . dramatic," which his boss delivered "in his terse, businesslike way." Pershing's delivery lacked charismatic sparkle, and he halted every few words filling frequent pauses with "eh, eh, eh." Still, his rough and uneven delivery combined with his reassuring bearing to reach the perfect pitch. It was "[h]is manner and his expression, more than his speech," George Marshall observed, that "fired the officers of the 1st division with the determination to overcome the enemy wherever he was encountered." Pershing's chief of staff, Col. James Harbord, agreed, telling his diary later that night that the Big Chief's "very stirring talk" was "made in that simple, direct manner which is supposed to appeal to the American soldier, and in which our General quite excels."

One company commander noted General Pershing's "earnestness impressed all hearers," but it was the specter of battle that lingered sharply in most ears, as if his words served as final confirmation of what the coming days and weeks held. "All who heard" Pershing's remarks, the same captain estimated, "were convinced that he contemplated an offensive use of the division, and that soon." Another young officer, Capt. Edward Johnston, spotted a sobering effect of the message on the gathered men. There was, he perceived, "a certain lack of Napoleonic enthusiasm on the part" of the officers, who seemed "rather serious." Still he sensed no "atmosphere of gloom" but "a certain air of anticipatory interest." "And why not? The Great Battle was bound to be interesting."

"I did not come here to make a speech," Pershing continued. "I am not given to speech-making, so only a word more and I shall close." He turned to the herculean task ahead, likening it to a noble crusade: "You are about to enter this great battle of the greatest war in history," and striking a distinct note of national pride, he reminded them, "in that battle you will represent the mightiest nation engaged." That thought alone, he nudged them, "must be to every serious man a very appealing thought, and one that should call forth the best and the noblest that is in you."

Anchoring his statements firmly in the allure of world history, Pershing declared, "Centuries of military and civil history are now looking toward this first contingent of the American Army as it enters this great battle." Reminding them of the "young and aggressive nation" they represented, he narrowed his appeal to their national past. "We come from a nation that for one hundred and fifty years has stood before the world as the champion of the sacred principles of human liberty." It was the United States, now personified in these officers and the men they led, that had returned "to Europe, the home of our ancestors, to help defend those same principles upon European soil."

In a finality crafted to arouse dormant enthusiasm, Pershing asked, "Could there be a more stimulating sentiment as you go from here to your commands, and from there to the battlefield?" He concluded:

> Our people today are hanging expectant upon your deeds. The future is hanging upon your action in this conflict. You are going forward, and your conduct will be an example for succeeding units of our army. I hope the standard you set will be high—I know it will be high. You are taking with you the highest hopes of the President and all of our people at home. I assure you, in their names and in my own, of our strong beliefs in your success and of our confidence in our hearts that you are going to make a record of which your country will be proud.

With that, his short speech came to an end and he stepped back. General Bullard stepped forward and "said a few words" in closing. "There was no effort on the part of either to be dramatic," a colonel later recalled; "the scene and occasion required no emphasis."

Most, but not all, who witnessed the scene were impressed. George Marshall noted that Pershing's remarks "made a profound impression on all those present." But Maj. Robert McCormick, the coeditor and publisher of the *Chicago Tribune* who was presently answering the call of national service as an artillery officer, dryly described it as "a weak speech saying we were to go in line." And as the crowd dispersed, Lt. Lansing McVickar of Massachusetts asked his friend, Lt. Earl Bonham of Indiana, "[W]hat did you think of the General's speech?" Bonham quipped that he "shed a few tears, but did you [notice] the boots?"

For those who found omens in such an occasion, the speech filled them with a foreboding of the prospect of war, as well as their own mortality. "We began to think when our offensive training schedule was published and actually knew that the end of our lives had come when General Pershing bade us all farewell," noted a lieutenant in the engineers. Another later remembered walking away from the speech "with a rather creepy feeling because I didn't fancy at all getting killed."

But for most of these young leaders, General Pershing's speech was a stirring summons, and it gave immortal expression to the durable virtue of valor in the cause of country. His words not only ignited the emotions of many present, but left a lasting impression on all. Years later, one lieutenant in attendance would recall, "A picture that vividly comes to mind whenever I think of the war is . . . when General Pershing made what I have always considered his valedictory address to the First Division." General Summerall would later describe the scene as "one of the outstanding incidents in the life of the command."

Pershing's confident but muted delivery anticipated the historic gravity that hindsight would later assign the moment. His supply officer (and future vice president), Col. Charles Dawes, described the occasion as both "solemn" and "historical," marking "the real entry of our nation into actual battle." The scene became legendary among division officers not for any feat of oratory but for Pershing's presence, and mostly for his final confirmation that they were to be sent into battle in a cause worthy of their "supreme sacrifice."

The next morning these officers would organize their men and begin a three-day trip to the front lines. Their destination was a sector facing an enemy entrenched in the small farming hamlet of Cantigny. Captured by the Germans two weeks before, Cantigny sat on a hilltop jutting into and overlooking the Allied lines, representing the westernmost tip of the recent German thrust. The division's task would be to push the Germans back and recapture the village—a feat that would not only wrest from the Germans a dominating observation point but would also loudly announce America's presence in the fighting line. Along the whole of the 468-mile-long Western Front, there was perhaps no better place for such a statement than Cantigny.

Six weeks to the day after Pershing's courtyard speech, at dawn on Tuesday, May 28, 1918—the 1,394th day of the war—the United States finally entered the fight as American riflemen climbed "over the top" of their trench parapets and crossed no-man's-land into history. It is no spoiler to reveal here that they were successful, and their long path to victory is the story you are about to read. It is my attempt to tell how a few thousand young soldiers found themselves thrust abruptly into manhood in a bloody struggle for survival within the ghostly remains of a small French village.

Doughboys who fought to capture Cantigny were met with a violence never before experienced by uniformed fighters of the United States. In the two-and-a-half day fight, men were shredded by machine-gun fire, blown to unrecognizable bits by mortar blasts, and knocked into instant death by the concussive detonations of high-explosive shells. Over one-fourth were wounded and nearly one-tenth killed in action, marking a higher casualty rate than that suffered by the Continentals at Saratoga, either side at Antietam, or even the Allies on D-Day.

For all the satisfaction that victory brought, Cantigny exposed the sad reality that the newly arrived Americans were not exempt from the inescapable butchery of the Western Front. Though the battle was a small operation—just over 4,000 Americans fighting a smaller number of Germans—it served as a harsh awakening for the AEF high command: a forced realization that despite noble efforts to fight a new and different way from its allies, the United States could not help but surrender itself to the grim embrace of total war. Beginning with the first reports of killed and injured to flow from the dirt of the village to field commanders' muster rolls to AEF casualty totals cabled across the Atlantic on May 29, each day for the next five and a half months, newspapers back in the States published heartbreaking casualty lists, which by fall would reach a daily scale unseen in American history, before or since.

After the Armistice, 116,516 envelopes were mailed from the War Department, each addressed to the closest surviving relative of an American killed in action during the war. Enclosed was Graves Registration Service Form #120, which gave a widow or father or mother or sibling the one-time option, at government expense, of shipping the remains of their loved one home to the cemetery of their choice—to include Arlington—or to be buried at one of the newly constructed US National Cemeteries scattered throughout France and Belgium.

The bodies of men killed at Cantigny whose families did not request them shipped home were buried in the Somme American Cemetery and Memorial in Bony, France. Like the battle in which they fell, the cemetery is small—actually the smallest of the five military cemeteries in France dedicated exclusively for the burial of Americans killed in the First World War. Residing on fourteen acres of beautiful and peaceful rolling northern French countryside forty-eight miles from the battlefield, the Somme American Cemetery holds the graves of 1,844 of our military dead. Names, units, and dates of death are carved into the faceless, white marble headstones, Latin crosses or Stars of David frozen in eternal rows of military formation. Inside the small stone chapel at the southeast end of the cemetery are the tablets of the missing. Below an inscription honoring the fallen "who sleep in unknown graves" are carved the names of those whose remains were never found. There, 333 names are arranged alphabetically, followed by rank, unit, date of death, and home state. Individual soldiers are memorialized in orderly etched rows, lit by subdued sunlight through a cross-shaped crystal window.

Scanning the heartbreaking list for "May 28, 1918" and the two days following, visitors can see that the battle of Cantigny accounts for one-quarter of the chapel's carved names, each signifying someone last seen fighting in the dirt and among the ruins of the village. Outside, located mostly in Plots C and D, more than 100 headstones memorialize men whose lives ended during the battle. Together with those whose remains were shipped back across the Atlantic to rest nearer their family, more than 300 doughboys were killed in the two-and-a-half-day fight for the village.

But as with every battle before and since, the struggle for Cantigny did not end at the cemetery, and it was on the battlefield around the village, where so many breathed their last, that the future of the war was written. Marking the first time that an American unit would capture enemy territory, the 1st Division's improbable victory in what Pershing called "this great battle" was the first American dent in the impregnable armor of the Western Front. Making far more than a single statement, Cantigny was the doughboys' baptism by fire, and for those who survived, it became the crucible by which they would measure all subsequent experience, in large-scale fighting at Soissons and the grand Meuse-Argonne offensive.

Historically, the fight for Cantigny was the first American clash with the German Army, a conflict between two world powers that would see many bloodier fights over the next twenty-seven years. Tactically, the operation previewed modern military methods, marking the first time American soldiers fought with the intricate support of artillery, machine guns, flamethrowers, grenades, gas, tanks, and airplanes, signifying the establishment of combined arms and the birth of our modern Army. Thus, May 28, 1918 was the US military's coming-of-age—the day it crossed a historical no-man's-land that separated contemporary fighting methods from the muskets and cannon of the nineteenth century.

The 1st Division's casualties in the battle tolled more than 1,600 men. Thinking as one does in the context of the First World War as a whole, this number is small, but the scale of turning points is not always grand. Not always is a vital battle of war marked by the magnitude of Operation Overlord on D-Day, the desperate struggle of the Marines on Iwo Jima, or the romantic attachments of historians to the pivotal battle of Gettysburg. Often the tide of events reaches a peak on the corner of a small foreign field with relatively few witnesses.

Cantigny was such a moment, reminding us that in history's malleable narrative, scale is no measure of significance. The decision to attack the Germans first at this small village would prove momentous, and the surge stirred by the battle's timing and outcome would not only elevate the AEF's role on the Western Front and in the World War, but would prove America's first small step toward a colossal Allied victory.

The first reports of American victory at Cantigny made their way into print by the second morning of the battle, May 29, 1918, even as General Bullard's soldiers hung on tenuously to their positions in a struggle against death under a rain of enemy steel. Triumphant headlines monopolized the front pages of newspapers: "Americans Take Town Alone," "Sammies Shout 'We're on Our Way to Berlin' As They Take Village," and "Yankees Yell

As They Take Cantigny," all bought up by a public thirsty for good news from "over there." It had been thirteen long months since the citizenry had been stirred by President Wilson's eloquent call to arms—"The world must be made safe for democracy"—and since then, communities had seen their high school students and local businessmen flock to the colors in growing numbers. Hometown papers carried daily articles about local boys in training, and published letters home in devoted sections, "News from the Front," or "Letters from the Trenches."

So when morning headlines carried bulletins of America's first victory against the Germans—against "Kaiser Bill" and his dreaded "Huns"—a national pride was ignited that would endure unmatched by any subsequent news until war's end. In the years after the Armistice, each May 28th would see editorials celebrating the battle, often including interviews with local veterans of the storied attack, occasionally enlarging the deeds of many into exaggerated legend. John Pershing and Robert Bullard, even in retirement, would each preside over "Cantigny Day" ceremonies, which often coincided with Memorial Day.

Through the 1920s and '30s, "Cantigny" remained a symbol of American sacrifice and triumph, a uniting emblem that finally exorcised the dividing demons of the Civil War in a way the Spanish-American War never could. But then came Pearl Harbor. And D-Day. And the Bulge. And in the wake of these epochal events, the 1st Division's attack at Cantigny lapsed into footnotes, its story left to slumber for a century.

This book is my effort to pull America's first fight of the Great War out of the dark shadows of a forgotten past. It is an attempt to memorialize the battle by revisiting a few of war's irreducible truths—that victories in combat are the collective actions of otherwise ordinary citizens, that statistics cannot tell sacrifice's story, and in war, no matter how many millions are killed, soldiers die as they lived, one by one by one. The last Cantigny veteran died in the late 1990s, and with the passing of Frank Buckles in early 2011, the living narrative of the doughboy on the Western Front was forever sealed. Any attempt to breathe life into names chiseled in the faceless marble crosses at the Somme American Cemetery or to pierce the anonymity of featureless lists on the tablets of the missing entombed in the cemetery's chapel can never be complete. Soldiers' private writings, official reports, and memoirs are now all we have, but they add rich color to fading, sepia-toned photographs. They reveal the transformation of farmhands from Kansas and factory workers from Michigan into soldiers. They shed light on the difficult transition of a handful of professional Army officers—veterans of quieter times—into commanders of the first American fighting force on a world stage. And they chronicle the front-line education under machine-gun and artillery fire that turned college students and young professionals into leaders of men.

The diaries and letters of Cantigny veterans contain expressions of dread or nerves otherwise hidden beneath layers of youthful bravado. They uncloak the men who fought to the high ground of the village, revealing an inner spectrum of adrenaline, strength, fear, and sadness. Many were mere boys who had sprinted to enlist, propelled by images of battlefield glory. But the blood and death that soon besieged them forced a realization that war was no adventure—it was dark, confusing, brutal, and harrowing. Those who survived would go on to work as accountants, railroad engineers, and insurance salesmen; they would be elected mayor and US senator; and a few would continue military service as generals in World War II and Korea. Though they helped bend the course of a world war, they allowed neither the battle nor the war to define them, and most only spoke of it—if at all—when corresponding with old Army friends who had shared their experience, or when pressed by family members or an occasional print reporter.

This book chronicles that small part of their life's journey—the passage of the men of the 1st Division in World War I, from enlistment to training to France to the trenches to what General Pershing envisioned on that frosty April morning in a small French courtyard: a "great battle of the greatest war in history." It is the story of the first "over there."

CHAPTER 1

Let 'em Come

Again that morning the sustained din of far-off artillery filled the expected hour of sunrise as darkness lifted from the American trenches. Light fog blanketed no-man's-land—three hundred boundless yards of ripening beet plants, wheat stubble, and butchery ascending toward the German lines. Beyond the tangle of barbed wire at the unreachable crest of the hilltop, dark rooftop silhouettes of the village of Cantigny materialized against the morning's leaden sky, framed by a horizon of piney woodlands in the distance.

Once a serene farming hamlet graced with orchards and idyllic red-roofed homes, Cantigny was now a barren maze of hollowed ruins staring back at the American lines across the forbidden plateau. Its smooth walls and rooftops had been whittled to jagged profiles by weeks of artillery fire, and though the village seemed vacant and lifeless, its stone cellars and outlying trenches were stiff with Germans.

By this, the final week of May 1918, tranquil moments on the front lines had grown rare, but for once, above the low rumble of remote shelling, no crashing of nearby artillery or chatter of machine-gun fire attended the emerging dawn. The temperature climbed out of the low fifties, but down in their trench where the bite of the night air lingered, the doughboys lay curled on the cold dirt floor or propped against the hard chalk walls, stealing what sleep they could before daybreak. They had arrived at the front lines only three hours earlier, after a long march lugging their weapons, supplies, and ammunition through crushing shellfire, and what little rest they were able to grab was surely insufficient to equip them for a new day staring down the German lines extending out the north side of the village. As the light fog and overcast sky battled the first glimmers of daylight, the sleeping figures in the trench line dressed in khaki, brown boots, wrapped leggings, and stiff, high-necked collars were lit faintly in colorless relief.

These fifty men formed 3rd Platoon, Company E, 28th Infantry Regiment

15

of the US Army's 1st Division, and together they held a short 150-yard stretch of the 468-mile-long Western Front—a ragged line of carnage clawed out by forty-five months of the bloodiest fighting in human history. The scene repeated itself in trenches snaking north to the English Channel and south to the Swiss border in alternating shades of French blue, Belgian navy, and British tan. The sight of American khaki in the front lines was a recent development, and though many of these doughboys had just endured their first French winter and some had been in-country nearly a year, they were still considered the new guys—the untested "Yanks."

For twenty-five-year-old platoon sergeant Ray Milner of Titusville, Pennsylvania, who stood six feet two inches tall, keeping his steel soup-bowl helmet down below the four-and-a-half-foot top of the trench parapet took strained effort. Bent at the waist, he worked his way up and down the line quietly rustling the men, one by one, awake for their morning stand-to. With six years of Army service, Milner was a seasoned veteran when measured against the inexperienced faces he was waking up. Some were just boys, like Pvt. Homer Blevins of Fresno, California, who at seventeen was the youngest in the platoon. Most had volunteered for service in the months following America's entry into the World War the year before, and many others had been drafted, trained, and added to the unit in the past few weeks—fresh replacements for those lost to snipers, shelling, mustard gas, or the influenza of a harsh winter that had dragged on well into spring.

It was Monday, May 27, 1918, a detail almost universally unnoticed by soldiers who had long before shed their previous life's mental dividers of workweeks and weekends. Time passed in clusters of days marked only by greater or lesser mortal danger—ten days of cheating death in the trenches, ten days "rest" billeted in drafty barns and cottages of some anonymous French village, then ten days in "reserve" up closer to the front, where the perils of mustard gas and aerial bombardments were often worse than at the front lines. Then over again the sequence repeated, and for how long nobody knew.

Three days earlier, this monotonous cycle was finally broken as these soldiers were ordered from the front lines and trucked twelve miles away to a training area for "battle rehearsal." As General Pershing promised six weeks before in his sendoff speech to the division officers, the 1st Division had been chosen out of the five then in France to enter that "great battle of the greatest war in history." Rumors had since circulated among the men about when the "great battle" would finally come, and where, and which unit would get the coveted assignment.

Back at the rehearsal area, these men had learned it was their regiment—of the division's four—ordered to retake the prize of Cantigny from the German Army. Field Order No. 18, which had descended from the typewriter of a young lieutenant colonel on the division staff, George C. Marshall, laid out the attack operation in great detail, and its thirty-nine pages of supply lists, mission assignments, and artillery barrage schedules formed the script for history. Thirteen months after President Wilson had called them to service in "the most terrible and disastrous of all wars," and ten months after landing in France to join the Allied cause, the Americans—the "Yanks," "Sammies," or "doughboys"—were finally entering the fight, and the soldiers of Company E's 3rd Platoon would be in the first attack wave going "over the top."

The first day of battle, "J-Day" was set for Tuesday, May 28, and with two and a half days of battle-plan rehearsal complete, most of the regiment would be spending May 27, "J minus 1," relaxing back at the training area before moving up to the front lines after dark.* But for the men of Company E there would be no rest. The four companies of their battalion had been ordered again to the front the previous night, May 26, two nights before the attack and a full day earlier than the rest of the regiment. Having taken over the front-line trenches well after midnight, some being rustled awake by Sergeant Milner had managed to squeeze in two or three hours of sleep, but many had found no rest, and fatigued by the night's long march they were running on fumes. As dawn struggled to break, their collective hope was for a quiet twenty-four hours on the front lines before the shrill whistles blew the next morning at Zero Hour, sending them over the top and into the maelstrom of war.

Up and down its length the trench began stirring with hushed activity as soldiers sat up, buckled on their canvas web belts, hung their gas masks over their chests, and strapped on their cold steel helmets amid stretching yawns and gulps of cold coffee. Sidestepping slowly through them, moving from soldier to soldier, his stout frame buckled tight in his officer's Sam Browne belt with holstered Colt .45 pistol, was their platoon leader, Lt. Charles Avery.

---

* The military use of "D-Day" to designate the start of a combat operation did not begin until August 1918, three months later.

Just fourteen months earlier, Avery was a field reporter for the *Kansas City Star*. The United States entered the war the day before his twenty-fourth birthday, and though married with a three-year-old son, he quit his newspaper job, volunteered for Army service, and was admitted to officer school. After three months training at Fort Sheridan, Illinois, he received his commission, said good-bye to his family, shipped off to France, and was placed in charge of 3rd Platoon by March. In just his second month as platoon leader, Avery displayed an effective leadership that seemed instinctive, but it was his light, personal touch that earned the swift respect of his men. A fellow Company E officer portrayed Avery as "the fun maker" who "bubbled over with fun and scintillating wit."

A few minutes past 5:00 a.m., as Lieutenant Avery and Sergeant Milner ensured the last of their men were awake, the calm hanging over no-man's-land was broken by the familiar low rumble of German artillery fire. The soldiers braced at the whistles of incoming salvos, and the distant drumfire continued as the first shots hit halfway across the plateau in crashing thuds of smoke and flame. More shells followed, humming a medley of ominous tunes as enemy gunners dialed in the American lines, marching the footfall of detonations closer to Avery's hunkered doughboys.

The blasts reached the trench in eruptions of fire and dry earth. Packed spoil of the parapet collapsed and earthen walls caved in as sheets of white flame and hot shrapnel filled the air. Lieutenant Avery scampered up and down the line checking on his soldiers, who were curled up, white-knuckled, hugging the dirt. "No such thing as a dugout in the sector, so we lay like lizards in the bottom of the trenches," one man wrote home. "The awful explosions would come, the ground would rock, then dirt would fall in on us." The onslaught was relentless, pounding minute after unending minute for an eternal hour, rupturing eardrums and stretching some men to their psychological breaking point. As their captain would later say of enduring such bombardments, "nothing can be done but wait, and wait, and wait."

Steel shards and flames sliced through the cramped space, and yells and screams punctuated the thunder of shelling. The undaunted Sgt. Ray Milner, still walking up and down the line and loudly encouraging his men, was the first to fall. In a blinding flash, his standing figure was "wrapped in smoke and fire," as Lieutenant Avery would later relay; "when the scattered mist of high-explosive fog and the uprush of earth had cleared away, the sergeant lay dead in two pieces, his trunk severed below the shoulders."

The entire platoon was trapped in the deadly vortex, and between exploding flashes men dropped wounded and dead. Eighteen-year-old Pvt. Charles "Ollie" Shepard fell on the dirt trench floor, "killed instantly by piece of shell in back" a watching comrade would later recount. Likely hit again and buried in the shelling that continued, young Ollie's body was never seen again. Another blast got the platoon's youngest, Pvt. Homer Blevins, killed "instantly" when "a shell exploded alongside" him, a nearby private reported.

Surrendering to the grim lottery of shellfire, twenty-three-year-old Cpl. Chester Melton and twenty-five-year-old Pvt. Fred Turner both shriveled into fetal bundles on the trench floor. A shell hit near Private Turner, and when the smoke cleared he lay motionless in the dirt, seemingly untouched. A fellow private, Franklin Berry, found Turner lifeless, with glazed eyes fixed in a death stare. "It was more concussion than wounds that killed Turner," Berry estimated, because "there were only a couple of scratches on him but he was as limber as a rag just shook to death from concussion." Corporal Melton, in sad contrast, had simply disappeared. None of his comrades remembered seeing the blast that killed him, and no trace of him was ever found, leaving his carved name on the Somme American Cemetery's tablets of the missing as the sole monument to his memory.

Three hundred yards behind them, in the captain's small command bunker, the company's second-in-command, Lt. Irving Wood, was worried and restless. He had been listening intently to the sounds of the bombardment, but repeated checks with the guard outside revealed no runners or messages from the front lines. The commander, Capt. Edward Johnston, was asleep, and as the roar of shelling hit full crescendo, Wood decided to wake him.

"Captain, I don't want to wake you up about a mere bombardment, but this has been getting steadily louder, and I don't like it." Lieutenant Wood was leaned over, shaking his captain's shoulder. The urgency in his voice was obvious as the packed walls of the earthen bunker telegraphed the distant barking of artillery blasts. Captain Johnston, only an hour into sleep and still in uniform, sat up on his canvas cot and adjusted his eyes. A faint hint of dawn leaked in through the curtain hung over the entrance invading the frosty dark of the dugout just enough to reveal a "somewhat concerned" expression on his number two's face.

"Lieutenant Desmond here," Wood continued, gesturing to a soldier stepping in, "says that this is heavier than usual." It was Lt. Thomas Desmond, or "Desperate" Desmond as his own men called him, though to these officers he was a face from another unit, the 18th Infantry, which Johnston's company had relieved in the front lines just hours before. Desmond and his men had held the trenches for the past three nights while Company E had been rehearsing for the next day's battle. Assigned to stay behind as a "liaison officer" to help acquaint the newly arrived platoons with newly dug trenches, fields of fire, and enemy activity, Desmond agreed that Wood's worry was well placed but added, "[I]t's hard to tell; the old place has been picking up lately, and they've doused us two or three times a night."

Captain Johnston was uneasy being this far from his men. His small command bunker had been hastily constructed by the French Moroccan unit that first defended this sector the month before. Dug into the face of the slope that descended away from the front, it placed Johnston three hundred yards behind the trenches. On arrival two hours earlier, he thought it "too far from the platoons." Now the distance forced a dilemma: remain to gather delayed information about the bombardment and keep command intact, or walk up to the front and expose himself to the shelling. Johnston brooded as he and the two lieutenants "stood still in the hush appropriate to such moments," he would later record, as "they listened to the clatter from without." Only three months into his command of the 250 soldiers of Company E, he was becoming quickly acquainted with such lonely decisions.

At just twenty-one years old, Edward Scott Johnston was the youngest company commander in the division. One of seven siblings from Bloomington, Indiana, he had enlisted in the Army National Guard two years before, while a student at Indiana University. His unit was activated for service on the Mexican border, and he volunteered for officer training, securing his commission in the Regular Army the same year. When America entered the World War the following spring, young Lieutenant Johnston's service, although brief, earned him promotion and he shipped off to France with the 1st Division.

Johnston had walked the gangplanks onto French soil with the first American soldiers in the first convoy to arrive the previous June. Since then, he had endured with his men each arduous slice that made up the hell of the Western Front. He had attended the solemn funeral of the first three young Americans killed in action the previous fall. He had survived nerve-shattering bombardments in two previous sectors and buried the grisly remains of young soldiers blown to pieces. He had endured the "hard winter" when "[s]ocks had to do duty as gloves" and "[s]hoes had to be held together with rags and string." He had led intelligence patrols out into no-man's-land, low-crawling on his belly, armed only with a pistol and hand grenades, where the faintest sound could trigger a German flare, then machine-gun fire, then death as certain as in a shooting gallery. He had seen gas shells fall from the sky and hiss out mustard clouds, causing men caught without masks to puke pools of blood as they gasped helplessly for air, and their skin boiled up into melting blisters. And just three weeks prior, he had witnessed his own battalion commander—his beloved major whom he called "a warm and living symbol of what we all were at our best"—crushed to death when a German high-explosive shell hit his headquarters.

It was that "soul-searching experience"—the death of his military mentor—that had affected Johnston most. He would later admit wondering to himself, "If this man can be slain, who can escape?" But like all other trying episodes in his service, it served only to buttress his indefatigable drive, and in what he gained from each experience he outpaced not only his men but his lieutenants, all of whom were his senior in age. It seemed that nature had parceled out to the young captain an unfair excess of those qualities that make good leaders.

Lieutenant Wood wrote of Johnston to the sister of a fallen soldier after the war: "[W]e were particularly blessed with a captain, who exacted our profoundest admiration both as an officer and a gentleman; as an officer I have not yet met his equal." In the same letter, Wood likened Company E to "a happy family, bound together by the ties of good fellowship in a great common cause." After eleven long months in France, Johnston himself felt his band of soldiers could finally feel "the confidence born of unity—the sense of being one no matter what betide." His company, he would proudly state, "was certainly the best in the regiment," and it was his four platoon leaders—lieutenants "all of unusual ability and character"—whom he would credit.

The welfare of these men—Johnston's officers, his soldiers, his "family"—consumed his thoughts as he listened to the shellfire from his dimly lit dugout in such a lonely moment of command. Without a spoken word, Johnston pushed the curtain aside and walked out past his posted guard and over to First Sgt. Conley Hawk's dugout. "Daylight had come," he noticed as he stepped out into the open, "but a gray and sullen sky indicated that the sun might be late in appearing." Johnston grabbed his first sergeant and two runners and together they rushed up the slope toward the approach trench.

Through the gray morning half-light toward the front lines they could see "[t]he bombardment on the plateau was intermittent, though fairly severe." Out of the fog walked a French lieutenant who had been staking out a path for his tanks for the next day's attack. Simultaneously, the French tank commander, the "plump and placid" Capt. Emile Noscereau, ran up and asked, in English, "The Boches are going to attack in a moment?" In a thick French accent, the lieutenant assured Noscereau and the rest, "Oh, no. I have just come from the front trench. It is merely a bombardment, for the most part by our own artillery."

Somewhat reassured, Captain Johnston left the two runners in a portion of the approach trench with instructions to give immediate warning in case of any attack. As he returned back down the slope with First Sergeant Hawk and they split off to head to their respective dugouts, Johnston instructed his topkick to "keep in frequent touch by runner with the observation post." Reentering his command bunker, Johnston passed Lieutenants Wood and Desmond, and in a tone he later admitted carried "a touch of severity," he declared: "I intend to get a bit of sleep. Let me be called if something important develops, and only then."

Back up in the front lines, the bloodletting continued. A mortar shell hit and "instantly" killed two more privates, Mike Dummitt of Detroit, Michigan, and James Adams of Kaysville, Georgia. The wounded writhed in pain on the dirt floor among a jumble of shovels and packs and dropped rifles. With no room in most of the cramped trenches for stretchers, many were dragged or carried, bleeding and with broken bones, out communication trenches for a long, painful journey to the first-aid station then driven by truck to a field hospital. Company casualty reports soon painted a picture of the peril at the front: "shell wound penetrating left leg," "compound fracture left arm," or "perforating wound of scalp."

For the survivors, some injured and others paralyzed with fear, added to the thunder above and the screams around them was the familiar rattle of German machine-gun fire from across the plateau. Bullets sliced through the dirt parapet above, shooting sprays of soil into the trench and thumping against the rear trench wall in chalky bursts. The intrepid Lieutenant Avery, still moving up and down the line checking on his men, heard yelling from across the plateau, barely audible over the deafening siege of noise. Between gusts of enemy machine-gun fire he stole a glance over the top of the trench and noticed in the German lines "movement there . . .

unquestionably something: a bobbing of helmets, a shifting along the line of the parapet." Simultaneously, the enemy shelling stopped.

Avery recognized the stirring in the German line and the sudden lift of the barrage as a clear signal: this was not another routine morning bombardment. It was an attack. Or a raid, at least, and he needed to notify the artillery. He scrambled back through the trench, found his Very pistol, checked it had a cartridge, aimed it high, and fired. The magnesium flare fizzed up and split into three stars that glowed white against the gray, overcast sky, signaling the artillery two miles behind the trenches to lay down a barrage beyond Avery's position. He waited. Hearing no response behind him, he impatiently loaded another flare cartridge and fired again, then again and again until finally he heard the unmistakable drumfire of the division artillery.

"There was a tumultuous thudding from the rear," Captain Johnston would later report, followed by "a rushing across the sky," a comforting sound for Lieutenant Avery and his men. But relief turned to alarm as the rushing sound changed pitch, then went eerily silent. Avery's men braced, and the shells hit. Detonations again filled the trench, this time in concentrated groupings fired by their own guns. The division artillery evidently had the wrong coordinates for 3rd Platoon's position. Avery grabbed one of his men from the trench floor and yelled, "Go to the captain. Tell him the Boches are attacking, and our barrage is falling on our own trench!" The runner shuffled out the communication trench as Avery rummaged through his box of flare cartridges, clutched a handful of single-star whites, and shot them up one after another to signal the artillery to "lengthen the range."

"The trench had become a scene of horror," Captain Johnston would later report. "[I]n places it was no longer a trench, but merely a smear on the ground." Trapped in the prolonged pounding of his own artillery, Lieutenant Avery moved up and down what was left of his trench, lining his remaining men up at the parapet with their rifles ready to defend against the German infantry attack he knew was imminent. One of them, Pvt. William Cameron of Superior, Wisconsin, was standing with his rifle when a shell "exploded at his feet," killing him "instantly," a comrade would report.

Avery continued moving down the line pulling five-round clips from the ammo belts of his fallen soldiers and redistributing them by the handful to the surviving remnants of his platoon, actions for which he would be awarded the Distinguished Service Cross. In the words of the citation, Avery "exhibited unusual courage in holding together his handful of men, after one-third had become casualties, and distributing ammunition to remaining men." Suddenly he was enveloped in a massive explosion. Thrust down and crushed, things went dark as masses of earth collapsed, pushing him down with mounting force. Folded awkwardly, his head was smashed against his legs, which were still stuck out in a standing position. Dirt clumps and debris sifted past his ears, and from above he could hear only the faint, muffled sounds of men's yells. To the remains of his platoon, Avery had disappeared from sight, buried alive.

Manning the trenches to the left of Avery's position were the men of Lieutenant Curry's 1st Platoon. Untouched by the bombardments, the soldiers here were lined up at the parapet with bayonets fixed and rifles ready. Their leader, John V. Curry, twenty-two and a native of Plains, Pennsylvania, was Avery's best friend. The two had completed officer training together, shipped off to France together, and two months earlier arrived for duty with Company E together. In the morning the platoons they led would be assigned to advance side by side in the first wave of the attack. For the past ninety minutes, Curry had seen the prolonged high-explosive barrage that had been ripping up Avery's stretch of trenches. Though Curry had no idea his friend was buried alive, he readied his own platoon, still at full strength, to defend his own line and Avery's against any German infantry attack.

The barrage lifted from the front lines, and Curry could hear a series of loud, rhythmic detonations behind his position. Enemy guns had laid down a box barrage, patterned to trap the Americans up in the targeted trench and prevent reinforcements. For the Germans, ever methodical in their tactics, this was their cue to attack.

All American eyes in the front lines were fixed on the German trenches, and each soldier strained and repositioned himself to get a clear line of sight. The ground of no-man's-land, covered with a blanket of knee-deep wheat, ascended gradually toward the German lines which, tailored by war's calibrations, bent closer to the American trenches there than at any other point in the two-mile-long division sector. Above the wheat and through the fog and acrid smoke blanketing no-man's-land, field-gray figures crowned with coal-scuttle helmets emerged from the earth. The watching line of doughboys leaned glued to the dirt of the trench front like guard dogs forcing restraint until the signal to attack. Flinching and ducking instinctively as enemy machine guns strafed the parapet with covering fire, they pressed their cheeks against the wooden stocks of their rifles, each soldier lining up over the sight post of his barrel a walking gray figure to drop, awaiting the order to fire.

In the trench beside 3rd Platoon a machine-gun crew waited, concealed behind a clump of trees. The gun-crew chief, twenty-year-old Cpl. Richard "Dickie" Conover of Newport, Rhode Island, stood peeking over the parapet, waiting for the approaching Germans to get closer to give the order to fire. The loader held a stiff twenty-four-round ammo strip out from the receiver with an open box of more stacked at the ready. The gunner leaned in on the shoulder rest and eyed the approaching enemy down the long steel barrel of the Hotchkiss, tightly gripping its wooden handle, his trigger finger ready to squeeze out grim retribution.

Most of these doughboys had spent weeks and months in trenches learning to hate the Germans—the "Huns," the "Boches," "Fritz," "Jerry"—an unseen, faceless adversary that lingered beyond the barbed wire and darkness of no-man's-land, stripped of human qualities. Now as they eyed the kaiser's soldiers approaching steadily, loaded with grenades and clutching Mauser rifles with fixed bayonets, individual human features began to emerge. Encountering for the first time the face of the enemy in a clash of kill-or-be-killed, these young Americans saw war instantly reduced to its tragic potential. One private muttered nervously, "By God, I'll bet they are as scared as I am." A sergeant defiantly whispered, "Let 'em come. None of them will go back."

The "bit of sleep" Captain Johnston had intended to get never came. "A dull but rhythmic thudding, that had woven itself into the very stuff of dreams," as he would later describe it, continued from the front, keeping him and Wood and Desmond wide-awake in the gradual growing light of the bunker. Johnston's concerns over the ambulatory nature of his command mounted, and he lamented aloud to himself what "bad business" it was to be "this far away from the outfit."

Before the words had left Johnston's lips, a soldier dove through the curtained entrance and landed on the dirt floor. It was Lieutenant Avery's runner, who had sprinted and dodged his way through the shellfire down the communications trench from the front lines. "Gray with dirt, and somewhat rumpled as to appearance," the young private stood up, saluted his captain, caught his breath, and delivered Avery's message: "Sir, the lieutenant directs me to say that our own artillery is firing on the 3d Platoon trench."

But the winded runner neglected the first part of Avery's message—that the Germans were "attacking." And neither he nor any of the officers present could know that Avery was slowly suffocating under a crushing heap of upturned earth. Acting on the only information he had, Captain Johnston instructed the runner to return and inform Avery that for the moment 3rd Platoon "simply had to grin and bear it" and that Johnston would be on his way up shortly. He then scribbled a message reporting the friendly fire, gave it to another company runner, and with a slap on the back sent him sprinting to the battalion commander's bunker.

As Johnston buckled on his gear and announced to Lieutenant Wood, "I'm going up to look at things," the curtain swung aside again and into the small, crowded bunker popped the battalion intelligence officer, Lt. Benjamin Gardner. As a former Company E platoon leader, his was a familiar face. "[T]he courteous calm of our distant southwest was his usual demeanor," Johnston noted of the lanky Texas native, but in this moment his animation was unmistakable; "rarely had he been seen in a state of so great excitement." Apparently the surgeon at the first-aid station was reporting high numbers of wounded coming in, and the battalion commander had sent Gardner to get a report.

Just as Captain Johnston was assuring Lieutenant Gardner it was only a bombardment, concrete news from the front finally arrived. It was a runner from Lieutenant Curry's platoon, who caught his breath, saluted, and relayed, "Lieutenant says Boches are attacking."

Johnston wasted no time. "Notify battalion." His brisk command hung in the air of the bunker as he and Gardner swished out the canvas curtain and headed toward the front.

From behind their patch of trees in the front-line trench, Cpl. Dickie Conover and his machine-gun crew could see the Germans approaching in two waves, each of about two dozen men. Young Conover was the ideal embodiment of America's presence in the Allied lines, perfectly situated to play his part dismantling the German myth that the doughboys could not fight. Back home, he had been a star athlete in prep school, a member of the rowing team, football team, and captain of the hockey team. Within two weeks of America entering the war, Conover was on a ship crossing the Atlantic to serve with the American Field Service, where he trucked ammunition to the French front. Once the US Army finally caught up with him in France, he enlisted and joined the machine-gun company of the 18th Infantry. Now over the din of the artillery barrage, he yelled to his

GERMAN RAID ON COMPANY E
MAY 28TH, 1918

gunner to wait just a little longer to fire—wait until the enemy got a little closer.

As the line of Germans reached the thin, single strand of barbed wire about fifty yards from the American trenches, Lieutenant Curry yelled "Fire!" The loud "steady, even popping" of over seventy rifles firing was swallowed by the hanging fog, and the charging gray figures dropped mid-stride beneath the wheat surface, some for cover and others injured and dead. As the American rifle fire continued, rustles in the grain evidenced German movements as coal-scuttle helmets appeared in flashes of forward sprints and gray-sleeved arms swung above the wheat tops slinging stick grenades toward the American trench line.

In a crackling frenzy, Curry's doughboys continued firing into the fog and wheat, popping their five-round clips at muzzle-flashes, movement, or any signs of a live enemy. Down on the trench floor, handfuls of men huddled to duck grenade blasts, while others lay shaking, seized by the shock of combat. Above, rifle volleys continued to send bullets slicing in both directions as more Germans fell and still more grenades came flying end-over-end into the trench. Buried down below and still struggling to breathe, Lieutenant Avery could hear only "the thin crackle of rifles" from above as the broken remains of his platoon stood their ground.

As the second wave of Germans reached the wire, Corporal Conover's machine gun opened up, the flashing white flame on the end of its barrel slueing left and right as it shot out a zipping torrent of bullets from behind the trees with a sustained, deadly rattle. Nearly every standing figure in no-man's-land was mowed down, cut to ribbons. As Captain Johnston would later report, "the rear line of attack went down into the wheat as if swept by a scythe."

Over on the far left, in front of 1st Platoon's trench, the Germans had lunged past the wire and were only yards away, tossing grenades and firing Mausers from kneeling positions in the wheat. The attackers pushed closer and rifle fire was exchanged at almost point-blank range. Without warning, one of Lieutenant Curry's men, twenty-three-year-old Pvt. John Drbal, threw down his rifle, climbed over the parapet, and ran toward the Germans with his hands up, motioning surrender. Five Germans gathered around him and he yelled something to them. "Whatever it was, it meant a lot to them," Curry later reported with lasting astonishment; "I guess it was about the attack tomorrow. They were certainly excited."

The soldiers of 1st Platoon absorbed the scene in stunned bewilderment. As one of the Germans blew a whistle and signaled to return back to their own lines, Curry's men unloaded their rifles on the group. "All six of them went down," Curry noted. "We were careful not to let them crawl away. Couldn't let *that* bunch go—any of them." Captain Johnston would report that "the group of six figures . . . gray and olive drab alike, they fell in a huddle amidst the wheat, and lay still."

John Drbal Jr. had been recently drafted out of Wisconsin, the older of two sons to Bohemian immigrants. When his shot-up body was recovered from no-man's-land, Curry would identify him as a "new replacement" and place on him the blame for "other trouble" from the past month, "distorted messages" and "false orders." Captain Johnston would later wonder at great length about this "deserter, traitor, spy" from his company, and the battalion commander would estimate him to be either "a desperate cold calculator, or a misguided young fool." Any truth that survived Private Drbal is now lost to time, and he lies under a Latin cross in the Somme American Cemetery, resting forever in the ranks of those who wore the same uniform.

Over on the far right, still directing his machine-gun crew, Corporal Conover sighted commotion to his left toward the 3rd Platoon trench. In the midst of the mayhem, obscured by fog and lingering smoke, a small clutch of German attackers appeared to be forcing their way into the front line still being desperately defended by the decimated remains of Avery's men. Before Conover could react, he saw the gray forms reemerge holding two doughboys at gunpoint, rushing them back across no-man's-land.

With a dogged determination to rescue his comrades that left him blind to the enemy machine-gun bullets still sweeping the parapet and plateau before him, Conover grabbed his rifle, climbed out of the trench, and yelled for his crew to cease fire and follow. He ran forward a few feet beyond the parapet to get a good angle, lay down in the open ground, and fired. His crew climbed forward with their rifles and joined him. "[W]e all started to pick off the Germans who were taking the Americans back," one of them later recounted. They were successful in finding their marks, and both American soldiers captured by the Germans made it back to the line unharmed.

But their muzzle flashes betrayed their position, and enemy machine guns ranged in. Unfazed, Conover was still "cool, enthusiastic and was doing good work," according to the soldier lying next to him. Like the first few heavy drops of an arriving rainstorm, enemy bullets pelted the dry dirt all around, and in a few moments the crew noticed Conover was gone. Finding him lying shot in the bottom of the trench, the crew climbed back in and asked their corporal if he was hurt. He noticed one of them was empty-handed and said, "I'm through, take my rifle."

Those were his last words. His lieutenant would later say he "had a smile on his face and he died with the knowledge that he had done his utmost in performance of his duty." Conover was buried in the trench where he fell. The following Christmas, his father, serving in Europe as a chaplain, would visit the very place his son died. In the mud he improbably found the last letter he had sent Dickie. It closed with the words "in spite of all the turmoil and death in which you are living, you can be at perfect peace in the arms of your Heavenly Father." Two years after the war's end, Cpl. Richard Stevens Conover was finally removed from the dirt of the trench and reburied in the Somme American Cemetery, where he rests today.

Johnston and Gardner arrived at the front after scrambling "over blocks of earth and debris" and sliding "down into new and deep depressions" through the approach trench heavily damaged by the box barrage. On the way up, they encountered men crawling out from under demolished sleep dugouts and shell-shocked soldiers who seemed "temporarily dazed and deafened" and "unable to answer questions." To the left, Johnston saw Lieutenant Curry and his men still firing their rifles over the top. Out in the wheat of no-man's-land, there was a "flurry of movement," which Johnston estimated was "the last desperate rush" of the German attackers. "A few figures were all that could now be seen to the front, moving about through the wheat at some distance; now and then one of them fell." The few German survivors were backpedaling through the killing field to their own trench. Johnston ordered a cease-fire, and the fight was over.

The lifting fog and rising sun revealed a no-man's-land scattered with the gray uniforms of the German attackers, some injured and many dead. Surveying the damage, Johnston estimated that "only three or four" of the Germans "returned alive to their own trench." In the bottom of the trench near him, a German lay wounded with a bloody leg. He had made it all the way to the American line when he and one of Curry's soldiers clashed with bayonets. Each had fired at the other, a bullet hitting the German's thigh and his own merely splintering the American's wooden rifle stock. Another German, unharmed, simply walked out of the wheat up to the trench and surrendered. Both were immediately taken to the rear as prisoners.

As Johnston made his way over to 3rd Platoon's position to look for Lieutenant Avery, he found "not a trench, but a twisted conglomeration of weapons, dirt, dead, and wounded." He began coordinating cleanup and reorganization as medics dressed wounds and stretcher bearers removed the wounded. Soldiers dug for Avery, a task made more difficult by a collapsed trench that shrunk the space to work in and compounded the places to dig. Lieutenant Curry came over to assist, calling his friend's name out and listening for a response.

Buried deep, Avery could only hear voices directly over him, and more than three hours would pass before he heard the faint sound of Curry's voice from above. "[H]e was immediately over me he called my name and I an-

swered," Avery later remembered. As muffled sounds of recognition, digging, and Curry's "calls of encouragement" came from above, he knew he
would make it. He was pulled out "almost suffocated, and in pitiful physical condition," Johnston observed. Avery had been buried for three and a
half hours, and rescue had come just in time. "Ten minutes more and I know
I should have suffocated."

In a "tender way," Avery noted, Curry helped lift him onto a stretcher.
Though paralyzed on one side, exhausted, and nearly suffocated, Avery still
had, in Johnston's view, "a proud mental state," asking for news and updates
about the raid. As he was carried off, lying on the stretcher smoking a cigarette, his buddy Curry wished him well. Avery later recalled of the moment, "I think we both cried a little."

But the morning would still claim one more life. Either in response to
an errant flare or a distorted message—details are conflicting—the division artillery fired again on the front lines. A few detonations, then silence.
Two more soldiers were badly injured and one, the liaison officer, Lieutenant
"Desperate" Desmond, lay dead. One of the high-explosive shells had
slammed the twenty-two-year-old Randolph, Massachusetts, native so hard
against the trench wall that it cracked his skull and shattered his pelvis
and most of his ribs. He likely died instantly. A private sprinted out of the
communication trench and down the slope, and delivered the news to
Captain Johnston, who was headed back to his bunker to file a report. Johnston would later remember that the runner "sat down suddenly, this steady,
brave, young soldier, and tears rolled down his face."

Of the raid, German reports would list forty-two of their fifty attackers
as casualties. Their commander had sent them forward with urging "that
prisoners must be taken at all costs," but the few survivors who managed to
make it back to the safety of their own trenches did so without prisoners
and without information. Their mission had failed in every respect. For the
Americans, as the rush of adrenaline faded, they knew only what their five
senses told them: that the scent of cordite and shrieks of otherwise fearless
grown men had left some with the palpable taste of fear and others with a
thirst for revenge. They could not yet know the final numbers or where
precisely this enemy raid fit into the big picture, but they knew they had
successfully defended their line and allowed no prisoners to be taken.

The cost was heavy. Company E suffered nine men killed and a dozen
injured; Company H, in the trenches to the right, had twelve men killed—
including a platoon leader—and twenty injured; and six members of the

18th Infantry were killed. In all, over fifty men had been plucked from the center of the first wave of the following day's attack.

For most survivors, this fleeting episode was their first taste of war, and they bore its imprint. The expressed carnage, whether nerve-shredding proximity to deadly shell blasts or the sight of a friend's final moment, left some shaking, their psyches fractured by combat exhaustion—what then was still universally termed "shell shock." But for many it roused dormant courage from within, and it demolished any remaining myth of German invincibility ingrained in their minds. They were no longer the uninitiated, and when the whistles sounded the next morning, they would go over the top as veterans.

Captain Johnston returned to his bunker for rest that would not come easy. His company stood at the starting line, less than a day from Zero Hour, bloodied but proven. The courage of his men under fire urged thoughts of his late battalion commander and mentor, who "had told them everything they would have to do," and "[w]hen the time came, they simply did it." Like a proud father, Johnston wrote that his lieutenants led "with courage and with dogged endurance," and the "[i]ndividuals and platoons cooperated to good effect" with "admirable unity of purpose." Doubtless it would be "a source of gratification to higher authority."

The next morning at dawn, Captain Johnston's men would go "over the top" and into the breach, forming the center company of the first wave of the first American battle of the war. Their crossing of no-man's-land would be their final steps in a long journey to war. It was a journey that had begun thirteen months earlier, when the United States declared war on Germany, abruptly transporting the reality of carnage and bloodshed of the Western Front across the Atlantic and into American homes. Before then, most of these young men had been living lives peacefully undistracted by the worlds falling apart in Europe. With a sudden call of duty they had flocked to the colors, answering their president's call to fight to make the world "safe for democracy."

It was a time that suddenly seemed a lifetime ago, before the irretrievable deaths of the morning raid, and a world removed from the men resting up in the front lines, many of whom would breathe their last the next day.

It is there, America's entry into the World War, that their journey—and our story—begins.

CHAPTER 2

The Advance Guard

For most Americans, the bloodshed and thunder of the first two and a half years of the Great War was no more than a distant noise. Only tragedies that touched home—the death of 128 Americans aboard the *Lusitania* and injuries to two dozen more aboard the *Sussex* when each was torpedoed by German U-boats—raised voices of outrage, but still few desired war. This "lack of belligerence," Woodrow Wilson's biographer, John Milton Cooper, notes, "was not surprising. Newspaper and magazine coverage of the carnage on the Western Front and the recent use of poison gas left no room for illusions about the horrors of this war." The British Army had suffered more casualties in just the first hour of the Battle of the Somme than America lost in the entire War of 1812, and in the first two days of that same battle had more deaths than the thirteen colonies in the American Revolution. Just nine months of defending Verdun had cost the French Army more casualties than either side in fighting the entire American Civil War. In the United States, daily news of bloodshed on such an incomprehensible scale left few clamoring for America to get involved.

For his part, President Wilson stressed that "[t]he United States must be neutral in fact as well as in name during these times that are to try men's souls." Through the crises that hit home, particularly times when there were public calls for military readiness or involvement, Wilson urged Americans to "put a curb on our sentiments." But the need for some level of preparedness was a growing national attitude, and many wealthy, influential business leaders set up and funded military training camps, with Army Chief of Staff Gen. Leonard Wood's encouragement, to train and prepare a large class of citizen reservists in case of war.

Most of these training camps were aimed at university men, and the one that attracted most established businessmen and prominent leaders was organized at Plattsburgh Barracks in Plattsburgh, New York. The camp was promoted by former president Theodore Roosevelt and attended by such notables as two of his sons, Archie and Theodore Jr., as well as the mayor of New York City. More than 20,000 young and middle-aged men of means attended in the summers of 1915 and 1916, spawning the "Plattsburg Movement" (the *h* in the town's proper name was left off in most publications at that time) that stressed a "call to duty" and the "special responsibility of the privileged to exert leadership in the country."

But it was not until Mexican revolutionary Pancho Villa crossed the border and killed civilians in Columbus, New Mexico, in March 1916 that President Wilson and Congress, slowly and somewhat reluctantly, embraced the urgings of the "Plattsburgers." Their official embrace took the form of the 1916 National Defense Act, which increased the size of both the active Army and the National Guard, provided federal funding for more military training camps (based largely on the Plattsburg model), and created the ROTC for colleges and universities. But with a five-year implementation period and much of the Army already getting deployed to the southern border to deal with Pancho Villa and his rebels, the United States military would still be far from prepared for any kind of involvement in what had become now the greatest war in mankind's history.

By the opening months of 1917, the *Lusitania* tragedy was twenty months gone, Wilson had been reelected to a second term on the slogan "He kept us out of war," and the World War was still an ocean away. It seemed the United States might remain uninvolved, but across the Atlantic in the top-secret inner sanctum of the British Admiralty, Room 40, where German messages and telegrams were decoded by British Intelligence, the storm that would draw America into the war broke quietly. It was a coded telegram from the German foreign secretary, Arthur Zimmermann, to the German ambassador in Mexico. Intercepted and decoded by British Intelligence, the telegram offered German support for Mexico to reclaim by force its former territory from the United States, an area comprising land in Texas, New Mexico, and Arizona. England eagerly shared this "Zimmermann Telegram" with President Wilson, and its public release in the United States, coinciding with the announcement of Germany's renewal of unrestricted submarine warfare, raised the Americans' call for intervention to a fever pitch.

War swiftly staked a claim on the nation's passions, a sentiment encouraged by most newspapers. In Chicago, thirty-six-year-old Robert McCormick, the publisher and co-editor of the *Chicago Tribune* and an outspoken interventionist, had thus far used his newspaper over the course of the war as a vehicle to campaign in print for better preparedness. As his biographer, Richard Norton Smith notes, McCormick "never saw a fight he didn't want to get into," and he had recently been dividing his time between running his paper and serving as a major in the Illinois National Guard, a commission he had obtained from the governor. Early in the war, McCormick had traveled to both the Western and Eastern Fronts as a war correspondent. More recently, he had led a group of state guard volunteers down to patrol the border during the Pancho Villa episode, using his own funds to supply horses, uniforms, and weapons. Now with the recent developments, McCormick used his paper to loudly call for a Draft, conservation of food and fuel, and volunteers.

Some young men, animated by the same national spirit as McCormick, did not wait for a declaration of war to enlist. On the first day of March, in New Castle, Pennsylvania, with the headline of his hometown paper reading "Wilson Confirms Fact of German Plot Against U.S.," William "Billie" McCombs enlisted for service in the Army, and his brothers Thomas and Arthur soon followed. In Denton, Texas, seventeen-year-old Levy Wilson and his two younger friends, Orville Klepper and Emory Smith, both sixteen, also volunteered. All dropped school to enlist and soon dubbed themselves the "Three Musketeers," a name their hometown paper would eagerly employ in subsequent stories covering their military service.

At long last, on the evening of April 2, 1917, the president who had won an electoral victory just five months earlier on his record of staying out of war submitted to his "distressing and oppressive duty" to ask Congress for war. In pin-drop silence before a joint session of Congress, Wilson declared, "the right is more precious than peace," and resolved that the United States become "one of the champions of the rights of mankind" and join those already at war. He admitted it a "fearful thing to lead this great peaceful people into war," but with his call to arms, the American citizenry was by and large now willing to enter what their president called this "most terrible and disastrous of all wars." In conspicuously passive tones he declared, "The world must be made safe for democracy." And to close the speech that would become one of the noblest passages in the American canon, Wilson intoned gravely, "[T]he day has come when America is privileged to spend her blood and her might for the principles that gave her birth and happiness and the peace which she has treasured." Paraphrasing Martin Luther, he closed, "God helping her, she can do no other."

Four days later, on the morning of April 6, by overwhelming votes of 373 to 50 in the House and 82 to 6 in the Senate, Congress passed a joint resolution declaring that a state of war existed between the United States and Germany, authorizing Wilson "to employ the entire naval and military forces of the United States" against Imperial Germany. In the early afternoon at the White House, President Wilson signed it, and America was at war.

With a population of 103 million, the United States entered the World War as the second largest power after Russia, which would be exiting the Allied forces by year's end. But as they related to America's armed forces, the numbers were far less encouraging. The Regular Army, currently scattered from the Mexican border and Panama to San Francisco, the Philippines, and China, had fewer than 5,800 officers and 122,000 men. Counting the existing National Guard and Marine Corps, the United States could muster a total land force of only around 220,000 men. In contrast, the massive Army of the German Empire, which united the armies of Prussia, Bavaria, Saxony, and Württemberg, numbered over 5 million and was currently fighting on two established fronts where it had been at war for nearly three years.

President Wilson's address had called for an "immediate addition to the armed forces" of "at least five hundred thousand men." To raise the number needed, the War Department concluded a mandatory national draft would be necessary, but that would take legislation and time to implement. As the sun set on April 6, it was clear that the pressing need for manpower could be answered only by volunteers.

The next morning, the front page of Janesville, Wisconsin, newspaper, the *Janesville Daily Gazette*, carried an image of the flag with the headline, "Citizens of Janesville: The National Congress has declared that a state of war exists between the United States and Germany." That same day, twenty-two-year-old Otto Hanson, who had emigrated from Denmark just four years earlier, entered Janesville's Army recruiting office and became the first from his adopted hometown to enlist after the declaration of war. In Davenport, Iowa, Albert L. Agnew, only sixteen, lied about his age and enlisted without his father's consent. He would later say it was his size that allowed him to pass for an older man.

Some volunteered together, bound either by blood or close friendship. Earl G. Simons, a nineteen-year-old only child from Altoona, Pennsylvania, applied for enlistment with his younger buddy, Harry G. Banzhoff, only seventeen. In Harthington, Nebraska, Carl M. Lange and eleven friends enlisted together. And in Burlington, Iowa, seventeen-year-old Vernon C. Mossman and his older brother, Ray, twenty-four, signed up together. By war's end, five sons from the Mossman family would enlist.

Fired by the same sense of national duty, many college men dropped their books mid-semester and flocked to the colors. Twenty-year-old Samuel J. Ervin Jr. from Morganton, North Carolina, who would one day represent his state in the US Senate and gain acclaim as the chairman of the Watergate Committee, was a senior at the University of North Carolina. He and his classmate Samuel Iredell "Si" Parker, from Monroe, North Carolina, were both only one month away from completing their studies and two months from their planned graduation. Neither Sam nor Si postponed their service until final exams or waited to be drafted: both immediately volunteered, were selected for Army officer school, and by May were headed to Georgia for training.

A good portion of the privileged class offered itself over to service. *Chicago Tribune* publisher Robert McCormick again donned his major's goldleaf rank and National Guard uniform, inviting volunteers to apply directly to him at his newspaper's downtown office. And for any *Tribune* employees who signed up, McCormick offered to continue paying their current wages for the length of their service. The old "Plattsburgers" jumped in, men of education and means still united in the common cause. Some, like Theodore Roosevelt Jr. and his brother Archie, who had attended camps in 1915 and 1916, volunteered for front-line service. In all, 90 percent of those who attended Plattsburg camps over the previous two years would see service in the war.

Thousands of young and middle-aged men volunteered to fight, and they came, as historian Gary Mead notes, "[f]rom town and country, salon and factory, farm and schoolroom, they came in an apparently endless stream." Their reasons for volunteering were as varied as their backgrounds. Young Emory Smith, one of the "Three Musketeers" from Denton, Texas, recalled it was being chased by a teacher that gave him the idea to serve: "I made such good progress in running from him that I thought I ought to do well in running after the Dutchmen [*sic*]." Twenty-year-old Herman "Dick" Dacus of St. Louis, a secretary in the city's civic league applying for officer training, later reasoned, "We were at war, I was single and sympathized with the French and British and disliked the German sinking of unarmed merchant ships, etc." Frank Groves of Lebanon, Oregon, later said simply he "wished to volunteer—Father signed for me without question."

Once signed up for duty, each enlistee was quickly shipped off for physical exams then off to a training camp and thrust into military life. The diary of Ruben J. Nelson, a nineteen-year-old enlistee from Kennan, Wisconsin, reveals the common initial experience of early volunteers: "[A]pplied for enlistment on April 10, 1917. Left for Escanaba, Mich. April 12, 1917. Passed examination . . . Left for Chicago, Ill. . . . From Chicago, for St. Louis, Mo. . . . Reached Jefferson Barracks, Mo. April 17, 1917 and passed examination and sworn into regular Army Service on April 18, 1917. Clothes issued and soldier life begins. April 19th, 1917 drill. School of a soldier. Drill squads right & left. April 20th same thing over."

Their training included marching, tent pitching, manual of arms, and guard duty. Enlistees were immersed in the rudiments of military structure, but there was little to no weapons or combat training. "None of the new weapons developed since 1914 were then available," one volunteer noted, adding that the only rifles they had for training were "pre-war vintage." Another trainee observed that "the training did nothing to equip us to take care of ourselves as a combat soldier." For these thousands of boys with no previous military experience who were to make up the bulk of America's fighting force, this initial bit of instruction gave them at least a minimal level of regularity and discipline. Adequate preparation would take more time.

But for the armies of the Allied nations currently fighting the war, there was little time. A series of recent bloody winter offensives on the Western Front with little to no results had cost the French Army dearly in lives and morale, and nearly half its divisions currently in the trenches were, as historian Allan Millett describes, "in active mutiny or sullen noncooperation." Barely capable of holding on defensively in many sectors, the French would be incapable of any offensive action without fresh troops, meaning Americans. It took only three weeks after the American declaration of war for the impatient French and British to deliver their pressing request to President Wilson in person.

Marshal Joseph Joffre, the revered former French commander who in the first months of the war had stopped the Germans and pushed them back to their current line, arrived in Washington in late April with France's minister of justice and former prime minister, René Viviani. They were desperate for a visible sign of American presence in the trenches to cure the depleted morale, and they pressed Wilson to send what troops he could immediately.

Wilson's conversation with Joffre, who at war's outbreak had overseen the mobilization and deployment of an army of a million in just days, turned to a detailed assessment of the logistics involved in organizing and shipping massive numbers of American troops across the Atlantic. This meeting followed one with a British delegation, sent to request American troops to fill gaps in the front caused by casualties, and for a stronger naval presence to protect shipping. "Wilson was," in his biographer's estimation, "getting a better idea of what waging this war would require."

Wilson gave his new allies no immediate answer but privately decided to send a contingent of troops as soon as feasible, and he delegated the task of selecting a leader for this deploying force to his secretary of war, Newton D. Baker. Diminutive and bespectacled, the former mayor of Cleveland had no military experience, but his analytical mind and cunning discernment equipped him as a quick judge of character. Undaunted by bemedaled uniforms, Baker had in his thirteen months heading the War Department coldly and accurately assessed the Army's senior generals. He bore well-founded worries about the insubordination and political ambitions of the senior Army leader, the aging former chief of staff, Maj. Gen. Leonard Wood, and held a strong preference for someone with recent field command of large forces. Surveying the small field of generals, his objective left him with one choice: Maj. Gen. John Pershing.

Pershing was a Missourian whose first paid occupation was teaching school—experience that afforded him invaluable practice in leadership at a young age. He was twenty-one when he finally entered West Point, one class behind Robert Bullard, who later recalled him in his cadet days as "plainly the estate of man while most of those around him were still boys." His fourth year he was selected class president and First Captain, the first of many honors to mark his ascending star. As a young lieutenant, Pershing led the African American "Buffalo Soldiers" of the 10th Cavalry Regiment, a job he performed so effectively he was selected to return to West Point as a tactics instructor. There the cadets under him, frustrated by his unbending manner, gave him a nickname that mocked his time with the 10th Cavalry, an epithet that would stick through his career—and which history would later sanitize—"Nigger Jack."

Pershing sailed for Cuba at the outbreak of the Spanish-American War, where his regiment and Theodore Roosevelt's fought together in the 2nd Cavalry Brigade and where he was described by a fellow officer as "cool as a bowl of cracked ice" when under fire. In 1906, after service in the Philippines and Japan, Pershing was promoted by President Roosevelt from captain directly to brigadier general, leaping past more than 800 senior Army officers in rank.

Pershing was now at Fort Sam Houston, Texas, commanding the Army's Southern Department at the border, having just returned two months earlier from a year-long mission leading the "Punitive Expedition" into Mexico. He and his force, which had expanded from 4,000 to 11,000 and constituted the largest American military detachment deployed since the Civil War, had trailed Pancho Villa through hundreds of miles in Mexico. Though their target was never captured, Pershing had shown adept leadership in keeping his growing organization together and diplomatic skill in avoiding an international clash with the existing Mexican government. While Pershing was ranked sixth in seniority among the Army's major generals, none other had such recent field experience or had ever led a force so large.

In early May, pursuant to instructions from Secretary Baker, Army Chief of Staff Gen. Hugh L. Scott sent a telegram to Pershing with instructions to select "four infantry regiments and one artillery regiment" from his Southern Department "for service in France" and to report to Washington at once. Eight days later, in Washington, DC, on May 10, Baker's personal meeting with Pershing confirmed his previous instinct that he was the right man for the job. Pershing was to form an expeditionary division, and the designated units would be expanded to "war strength" with immediate supplements of newly trained manpower. At the time of this meeting, the Selective Service Act, which would authorize conscription to supplement volunteers and reach the new goal of 1 million men, was still awaiting passage in Congress. Although this Draft Bill passed a week later, the service registration deadline was not until June, and the first selection lottery would not occur until mid-July, leaving the makeup of Pershing's initial expeditionary force entirely reliant on volunteers.

The four infantry regiments Pershing chose to make up the fighting line of this yet-unnamed expeditionary division were the 16th, 18th, 26th, and 28th, which were scattered at three camps in Texas and one in Arizona. Newly minted doughboys arrived at each garrison after abbreviated training, but most regiments remained at their prewar strength of fewer than 700 men each (three battalions of four 50-man companies, plus officers and staff). Pvt. Ruben Nelson, the nineteen-year-old from Wisconsin who had passed through physical exams in Chicago before training at Jefferson Barracks in St. Louis, described in his diary arriving at his new unit, the 18th Infantry, in Douglas, Arizona, in early May: "Find Co. of 70 men and one officer. All old soldiers." With prewar military experience at a premium, half the existing men in these units had been promoted and parceled out to other new units and training camps, and fresh volunteers like Private Nelson were to beef up each regiment to about 2,400 men before deploying.

Word that a division was being formed for immediate deployment to France spread quickly through the ranks of the thousands of young men then in training, and many who were eager for front-line duty sought assignment to one of the chosen regiments. One of the "Three Musketeers" from Texas, Pvt. Emory Smith, later recalled his disappointment in discovering he "was not on the list of those to be transferred" when "sixty men were needed for the 28th, which we knew would go across." Emory was determined to go fight. "I swapped places with a boy who did not want to go," but then the boy "later decided he wanted to go and we swapped back." Finally, Emory noted proudly, "I swapped a third time before I got permanently on the list." Pvt. Orville Klepper, Emory's fellow "Musketeer," recounted his own commanding officer asking for volunteers to go to France. "Every man stepped forward," Klepper recalled. His commander asked him his age. "Eighteen, Sir." "Why do you wish to go to France? Don't you think you are too young?" "No, Sir, that is what I enlisted for—to fight." "All right my boy, I like your spunk." "So," Klepper proudly noted, "I became a member of the 28th Infantry."

Far more challenging than training new recruits was the task of finding and training men to lead these thousands of enthusiastic volunteers and harness their unbounded confidence. Of the 5,800 commissioned officers in the standing Regular Army, nearly 2,000 of them had less than one year experience. Leaders—platoon leaders, company commanders, artillery battery commanders, staff officers—were needed and fast. It was mostly young men and middle-aged men of means who applied for commissions—college students, college graduates, and businessmen. "These volunteers," Secretary Baker observed, "left positions of responsibility and profit, dropped their personal affairs and devoted themselves wholeheartedly to the new business of war."

Those who had applied for officer duty in April and early May now reported to begin their training. Sam Ervin and Si Parker, the UNC seniors who had volunteered in April, arrived at Fort Oglethorpe, Georgia, to begin three months of instruction. Many of the old "Plattsburgers," to include the Roosevelt brothers Theodore Jr. and Archie, returned to the Plattsburgh Camp to complete the same training as the new men. In all, 43,000 officer candidates, men ages twenty-one to forty-five, began their ninety-day training in mid-May at sixteen new reserve-officer training camps across the United States.

The precious field command and combat experience of senior Army officers and NCOs (non-commissioned officers: corporals and sergeants), soon to form the basic framework of the deploying forces, was for the time largely employed in training future officers. Robert Bullard, then a colonel, was placed in charge of the officer training camp at Fort Logan H. Roots in North Little Rock, Arkansas. "Like cadets at the U.S. Military Academy," Bullard observed, "the student officers were largely relieved of the usual fatigue work of soldiers, devoting their time to study, care and understanding of their equipment, to drill and to practice in instruction of others less advanced."

Bullard's camp and the others each had 2,500 officer candidates drilling and training under veteran army officers and NCOs. These seasoned instructors impressed their educated but impressionable students. Richard Newhall, a twenty-nine-year-old Harvard PhD from Massachusetts, was receptive to his captain's teaching: "He knows how to handle men and that is something which I would like very much to learn," he observed, impressed that the captain's "excellence" came "from personality and experience rather than from an encyclopedic knowledge of the different manuals." The NCOs impressed as well. Officer candidate Herman "Dick" Dacus from St. Louis, in training at Fort Sheridan, Illinois, noted that he "learned quickly to obey acting non-coms" and "was fortunate in having an instructor who did a fine job of teaching us how to give commands so that they could be heard and understood."

General Pershing's telegram from General Scott and meeting with Secretary Baker had left him believing that he was to organize and command only the first deploying division, but a subsequent phone call from Baker revealed he was being handed the colossal task of leading the entire American war effort in Europe. General Pershing was being sent to France as "Commander-in-Chief," and he was to select a staff and prepare to sail as soon as possible. In a rare betrayal of his own emotions, Pershing would later admit that this weighty responsibility "depressed" him: "Here in the face of a great war I had been placed in command of a theoretical army which had yet to be constituted, equipped, trained, and sent abroad." But his self-doubt quickly evaporated as he flung himself into the gargantuan task.

In what would become their one and only meeting during the course of the war, President Wilson had General Pershing to the White House on May 24. Of the president, Pershing was "impressed with his poise and his air of determination," and found him "cordial." "General, we are giving you some very difficult tasks these days," Wilson said, following a brief conversation about shipping. "Perhaps so, Mr. President," the general replied, "but that is what we are trained to expect." Pershing was somewhat surprised that Wilson said nothing of the part the American forces were to play in the Allied lines, but the omission did not signal detachment so much as confidence. The president and his secretary of war were giving their new AEF commander-in-chief their full assurance of trust and support, so much so that Pershing would, over the course of the World War, enjoy unfettered autonomy—what Wilson's biographer describes as "complete freedom in conducting operations."

President Wilson's single directive to Pershing was to "cooperate as a component of whatever army you may be assigned to by the French government" until the troops are "sufficiently strong to warrant operations as an independent command," at which point he was to lead the AEF as "a separate and distinct component of the combined forces, the identity of which must be preserved." Sure in his command of nuance, Wilson's concise and carefully worded orders to Pershing embodied his clear response to the pleas of Britain and France for American forces. There would be no "amalgamation"—no folding of American soldiers and Marines into French and British units to plug holes in the weakened Allied lines. American forces would organize, ship to France, and fight in the trenches under their own officers and under the American flag, no other.

Now firmly in command and propelled by the president's boundless confidence and his own broad mandate, General Pershing acted with a promptness and decisiveness that revealed his managerial genius and marked gift for organization. The pace of forward motion rapidly shifted from a glacial slowness to a frenetic speed as Pershing organized a headquarters staff and selected leadership for the expeditionary division, turning abstractions into institutional realities.

In a heavy rain on the foggy morning of May 28, General Pershing and his handpicked staff—in civilian clothes to avoid excessive press attention—walked the pier at Governors Island, New York, and boarded the British steamship RMS *Baltic* to sail for France. Among those at the pier to see them off was Capt. George C. Marshall. Like many other young Army officers, Marshall had desired a coveted place on Pershing's staff but was not one of the forty-two selected. As he watched the general and his party set off to become the first American troops to land in France, he was left "in a most depressed frame of mind over being left behind." Marshall now craved an assignment with the division then being assembled for immediate shipment to France, recently named the "First Expeditionary Division." Ideally he wanted the job of Operations Officer, "but as this seemed out of the question" in his mind, he decided to "let fate determine my assignment."

George Catlett Marshall Jr. was thirty-six and a native of Uniontown, Pennsylvania. Six feet tall, with intense blue eyes and brown hair unfrosted by any hint of gray, he was still boyishly youthful. Marshall already had fifteen years of service in the Regular Army, which he had marked with quiet professionalism. His father, George Sr., originally from Kentucky, had carried a rifle in his hometown militia and had been a prisoner of the Confederate Army during the Civil War. George Jr., the second son and youngest of three children, sought to gain his father's favor and outshine his older brother by graduating from VMI and gaining what neither of them had: an officer commission in the Army.

As a young lieutenant, Marshall exhibited a military acumen that would later assume legendary proportions, quickly proving equal to any assignment. With an attention to detail that seemed instinctive, he commanded a cavalry force tasked with mapping two thousand square miles of the Texas badlands, resulting in an atlas the chief Army engineer called "the best one received and the only complete one." While still a lieutenant, Marshall completed an advanced infantry course at Fort Leavenworth, where he graduated first out of a class of fifty-four captains and majors, one of whom was future general Douglas MacArthur.

Marshall served in the Philippines, where he witnessed with no small measure of disfavor the brutal American military reprisals against local guerilla attacks, disorder that helped form his measured approach to leading soldiers. "Once an army is involved in war, there is a beast in every fighting man which begins tugging at its chains," he voiced at the time, adding that "a good officer must learn, early on, how to keep the beast under control, both in his men and himself." It was a phrase that would reflect his professional touch throughout his career.

Now a captain and aide-de-camp to the Eastern Division commander, Maj. Gen. Franklin Bell at Governors Island, Marshall craved a place on Pershing's staff, but he declined his boss's offer to lobby for an assignment for him and left it to "fate." This force of fate that was destined one day to mark Marshall's career with a promotion to five-star general and place on him the mantle of Army chief-of-staff, defense secretary, and secretary of state, took its first providential turn here when he was chosen to ship for France with the First Expeditionary Division. Marshall received General Bell's blessing and reported for duty at Penn Station.

While fate had thus far left Col. Robert Bullard down in Arkansas leading an officer training camp, on the very day General Pershing and his staff sailed for France a telegram arrived for Bullard summoning him to report to Washington "for extended foreign service." Ever governed by an unquenchable thirst for front-line field duty, Bullard leapt at the chance and was on "the next train."

Though not Pershing's choice, the man selected to command the First Expeditionary Division was Maj. Gen. William Sibert, a West Pointer who had proven his own organizational skill as an engineer officer in the construction of the Panama Canal. The division under his command would consist of the four infantry regiments Pershing had selected, which were then on their way to Hoboken, New Jersey, by train from their camps in Texas and Arizona. On arrival, the regiments would be combined to form a "square division," with two brigades of two regiments each. On Colonel Bullard's arrival at the War Department, he learned he was promoted to brigadier general and was assigned to command one of the two infantry brigades. When Captain Marshall reported to General Sibert, he was granted the role he most desired: division operations officer.

The four regiments of fresh soldiers arrived in a steady stream over the course of three days. Each arriving group was held away from the Hoboken pier until nightfall when, under cover of darkness the lines of fresh khaki and duffel bags and brown boots shuffled slowly onto the waiting transport ships. One night their newly appointed operations officer, Captain Marshall, stood at the shipping-office window "watching the endless column of infantry pouring slowly through the courtyard into the covered docks." As he would later recall, "Except for the shuffle of their feet there was little noise." The silence gave him pause, and he remarked to another officer, "The men seem very solemn."

The officer replied, "Of course they are. We are watching the harvest of death."

At long last, on June 14, as Pershing and his staff had done two weeks before and as 2 million American troops would over the coming seventeen months of war, the four regiments of the First Expeditionary Division weighed anchor and sailed from Hoboken for France. The soldiers rode on twelve transports divided into three groups of four, each group escorted by a battle cruiser and six destroyers. Private Nelson noted in his diary: "Set sail for France. Big game starts. With three other transports convoyed by Battle cruiser *Charleston* as flagship and six Destroyers . . . everyone is seasick but myself." General Bullard, in the same convoy, noted in his own diary: "About 1 p.m., June 14th, we put to sea with convoy naval vessels—the cruiser *Charleston* and three torpedo-boat destroyers, with one collier."

The sailing was smooth with gentle seas. They ran lifeboat drills by day, and after dark, to avoid detection by German subs, portholes were covered and no lights or smoking was permitted on deck. The first few days were unremarkable, though not without discomfort for those unaccustomed to nautical life. "Everyone was ill," Pvt. Frank Groves later remembered, "Troops got dysentery from eating spoiled meats." The adjustment curve for most was steep. "Everyone was new to everything," George Marshall observed, "the men to their organizations, the sailors to the ship, and the officers of the Headquarters to each other." But these land-based Army soldiers settled in, and many found some pleasant moments in their passage. A series of Pvt. Ruben Nelson's journal entries reads: "On 19th day we run into school of porpoise. June 20, 1917 I see a big shark. Some fish. From now on there is no one seasick aboard and everything is a pleasure."

"On the 24th we run into a sub zone and I get job in observation," Private Nelson wrote, marking their entry into the danger zone known to be patrolled by German U-boats. "We were soon zig-zagging as though we were among hostile submarines," General Bullard noted. At night, all lights on deck were extinguished and men took shifts on sub watch duty. When the first submarine alarm sounded and shots were fired by the destroyers, the men were all ordered above deck to stand by. "Immediately all the ships changed their course, increased speed, and began to zigzag off in different directions," Captain Marshall, riding up in the lead transport, noted. Fortunately it proved to be a false alarm, though not without giving a fright to most on board. Bullard admitted in the privacy of his diary that he "slept little until 1 a.m., and then with all my clothes on. I was badly scared; we seemed so helpless." But the brief, tense crisis revealed to him the "absolute obedience of the troops" on his vessel, evidence of military discipline which he found "most encouraging."

After twelve days sailing across the mine-littered Atlantic, the shores of France became visible to the men in the lead convoy. As they stood on deck and squinted to see the emerging outline of houses and details on the shoreline, their untapped enthusiasm—to land, to fight, to do something to be part of the action—revealed itself in loud cheers. Private Nelson described the scene in his journal: "June 28th 1917. Big day. We see land early in morning. Mademoiselles to wave at. The Battle Cruiser Charleston steams alongside and we give three cheers for the Navy." Of seeing the French shoreline, General Bullard noted "the thing that impressed these unaccustomed eyes was the cleanness, neatness, and especially the finish of the villages and houses along the banks." Captain Marshall shared Bullard's view, effusing that "the green hill slopes and little cottages along the northern shore gave us all an agreeable impression of what France was to be."

One by one the transports docked at Saint-Nazaire, were tied to the pier, and the ramps were lowered. The French populace gathered to greet the doughboys. "There was not a cheer," Captain Marshall noticed, "and the general aspect was that of a funeral." Drained by almost three years of war and the loss of so many sons and brothers and husbands and fathers, the crowd was mostly women and children and seemed to be "in mourning." "There was an air of grimness and sadness among the onlookers," one lieutenant observed; "The garb was universally black, for everyone had lost relatives." Here on display were the broken people Field Marshal Joffre referenced in Washington two months before when he had urged President Wilson for an immediate American presence in France. These men walking down the gangplanks were Wilson's answer, America's first offering: the first 12,000 soldiers of what would by war's end number over 2 million.

No metaphor is too large to encompass the scene and all that it represented. As the four regiments of soldiers emptied from their dozen transports and gathered on the piers at Saint-Nazaire, France, the infantry of the 1st Division stood as one for the first time. Since that day, the division has remained on continuous active duty without interruption. The institution would distinguish itself over the coming century in action in the Argonne Forest, North Africa, Normandy, the Bulge, the Tet Offensive, Desert Storm, Iraq, and Afghanistan. The doughboys who first landed on French soil that sunny June day in 1917 embodied not only the "Fighting First" and "Big Red One" in its earliest form, they symbolized America's promising beginning as a world power on the global stage. They were, in General Pershing's words, "the advance guard of America's fighting men."

CHAPTER 3

Must Not Fail

On July 20, as a blindfolded War Secretary Newton Baker pulled a registration number from a jar in the Senate Office Building in Washington, DC, to begin the national draft, the 12,000 doughboys of the 1st Division's four infantry regiments crossed the French countryside toward their first phase of training in Gondrecourt. By foot and by rail (in "forty-and-eights," which could be crammed with either forty men or eight horses) they passed the picturesque landscapes that had once inspired Van Gogh, Renoir, and more recently, Monet. But the drafty barns in thatched-roof villages where the men quartered and the potent stench of stacked animal dung that carried through the hot country air did little to prompt inner artists. "The towns in which the division was billeted were dirty and uninteresting," one lieutenant recalled. Officers slept in the spare beds of family farm homes, while enlisted men slept up in barn haylofts, described as "often dilapidated, always dark, and invariably cold."

The doughboys spent their first month in France residing in cramped, inadequate wooden barracks hastily constructed by German POWs. The only extent of training possible was a daily march along the sandy shorelines where the Loire River Estuary met the Atlantic Ocean, good for physical conditioning but short on improving military deportment or learning to fight. Over these first weeks, even logistics presented great difficulty. "The nearest open ground, free from crops," Captain Marshall noted, "was on the coast some nine miles distant." Horses and draft mules had not yet been shipped, and the division had only one automobile, a three-passenger French sedan for use by the division commander, General Sibert. This "dearth of transportation," as Marshall called it, forced the soldiers and officers, including both brigade commanders, to hike eighteen miles a day to get to and from the training area.

The division sent a battalion to march in the specially arranged July 4 parade through Paris, where General Pershing cast his exacting eye on the green troops and fretted over their "untrained awkward appearance." Ten days later, the division's top brass attended the Bastille Day parade, where the review of a perfectly drilled French unit threw into stark relief the experience gap between veteran French fighters and the fresh American troops. "It was a fine, fine sight," General Bullard soon effused to his diary. "Everything was cocky and snappy. They were in full uniform, though just from the front, and horses and men were beautifully kept." Military neatness and ceremony did not rank high in his dogma, and his candid remarks revealed not only his high regard for the striking appearance of the parading French poilu, but also an inner frustration with the state of his inexperienced troops. As one of two brigade commanders in the division, Bullard had seen little over those first three weeks in France to suggest that progress in molding these young Americans into fighting soldiers would be anything but slow.

As members of the only AEF division to land in France before the draft, each man there was a volunteer. Theodore Roosevelt Jr., serving as a major in the 26th Infantry, later wrote, "The men of the newly arrived division were as courageous as the men" who had already seen fighting on the Western Front. "Their intelligence was as good," he insisted, "but they did not know the small things which come only with training and experience." The average 1st Division soldier was twenty-four-years-old, had completed at least some high school, and could read and write. Excluding the old Regular Army veterans who filled leadership positions, most were unmarried and very few had children. Their prewar occupations varied from store cashiers and teachers to farmers and clothing salesmen. Stockbrokers from Manhattan marched, trained, and slept beside railroad workers from Nebraska.

All forty-eight states were represented, as well as the US territories of Hawaii and Alaska. The division offered a panoramic view of America, with an ethnic makeup as diverse as the proprieties of 1917 would allow, including Polish, Russian, and Italian immigrants; natural-born Irish, Mexican, and German Americans; as well as American Indians. "They call us the foreign legion," one private remarked; "I don't blame them, either. They expected American soldiers to be American, and we handed them an army made up of forty different nationalities." And while the official 1st Division History published in 1922 boasted, "The Division was truly representative of America," conspicuously absent were any black soldiers. In a sad testament of the times, while over 350,000 African Americans would serve in Army uniform during the war, most would be relegated to Services of Supply duty, and all would serve in segregated units. Only a few black regiments would ever see combat, most under French command. One in particular, the 369th Infantry ("Harlem Hellfighters"), would serve with such distinction that France would award 171 of its soldiers the Croix de Guerre, an honor greater than they would ever live to see from their own nation.

The first stage of formal training began in late July at the well-worn drill grounds on the northern French plains near Gondrecourt, situated so near the front that the "troops lived daily and hourly with the sounds of the guns of St. Mihiel in their ears." "There was a constant rumbling of guns from the distant front," one lieutenant remembered of the persistent reminder of an un-waiting war that added urgency to the already abbreviated training schedule. "In the midst of war, we had to prepare for war," General Bullard wrote of these rushed conditions, a challenge that would be met by what he called the "hardest, most uncompromising and intensive system of drill that the American Army has ever known."

Through the summer months, with nearly every hour of every day filled with training, the soldiers got little rest. "There was nothing but drill every day and most of the nights," Pvt. Ruben Nelson noted in his diary. Major Roosevelt, commanding a battalion of the 26th Infantry, described the typical day: "First call about 6 o'clock, an hour for breakfast and policing. After that, the troops marched out to some drill ground, where they maneuvered all day, taking their lunch there and returning late in the afternoon. Formal retreat was then held, then supper, and by 10 o'clock taps sounded."

The first and primary focus was weapons training. "[T]here was no one with the command who had ever shot an automatic-rifle, thrown a hand grenade, shot a rifle grenade, used a trench mortar or a 37-millimeter gun," Major Roosevelt lamented. "The closest any of us came to any previous knowledge was from occasional pictures we had seen in the illustrated reviews." The rifle adopted by the US Army for use by its soldiers was the magazine-fed, bolt-action Springfield Model 1903—a reliable and accurate firearm even if there weren't enough to supply the expanding AEF (shortages would be filled by British Enfield Model 1917 rifles, rechambered to take .30 caliber Springfield ammunition). But the Springfield rifle and the Colt .45 pistol carried by officers—the latter chosen for its "knock-down" power proven in the Philippines—were the only weapons the Americans brought with them. All else, to include automatic rifles, machine guns, grenades, and artillery, would be supplied by the French Army.

These first American troops trained under the 47th French Division of Chasseurs Alpins, nicknamed the "Blue Devils" for their reputation of brave, "devil-may-care" fighting in the most active sectors along the Western Front. "They had a magnificent fighting record," Captain Marshall recognized, adding that they "made a wonderful impression on our men." The doughboys and these veteran "stocky, tough old timers" soon fostered what the Division History describes as a "friendly rivalry," and when the Americans beat the French in shooting contests, the "warmhearted Frenchmen were loud in their applause."

To improve accuracy, 1st Division soldiers practiced during downtime and off days on paper targets set up at distances of one hundred, two hundred, and three hundred yards on the rifle ranges. Top scores at qualification were awarded marksmanship badges; at practice, with rum and free cigarettes. When unable to secure shooting-range time, some enterprising officers improvised. Twenty-eight-year-old Lt. Clarence Huebner set up empty tin ration cans on strings at fifty and hundred-yard distances to give his men extra practice.

Over the previous three years of constant bloodletting between two entrenched adversaries in subterranean cover without exposed flanks, the rifle had been sidelined by more powerful, destructive, long-range weaponry that best fit into the puzzle of the Western Front's war by attrition. Artillery had dominated the fighting, but for front-line infantry, both the Allies and Germans were increasingly relying on grenades and automatic weapons.

In the large swath of open ground set aside for AEF training and dubbed "Washington Center," doughboys dug a maze of practice trenches into the hardpan under the guidance of French instructors. Complete with command dugouts, sleep holes, and front lines with second-parallels connected by perpendicular communication trenches, the replicated Western Front landscape provided an ideal setting for doughboys to gain familiarization with the tools of trench warfare.

In Washington Center's network of practice trenches, 1st Division soldiers learned how to properly throw grenades—not horizontally like baseballs, but on a high, lobbing trajectory to increase the chances of dropping into an enemy trench. Soldiers found the fuse timers to be unnervingly inconsistent. "Yeah, they tell you it is timed for 5 seconds," Pvt. Maurice Becker of the 16th Infantry complained in a letter home, "and then one goes off in three seconds, and the next goes off in seven, so Fritz can dump it back on you." Rifle grenades proved tougher to master and even more unpredictable. One young lieutenant later described them as "not too good—first military funeral I attended was that of instructor killed by one prematurely exploding."

Doughboys were issued the French Chauchat automatic rifle (pronounced show-shat), capable of firing over two hundred rounds per minute. Despite its heft at nineteen pounds, and even though, as one lieutenant complained, the thirty-round banana-clip ammo magazine "jammed frequently" from rocks and dirt particles, the Chauchat could be effectively operated on close-range targets by a single soldier from a fixed position or while running forward in a tactic known as "walking fire."

Automatic rifles and grenades were both products of the shifting realities of trench warfare, but no single infantry weapon had altered tactical decisions or shifted strategic realities for the armies on both sides of no-man's-land as much as the machine gun. Its defensive capabilities rendered frontal infantry assaults on fixed positions futile and deadly, as the British had learned at the killing end of German Maxims on the Somme. Offensively, its long effective range and high rate of fire rendered it an efficient tool to support an attack with indirect barrages on enemy positions over the heads of advancing infantry.

The Americans were equipped with the French air-cooled Hotchkiss, a powerful and reliable machine gun even if, at over one hundred pounds, it was the heaviest then in use. It required an eight-man team: a loader to carry the fifty-pound tripod mount, five ammunition carriers to haul the wooden ammo boxes, a crew leader (corporal or sergeant) to carry the spare barrels and parts, and a gunner to lug the gun itself. But for all its cumbersome immobility, when operated by a well-trained crew it could send 450 rounds per minute on enemies up to two miles away. And with a mount that absorbed recoil and allowed for precise, repeated firing when properly "nested," it could be used by troops in night fire on enemy targets fixed during daylight registration. Doughboys were instructed both how to effectively use the Hotchkiss to defend against infantry attack and to support an offensive, and as the Division History records, "French instructors were greatly surprised at the speed with which the Americans learned to operate and employ the gun."

But it was here where the direction of American training began to run afoul of the preferences of the AEF high command, specifically General Pershing, who believed the bloody rigor mortis of the Western Front could be undone only through a tactical shift to "open warfare." As he rationalized, the current murderous attrition of back-and-forth jabs could never achieve a decisive victory, which "must be won by driving the enemy out into the open and engaging in a war of movement." There was little value in familiarization with the existing methods of trench warfare, Pershing believed, because a "new army brought up entirely on such principles" would not only be "seriously handicapped without the protection of the trenches" but would lack "the aggressiveness to break through the enemy's lines and the knowledge of how to carry on thereafter."

The US Army's field regulations specified that "[t]he infantry is the principal and most important combat arm," and its tools were what Pershing called "the essential weapons of the infantry," the rifle and bayonet, not automatic weapons or artillery. Machine guns were deemed "emergency weapons" only, and the artillery was only a "supporting" arm—best when used for "the destruction of material objects, as buildings, bridges, etc." These guidelines had been updated and revised that year, but they were rooted in the fighting of the Civil War and Indian Campaigns and ignored the realities of the past two and a half years of Western Front combat. Playing off this sheet music of nineteenth-century tactics, AEF instructors were teaching their trainees that "the ultimate act" of battle was "the bayonet charge," a weapon one enlightened officer regarded "as obsolete as the crossbow."

Among General Pershing and his staff, the primacy of open warfare training—rifles and bayonets, not machine guns or grenades—was quickly enshrined as unassailable dogma, creating fault lines that would soon run deeply through the divergent schools of thought in the Allied coalition. The head of the French Army, Gen. Henri Philippe Pétain, did his best to impart to the Americans "the benefit of our dearly bought experience" in trench warfare, and he instructed his own soldiers to use "constant patience and extreme tact" to "counteract the idea that we are inexperienced in open warfare."

General Bullard, who received Pershing's confidence with a new posting establishing training schools throughout France for newly arriving AEF officers, spied the chasms lurking between American and Franco-British doctrines, but he saw no reason to embrace one tactical preference at the expense of the other. His generalship was informed by fighting experience in the Philippines, where the "utter discouragement and spiritlessness" of his men after months in trenches left him determined to forever avoid "purely defensive ideas of warfare." But while Bullard valued the offensive spirit fostered by the classic infantry training so urged by Pershing, his tours of the active British and French fronts confirmed the grim reality that flesh could not be thrown successfully against steel: the infantry could not achieve the first goal of open warfare, the breakthrough of well-fortified enemy lines, without the full support of heavy firepower—automatic weapons, grenades, and artillery.

This placed the man heading Pershing's AEF officer-training program squarely on both sides of the tactical question. Bullard appreciated the fighting morale and confidence cultivated by open warfare training, but he entertained the heretical notion that the weaponry provided by the French Army and the practical knowledge gained by the chipper tutoring from French veterans would be essential when time to give battle. With measured judgment that would reveal itself to great effect in the higher role he would soon fill, Bullard tacitly determined that soldierly instruction include thorough schooling in both tracks of methodology, a precarious balance he was forced to strike "very tactfully."

This underlying tension would define the AEF, and its resolution would determine success or failure when America's best and brightest entered the fight. A balanced tactical doctrine was forming fragile, exploratory roots in these first few thousand doughboys. With millions of young troops following on their heels, the fighting methods practiced and eventually employed in the first clash of arms would decide the role played by the emergent US military in the Allied march toward an elusive end to this "war to end all wars."

With rival hands tugging at the wheel of the AEF's ship, the course of tactical training had not yet crystallized. "Not only did no one know how to teach—no one knew what to teach," an officer later bemoaned of the time. But with new AEF divisions arriving in France (the 42nd and 26th Divisions had each landed by late September), training could not wait, however disjointed the leadership's visions. As one officer intuited, employing a simple metaphor: "Both tactics and equipment were tried on the dog with the First Division the only animal."

For the time being, the urgency of the un-waiting war demanded that the AEF's "only animal" gain experience in real trenches at the real front. Despite their completion of an exhaustive summer of training— "acclimatization and instruction in small units," the first of three stages planned for AEF units—war remained an abstraction for the soldiers of the 1st Division. The next stage of prescribed schooling, to "serve with French battalions in trenches in contact with the enemy," would send the dough-boys up to a small portion of the 468-mile-long strip of actual war. Men packed up their gear from their cottages and barn lofts, were issued steel helmets to replace their soft campaign caps, and after a daylong truck con-voy to the front lines at Sommerviller, the second stage of training began.

"The enthusiasm of the infantrymen reached its highest point," Captain Marshall noted of this passage, as doughboys rode trucks through "the final stage of their long journey from America to the front." Located south of the bloody Verdun front in the "rolling and attractive country" of the Lorraine region of eastern France, the Sommerviller sector was considered a "relatively quiet" front. Its opposed armies, content to launch offensives elsewhere, had settled into years of static coexistence—barking and snip-ing across lines clawed out by the fighting of late 1914. "Serious operations in this section of France," Marshall observed, "were not contemplated by either side." But for all this "quiet," gassing and shelling were daily, and any movement in daylight could draw fire.

As the first battalions entered the Sommerviller trenches for inaugural ten-day tours of front-line duty in late October, their electric sense of high adventure was palpable. One of the battalion commanders, Maj. Theodore Roosevelt Jr., admitted that on their way into the front lines, he and his men "were all very green and very earnest." But this romantic notion of the Western Front was unmatched by the dirty, monotonous reality of the sector. "The first thrill of service in the trenches soon passed," Marshall noted, "with a realization of the mud and other discomforts and the dearth of excitement." Even Roosevelt, whose eagerness for combat duty was re-nowned and whose enthusiasm, according to Marshall, "knew no bounds," later depicted the frustrating minutiae of the experience like a repressed fighter: "During the ten days we spent in the sector," he fretted, the thousand-plus men of his battalion were reduced to "shoveling mud the color and consistency of melted chocolate ice cream from cave-ins which constantly occurred in the trench system."

Eager doughboys anticipated—and many hoped for—a taste of front-line excitement matching the colorful war stories painted by their British and French instructors over the summer months: artillery clashes and trench raids and patrols through no-man's-land. But the tedium and dreariness of the first few days were barely broken by any action. "The artillery on both sides contented itself with a few ranging shots each day," Marshall noted, "and these were so directed as to avoid causing casualties." Furthermore, the Americans were prohibited from venturing beyond their own barbed wire, trapping them day and night in the muddy trenches, where an impatient thirst for a break in the monotony drove many uninitiated young soldiers to conjure up Germans where they did not exist.

"It is quite true," Lt. Richard Newhall later wrote of this time, "that when you have been peering out into the dark for a while the posts in the entanglement begin to put on German helmets and to creep towards you." Like many other recent graduates of the first round of ninety-day officer-training schools, twenty-nine-year-old Newhall was a brand-new lieutenant, a "90-day-wonder" or "shavetail." Less than a month in France, he was thrust into the responsibility of learning to lead the fifty men of his newly assigned platoon. "My own experience in the trenches was that my chief job was to restrain the men from senseless firing," he soon wrote his mother. Hearing automatic-rifle fire from his men's positions in the dark of night, he would discover they had fired on "a noise in the wire." "Do you think you can hit a noise in the dark?" he would inquire. "No, sir." Newhall would then send up a flare revealing no Germans in the wire or anywhere in no-man's-land, and "so the men calm down and things remain quiet."

Day after sleepless, muddy day slowly passed in this unnerving "quiet" until finally broken by the arrival of the American artillery. The 9,000 men of the three field artillery regiments that formed the 1st US Field Artillery Brigade had arrived in France in early August after shipping out from their home stations in Texas and Arizona. For an Army branch that spent half a century with a primary mission of coastal defense, and for gunners accustomed to 1885 model field cannon, the two months of schooling at the French artillery training grounds at Valdahon presented new guns and a steep learning curve. Equipped with the modern 155mm howitzer and the celebrated French 75mm—a gun with a hydropneumatic recoil that allowed rapid fire of over twenty shots per minute on the same target without reaiming and widely regarded as the greatest light artillery piece on either side of the Western Front—the American artillery took daily target practice, learned the effects of wind and temperatures on shell trajectories, and as the unit war diary recorded, made "rapid progress" before joining the division infantry at the front.

With orders to "generally reinforce the French Artillery behind trenches occupied by our Infantry," the first battalions of each of the three regiments of the 1st Field Artillery Brigade marched along dusty country roads behind their new guns, drawn by teams of sickly looking emaciated horses whose strongest days were long-before spent in years of service at the French front. On arrival at battery positions in the Sommerviller sector, the doughboy gunners received a warm welcome. "The enthusiasm of the French was tremendous when they saw the American artillerymen bringing up their guns. The *poilus* shook every man by the hand," the unit history noted.

After the first few days of desultory small-arms fire, shot aimlessly from the front line trenches by skittish doughboys at noises in the dark, Captain Marshall noticed that "[t]he enthusiastic activity of the newly-arrived American artillery tended to break the calm and stirred the enemy to retaliatory measures." The shot that cracked "the calm" was fired by twenty-three-year-old Sgt. Alex Arch of South Bend, Indiana, who pulled the lanyard of his 75 just after six a.m., October 23, and sent a sixteen-pound, three-inch-diameter shell—the first American shot of the World War—over the heads of the infantry, across no-man's-land into the enemy lines. More shells followed, "going over with a long, slow swishy sort of sound," one lieutenant described in a letter home.

German "retaliatory measures" began quickly, and a series of historic but unfortunate firsts followed. The same day America's first shot was fired, Field Hospital No. 13 reported the division's first injuries from enemy artillery. Two days later, the first officer, Lt. De Vere Harden of Burlington, Vermont, was injured when a German shell fragment struck his knee (Major Roosevelt, nearby when the blast occurred, ran to congratulate Harden "on having the honor to be the first American officer hit while serving with American troops"). Within a week, doughboys captured their first German after he ventured too close to the 18th Infantry Regiment's trenches on a night patrol. And then, after the first ten-day tour had drowsed to an end without loss of life, came the tragic but inevitable: America's first combat deaths.

The blow struck just after the second battalions of each regiment relieved the first, taking positions in the front lines during the dark, wet early morning hours of November 3. As with their comrades ten days earlier, the men of Company F, 16th Infantry Regiment—part of the very battalion that had marched in the Paris July 4 parade four months earlier—settled into muddy lines on the rim of a bald hill, "tense with the novelty and the sense of danger." At three a.m. came a "blinding flash and a crash and a roar" of a German box barrage, trapping over two dozen doughboys in the front-line trench and cutting them off from support. Most soldiers—heeding the advice of their French and British instructors—opened their mouths wide while the shells exploded, so their eardrums would not burst, yet many were deafened and a few were knocked unconscious. "Nothing but the boom of big guns and explosion of big shells could be heard," Pvt. Ruben Nelson, lying in a nearby trench, soon told his diary. From outside the barrage, he and the men of his platoon felt powerless to help. "The only thing we could do," Nelson noted, was "to flank the boxed sector with machine-gun fire."

Gray-clad, Mauser-wielding Germans in coal-scuttle helmets materialized in the smoke shrouding no-man's-land. Private Nelson noticed "about 300 Germans making our lines. We knew what was coming," he wrote of the moment: "Three hundred against thirty." Grenades exploded and rifle fire crackled and yells in German and English punctuated the clamor of the barrage. Although doughboy rifles and machine guns "burnt themselves up" to repel the raid, German attackers proved too many and swarmed the American trenches. The spur of first combat erupted in a bloody clash of rifles, pistols, and bayonets. Rookie defenders fought back in fits of unregulated adrenaline, their actions finding order only in reloading rifle clips and unjamming automatic-rifle magazines—involuntary flashes of muscle memory acquired in their summer of training. At the sound of a high-pitched whistle, the Germans leaped back out of the trench, disappeared as one into the darkness beyond the wire, and the confusion and noise ended as abruptly as it had begun.

The dead calm of the inky-dark night returned, but adrenaline was still flowing. "Our men were some nervous when it was over," Private Nelson confided to his diary, adding, "I'm wondering, What next??" Five Americans lay wounded, waiting for stretcher bearers to evacuate them for treatment. Eleven were missing—the first Americans captured by the Germans as prisoners of war. And three, Cpl. James Gresham, Pvt. Merle Hay, and Pvt. Thomas Enright, lay dead in the muddy trench bottom. Two had been shot, and one had his throat sliced open so deep his head was nearly severed. Captain Marshall, who happened to be with the French Army sector commander, Gen. Paul Bordeaux, when he heard the melee, made his way through tangles of collapsed trenches to the front lines and watched with men solemnly lining both sides of the approach trench, heads bowed and helmets removed, as the blanket-covered bodies were carried by stretcher bearers to the rear.

The next day, under a warm midafternoon sun, the first three Americans to fall in combat in the World War were buried with full military honors in a pasture edging the nearby village of Bathelémont. Companies of American and French troops stood in loose formation surrounding the fresh graves. A French chaplain stood in his trench coat and Adrian helmet and spoke a prayer from a small Bible. In his immaculate sky-blue uniform and visored coffee-can cap, General Bordeaux stepped forward and spoke in English through a thick French accent, adding inspiration to the solemnity.

"Men! These graves, the first to be dug in our national soil, at but a short distance from the enemy, are as a mark of the mighty hand of our Allies," Bordeaux began. Their sacrifice confirmed "the will of the people and Army of the United States to fight with us to a finish," and he asked that "the mortal remains of these young men be left here, be left to us forever." Envisioning an eternal monument to their memory, he crowned their eulogy with the gratitude of unborn generations:

> We will inscribe on their tombs: 'Here lie the first soldiers of the famous Republic of the United States to fall on the soil of France, for justice and liberty.' The passerby will stop and uncover his head. The travelers of France, of the Allied countries, of America, the men of heart, who will come to visit our battlefield of Lorraine, will go out of the way to come here, to bring to these graves the tribute of their respect and of their gratefulness. Corporal Gresham, Private Enright, Private Hay, in the name of France, I thank you. God receive your souls. Farewell!

A hastily assembled seven-man rifle squad from the 16th Infantry Regiment stood in rumpled khaki tunics and boots splattered with the dried mud of the trenches. At the sergeant's quick command, they chambered rounds with slams of their bolts, aimed their Springfields toward the cloudy sky above the fresh graves, and fired a volley. Then a second. And finally a third. As the crackle of shots faded across the countryside, a bugler played "Taps." It was the first performance in eulogy on French soil of the three-note melody that would stir emotions for fallen comrades thousands of times through the present World War and the one to follow.

In 1921, at their families' requests, the remains of all three soldiers were disinterred and shipped back across the Atlantic for reburial in hometown cemeteries in Iowa, Indiana, and Pennsylvania. A granite memorial, rebuilt after its 1940 destruction by occupying German forces, still marks where they were first laid to rest. Casting permanence to General Bordeaux's stirring but fleeting words from that brisk afternoon now a century gone, the gold-leaf inscription reads: *"Ici en terre Lorraine, reposent les trois premiers soldats américains tues a l'ennemi le 3 novembre 1917"* (Here on Lorraine soil rest the first three American soldiers killed by the enemy on November 3, 1917).

For the soldiers still up in the trenches, and for the battalions that followed through mid-November, news of the first casualties kept them on edge day and night, and the second and third ten-day tours passed slowly. "Our losses were slight during the remaining days which seemed like years," Private Nelson told his diary. "We were from the night of Nov. 2 always looking for a raid and it would be hard for a surprise attack to be pulled off." There were no more raids, but the Americans and Germans sent patrols forward each night, their paths crossing occasionally in no-man's-land in frantic, backpedaling clashes of pistol fire. And American casualties continued. Eleven more were killed and three dozen wounded—almost all at the hands of German shells, more of the "retaliatory measures" prompted by the division artillery's assertiveness—before finally leaving the sector.

"Must say [we] were glad to get out," Private Nelson scratched in his diary after he and his platoon, a "bunch of worn out and hungry Americans," crawled through a muddy communication trench away from the front lines, instilled with new confidence. "At the end of the ten days we were relieved," Major Roosevelt later wrote of his battalion, who "hiked back veteran troops, as we thought, to the training area." Lieutenant Newhall noticed the same fresh poise in the men of his platoon as they returned to Gondrecourt: "The men thought that now they were veterans. They had been to the front and returned safely. They knew shell fire or thought they did." With more American units landing in France every week to add to the ever-expanding AEF, 1st Division troops were proud to finally belong to a "veteran" outfit "actually at war at last." From Newhall's perspective as a platoon leader, it seemed that the proving grounds of the Sommerviller trenches had elevated both cohesion and morale: "From that time forward the esprit de corps was unmistakable."

"The Division Commander wishes to congratulate the soldiers of the Division upon their excellent conduct and cheerful demeanor during the past month at the front," read Major General Sibert's General Order to his troops as they returned from the Sommerviller trenches in late November. Entering the final stage of instruction, "training of the combined division in the tactics of open warfare," Sibert announced his confidence in them, his sureness to "depend on every individual soldier to meet the situation with the same fortitude and resolution" displayed in the first two stages.

But in Sibert as a commander, General Pershing did not share the same confidence. As other divisions arrived through the fall and winter months, the men of the 1st Division became known as "Pershing's Darlings." The Big Chief believed it "highly essential" that the first battles fought by American troops be successful to build Allied faith in the AEF, and it was widely accepted that the troops of his favored 1st Division would be the first to fight. But over the course of seventeen inspections stops at the division since June, Pershing had found Sibert to be absent or sick for most of them. And in the qualities Pershing held highest—drill, discipline, bearing—his "darlings" were still lacking, responsibility for which he laid at the commander's feet. "He is without much training since cadet days," Pershing's chief of staff noted of Sibert in his diary, "and has let his division run down."

In mid-December, after sending a message to all his division commanders imploring them to avoid the "note of deep pessimism" that was rumored to have invaded the morale of certain "general officers," Pershing replaced Sibert—the unspoken target of his message—with the man who had not only had a proven record leading citizen soldiers in battle but had also demonstrated effective leadership in quickly establishing a complex network of AEF officer-training schools throughout France—Maj. Gen. Robert Bullard.

If Ralph Waldo Emerson was correct in asserting that an "institution is the lengthened shadow of one man," the man casting the 1st Division's shadow for the remainder of the war would be Robert Bullard. While still en route in a sedan provided by AEF Headquarters, he impressed the enlisted driver by helping change a flat tire in the wet, frigid December air. Immediately upon arrival at Division Headquarters, Bullard gathered his brigade and regimental commanders and staff and announced: "If we cannot do the job, we will be replaced." His tone left no doubt that he would not be the first to go.

The division's lot in the war would henceforth be directly cast by Bullard's command decisions, each one thoughtfully pragmatic and rooted in his mostly self-cultivated abilities. He was no academic—he had graduated twenty-seventh in a class of thirty-nine from West Point. And although he could speak fluent French, had taught Latin and trigonometry for money before college, and had published articles in the *Journal of Military Service*, *Atlantic Monthly*, and *Field & Stream*, he was no intellectual. But he was a studied calculator of the motives that govern men, and readings of Colmar von der Goltz's *Conduct of War* and biographies of Confederate generals filled his spare hours and contemplative mind. His greatest teacher was experience, and his first decision as division commander stemmed from his most lasting lesson of combat, learned nearly twenty years before in the throes of fighting in the Philippines.

It was back in 1899, when a regiment of volunteer infantrymen led by then Colonel-of-Volunteers Robert Bullard entered battle with insurgents in the Philippine jungle. An artillery battery led by a thirty-two-year-old lieutenant named Charles Summerall effectively discharged the enemy from their positions, opening a path for Bullard's riflemen. "Under rattling fire from the enemy," Bullard noticed, the lieutenant "stood boldly forth in the open, directing the fire." So impressed was Bullard by this young artillery officer that twice more in the Philippines he would specifically request the support of his battery, and in subsequent action would find Summerall's service as good as he "saw rendered by any officer or man." Bullard, a career infantryman, took lasting note of such effective gun support, and seventeen years later, his first move as 1st Division commander was to replace the existing leader of his 1st Field Artillery Brigade with Brigadier General Summerall.

The son of a Confederate soldier and grandson of a Florida slave owner, Charles Pelot Summerall was, like Bullard, a product of the Deep South. As a boy he picked cotton and helped his father sell produce, and as a young man he taught school to support his parents and two older siblings. At nineteen, he beat out eleven others in a competitive examination sponsored by his local congressman, earning a ticket to West Point, where he graduated in the top third of the class of 1892 and, like General Pershing six years before, as First Captain. As a young lieutenant, Summerall sought out frontline service, and reports of his exploits under fire in the Philippines earned him an invitation to return to West Point as a senior instructor of artillery tactics. There his fire demonstrations impressed such visitors as Lord Kitchener of England and Princeton president Woodrow Wilson, and his students included cadet (and future general) George S. Patton.

Fiery and diminutive, Summerall stood five feet eight inches tall, and his short legs, long torso, and barrel-shaped waistline made him seem shorter still. But his unimposing frame had already cast a long shadow in a growing Army. He positioned himself perpetually on the tactical cutting edge, helping to spearhead the Army's move from an era of dated muzzle-loading cannon to modern, rapid-fire, breech-loading field guns. By America's entry into the World War, his career had spanned what he called a period of "marked changes," and in the early days of mobilization to France, his expertise earned him a spot as colonel on the Baker Commission's panel of experts, where he asked inconvenient questions and assertively sought to define a pivotal role for artillery in the AEF.

But General Pershing and his staff at AEF General Headquarters were still holding an inflexible adherence to the romantic notion of a rifleman's war, which artillery could only profane. In his role on the panel and with little deference or tact, Summerall professed "the infantry would pay in losses for lack of artillery." He pushed for a 75mm gun for every fifteen yards of American front, and a 155mm for every hundred yards, more than twice the number AEF planners were advocating. According to his later recollection of events, he was "viciously attacked" for even suggesting so much artillery, and Pershing—in Summerall's estimation, "furious"—privately admonished Summerall to "get together" with his staff's ideals. Dangling his point precariously near the line of insubordination, the undaunted Summerall responded, "Your staff was wrong," adding that he intended to return to Washington "to fight for what I know is best for our artillery."

Back in DC, Summerall tirelessly advanced the artillery cause, was appointed by the War Department to prepare the AEF field artillery instruction program, and was promoted to brigadier general and shipped back to France by September. Whether General Bullard knew of the early summer clash with Pershing is unknown, but it likely would not have mattered. Since his fighting experience with young Summerall's artillery in the Philippines, Bullard held a deep appreciation for combined arms even if, in practice, he exercised more subtlety than Summerall. As head of AEF officer schools, Bullard had exhibited a deft touch in harmonizing the opposing dogmas of Pershing's staff with those of the British and French. Now as division commander, he continued to contemplate large decisions through the lens of a tactical pragmatist, and his renewed collaboration with Summerall was set to bridge a wide gulf between his infantry and artillery—two arms at historic odds.

From the first moments of General Summerall's arrival at Division Headquarters on the bitterly cold afternoon of December 22, Bullard could tell the "influence of a master artilleryman and commander was felt." Now fifty years old, gray had started frosting Summerall's dark brown hair, but his warm eyes and handsome features remained youthful and disarming. He had the rare ability to issue "the severest reprimand in the quietest words," was unsparing in praise and recognition for the deeds of men under his command, and in them he quickly inspired what Bullard described as "almost fanatical support." It was "the hand of destiny," in Summerall's own estimation, that he had been chosen, and it would prove Bullard a master talent scout in a single move.

By the third week of December, the mercury dipped below zero, and "sunny France" was invaded by ice and snow flurries. "We have been enjoying a large quantity of snow recently," Lt. Sam Ervin wrote his "mama" back in Morganton, North Carolina, from the farmhouse where he billeted with two other officers. "In fact," he added, "the ground has been entirely covered for almost a week and the temperature has been quite low for some time." The doughboys had endured difficult conditions during their time in France—rain, mud, fear, homesickness—but never had they been tried so severely by the weather. George Marshall later remembered: "When we were not cursed with mud, we were frozen with the cold." Supply issues caused a shortage of gloves and winter coats, and the men, still sleeping in drafty barns under thin blankets, woke up each morning with feet so swollen they found difficulty putting their boots on. One soldier noted that these tough conditions "inured the men to withstand the worst exposure of campaign without weakening," and another quipped, "[T]he father of his country and Valley Forge had nothing on us."

The extreme cold hampered the final stage of training, made all the more important by the addition of new draftees. The first crop had recently arrived, anxious boys and middle-aged men of little discipline and uneven potential. "There were many Poles and Russians and Jugo-Slavs of various sorts," one officer noted, adding that "several could speak no English whatever." Eyeing these new conscripts, Major Roosevelt spotted a manifest need for crash training: "A large percentage had never shot any firearms, and still a larger percentage had never shot the service rifle." The rookie doughboys were spread among the veteran troops, and along with more fresh lieutenants from the second round of officer-training schools, they swelled each company to the AEF target complement of 250 men. And the division as a whole—now with the artillery brigade and newly arrived engineer regiment—reached Pershing's planned strength of 28,000 soldiers. It was a number twice as large as French, British, or German divisions, an immensity chosen for "staying power" on the battlefield.

These final days leading to Christmas and the New Year were spent in large-unit training, where, as Lt. Richard Newhall described, commanders and staff got swift practice "in handling men by the thousands, and accustom the men to act as parts of a large force." Leading one of the nearly 150 sixty-man platoons conducting the massive division maneuvers, Newhall wrote home, describing the "very bad, unusually cold and exceedingly wet" weather as "a test of endurance," a trial he rated as "harder than any front-line experiences before the big advance." In his own letter home, Newhall's bunkmate and fellow platoon leader, Lt. George Haydock, wrote of three straight days he and his men spent in "long hikes on slippery roads," getting only an egg and a piece of ham for supper, then an entire night manning simulated outposts on frozen ground in the biting cold. "It was the first time I had to handle the men alone," the twenty-three-year-old wrote, excitedly adding that he "learned a great deal." Even Haydock, a Massachusetts native and Harvard alum who knew the bone-deep chill of New England winters, was struck by the night's harsh cold: "We were on a high ridge with the coldest wind I have ever known blowing about thirty miles an hour straight on us."

This was as General Bullard wished. He embraced such arduous conditions, believing they hardened his soldiers, mentally preparing them to meet even the worst that could be thrown at them when the time came to enter combat. And events elsewhere were conspiring not only to move that time nearer but also to make Allied reliance on his division's eventual success even greater.

That fall, the French front had remained stagnant and British offensives in Flanders had resulted in a quarter million Allied casualties. The small bit of bright news—gains by the British at Cambrai, a first with the effective support of tanks—turned dark again by late November as German counterattacks recaptured the ground gained. But the darkest news came from the Eastern Front. A large part of the Italian Army, holding the Allied line at Caporetto, had recently crumbled under a joint German/Austro-Hungarian offensive, resulting in the capture of more than 300,000 troops and 3,000 artillery pieces. And Russia, now under Bolshevik rule following the overthrow of Tsar Nicholas II and the recent takeover of the Kerensky provisional government, was negotiating a separate peace with the Central Powers. Though the treaty terms would not be finalized until March, the cease-fire withdrew the massive Russian Army from the war, effectively ending the fighting on the Eastern Front and releasing more than sixty German divisions to pack up, board trains, and join the fighting in the west.

"Seemingly in an instant the cause of the Allies had been dealt a master blow," General Pershing would later lament. Since the first shots of the war had been fired three Augusts before, the prospects of victory had never seemed bleaker. Based on Allied Intelligence, Pershing had recently estimated German strength in the west at "a present total of 150 divisions"—a force the 170-odd Allied divisions had been unable to defeat and had barely been able to hold off defensively. Suddenly, on top of the loss of five British and six French divisions "rushed to Italy to save the situation" at Caporetto, five dozen German divisions were rushing west to tip the scales of the precarious balance at the front, endeavoring to knock the Allies out of the war before the slowly waking American giant arrived in force.

With only four AEF divisions in France, General Bullard understood that his 1st Division, the only one fully trained and deemed "fit for open warfare," would be the first American unit to face the German Army in pitched battle. His thoughts turned to his men—store clerks and farmers-turned-infantrymen, bending their minds sharply to fit into military routine, a life as foreign to them as the land they now populated, each soldier learning to lean ever more on those sharing his misery beside him, every tough step of every painful march in frozen boots through snow and ice fusing them together as teams of dozen-man squads within sixty-man platoons, led by college-students-turned-lieutenants still learning the difficult art of leading men in the dark of war.

Of all that the United States would throw at the German Empire, these men would be the first. Just a month previous, Bullard had confided to his diary a fear that "I think we came too late," and more recently he added concern over the slowness of training: "It is a very remote preparing." But with his soldiers on the brink, satisfied that preparations were finally "going at a high rate of speed," he gave no more voice to pessimism. "This was the stimulus," Bullard later revealed, and the rigorous drill schedule that carried his 28,000 doughboys into the New Year prompted no further nervous diary entries. From his perch as field commander on the fighting edge of America's forces, Bullard recognized that "the eyes of all the Allies and of all the world would be especially on" the doughboys of his 1st Division, and "if they failed the world would say that America would fail."

The year 1918 approached, and time marched ever onward. An even larger German Army loomed, threatening. Robert Bullard did not know where or when, but he knew it was his men who would bring a decidedly American production into the theater of war. Until that time and place was decided, he was resolute: "They must not fail."

CHAPTER 4

Adventure of War

"Your letter of Nov. 12 arrived this week and it was a dandy letter too. You can't imagine how much pleasure and inspiration I get out of your letters all so nice and tender and homey." By gas-fired lamplight in the drafty confines of a quaint farmhouse where he was bunking with another officer, Lt. Jim Hartney spent the first moments of 1918 writing his girlfriend, his "Dearest Margaret," back home in Minneapolis. Their correspondence, steady since Jim's time in Plattsburg Officer Training Camp the previous summer, simultaneously warmed the chill of her worry and his homesickness. Imploring her to not let herself "get all fussed up over a little old war," he added, "I hope the new year will have lots of good luck in store for both of us." He typically closed his letters with the understated "God bless you my sweetheart," or a quick "yours," and she would end her letters to him, her "dearest beloved," with "heaps of love." But the blank slate of a new year and rumors of impending action filled him with sufficient inspiration—and perhaps passing thoughts of mortality—to close this letter with deeper sentiment: "I love you, Margaret."

One week later, General Bullard gathered his top officers in his headquarters to announce a move to the front lines. A hot fire blazed in the chateau's stone fireplace, and Bullard, his slim figure wrapped in a wolfskin coat, shivering and suffering another severe bout of neuritis, forced a calm air of outward tranquility. Ever impatient with inaction, the dawn of a New Year renewed his frustration that "nine months had now passed since we had put ourselves in the war and we were still there by declaration only." But despite the physical aches now invading his body, his officers and staff noted his spirits soared with the announcement.

The division was moving into the Seicheprey sector, the southern face of the Saint-Mihiel salient. Bullard's soldiers were to relieve the Moroccan Division currently holding the four-mile front, and they would enter the trenches, for the first time, as a war-strength division—infantry, artillery, engineers, and machine-gun companies. This move was General Pershing's answer to recent Allied demands for amalgamation of American forces into their established units along the front.

In December, British Prime Minister David Lloyd George had pressed for "half-trained American companies or battalions" to be thrown into the trenches with British divisions. And the French had petitioned Washington, DC, directly for AEF infantry regiments to be divvied up to strengthen French units at the front. To these overtures, Secretary Baker responded by cabling Pershing that "identity of our forces" was from here on deemed "secondary to the meeting of any critical situation by the most helpful use possible of the troops" at his command.

As with the bulk of his wartime directives to Pershing, Baker's message was deferential. And while the cable signaled a slight shift from Wilson's order of the early summer, it again underscored Pershing's "full authority to use the forces" of the AEF as he saw fit. Pershing's most cherished strategic dream—consistent with Wilson's initial order—was a self-contained, all-American section of the front. Not ready to loosen his tight grip on that vision, Pershing employed his autonomy by translating Baker's words narrowly. He read "any critical situation" to mean "emergency," and at present, he saw none. But he did bend somewhat to the Allied entreaties, sending the 1st Division to man the Seicheprey front under French command. And by ordering the full division into the line as one, under its own flag, he wisely set a precedent of enduring importance, ensuring no AEF divisions would be split apart through the course of the war.*

"Everyone was relieved that the period of training was at an end," noted George Marshall, retained by General Bullard as operations officer and promoted to lieutenant colonel. With a shortage of trucks and no rail lines in the path toward Seicheprey, division troops would have to walk the twenty-four-mile journey, made all the more difficult by more severe winter weather. A "terrific blizzard" hit the night before their march, which they were forced to make in threadbare uniforms on what Marshall described as "roads heavily glazed with smooth ice." Pvt. Ruben Nelson vented to his diary, "The roads are full of ice and snow . . . many men fell out on this

---

* Black infantry regiments were the conspicuous exception, handed by Pershing over to the French Army for front-line service under French Corps command.

march." General Summerall would later describe the "bitter cold" and his shivering artillerymen coaxing exhausted, emaciated horses forward through "deep snow and ice on the roads." Their "progress was slow" as "horses constantly fell," and wheeled guns and supply wagons slipped sideways on the ice of paved roadways and overturned into ditches. One captain heard General Bullard remark that the first day of the five-day trek to Seicheprey was the "worst day he had seen troops out in 35 years of service." Years later, Marshall remembered this march, the bite of the north wind that "penetrated the thickest clothing," and the soldiers, "exhausted by their efforts to make progress against the strong head wind along the slippery surface of the highway." War aside, it was a journey of the type that would be retold well into old age by those who shared its difficult passage.

By the time the first battalions relieved the French troops in the muddy front lines near Seicheprey on January 21, the frost had thawed and signs of early spring appeared. "The weather is much better now, the sun out, the snow gone, and the mud fast drying," Lt. George Redwood wrote his mother in Baltimore; "Everyone is beginning to feel more industrious and energetic now that less time is put in keeping warm." Lt. Sam Ervin wrote his grandfather back in North Carolina, describing "spring weather" that "makes one desire to go bare-footed, a-swimming and a-fishing." But from back in the trenches, where all conditions—weather especially—were analyzed by the effect on war's calibrations, many officers viewed the emerging warmth as a spur for rekindled action. "[W]ith the prospect of spring," Lt. Richard Newhall later recalled, "came also the prospect of renewed activity which the men welcomed with excited enthusiasm."

The sector was swampy and, as one soldier described, "the front lines lay in low, marshy valley, so that the trenches were always awash with mud." Rain had replaced the snow, and as General Bullard observed, "men and officers were in the mud day and night." As with Sommerviller, no offensives had been staged by either side in this region, and the trenches on both sides had been well established by more than three years of static occupancy. Although told it was a "quiet" sector, doughboys cycling through the trenches in ten-day shifts quickly found it to be, in the Division History's words, "neither quiet nor restful." "This was a real fighting front," Lieutenant Newhall noted. "It was a sector of raids, patrolling, and intermittent bombardment." Lt. Irving Wood agreed, calling it "a very lively sector with raids, shelling and machine-gun firing going on all the time . . . a very nerve racking place." It was, as Major Roosevelt described, "our first real taste of war."

For most 1st Division doughboys, the Seicheprey sector was also their first real taste of the dreaded mustard gas. Since first introducing poison gas to the war two years before, the Germans had become proficient in dosing the Allies, mostly in high concentrations via explosive artillery shells shot deep behind the front lines into artillery emplacements to render gun crews ineffective or into billeting areas to cause mass casualties among sleeping units. Through February and March, division muster rolls swelled with gas casualties, and though typically not fatal, the repeated phrase "gassed in action" in unit morning reports did little to describe the gruesome effects of what Marshall called this "hideous phase of warfare."

Mucus poured out of eyes, and eyelids swelled with red sores, causing blindness that was typically temporary though sometimes permanent (ten years after the war, one engineer officer gassed at Seicheprey could still see only "a strong light"). All exposed skin rashed over red, then bubbled up into large blisters as painful as second- and third-degree burns. Those who breathed it got bloody noses and coughed uncontrollably as their throats closed, swollen with airway blisters. Gagging, choking, writhing men who made it to a field hospital in time to have air tubes shoved down their throats were still left with incurable tongue sores and often without a voice. Sgt. Clem Woodbury of Michigan wrote home after getting gassed: "I couldn't speak for about a month and the gas burns on my body were very painful."

Heavy and carried by fickle winds, mustard gas settled on the ground and pooled in unexpected places. An artillery officer noticed two men washing their faces in "water from a shell hole which happened to contain 'mustard' and six hours later they were scarred and burned terribly as with a hot iron." On another occasion he saw a French soldier "burned from sitting in the grass where a mustard shell had burst." Even a small whiff could leave men with severe cold-like symptoms, as well as diarrhea, nausea, and vomiting that persisted for weeks.

The feared brownish-yellow cloud shot immediate terror into soldiers who feared its effects more than bullets or shrapnel. The reach of German guns lobbing gas shells seemed to be limitless, and doughboys grew quickly familiar with the hollow "plunking" sound of a mustard-gas projectile hitting the ground, followed by the hiss of pressurized gas escaping, then men with eyes squeezed shut flailing to strap on ill-fitting masks. "As soon as the shells hit the ground they explode and great clouds of poisonous gas rise," Pvt. Stanley Mindikowski of Chicago complained in a letter home.

"No matter how soon you adjust your mask you get a whiff of that stuff, and if the attacks are repeated those little whiffs begin to work on you, and before you know it you're ready for the hospital."

Doughboys were issued the British Small Box Respirator, or "SBR," a cumbersome, uncomfortable mask most soldiers couldn't tolerate for longer than a few minutes. Pvt. Jesse Evans wrote in his diary that the SBRs "were not the easiest things to fight in," and one officer called them "painfully oppressive." General Bullard later shared his own aversion: "It seemed to me in all my trials and efforts that I should be smothered if I remained longer than three minutes in that gas mask." Many men managed to acquire the less-oppressive French mask, which was nothing but a filter that covered the face. "I put on the French because it is more quickly adjusted . . . It is cheese-cloth about an inch thick, soaked in chemicals," Private Evans told his diary.

Whichever version they preferred, soldiers went nowhere without their masks, and at the signal for gas—either a green flare or a klaxon horn—all else was dropped in place until masks were on. Strolling behind the front lines one night, Lieutenant Colonel Marshall heard the baritone wheezing of a klaxon and asked a nearby enlisted man, who was urgently throwing on his own SBR, whether the alarm was real or just practice. The man snapped back: "Put on your mask, you damn fool, and don't ask questions." When later learning of this episode involving his operations officer, General Bullard praised the alert soldier: "I was never able to find this young man, or I would have caused him to be promoted."

Far more than in Sommerviller the previous fall, in the Seicheprey sector, 1st Division soldiers endured the whole harsh reality of trench life, of which mustard gas was just one part. To the injuries caused by gas and sniping and shelling was added the insult of constant discomfort. "[T]here were vermin and rats and mud to the waist," Major Roosevelt later recounted. Maggots—soldiers called them "vermin" and "cooties"—invaded everything, feeding on dropped ration tins and rat carcasses and planting eggs in the boots and uniforms of sleeping troops. One platoon leader remembered waking from fitful sleep "picking out cooties and their eggs" from his underclothes.

"I carry a blanket with me and that is indispensable," Lt. Vinton Dearing wrote home, describing the eighteen-inch-tall, two-foot-wide dirt dugout where he shaved while lying down and seized the rare "luxury" of "sleeping with one's shoes off." Trenches themselves were described by

Lieutenant Newhall as "soaked with rain till they are masses of mud, strewn with equipment of all kinds." He wrote of "living in the mud and sleeping in a rat-infested dug-out," and rubbing down his feet each morning with whale oil to prevent trench foot, then checking to see that his men did the same. His good friend George Haydock had his own answer for trench rats: "we even had to go so far as to shoot a couple of them."

The rain of the French spring was relentless. "The men either huddled against the side of a trench or stretched their ponchos from parapet to parapet, and sat beneath them in a foot-deep puddle of water," Major Roosevelt recounted. Through the taxing conditions, young platoon leaders searched for ways to motivate their troops. Lieutenant Haydock wrote home: "It is pretty hard to ask a man to be on the alert for fourteen hours, standing in mud, and then get him to do any work in the day-time." This lack of any sleep strained many soldiers. Twenty-five-year-old Lt. Robert Anderson wrote his father back in Wilson, North Carolina: "The most disagreeable part about the trenches was the mud and water in one sector and over five nights with about four hours sleep in all."

During their ten-day shifts at the front, most troops survived on cold rations and very little drinkable water. "We had only two canteens of water each, for 24 hours," Lt. Dick Dacus later recounted, and it had to be stretched "for drinking, washing, and shaving." Pvt. Ruben Nelson wrote in his diary, "The only thing we lack is something to eat." When hunger hit them through the day, they had to depend on their reserve rations, described by one officer as "soaked and muddy hardtack" and canned beef dubbed "corned willie." Soldiers in the front lines were allotted one warm meal per day, carried forward to the sector's edge in Marmite cans on supply carts under the cover of darkness. Chow parties were sent out through communication trenches and across open ground in rear areas to retrieve food, a perilous journey of two miles or more through German shellfire.

"They just couldn't get that meat to us," Cpl. Patrick Slamon of Boston, Massachusetts, later remembered. "They tried hard enough, but no man could get through the fire that was laid down by the Germans and reach us." The few cans that made it through were filled with cold stew and potatoes, a thick soup Lieutenant Ervin called "slumgullion." George Marshall noted "a favorite method of preparing the meal" was to mix it up and pour molasses over the top, and he later remembered one soldier reasoning that "they might as well mix it up outside as well as inside." As General

Bullard later quipped: "Food and coffee were always cold and the water warm. But that is war."

Through the dragging minutes of the night's darkness, it was hunger and exhaustion that stretched men's nerves. In the daylight, with every inch of the American trench top covered by overlapping fields of German machine gunners and snipers, it was the fear of getting shot. As Bullard explained, "a head, a hand, any sign of a human body shown above the trenches anywhere immediately drew the fire of the enemy." But at all hours and in all weather, the greatest danger—and the most draining on the spirit of a soldier—was the shelling.

"I guess the worst thing is to sit in the bottom of a trench and listen to the shells come," Richard Newhall wrote his mother. "There isn't anything to do but sit tight and wonder where the next one is going to land." The incessant bombardments "are indeed very noisy things and make you move around with a crook in your back," Newhall's buddy George Haydock wrote home, "or else hang on to the front of the trench as if you expected it to get away from you." German artillery fired mortar rounds and shells of all kinds into the American lines, from 77mm "whiz-bangs" ("we were usually on our stomachs by the time the bang came," Haydock remarked) to the large 150mm "Jack Johnsons," nicknamed by soldiers for the famous heavyweight boxer.

The detonation of a German high-explosive shell sent lead balls and steel fragments the size of railroad spikes cutting through anything in their path—weapons, canteens, wooden trench supports, and human flesh. Some troops hit directly were cut in half, others had arms and legs ripped off, and a few disappeared, shot to unrecognizable pieces, reported in death records as "nothing left to bury." Many who were hit survived, like Sgt. Paul Chamberlain, who wrote home to Kansas from a field hospital after shrapnel tore into his shoulder: "There's a bunch of scrap iron in those Dutch shells and it got me." Some died simply from the concussion, found lying without a scratch as if sleeping, their bones shattered and insides turned to soup.

With unexplainable chance, some shells caused no physical damage at all. "Perhaps it is good luck," Lt. Jim Hartney admitted in a letter to his girlfriend, Margaret. "I've been through a couple of these bombardments and it is extraordinary how little damage is done." Hartney even witnessed six shells hit the chow party, which only "knocked the cups out of their hands but . . . left the men uninjured." The only commonality of artillery blasts was the shattering impact they could have on the minds of men, and contrary to the earthly proverb, what did not kill them often left them weaker. As George Marshall would describe: "A 3" shell will temporarily scare or deter a man; a 6" shell will shock him; but an 8" shell, such as these 210mm ones, rips up the nervous system of everyone within a hundred yards of the explosion."

Never one to be a silent spectator in events and determining the same for the division he was shaping, General Bullard issued an order: "Be active all over no man's land; do not leave its control to the enemy." His Alabama childhood had been filled with stories of the gloom and low morale that contributed to Confederate defeat: "I remembered the tradition of the loss of heart, aggressiveness, and morale of the Confederates shut up in the trenches at Vicksburg." And his own experience in the Philippines taught him that being "shut up in trenches" caused soldiers to lose "all aggressiveness, all spirit of offense." Now, resolute that his men would not fall prey to the same dejection, he directed that patrols for intelligence occur nightly and raids as often as possible, with coordinated artillery support.

Patrols consisted of a handful of volunteers stripped of gear to avoid the noise of buckles and metal clips, armed only with pistols, trench knives, bolt cutters, and at least one compass. Led by a single officer, the team would low-crawl to the German lines in the dark of night to note locations of enemy machine guns and scout for changes to their trenches. Bullard considered nightly patrolling "extremely dangerous but very necessary work." Pvt. John Johnston of La Crosse, Wisconsin, later remembered his own slow crawl across no-man's-land on patrol: "If you kept your head down there was no firing from the Germans, but the minute you lifted it (we crawled most of the time) they started the machine-guns."

Raids, with a purpose of capturing prisoners and stealing materiel, were far deadlier and more daring, and required more planning. Infantry officers coordinated with the artillery for an orchestrated storm on a small section of German lines. The 155s would fire a box barrage around the targeted trench while the 75s laid down a "creeping barrage" in no-man's-land, moving forward in pre-planned intervals behind which the raiding team would advance to the enemy lines, where otherwise civilized men were suddenly thrust into sharp spasms of violence that laid bare their basest, most primal instincts.

Pvt. Arthur Hansen of Reno, Nevada, volunteered to participate in a raid on the German trenches, and he described the encounter in a letter home. Led by a lieutenant, they crossed no-man's-land behind the artillery barrage, a journey he did not find alarming until they reached the enemy lines. "We got into their trench and started the slaughter. It was then that I killed my first man. He was a big, husky man—it is all bunk about the Germans being underfed—and he came at me with the bayonet." With his own bayonet fixed on the end of his Springfield, Private Hansen reacted in kind. "It was simply a case of being quick or dead, and that time I was quick and speared him on the end of my bayonet." Of the raid's grim toll, Hansen wrote with dispassion: "We killed as many as we could and took sixteen prisoners."

One artillery officer wrote home of the box barrage that his battery fired while supporting a raid: "Our artillery fire was so intense that when our infantry went over they found the trenches and dugouts demolished and only dead Germans in them, excepting one dugout in which there were ten who bravely refused to surrender and were blown out by hand grenades." As General Bullard recounted of the common trench raid, "[I]ts suddenness, its hand-to-hand deadly encounters, its carnage at close quarters with daggers, pistols, and fearful explosives, its shattering, bloody, merciless action, make it terrible to both raiders and raided."

The first successful raid evoked from General Bullard's typewriter a commendation for the critical role played by the artillery. But General Summerall, never timid when bold measures were required, needed no nudging from Bullard to take the fight to the Germans. His gun batteries had been under fire and gas attack day and night, and he ensured his gunners "vigorously replied." His 155s hurled high-explosive shells on known German artillery positions, his 75s lobbed gas shells behind the German lines at all hours, and he planted his trench mortar battery six hundred yards from the enemy trenches to inflict maximum, close-range damage.

A man of enterprising ideas, Summerall—dubbed "Sitting Bull" by his loyal men—rewrote the US Army's script on gunnery. He combined his headquarters with Bullard's for better coordination in planning, assigned artillery liaison teams to each front-line infantry unit, and arranged for phone lines to be run from infantry command posts back to the artillery batteries for better real-time fire support. Confidence soared as riflemen in the front lines no longer felt trapped in the event of enemy bombardments or raids. With one flare signal, a platoon leader up in the trenches was instantaneously connected with the full array of firepower scattered three and four miles behind his men. "The support from our artillery came the moment the red rocket went into the air," Pvt. Ruben Nelson wrote admiringly in his diary. "Almost before it was at its height our barrage fell."

Sitting Bull's inventive energy not only animated the entire artillery brigade but also served to consummate the marriage between infantry and artillery. And with machine-gun companies formed and integrated with front-line riflemen in first and second parallels for "defense in depth," and with a regiment of engineers working on fortifying trenches and taking on the perilous, nightly task of repairing barbed wire out on the edge of no-man's-land, all the disparate components of the division were finally working as one.

It is hard to pin down that elusive moment when the 1st Division became the "Fighting First," but it likely occurred during the eleven and a half weeks in the Seicheprey sector, a place that gave these doughboys their real schooling in the lifeless crucible of the trenches. They discovered that success "over here" was measured by yards of pockmarked, unlivable land, and sometimes it was marked only by mere survival. They now understood, with appalling clarity, the "Sausage Machine" of the Western Front—a comparison drawn by British soldier-turned-writer Robert Graves, "because it was fed with live men, churned out corpses and remained firmly screwed in place." They learned that life in the trenches was an assault on all five senses—sight stolen, lungs seared, and skin burned by mustard gas; hearing deafened by artillery blasts; fear and panic as palpable a taste as the cold "slumgullion" they forced down; with even breathable air fouled by the ever-present stench of excrement and death.

And like their British and French counterparts had learned time and again over the past three and a half years, the doughboys arrived at the frustrating realization that there, as elsewhere all along its length, the Western Front remained "firmly screwed in place." Winter ended as it began, with trenches full of cold, miserable men, a few hundred yards from enemy lines still maddeningly immovable. Then, as if marking the seasonal change with an exclamation, spring broke with a storm.

Just before dawn on March 21, over 200 miles northwest of the 1st Division trenches, a rain of shells from over 6,000 German guns struck the British 5th Army lines across a fifty-mile front in the valley of the Somme. The bombardment, brief but intense, "shook the entire battle front." An Army major over 40 miles away at the French headquarters in Compiègne likened the distant roar to "a surf of ten thousand breakers on an uneven shore." The crushing barrage was followed by a massed infantry attack, and with a concentrated blow of over sixty-four rested, full-strength German divisions—many recently transferred from the Eastern Front—against two dozen tired, depleted British divisions, the push-back was swift and a breakthrough threatened.

The onslaught was the opening of Germany's grand offensive, code-named Kaiserschlacht ("Emperor's Battle"). The attack was the brainchild of Gen. Erich Ludendorff, the strategic planner pulling the strings of the military behind the field-marshal baton of the aging chief of the German general staff, Field Marshal Paul von Hindenburg. "Owing to the breakdown of Russia," Ludendorff would later explain, "numerically we had never been so strong in comparison with our enemies." With 192 German divisions in the West and more on the way, and with American mobilization swiftly gathering steam, Ludendorff believed the circumstances "all called for an offensive that would bring about an early decision." Early enough, he hoped, to tip the scales against the Allies before the United States arrived in force. As he would reason, "This was only possible on the Western Front."

The massive attack force was led by Gen. Oskar von Hutier, whose innovative tactics on the Eastern Front had won such lopsided victories over the Russians and Italians that General Ludendorff built the entire spring offensive around—and ordered all involved troops be thoroughly trained in—the "Von Hutier method." His approach to a successful attack involved a brief but devastating preparatory bombardment, followed by a wave of *Stoßtruppen* (storm troops), who would advance quickly across no-man's-land behind a creeping barrage then prod enemy lines in a search for weak points to penetrate, avoiding strongpoints and machine-gun nests. Second and third waves of infantry would then follow, disable remaining resistance left untouched by the hurried first wave, exploit the ruptures in the lines and drive the enemy into the open. As *Remains of Company D* author James Carl Nelson explains: "The Germans had beaten Pershing to open warfare."

So far, the tactics were proving devastatingly effective. In the first day, German troops advanced over 4 miles into Allied lines, taking over 20,000 British prisoners. By the third day, the push-back was 12 miles deep, and four enormous German Krupp guns were moved close enough to bombard Paris (twenty shells would kill 256 Parisians in just the first twenty-four hours). In the days following, the Germans crossed the River Somme, portending a wedge between the British and French Armies. And within a week, Von Hutier's troops had captured over 90,000 Allied prisoners and 1,300 guns and pushed the lines in some places 40 miles west, threatening the critical rail and road junction at Amiens so essential to Allied supply lines.

On a front frozen through three and a half years of strategic impasse, where victories had been claimed over the capture of mere yards, the German Army's geographic gains were momentous. In Berlin, the kaiser proclaimed a national holiday to celebrate, gave schoolchildren the day off, and professed "the battle won. The English utterly defeated." He bestowed on Field Marshal von Hindenburg the Grand Cross of the Iron Cross with Golden Rays, which was, prior to this, historian Sir John Keegan would note, "last awarded to Blücher for the defeat of Napoleon in 1815." For the Allies, it was their darkest hour. An emergency meeting of Allied commanders on March 26 gave French General Foch overall charge of united Allied forces. French divisions were rushed north to help seal the breach, where British forces were running out of land and men. In London, Prime Minister David Lloyd George declared in desperate tones, "The last man may count."

Back down in the Seicheprey trenches, George Marshall worried that the German attack "threatened to bring the war to a sudden conclusion disastrous to the Allies," and General Bullard noted, "The whole Allied world, especially America, was shocked beyond measure at the might of this blow." Throughout the division's ranks, news of the offensive spread at viral speed. "The big drive is on now in the west," Lt. Jim Hartney wrote his "dearest Margaret" back home, where he supposed there was "considerable anxiety." Knowing her thoughts would turn next to the question of him seeing combat, he added: "Just what part we will play is questionable but whatever it is we pray that we may play it creditably and that good fortune may attend us all." Troops in the front lines heard "alarming reports . . . of the progress of a great German drive in Picardy," one captain would later recall, "and it was general felt by the rank and file that the division might take an active part on that front."

General Bullard himself wondered what part his troops would play. "Fighting had to be done at once," he believed, "or it would be too late." Even down in his sector, more than two hundred miles from the Kaiserschlacht drive, he "began to see long, calm processions of French troops going northwest to fill the great gap . . . They were very quiet, very serious, with the air of veterans who face everything." As yet, there was no word from

Pershing about a movement to the battlefront, though Bullard hoped it was imminent. Back in December, in the privacy of his diary, Bullard had confided, "[O]ur General Pershing is not a fighter . . . He is a worldly-wise, extremely ambitious, and confidence-inspiring man, but not a warrior. . . . I shall be very glad to find myself mistaken." Just weeks later, he found himself mistaken when Pershing sent Bullard's division to the fighting front at Seicheprey. And in the greatest crisis of the war, Bullard was soon to be proven mistaken yet again, as the Big Chief maneuvered to get America in the fight.

Up to this point, General Pershing had been working toward combining his first four scattered divisions, once trained, into a planned I Corps—a first step toward his assertive vision of an all-American sector along the battle front. But with news from the British front painting what he described as "an extremely dark picture of disaster," Pershing deemed this the qualifying "emergency" he had read into Secretary Baker's January directive, and he determined to "do everything possible to render assistance."

On the fifth day of the German offensive, Pershing paid a late-night visit to the headquarters of Gen. Philippe Pétain at Compiègne. The American placed at the French Army chief's disposal "any of our divisions that could be of service"—an offer he tempered with the voiced expectation of their eventual "assembly under their own commander." It was a meeting charged with historic consequences, an exchange of command decisions from which hung the fate of tens of thousands of America's best and brightest. Always precise in his words at such weighty moments, General Pershing was careful to not only frame his offer as temporary but also to use the word "divisions," still holding firm on his resistance to an amalgamation of any smaller AEF units. With his contribution to the emergency thus pledged, Pershing departed and gave orders to all AEF divisions to "be held in readiness for any eventuality."

Three afternoons later, Pershing carried his nation's offer to the field headquarters of the newly appointed Supreme Allied Commander, General Ferdinand Foch. Pershing used broken French, but his words were equal to the moment: "I have come to tell you that the American people would consider it a great honor for our troops to be engaged in the present battle. . . . Infantry, artillery, aviation, all that we have is yours; use them as you wish. More will come, in numbers equal to requirements. I have come especially to tell you that the American people will be proud to take part in the greatest battle of history."

It was obvious to Pershing that Marshal Foch was "very much touched," and the words of the American offer found their way into Parisian newspapers by the next morning, "written up in much better French than I actually used," Pershing would quip. George Marshall, who would himself one day master the delicate diplomacy of war by coalition, later judged this to be the moment when General Pershing "rose to greatness." By giving control of his prized divisions over to Pétain and Foch, Pershing had, in Marshall's view, "laid all his cards on the table and directed every move toward the salvage of the Allied wreck."

The next morning, in his journal at his Chaumont headquarters, General Pershing recorded, "At Pétain's request, the 1st Division ordered to battle line, which Mr. Baker said people at home would enthusiastically approve." The chief ordered the remaining AEF divisions—the 2nd, 42nd, and 32nd—into "quiet" sectors to replace French divisions needed for the front, and he sent the 26th to relieve the 1st at Seicheprey. General Bullard's men were ordered northwest for brief training before heading into the center of the German attack.

Of getting Pershing's order to move to the front, General Bullard would later write, "Never a commander received an order more gladly or started on a service to which he looked forward with more lively anticipation." After getting relieved in the trenches during the dark of night, division troops, loaded down with full packs, marched at dawn in long, muddy columns toward the town of Toul and loaded into trains. The move to a new front "was a matter of great elation," Lt. Richard Newhall noted. "We were going where there was real fighting in progress." Major Roosevelt perceived that the men in his battalion "were delighted" with the thoughts of impending battle: "Men do not like sitting in trenches day in and day out, and being killed and mangled without ever seeing the enemy," he explained, "and this promised a fight where the enemy would be in sight."

The swift movement of 28,000 men, 1,700 animals, and 1,000 wagons over a network of roads and railways already clogged with urgent movements of a national army of more than 3 million presented what one unit history called "a test of administrative ability," resulting in a "feat which will probably never be explained." Marching toward Toul, the columns of doughboys—end-to-end—stretched the entire 17 miles of roadway. At the train station, fifty-car trains loaded with 1st Division troops, guns, and supplies steamed off toward the front every hour, 'round the clock, for three days.

As with other journeys by rail across the country, the doughboys were crammed into their "forty-and-eight" freight cars for a clattering ride that continued day and night. "With straw in the bottom, we had comfortable quarters," Lieutenant Dearing wrote home of the boxcar he shared with half his platoon; "at night with our feet pointed towards the center we slept well." Each crowded car carried a box of bread and "corn-willie" in one corner, and an empty bucket for drinking, shaving, and washing in another. Only two stops per day were made, those for water and hot coffee. "To go to the toilet," one soldier later recounted, "one clambered around the end of the car to the couplings," where, in the cold wind at full-speed, soldiers relieved themselves with "pants down, in precarious balance."

The division's temporary destination was the open plains surrounding Gisors, a commune on the northwest outskirts of Paris—beautiful countryside bearing "no scars and no desolation of war," the Division History reminds us, as this land "had not been defiled by the enemy." Here, the troops were to train in open warfare before entering the front lines. They drilled day and night in pleasant spring weather on fresh plateaus of what Major Roosevelt described as "a beautiful peaceful country, the most lovely we had seen yet in France."

In the midst of training came word on April 9 that the Germans launched a second offensive against the British lines, this one up in Flanders, threatening a breakthrough to the coast that would cut off a large number of Allied units. German troops advanced ten miles across a 24 mile front, prompting England's Field Marshal Sir Douglas Haig to issue a desperate plea to his Tommies: "Every position must be held to the last man. There must be no retirement. With our backs to the wall and believing in the justice of our cause each one must fight on to the end."

Events moved with even more urgency as the division prepared to be thrown into the line to help the Allies. "Where would we be put?" General Bullard wondered to himself at his chateau headquarters, shaking with chills and nearly crippled again by a new attack of neuritis. The week before, just as his division was departing Seicheprey, he had been forced into the hospital, struck by the "excruciating pain" in his arm and shoulder. But after four days—and with the help of his loyal medical officer's concocted story of a car-door mishap—Bullard successfully "jumped" the hospital to rejoin his men, even though the pain remained so debilitating he would carry it, as he would later write, "until [he] was a shadow."

Amid the "constant sound of heavy cannonading" from the front some forty miles away, lectures and drill filled daylight hours, a training schedule capped off with a division-wide maneuver witnessed by General Pershing himself. Standing out immaculate in his shined boots and creased trousers beside General Bullard—who struggled to conceal his physical pain—the chief's confidence in his favored 1st Division was buoyed by the sharpness and discipline on display before him. "Both officers and men were in splendid condition, notwithstanding their long rail journey," he noted, "and all were ready for the test of actual battle." Looking around him, Pershing noticed "[t]he countryside was radiant with its green meadows and early flowers." This contemplation of the aesthetic, rare for him, was doubtless prompted by thoughts of where he was sending these soldiers. "[O]ne could not help thinking," he later revealed, "how different would be those other fields on which this unit was soon to be engaged."

After a chilly day of rest, during which the men wrote letters and began packing while the officers all went to see Pershing's "Farewell to the First" in the courtyard of Bullard's headquarters, the division set off at dawn, April 17, for their three-day march to the front lines. Pvt. Ruben Nelson wrote in his diary, "[W]e started on a long march not knowing where to." For troops who had spent the past month moving from muddy trenches to cramped boxcars to 'round-the-clock drill, the march through the French countryside was a pleasant one. "Spring was on the land, the trees were budding, wild flowers covered the ground, the birds were singing," Major Roosevelt noted. "Our dusty brown column marched up hill and down, through patches of woods and little villages." Lt. George Haydock saw "some wonderful old houses and gardens, and landscapes that make me feel as though I were in a dream" as he led his platoon across the rolling French plains. "It's a queer world and a crazy war," he said. Lt. Jim Hartney's impression was just as agreeable, writing in a letter home, "Our move has been to quite an extent a pleasure trip . . . 'Touring France' we call it."

Many of those "Touring France" were urged into the same sentiment. "I wouldn't change places with anyone in the states now," Lt. Vinton Dearing wrote his mother in Massachusetts, "not until the war is over or I have accomplished something worthwhile." Lt. Irving Wood later described the passage as "more like a pleasure jaunt than a march into battle," though signs of the war began growing. Refugees from villages recently overrun by the

Germans—the elderly, children, mothers bearing babies and every posses-
sion they could carry or haul by wagon—streamed away from the front.
Green pastures and flowered fields progressively crumbled into brown earth
and scorched villages. And, as Lieutenant Wood described, "each day
brought the sound of the guns closer." A war correspondent making the
journey with the 1st Division described reaching a point "where the rumble of guns, like distant thunder, is heard."

"This was what we had crossed the Atlantic to do," observed Lt. Richard
Newhall. Ever characterized by a razor-sharp discernment, the tall, slim,
bespectacled Harvard PhD-turned-platoon-leader could, with scholarly
detachment, recognize the emotions and human reactions of the soldiers
under his charge. "They knew the discomforts of trench life" and "had
experienced some of the lesser horrors of shell fire," he noted, "[b]ut they
were still innocent of modern warfare in its complete hideousness."

The men of Newhall's platoon—as with the division as a whole—spanned
a generation, some in their late thirties and others still teenagers. Just months
before, they had been clerking in banks, laboring in factories, or attending
high school. Now service in the cause of country, that great equalizer of
class and age, was merging them into a single, uniform force. It was apparent to Newhall that, for them, "the war was still an adventure," and among
them he spotted "an eagerness to go 'over the top,' which was born of igno-
rance and the spirit of adventure." Newhall carried no illusions about the
challenges and dangers of this "adventure," but it was curiosity that animated his troops, who "did not know what they were going into, and they
were intensely eager to find out."

And so Newhall led the soldiers of his platoon, sixty men of the division's
endless stream of 28,000, formed in khaki columns stretching along dusty
roads from horizon to horizon, with packs on their backs and rifles over
their shoulders, marching with a firm step toward "the sound of the guns"
and the "adventure" of war.

CHAPTER 5

Life and Death

Of Germany's nearly 3 million troops in France, its two battalions of soldiers occupying the cellars and trenches in and around the hilltop village of Cantigny were the farthest west, deeper into Allied territory than any of the kaiser's forces had been since the first months of the war. Until the German offensive, this sleepy farming hamlet was home to few more than 100 souls living in its cluster of quaint, slate-roofed cottages. Among them sat a school, a bakery, and a single stone church, and in the low-lying fields surrounding the village were crops, mostly beet plants and wheat. From Cantigny's commanding perch, one could see thick patches of forest interrupting the green plains that rolled toward the horizon in all directions. And from the center of town, roads descended down into the plateau toward all compass points: north to Grivesnes, east to Courtemanche, southeast to Montdidier, northwest to Le Plessier-Hameau, west to Coullemelle, and southwest to Villers-Tournelle.

In late March, as von Hutier's 18th Army drove westward and the thunder of its guns grew louder, Cantigny's residents grabbed what they could carry and fled their homes. German infantry overran the village before Moroccan fighters from a French Colonial division finally stopped their advance. Twice the Moroccan infantry recaptured the village in determined attacks, but each time the weight of German artillery proved too great, and the French Colonials were driven back out. Since then, German forces had entrenched themselves firmly in village structures crowning the hilltop, forcing the Moroccans to settle into fresh lines forming a pronounced salient that jutted sharply back into Allied territory.

German troops converted Cantigny's cellars and stone buildings into command posts and armed bunkers, and during the night's darkness, they fenced the west face with barbed wire and a newly dug trench line. Along its length, they positioned machine guns that covered, in overlapping fields of fire, every inch of the wheat-covered plateau that sloped down toward the newly dug-in French. German artillery set up shop in positions concealed under the thick canopy of forest patches behind the village to the east, each gun ranged in on the fresh French lines. On the other side, French artillery was moved forward, thrown into emplacements in wooded hilltops to the west, and Moroccan troops manned improvised lines of shell holes, staring up at the village that stared back down at them across a fresh, almost immaculate no-man's-land.

And so new lines were clawed out, and nearly 40 miles west of where it had sat contested but stubbornly unyielding for three and a half years, the Western Front stomped its hobnailed boot down on Cantigny. Gradually the virgin ground began fraying with the hallmarks of war. Up in the village, cottage walls were sandblasted by daily and nightly shelling, and with glass shattered out of window frames and tile roofs whittled away, by mid-April most homes were empty shells. Others had been reduced to structural insignificance or outright leveled. And out in no-man's-land, amid the red poppies and purple thistles of spring, the bodies of both sides' dead bloated under the April sun, grisly omens to greet the American newcomers.

The 1st Division troops entered the small, recently abandoned towns behind the front lines of the sector on April 22, where General Summerall noted the "sound of guns in the line warned us of what awaited." General Bullard set up Division Headquarters in the stale brick wine cellar of a manor house in Mesnil-Saint-Firmin, where it was apparent to George Marshall that the residents had been forced to evacuate without warning. "Silver, linen, clothing, and other intimate personal effects had been abandoned," and he noticed a "partially completed letter" on a desk and discarded clothes strewn about. Marshall and other members of the division staff moved into "improvised double-decked bunks" down in the cellar, safe from the detonations of long-range German shells.

Just three and a half miles from the front lines, Bullard noted that his headquarters placed him and his staff "nearer the enemy than ever before." From there, Marshall could hear a "continuous roar of the distant guns [that] filled the air." General Summerall's field artillery batteries scattered to build a response, digging gun emplacements throughout the countryside while the thousands of division infantrymen billeted by platoon in this and other small hamlets that dotted the rear of the sector. Stranded within range of enemy shells, most of the population of these parishes had vacated weeks earlier. "[Y]ou hardly ever see anybody except old women and men," one lieutenant wrote.

Even in these towns two and three miles from the front, the force of the German onslaught was apparent. "The guns could be heard from this billet rumbling like thunder," Pvt. Bert Tippman wrote home to La Crosse, Wisconsin, "and the ambulances were speeding toward the front and at a pace to cheer the heart of any La Crosse traffic cop." Curiosity over what awaited him up in the trenches got the best of Pvt. Ruben Nelson, and he went with a comrade to explore. "On the evening of the 23rd I took a new man and went for a walk toward the French lines," he wrote in his diary. "I walked nearly to the lines and . . . could see we were in for a merry spell as soon as we entered the lines. I was already carrying $5,000 war risk insurance and when I went back I soon made arrangements for $5,000 more."

Thoughts of mortality gnawed at the mind of every doughboy headed toward the front lines in a way they had not when entering the trenches at Sommerviller or Seicheprey, though most soldiers took no counsel of their fears. "All Allied eyes were cast upon the First U.S. Division," Sgt. Don Butcher noted. "Every man from colonel to buck private knew what he was up against, but felt with perfect confidence what the results would be."

After nightfall on April 24, the soldiers of the 1st Battalions of the 16th and 18th Infantry Regiments walked through open fields and wooded patches toward the front lines, where they were to relieve the French Colonials. Prior to departing, Private Nelson's captain organized the 250-plus men of his company for a quick pep talk. "He said we were going into a place where only few would come out," Nelson told his diary. "The men seemed to think he was crazy and some remarks [were] passed about his mental condition."

But as Nelson and the others trooped forward in small groups—a precaution against excessive losses from enemy shells—they soon realized their captain had not overstated the danger. "Not far after we split the Co. into sections, we came into artillery fire," Nelson noted. "I had not gone but a short way when one of my gunmen was struck by shrapnel. The first to go on this trip. Making the relief I lost five men." Another private wrote home that a whiz-bang shell "burst at the roadside" near him on the march to the front. "Another bursts nearer just as we dive in a trench," he added, "and here we stay during the night and the shells shake the ground all night."

Each platoon arrived at the front with the mission "to hold its position," but soldiers found Moroccan troops bunched in shallow shell craters un-connected by any discernible trench lines. "To say that we took over a line rather overstates the case," General Bullard would later write of his men, who had "moved forward to a front that was little more than a succession of shell holes connected by shallow ditches." Gone were the established French lines of Sommerviller and Seicheprey to which the Americans had grown accustomed: zigzagged trenches five and six feet deep, built up with sandbags and wooden supports, complete with dugouts, command posts, and second parallels connected by communication trenches. There facing Cantigny was what one lieutenant described as "a position consisting of practically nothing but a series of foxholes in a field of uncut wheat or in woods, when the French troops had stemmed the German tide at the point of its furthest advance."

The Americans filed into the skimpy fieldworks during the dark of night, but when dawn's first light came, it exposed the battlefield's vilest features, laying bare a no-man's-land littered with the unburied dead of the recent fighting. "Dead Colonials still lay in the fields," observed Lt. Richard New-hall, "grim reminders of the battle which had halted the German advance." One private wrote home describing "large numbers of large black buzzards eating the dead all over the battlefield." He described two dead Moroccan soldiers frozen "in a kneeling posture out beyond the trench," one of whom "had a fine looking revolver hanging in a holster from his belt." That night, on a patrol, another soldier went for the gun, and "[w]hen he touched the soldier he fell apart. He had been there so long that he was rotten."

The Colonial troops, depleted and exhausted by repeated attempts to re-take the village and by holding ground covered by enemy guns up in com-manding perches in and around Cantigny, had been unable to consolidate their unprotected position. "Trenches were shallow and scanty," Major Roo-sevelt complained, "and dugouts were almost lacking." The doughboys were forced to take cover behind parapets that were nothing more than "newly thrown-up earth," the Division History notes. A 16th Infantry cor-poral sitting up in his new position scratched his early impressions in his diary: "In front of Cantigny, in woods on hill. . . . Boche on hill across val-ley and in town of Cantigny. Heavy shelling; gas day and night. Parks and Wynn killed by shellfire. Relieved Algerians. No trenches, they stopped the Boche there." During daylight hours, the Division History records that soldiers "would peer through an opening in the clods of earth . . . in an ef-fort to spot the enemy." At night, between artillery bombardments, men scratched furrows and dugouts with entrenching tools in efforts to improve their defensive lines. A quotation spread—perhaps apocryphal but nevertheless accurate—attributed to a French officer: "It's not a sector, but it's a good place to make one."

For the Germans, only in the past fortnight had Cantigny become a prize worth defending, and they had promptly established trenches and defensive positions in and around the village. The 30th Reserve Division held the German lines until May, when it was relieved by the three infantry regiments of the 82nd Reserve Division, part of the left wing of von Hutier's 18th Army, a veteran unit recently redeployed from two years of service on the Eastern Front. The 272nd Reserve Infantry Regiment held the lines north of Cantigny and a few positions in the village itself, and the 271st manned most of the positions in the village and the lines to the south. Two 800-man battalions—one from each regiment—held their assigned front lines, designated as "combat" battalions. "Support" battalions held positions in the woods one and a half to two miles behind the front, and "rest" battalions billeted six to eight miles in the rear. Every ten days they shifted: rest battalions to support, support to combat, combat to rest.

Rated by Allied Intelligence as third-class on a scale of four, the troops of the 82nd were employed here as "sector-holding troops" while the 30th and other units were redeployed to rest for the next wave of Kaiserschlacht. The makeup of the division embodied the strain placed on Germany's manpower after nearly four years of war, with soldiers ranging from seventeen-year-old boys—drafted more than two years early by national necessity—to men in their mid- to late thirties, pulled from *Ersatz* (reserve) and *Landsturm* (home guard) duty.

Although a pale shadow of the earlier Imperial Army, these troops were, in one American officer's estimation, "by no means inferior," and they "fortified their positions with diligence and skill and patrolled energetically, conducting small and large scale raids with vigor." Lt. Dick Dacus agreed: "The Germans were good. Their water-cooled machine guns were far better than our air-cooled Hotchkiss," and "[t]heir 'potato masher' grenades were better." Each infantryman carried a Mauser rifle, officers a Luger 9mm, and in the front lines, platoons stockpiled "potato-masher" stick grenades, especially effective tools for trench fighting.

German fighters employed the water-cooled Maxim machine gun, fed by 250-round belts and able to fire more than 450 rounds per minute. Its sound when firing to full effect prompted doughboys across no-man's-land to call it a "typewriter," and its effectiveness in defending entrenched lines across open fields had been proven with devastating results against offensives by the French and British (most of the 19,240 British soldiers killed on the first day of the Somme attack were felled by Maxims). Each of the two battalions holding Cantigny and front lines included four 200-man infantry companies armed with six Maxims positioned so that every approach across the plateau before the village was swept in shredding crossfire.

Beyond weaponry, each regiment boasted 50 to 100 *Stoßtruppen*—the unit's strongest, ablest, and fastest riflemen, given double rations and extra training, used mostly to launch patrols and deadly trench raids. And always there was the unseen menace—the patient veteran German snipers, perched in building windows or nested back in the cover of the wood lines, peering through scopes down the length of their Mausers. They inflicted instant death on doughboys so distant that those in the American trenches would see a soldier's head snap back and body collapse in a lifeless heap a full second before the echoing shot sounded from across the plateau.

But most imposing was German artillery, with guns ranging from the 77mm, which fired "whiz-bang" and gas shells, to the imposing 280mm, capable of hurling a six hundred-pound, eleven-inch-wide, high-explosive shell over ten miles away. From emplacements scattered in the wood lines and elevated towns beyond Cantigny (French observation pilots had thus far pinpointed over ninety separate gun positions), German batteries had inflicted demoralizing damage on French Colonials, and now unleashed the same on the Americans.

For the Americans, building the sector's defenses—miles of duplicate trenches and barbed wire, hundreds of dugouts, and dozens of command posts—was the first priority. "The engineers were called on to do all this work," Lt. Moses Cox of the 1st Engineers Regiment noted. "Here is where we worked day and night, often with only two and three hours sleep out of twenty-four hours." It was a mammoth task made ever more daunting by incessant enemy shelling. "They simply rained shells everywhere," another engineer fretted. "We stuck up wire, built a lot of dugouts and dug defensive positions, and the Boche tried to dissuade us from the work by constantly hammering at us."

With every inch of the new lines covered by German snipers and machine gunners up in the village, the engineers could only work during the few hours of darkness each night. Lt. Vinton Dearing wrote home that it was "light from 4 a.m. until 10 p.m." and added, "It is the first time I ever thought there could be too much light." In the fleeting darkness, field signal troops worked feverishly to lay and conceal miles of phone lines connecting headquarters with all command posts and all command posts with the front. With shellfire dicing up the wire, repairs were needed multiple times nightly. Work progressed slowly, one officer explained, "because of enemy fire and the shortness of the nights which by summer were less than six hours long."

"I know of no duty which new troops dislike more than digging," General Bullard observed. But the digging, slow and exhausting, was necessary, and to make greater headway, infantry from the regiments in reserve were sent forward with picks and shovels, pressed into helping the engineers. "Here we worked for more than a month at night building trenches," Lt. Irving Wood wrote, "putting up wire and always on the alert." In one three-night stretch, a three-and-a-half-mile-long communication trench—four feet deep all along its length—was completed: a "remarkable achievement" credited in the Division History.

The ground was dry and the dirt chalky, and when enemy shells were not falling the digging was relatively easy. As one officer noted, this "permitted deep and dry dugouts, and if any sector needed deep dugouts, this one surely did." But the light-colored, chalky subsoil made all freshly dug trench locations stick out as obvious targets from even a great distance. One lieutenant observed that "all the trenches in the sector had parapets of white," and another soldier complained that new trenches "showed badly on aerial photographs and all new works were taken under fire."

The clangs and dings of shovels and picks carried nightly across no-man's-land, and each time the swift answer by German artillery lit the sky. Despite the danger it signaled, many soldiers could not help but absorb the light show's ominous brilliance. During "pitch black nights," Lieutenant Dearing wrote his sister, "the flash of guns gives a bizarre effect which you would pay three dollars to see in an opera." But with high-explosive shells sailing with preregistered accuracy into the midst of trench-digging crews, the work was dangerous and losses mounted. One evening, a mortar round landed between two privates who were digging, leaving no trace of either man. Another night, a high-explosive shell hit a group of engineers working on barbed-wire lines, wiping out all six with a single blast. Death became a daily spectacle, and the division's manifest of casualties grew steadily larger. After the war, one platoon leader in the engineers recounted of this time: "I averaged more narrow escapes per day in our first month there than I have before or since."

Thousands of doughboys hunkered in the freshly dug front lines, fulfilling their division's mission of holding the position. Every unmistakable boom from the German lines was followed by a whistle that pitched higher, then stopped, and in the thick adrenal instant that followed, a reflexive choice was triggered in each man—whether to stand or sit, whether to move to the front of the trench or the back, whether to stand next to a newbie replacement or far away—an array of decisions mentally comforting but unavoidably futile. Such constructed choices gave soldiers trapped in their small earthen ditch some false hope of escape from war's bloodiest potentials, some feeling of control in the awful lottery of indiscriminate shellfire. The sum was a psychological battle each man fought with himself, with his unchangeable station, and with a faceless enemy on the far side of those awful explosions.

"Men lived in that sector under the most extraordinary game of life and death ever invented," twenty-two-year-old Lt. Jeremiah Evarts of Windsor, Vermont, later wrote. "Sometimes a direct hit on the parapet from a 77 would bury the occupant undamaged under a couple feet of earth," he noted, adding, "[a]nything larger than a 77 meant no further worry." Another lieutenant later explained, "We kept shovels and tools in small piles to dig our men out when a shell would hit in the ashy and dusty soil and succeeded in unearthing many a man from smothering after a shell had buried him alive."

German guns of all sizes—77s, 105s, 210s, and 280s—hammered away on American positions around the clock. "Guns and machine-guns on both sides were always barking," Pvt. Ruben Nelson told his diary. "Never was there a minute of silence." One lieutenant later remembered "the Germans shelling us almost every 15 minutes and at no time more than ½ hour intervening, during the day." The fusillades typically came in waves between momentary lulls. Major Roosevelt described the repeating scene: "First a few flashes can be seen, which increase until on all sides you see the bursts of the shrapnel and the noise becomes deafening. Then it gradually dies away and a thick acrid cloud of smoke lies over everything."

"[S]hells come over so big they look like beer-kegs," Pvt. Levy Wilson, one of the "Three Musketeers" from Denton, Texas, wrote home. "I run in the little door of my dug-out so much every time I hear one of the 'beer-kegs' loaded with railroad spikes." High-explosive shell and mortar blasts would creep toward the American lines with a heavy footfall, and the inevitable direct hit would wreak indescribable havoc in the confined trenches. Soldiers stood or lay braced to absorb each detonation, and those not chopped to pieces by shooting shrapnel came unglued with frayed psyches. They were struck in the chest by the concussion waves, the air was sucked from their lungs for several gasping seconds, and they were deafened for minutes or longer. When they could finally breathe, they were choked with whiffs of cordite and sulfur. When their hearing returned, they were met with more menacing rumbles from the German lines and steeled themselves for the next onslaught. "In a very heavy bombardment when there was no respite," Lieutenant Evarts explained, "one became gradually taut and then practically speechless after a time."

Repeated cannonading gave the troops a forced lesson in the whistles and screeches produced by different shell sizes. "They gave off different sounds," one company commander observed, "and the men named them for various railroads such as the Missouri-Pacific and the Southern." Pvt. John Johnston noted that one-pound shells "largely imitated the lonesome night howl of a hound dog. Sometimes it almost drove a man crazy—the sound was so continuous and doleful and unholy." Seasoned men could soon discern whether the whistle signaled danger. As Lt. George Haydock wrote, "[W]e soon learned the different noises and got over wasting energy," and he added that when the sound heralded a direct incoming, "I have seen my entire platoon, self included, disappear off the face of the earth in a plowed field, and in less time than it takes to tell."

The 1st Division records reveal that German guns fired an average of 3,400 shells into American lines each day in the Cantigny sector—an average of more than 140 per hour and 2 every minute. All day. Every day. And this astonishing weight of metal was not directed solely on the front lines. As General Summerall recorded, thousands of shells "were hurled daily against our poorly prepared front lines, our battery positions, our roads and posts of command."

The ground behind the front lines descended into a flat, low-lying plateau that was shelled so heavily the men dubbed it "Death Valley." Pvt. Bert Tippman noted, "[I]t certainly earned its name," describing the "shell-torn valley" in a letter home: "The ground is plowed up and the trees are all broken and splintered." An officer later recounted the name came from "the knowledge that one would always run into shells upon entering this valley," and a medic wrote, "the valley was one big shell hole because there was one shell hole after another, all the way to Villers-Tournelle," a town two miles behind the lines.

The Germans shelled "Death Valley" so heavily because it encompassed all lanes of approach for supplies and ammunition and food and troop relief for the American front lines. "At night every road was swept with a fire of murderous accuracy," a captain later recalled. The vital supply arteries became so "badly torn up by the intense artillery fire," one platoon leader lamented, "that it was hard for even a one mule ration cart to pass."

Big German guns had sufficient reach to pummel the towns where reserve troops billeted two, three, and four miles behind the American lines. Villers-Tournelle was dubbed the "City of Suicides," because, as Cpl. George Ross of Clinton, Indiana, wrote home, "there was someone killed at all times, day and night" and "it was just suicide to go in there." Visiting a regimental headquarters there one evening, General Summerall was forced to run for cover, betraying a panic he typically avoided in front of his men. "Shells were bursting frequently," he noted. "Mangled bodies were in the streets." Back in Mesnil-Saint-Firmin, Summerall bunked in an upstairs bedroom of the division headquarters manor house until a high-explosive shell exploded beneath his window one night, "completely wrecking it." From that point forward, he slept in the wine cellar.

Daylight discipline so punctiliously obeyed by doughboys in the front lines had to be followed by those in reserve and rest areas as well. Daytime gatherings of troops in the open could be spotted by enemy observation pilots, who would transmit the targets back to German gun batteries. Cpl. Earl Seaton, a signalman with the 16th Infantry, remembered hearing incoming shells as soon as the line gathered for chow near Villers-Tournelle one afternoon: "The Germans evidently spotted the kitchen coming up and started shelling," he wrote, adding that he had already picked out a safe spot to flop in case one hit close. He and the others heard the distant "whomp" from behind the enemy lines, "then the topoff as the shell reached its highest and started down, growing louder and louder." It hit the tile roof of a nearby building and detonated as it hit the ground, causing extensive damage. "Several men were killed, one was gone completely," Seaton noted, and on the ground near him he saw "a leg with shoe and puttee leggings on it, cut off above the knee." Men grabbed their mess kits and scattered, and in the midst of the jumble of fleeing khaki, more shells hit. One man watched as the soldier he was running behind "was cut off at the hips. The legs stood for a moment, as the blood oozed out, then collapsed."

Most bombardments were aimed at the division's artillery batteries, many of which, despite great efforts at camouflage and concealment, were spotted by enemy pilots and plotted on German artillery maps. The field logbook of one 75mm battery noted its positions were "constantly subjected to a fierce fire" and "completely destroyed twice." Officers and NCOs, forced by chewed-up phone lines to run orders and messages between gun pits and observation posts for coordination, suffered the highest casualties. In the 7th Field Artillery Regiment, six NCOs were killed and a dozen injured in the short space of a single week.

One artillery major wrote in a letter home, "[O]ne of our Captains was buried by a shell yesterday." On another occasion, he saw the blast of a German whiz-bang wrap a motorcycle messenger lifeless around a tree, and was himself knocked unconscious by a shell blast. The writer was Maj. Robert McCormick, the *Chicago Tribune* publisher who had donned his Army National Guard uniform at America's entry into the war. When the 1st Division crossed the Atlantic, McCormick had mobilized his clout, connections, and resources to win a spot initially as an AEF intelligence officer, then finally at the front in his present role, commanding an artillery battalion of eight 155s. Like other artillery officers in this sector, Major McCormick spent his crowded days either dodging enemy shells while visiting his batteries and observation posts, or hunkered in a dugout or damp cellar near his guns, forced by German metal into what his biographer would call "a molelike existence."

One of McCormick's gunners, Pvt. Arthur Cunningham of Clinton, Indiana, wrote home: "While in this sector I wouldn't have given seven cents for my chance of ever coming home again. At one time there were seven of us sitting in the gun ditch and the Boche dropped a shell in one corner of it. Six out of the seven were wounded." Cunningham added that two were sent home disabled, two returned to the battery, "and I have never heard from the other two."

Compounding the danger from above was something entirely novel to the doughboys: airplane attack. Still under French Corps control, the division was supported by a squadron of French Spads, biplanes that flew high over the German lines mostly for aerial photography and artillery observation. But command of the skies remained decidedly tilted in the enemy's favor as German fighters—armed with machine guns and small, hand-dropped bombs nicknamed "grass-cutters"—flew in a constant, menacing stream over American positions. Lt. Vinton Dearing wrote home, "There is almost a continuous hum of airplanes over our head," and Pvt. John Johnston noted "a danger, on bright days, from airplane attacks."

General Bullard observed that often, especially after dark, German bi-wings buzzed so low that one could "almost feel the whiff of [their] wings." It was not even fifteen years into manned powered flight, and many doughboys had only ever read of airplanes, making the assaults from above both bewildering and frightening. Bullard noted that soldiers "became sometimes almost hysterical in the feeling of helplessness and defenselessness that comes over a man at seeing or hearing the enemy circling deliberately above him and earnestly seeking to take his life."

It was also in the rear areas of the sector where most mustard-gas attacks occurred. Battery emplacements became a favorite target for German gas shells, forcing American gun crews to toil for hours in their suffocating gas masks. Most bombardments on the towns of Villers-Tournelle and Mesnil-Saint-Firmin had gas shells mixed in with the high explosives, and more than 700 gas shells fell in and around the town of Coullemelle in one single afternoon. The heavy, oily mustard clouds settled in the lowest areas, most of them rolling down and pooling in Death Valley. There, troops who were fortunate enough to make it through its gauntlet of shelled pathways unscathed by artillery shrapnel were often burned by the lingering gas.

In the face of this unrelenting onslaught, General Bullard unleashed Summerall on the enemy, and as before, Sitting Bull proved equal to the moment. The gunners of the forty-eight 75s, twenty-four 155s, and dozen trench mortars had learned the rudiments of their craft on the proving grounds down in Seicheprey, and now they imposed their will on the enemy by sheer weight of steel.

During every minute of darkness, American guns hurled shells into the far side of Cantigny, pummeling reserve positions and all roads of approach, cutting off supply and relief for German infantry hunkered down in the village. To this end, the French eagerly provided an inexhaustible fund of shells, trucked to the division front by the ton. "Our ammunition supply," the 7th Field Artillery Regimental History would note, "was practically unlimited and gun crews were active in the pits twenty-four hours a day." In contrast to the Seicheprey sector, where over the course of eighty-one days, the artillery brigade averaged firing fewer than 1,500 rounds per day, facing Cantigny, the same guns heaved 9,000 shells—high-explosive and gas—into German lines daily. Summerall observed that this sustained, blistering fire "paralyz[ed] the enemy's movements" and caused what Marshall described as "demoralizing losses."

Gunners were given daily fire schedules based on intelligence updated daily with aerial mapping and reports from nightly infantry patrols. Counter-battery fire (direct fire on enemy batteries) was aided by the new science of acoustic ranging, using equipment and methods taught by the French Corps artillery. And as before, liaison was established with front-line troops for immediate support to repel raids or enemy attacks.

One afternoon up in the trenches, Lt. Jeremiah Evarts noticed the blasts of a few desultory German shells just behind his platoon's line. Recognizing this as possible adjustment fire by the enemy for a planned raid on his trench, he told his artillery liaison to expect a call-for-barrage that night. Later, after darkness fell, Evarts noticed that "the whole German sky lit up in a great red glare" and "what seemed like a thousand shells exploded along the parapet." He grabbed his Very pistol, fired a flare, and in seconds "the blazing, crashing wall of steel from the barrage of the 6th FA landed just inside our wire and moved along over to Germany," forcing the gray-clad enemy back into their trenches. As Summerall later wrote proudly of his gunners, "[S]o prompt and rapid was the response to every call that they were jestingly called 'rapid firers' and the men had a saying that they kept two shells in the gun and three on the way."

In mid-May, the 2nd Brigade—the 26th and 28th Infantry Regiments—entered the front lines, relieving the 1st Brigade. These soldiers were soon drowning in the same baptism by fire as their predecessors. Capt. Charles Senay, commanding Company C of the 28th Infantry, later recalled: "I relieved Red Kelly of the 18th Infantry. He told me that the fire was so intense that I should not attempt to inspect all of the area. A number of men had been killed in his company. The first man that I lost was by a rifle grenade. He was slightly forward on outpost. A nervous soldier in the line dropped a rifle grenade when he observed slight movement and blew out his buddy's brains. On another occasion I lost four men from one shell burst."

The 1st Brigade soldiers trooped back to the rear, and members of the 18th Infantry retired into the depopulated ruins of Villers-Tournelle for well-earned rest. Darkness fell, a rumble sounded from the distant German lines, and abruptly the world detonated. The homes and barns where men were billeted were flayed open as the screaming shellfire—an awful mix of high-explosive and gas shells—kept coming. Soldiers not knocked unconscious or shredded by the hot metal struggled through the choking, burning melee to put on their masks and find cover, their paths lit only by the orange flashes of artillery blasts.

For an hour and a half the shells fell, some hitting as far back as the field hospital where many of the casualties were initially carried. One of them, Sgt. Clem Woodbury, later recounted, "It was terrible to realize that there were men there unable to move and expecting to be blown up any moment." By the time the night fell silent, 15,000 shells had fallen and more than 800 casualties were suffered, most caused by mustard gas—the highest concentration the division soldiers had yet endured. A masked George Marshall came from Division Headquarters, noticing that "[f]or a quarter mile outside of the little village, the soggy, wet ground was peppered with fresh shell craters, most of them containing mustard gas." Troops were moved out of the gas-swamped cellars and buildings of the village and into cots on open fields. A temporary canvas field hospital was pitched, and within five hours received 249 gas patients. By the end of the week, the number would climb to almost 700. Having just endured ten days in the front line trenches, the doughboys of the 18th Infantry learned the bitter reality that nowhere in the sector—no trench, no dugout, no barn, no cellar, not even a hospital—offered sanctuary from the slaughter.

Slowly the landscape began hinting at the surrounding savagery. Green foliage cover was blown out of trees and trunks were splintered by the daily showers of steel. Much of the green in the fields between the American and German lines turned dirt-brown, dimpled by shell craters. As with the British and French Armies since 1914, the troops of the 1st Division were unwittingly sliding into the ways of war they were brought over to end. It was the same stalemate with new scenery and fresh khaki. Without a mission grander than "holding the position," the collective acts of all of Bullard's riflemen could serve only as heroic gestures of futility. And without engaging the enemy in actual battle, all the steel in the Allied arsenal fired by Sitting Bull's gunners could do nothing more than perpetually erode and exhaust the same German regiments across the same fields in the same lines from the same low ground.

That his soldiers must launch an attack on the enemy, General Bullard needed no convincing. He gazed at the battlefield through a lens focused for action, and no impulse was more deeply rooted in his nature. He and every one of his officers had stood in that frosty courtyard and witnessed General Pershing's clarion call—one that envisioned "great battle," not defending a line. Bullard was driven to seize the initiative and execute an important stroke, but through the first weeks in the sector, the AEF and French Corps commands seemed focused only on reacting to the enemy. The Allies expected a third German offensive after the first two, which though begun with great local tactical success had since sputtered and stalled, reaching what one French officer called their "mechanical limit." Most presumed, given the expected German target of Amiens, that this third wave would be launched from Cantigny, and Allied Intelligence indicated this was to occur in mid-May.

General Bullard and his staff planned the division's role in a joint offensive, meant to be launched with the French divisions on both flanks as a counterattack response to the third German offensive. The 1st Division's part involved three regiments, reinforced by a battalion of the 1st Engineers, the artillery, and twenty French tanks, to sweep through Cantigny and beyond to "capture the plateau north of Mesnil St. Georges." This would advance the lines one and a half miles beyond Cantigny itself, capturing not just the garrison entrenched in the village but also German artillery and reserve positions in the thick wood lines of Framicourt and Courtemanche.

But the trigger for this counterattack—a German attack—did not materialize. "The days passed without a hostile advance," George Marshall noted, and by mid-May, the joint counterattack was called off. This did not disappoint Bullard, who remained determined that if there was to be action in his small theater of the large war, his soldiers would play the protagonists. And he was determined to move his men out of the vulnerable low terrain. Topography—that arbitrary variable by which so much of war's outcomes are determined—still favored the Germans, perched up on their commanding high ground. One American captain commanding a company down in the front trenches complained, "The Boche could look down our throats." Taking the enemy's roost in Cantigny would at least tilt the immovable landscape in the 1st Division's favor.

For his part, General Pershing was just as impatient for his favored division to strike, and he issued an order giving Bullard the green light to take Cantigny. The purpose, Pershing would later write, was for the 1st Division "to improve its position" and deprive the Germans of "the advantage of higher ground." But for the Big Chief, this served only as comforting pretext. The morale of the Allies, after losing dispiriting amounts of land and men to Kaiserschlacht, was at its lowest ebb, and faith of the Allied high command in AEF competence was no higher—a doubt given some resonance by a recent poor performance and heavy losses of 26th Division doughboys in the face of a heavy German raid down in Seicheprey.

An all-American offensive victory would serve to buttress Pershing's vision of strategic self-sufficiency and strengthen his argument that AEF divisions were capable of holding their own front against the enemy. "[A]t this moment the morale of the Allies required that American troops make their appearance in battle," Pershing later wrote, revealing his truest motives for ordering the 1st Division attack; "if successful, it would demonstrate that we could best help the Allies by using our troops in larger units instead of adopting their plan of building up their forces."

General Bullard could not have been happier to take action, and he needed no higher purpose than that of capturing the high ground. "Before we came Cantigny had been twice taken and twice lost by the French," he wrote in his diary. "Now, to try out the division and to remove this threat, I was allowed to plan an attack upon this village." And in his division, he could hold no higher confidence, calling it "the best equipped, best officered, and best prepared for service that ever the United States sent to begin a war."

But the small village presented a large challenge, the most difficult of all military maneuvers: a frontal assault on a fortified position. And this would not be a joint Franco-American offensive, launched in tandem with French divisions to the left and right. It would be a solo American effort—what Marshall called a "new and distinctly American operation"—with American prestige on the line.

In this, as with so much else, the 1st Division was wading into uncharted waters, at least in the context of the AEF, and Bullard did not wish to wade blindly. He possessed the rare gift of managing the conflicting forces of pressure and prudence, and for him, this attack was no mere symbolic gesture. The future of America's role in the war was written on these fields, and in the streets of that small village. On the grand scale of the Western Front, the operation would be small, but its causative ripples would be far-reaching. With a field commander's vision that never outdistanced reality, Bullard committed all the resources of his own mind and the minds of his commanders and staff to construct a plan to take Cantigny, and he planned for nothing less than total victory.

CHAPTER 6

Marshall's First Plan

It was "out of a clear sky," George Marshall noted, that orders came "to prepare an operation for the capture of the heights of Cantigny, without the assistance of any French divisions." Over the previous eleven months as the operations officer in the fishbowl world of Pershing's favored unit, Marshall had revealed a matchless gift for planning. He had employed his organizational thoroughness to tackle one mammoth logistical challenge after another, from orchestrating the movement of tens of thousands of men and supplies to harmonizing training schedules with the French Army and planning raids on enemy trenches.

Now Marshall, whose name would forever be indelibly linked to a larger, farther-reaching plan, was ordered by Bullard to construct a plan to capture Cantigny from the enemy. But in the improvisational spirit of open warfare, which Pershing had been urging at every turn, Marshall's assignment seemed almost unfeasible—an attempt to impose order and reason to the disorderly tumult of unpredictable combat. As a military proverb then still young but already growing in legend, that of the former German field marshal Helmuth von Moltke (the Elder), proclaimed: "No battle plan survives contact with the enemy."

But Marshall's assignment was no open-ended mandate, and the tactics applied would not be open warfare. "By direction, this was to be an operation with a strictly limited objective," he would later write. The mission was "bite-and-hold": capture Cantigny, moving the American lines one mile east, eliminating the low-ground salient by biting off the enemy's high ground, then hold the new position against the inevitable counterattacks. It was a straightforward objective inspired by the straightforward Bullard, and Marshall was to plot the ground attack by the infantry and formation of new lines by combat engineers while General Summerall and his own staff planned the artillery support.

But for any stratagem to find success, Marshall needed a comprehensive picture of enemy dispositions. He needed to identify which structures in Cantigny had deep cellars, and of those, which were used as command posts and which were used for ammunition storage. He needed updated mapping of each German front-line, communication, and reserve trench surrounding the village, as well as those stretching north and south and the lines of barbed wire before them. And he needed the exact placement of each enemy machine gun and its field of fire to give Sitting Bull's gunners accurate targets to neutralize. Finally Marshall needed the effective strength and location of each component of the enemy combat battalions holding the targeted positions, down to each company, platoon, squad, and outpost sentry, as well as locations of their reserve and rest battalions back in the thick woods beyond the village.

To satisfy the gargantuan appetite Marshall and his fellow staff planners had developed for such data, front-line infantry commanders were pressed for enemy intelligence, and the regiments in the trenches were stirred into action. "We have taken no prisoners since arrival in this sector," the commander of the 26th Infantry told his subordinates, adding that, thus far, "[t]he information gained by us of the enemy has been practically nil." He ordered patrols and raids to capture "One or more prisoners," and his regiment and the 28th were soon launching nightly hunts for information.

"I've had a patrol out every night," Cpl. Tom Carroll told his diary, describing his experience after a slow, painstaking crawl across no-man's-land: "Got to main road, very dark, heard Boche talking. Peeked over road, could see nothing. Heard snap of grenade detonator. Grenade hit my back, but didn't explode. Machine-gun opens up and we see gun right across from us. We each throw a couple of grenades, and as flares are going up we run like hell back to our side." The next night, he and the others sneaked out to the same spot to capture the machine gun, but "ran into 34 Boche laying for us." In a point-blank flurry of pistol and rifle fire, Corporal Carroll was grazed by a bullet in his scalp. "I saw two Boche go down before the blood started to run into my eyes, blinding me," he wrote, "but we all got back safely. All we had was pistols. If we had an automatic-rifle or two we could have taken them."

On some nights, two or three patrols explored different parts of the sector simultaneously. Platoon leaders and company commanders rotated the lead job, gathering six- to fifteen-man teams of two or three NCOs and volunteers—always including at least one soldier who could speak German in case they came close enough to enemy trenches to pick up conversation. With faces rubbed black with mud or burnt cork, they would climb over the top just after midnight and low-crawl through the wheat stubble, keeping a heading with a luminous compass. As on previous patrols, their instructions were to look for "enemy working parties, enemy strongpoints, breaks in wire, shell holes" and to note exact locations. If all went smoothly, they would return by two thirty or three a.m.—time enough to avoid getting trapped out in no-man's-land by the light of early dawn. Officers would then fill out reports of what was observed and heard, sometimes with hand-drawn maps, and pass them to battalion intelligence officers for relay up the chain.

Stacks of these reconnaissance reports filtered back to Division Head-quarters daily, most with valuable data for Marshall to plot on his planning map. In one report was the following: "A machine-gun fired on us from a point 50 yds south of the lone tree immediately in front of 4th platoon. A sniper's post was discovered on my return." In another: "moved towards enemy's trenches about 200 yds when a series of flares sent up by the Boche drew machine-gun fire on the patrol. The enemy could be plainly heard dig-ging and hammering as though driving stakes. Patrol moved to right and found evidence of former snipers' posts in several shell holes." And still an-other: "MG active and flash seen near [map coordinate] 218.321 at trees. Will identify spot later by daylight."

Junior officers in every company got at least one turn each at the perilous duty, the rotations at times meeting with uneven results, but there remained one constant: every night, in every type of weather, a patrol to the enemy lines was led by the 28th Infantry's fearless 3rd Battalion intelligence offi-cer, Lt. George Buchanan Redwood. A twenty-nine-year-old Baltimore na-tive and Harvard graduate, Redwood was handsome, intelligent, and well liked. When war had first erupted in Europe, his widowed mother worked to persuade him—thinking mostly of his young brother for whom he had become a father figure—not to join the Canadian or English Army. But when America entered the war, Redwood left his advertising job, attended the first round of officer training, shipped off to France in September, and was assigned to the 1st Division.

A devout Christian, Lieutenant Redwood filled his spare hours with read-ings of his small Bible and books like *A Good Samaritan* and *Out-of-Doors in the Holy Land*, and after attending British scouting school, he studied German tirelessly until, as one soldier commented, he could speak it "like a Hun." He won renown in late March down in Seicheprey when he led a ten-man raid in the driving rain of dawn across no-man's-land, fought off an enemy force that outnumbered his two to one, and returned with four frightened Germans at the point of his Colt .45. It was the first American raid to capture enemy prisoners, and stories of Redwood's daring made their way into the *Stars & Stripes* and back in the States in newspapers from coast to coast. He was awarded the French Croix de Guerre and the Distinguished Service Cross for his "extraordinary heroism," but the humble Redwood was quick to deflect praise, calling the raid merely "our little adventure."

His friend and fellow lieutenant Sam Ervin remarked that Redwood "did not know what fear was," and described him as "the incarnation of the Christian soldier." At the beginning of each patrol, he was known to kneel with his fellow soldiers and pray, and a member of the infamous Seicheprey raid later recalled that Redwood promised if they "took prisoners he would read us the Gospel on Easter Sunday." So successful was he at the art of scouting, he would slip into enemy trenches in the dark, grab materiel—sometimes even snatching their rations and coffee—then slip back out without notice. "The joke of it," one private remarked, "was that he captured them from under the Germans' noses, and if any of them spoke with him he would reply in German and they would not know but that he was one of them." One doughboy said Redwood had "the best reputation I ever heard a man get," and another claimed, with pardonable exaggeration, that patrols led by Redwood always "brought something back that could walk."

For a stretch of twelve straight nights, Redwood, the "scout officer," as he referred to himself, patrolled out into no-man's-land, often alone. "He would come in about daylight covered with mud from crawling around the trenches and under the barbed wire, and looking like anything but an officer," a fellow soldier recounted. After grabbing a bite to eat and catnapping, he would "do the same thing the following night until the entire situation was clearly developed," providing Division Headquarters with a bottomless fund of timely and accurate enemy intelligence. But over three miles away, where Marshall worked by gas-fired lamplight in his stale, wine-cellar workspace, the squiggly trench lines and penciled-in Maxim nests on his flat map board—all shaped by aerial photography and the patrol reports of

Redwood and others—could still not accurately render the topographic folds and ridges of the landscape over which the attack would be made.

To gain a firsthand feel, Marshall and other staff officers began personally taking nighttime ventures to the front. They would depart after midnight, ride one mile by car, leaving their driver to wait in a shell hole while they found their way—by guide or by compass—through Death Valley and up the slope into the narrow communication trenches leading to the front lines. "During the night we could check up [on] most of the dispositions of the troops," Marshall later recounted, "but it was only possible to size up the terrain in the short period at dawn just before sunrise," when there was enough light to make out details of the village but still dark enough to conceal their movements.

One morning, Marshall crawled with two others into a level stretch of no-man's-land, where, he would later recall, "we studied the lay of the ground until shortly after dawn." The sun rose surprisingly quickly, and they were "confronted with the necessity of either remaining in that locality until nightfall or exposing ourselves in an endeavor to get back to Division Headquarters." They low-crawled slowly back toward the ridge and found slight cover in a one-foot-deep ditch leading back to the division lines. But they were still four or five hundred yards from safety when an enemy machine gunner spotted them, and the Maxim's dreaded rattle sounded. The three officers flattened out and inched their way back, "crawling with our hands and toes," as Marshall described, while bullets gouged the earth all around them. Of the incident, where history came perilously close to being bent sharply by some anonymous German machine gunner, Marshall would later admit: "I think each of us was considerably disturbed over the possibility of being shot in a rather ignominious fashion and we were all very glad when we reached the cover of the ridge."

With better familiarity of the lay of the land, Marshall and Summerall and their planners hammered out drafts of the attack plan, and gradually, from the daily and nightly clacking of typewriters, Field Order No. 18, "having for its object the capture of Cantigny," took shape. The artillery support would borrow from the German artillerist Col. Georg Bruchmüller, whose tactics were being successfully employed in Kaiserschlacht. Instead of a long destructive bombardment of the targeted position—which would forfeit surprise and give the enemy time to prepare a defense and counter-attack—a short but overwhelming preparatory bombardment of the village would precede the infantry attack.

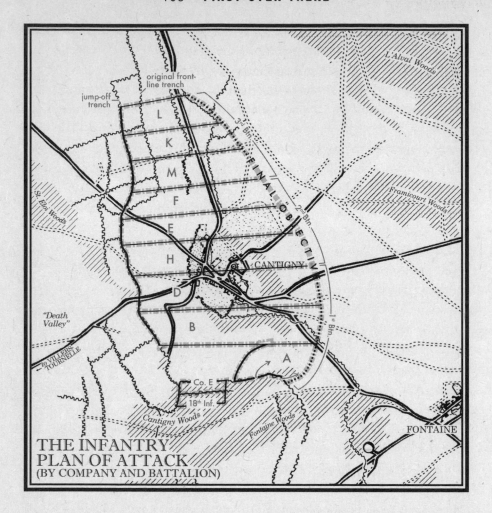

THE INFANTRY
PLAN OF ATTACK
(BY COMPANY AND BATTALION)

For this purpose, the guns of the 1st Field Artillery Brigade would be augmented by thirty-seven batteries of French Corps artillery, all totaling 386 guns placed under Sitting Bull's command. For one hour, these guns—ranging from 75s up to the immense 280s—would pummel Cantigny, the enemy lines surrounding it, and known enemy artillery and reserve troop positions back in the woods. Minutes before H-Hour—"Zero Hour" as most called it—the bombardment would cease and 75s would fire in unison to form a curtain of explosions out in no-man's-land. At Zero Hour, a regiment of infantry, three battalions wide and augmented by three machine-gun companies and a company of engineers, would go "over the top" and advance in three waves toward the barrage line.

This "creeping barrage" was to advance punctually one hundred yards every two minutes, leading the first wave of attackers across no-man's-land.

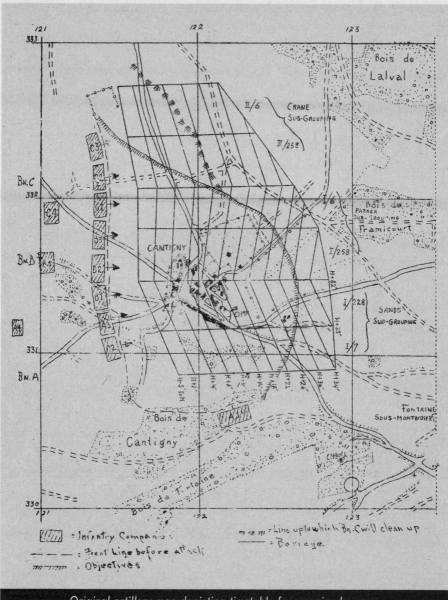

Original artillery map depicting timetable for creeping barrage

The middle battalion of infantry, assigned to sweep through the village itself, would be supported by a battalion of a dozen French Schneider tanks to help overcome machine-gun nests and strongpoints, as well as a team of ten French flamethrowers to aid in "mopping up the caves and the undergrounds" of the enemy. Once the creeping barrage reached the village, it

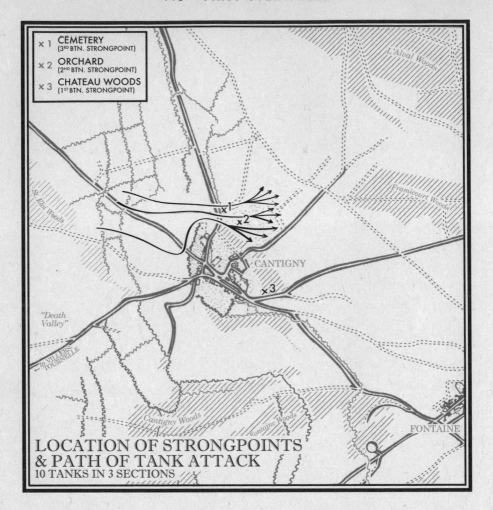

CEMETERY
(3RD BTN. STRONGPOINT)

ORCHARD
(2ND BTN. STRONGPOINT)

CHATEAU WOODS
(1ST BTN. STRONGPOINT)

LOCATION OF STRONGPOINTS
& PATH OF TANK ATTACK
10 TANKS IN 3 SECTIONS

would pause, allowing the second and third waves of infantry to catch up, then advance every four minutes until reaching the objective on the far side. There new lines would be dug into open ground facing the pushed-back Germans, a point that was to be reached thirty-four minutes after Zero Hour if all went as planned.

Success would require the skillful choreography of aerial observers, artillery, infantry, engineers, tanks, and flamethrowers. It was uniform coordination of combined arms reduced to science—a first for American combatants—and there was no room for error. Riflemen were instructed to "follow the barrage as closely as possible." Two and three miles away, the teams at each 75 firing the creeping barrage would be given charts for timed elevation adjustments, full of instructions "to absolutely *prevent firing at the wrong range*" and emphasizing that "all successive lifts must be absolutely by the synchronized time," as even the slightest miscalculation could land an explosive shell in the middle of a fifty-man platoon up in the first wave.

But even if all parts were perfectly executed and the objective reached, victory would be far from inevitable. All along the Western Front was ground that had been captured then lost to heavy enemy counterattack, most recently Cantigny. Each shell-torn village or pockmarked hill that had slipped back into the grip of the German Army served as an object lesson for military planners—a series of cautionary tales urging a better way. Marshall and Summerall would not be herded into repeating the same mistakes, and thus they devised a second well-orchestrated phase to hold the ground gained.

If successful in reaching their objective, the troops would be exposed in an open field on the far side of the village, where they would have to dig trenches and string barbed wire within range of German artillery and machine guns in the wood lines. To protect this process, the heavy, long-range guns and howitzers of the French artillery would be needed. In the words of the plan, "the counter battery artillery must be extremely vigilant and ready to intervene energetically against any enemy battery" throughout all of J-Day and the days following. If every rifleman dug his line, if every platoon leader ordered well-placed outposts and machine-gun nests, if every artillery observer spotted enemy batteries and every French and American gunner adjusted their fire accurately—if every doughboy breathed life into his typed role in Marshall's large blueprint, then the machinery of the 1st Division would, as Bullard envisioned months before, "work independently of the quality of the hand that turns the crank," and the battle could be won.

And so the script for America's first battle of the World War was written. It embodied the painstaking distillation of hard-won intelligence and application of a division-wide harmony of action first practiced down in the muddy trenches of Seicheprey. This was no visionary leap, and neither did it embrace open warfare, with flexible objectives and elbow room for low-level small unit adjustments to exploit local success. Rooted firmly in the tried tactics of trench warfare, this was a limited plan with a fixed objective, known enemy infantry and battery positions, heavy dependency on artillery support, and little perceptible room for adjustment. Its rigid structure left little to the vagaries of chance. Everything down to the number of rounds in each rifleman's ammo pouches and the contents of each soldier's pack was chiseled into the stiff division operations plan. As one officer later noted, this plan left "optional with the regimental commander the designation only of the particular individuals who should carry the long handled shovels."

In a dirt bunker dug into the face of the slope ascending from Death Valley toward the front lines, seated on his dismounted horse saddle atop a propped-up ammunition box, was the leader of the 28th Infantry Regiment, Col. Hanson Ely. The fifty-year-old Iowa native was, in Bullard's words, a "giant of a man." When not hunkered in his cramped dugout, he stood six feet two inches tall and bore the type of broad-shouldered, barrel-chested physique that hatched wartime legend. He graduated West Point near the bottom of the class of 1891, where his feared reputation as a skilled boxer thwarted many fights among his fellow cadets, arming him with an effective metaphor he eagerly employed as a preparedness advocate before America entered the war.

After teaching military science as a lieutenant, Ely drilled volunteer regiments for deployment to fight in the Spanish-American War, where he served as a supply officer. He saw action commanding mounted scouts in the Philippines, was promoted to captain for bravery under fire, and after observing maneuvers of the German Army and completing Army War College, he commanded a battalion in the Vera Cruz Expedition in Mexico. When America declared war, he was promoted to colonel and became one of the first AEF officers to arrive in France as part of the Baker Mission in May 1917. So extensive was his experience when he joined the 1st Division as chief of staff that Bullard would later write, "[F]ew officers of any army were as well prepared for the war as he was in both theory and practice."

Physically, Colonel Ely was equally intimidating to eyes and ears, with a manner and tone that provoked fear rather than persuasion. His men called him a "steam-roller," and General Bullard noted that he "smiled little," his voice was "gruff," and most of his words were forced out through flexed jaw muscles between clenched teeth. Because Ely "relied on the force of hard blows," having "never cultivated the qualities of tactfulness," Bullard felt his leadership style—often explosive and usually abrasive—was better suited for command than staff, and placed him in charge of the 3,700 men of the 28th Infantry before the winter move to Seicheprey.

As a commander, Colonel Ely had no gift for sustained analysis, and his decisions were sudden and firm, sometimes made without full facts. Back in Seicheprey, when he heard wind of a rumor that Lt. Sam Ervin had fallen asleep at his post, Ely ordered him out of the regiment. But the rumors were false, and even after the division's judge advocate cleared Ervin of the accusation, Ely would not relent. Though Ervin had the option of serving as a billeting officer behind the lines, his sense of service had been inalterably wed to front-line duty with his buddies in the 28th. It took the lobbying efforts of Ervin's friend Lt. George Redwood to convince the unforgiving Ely to accept Ervin back into the regiment, but Ely would not readmit him as an officer. Thus, so he could stay with the 28th Infantry, Ervin resigned his commission and enlisted as a private.

At Cantigny, in his fifth month of command, Ely had learned days earlier that his 28th Infantry would be charged with making the attack on the village. He would later remark that his regiment "was chosen, because of its splendid discipline, to bear the brunt of the attack." But the true reason was less rousing. Bullard's first choice had been the 18th Infantry, which had already completed a tour in the lines facing Cantigny, but the heavy casualties it suffered in the Villers-Tournelle gas attack removed it from consideration. And with the 16th and 26th only familiar with the south end of the sector, the logical choice was the 28th, whose soldiers had gained intimate familiarity with the landscape over which the attack would be launched. So from the confines of his bunker—which one officer noted was "about the size of a piano box"—with a handful of orderlies and a single field telephone from which lines led to the command posts of each of his three battalion commanders, Ely ordered that the twelve infantry companies of his regiment prepare for a move to a training area for "special instruction."

After dark on Thursday, May 23, the soldiers of the 18th Infantry entered the front lines, relieving the soldiers of the 28th, who in turn shuffled down the communication trenches with their rifles and full packs, crossed Death Valley and loaded into waiting trucks for a twelve-mile ride to a training area. Lt. George Haydock noted it was "a long, hard, all-night pull," after which he and his platoon "were greeted by a hot meal, which is a luxury in itself." Troops billeted in nearby villages, and after welcome sleep away from the perils of gassing and shelling, by dawn they were assembled on the edge of a large plateau to rehearse Marshall's plan.

"Ground was selected as near like the actual terrain to be operated over as possible," Colonel Ely observed. The training area was a vast, open farm field, with low ground rolling up on a slight incline to a patch of trees on a hilltop, meant to simulate Cantigny. Off to the side of the field, on a twenty-by-thirty-foot sand-table with scaled models of the village structures, trenches, and surrounding battleground, company commanders and platoon leaders were shown the direction of their specific parts of the larger attack and the objective line each was to achieve. "In addition," one platoon leader later recalled, "officers and non-commissioned officers were shown lantern slides of aerial photographs of the area over which the attack was to be made."

From trenches on the edge of the field, dug to simulate the American front lines, junior officers walked through their platoons' and companies' lines of attack, complete with landmarks and compass headings. They were then joined by their NCOs to work out the part for each squad and supporting machine-gun team. Then a full walk-through was conducted, giving each soldier familiarity with the part he was to play in the assault. The eighteen platoons forming the first wave practiced moving forward from the trench at a brisk walk, keeping in line with the men to their right and left, and following closely the creeping barrage, which was, Colonel Ely noted, "represented by men carrying tree branches." The second wave— infantry platoons and machine-gun teams—followed, then finally a third wave of carrying parties, who on J-Day would be loaded with ammo boxes, barbed wire, and wooden stakes.

"During next two days the entire Regiment was put through the entire operation," Colonel Ely noted. "The marching up to and taking position on jumping off lines, jumping off, following moving barrage . . . keeping direction and rate of march, halting at the proper objectives and beginning to consolidate same, sending out of patrols and covering parties in advance of objective, organization and use of carrying parties and moppers up." Ely was intent that every man in his regiment drill his own part until it became muscle memory. "[W]e practiced for the attack for three days," one lieutenant later recounted, and another added that "[a]fter each rehearsal detailed critiques were held and errors pointed out." Lt. Dick Dacus described a humorous moment at one such evaluation: "One French General gave a long critique to the assembled officers, in French of course. When he finished, General Bullard, wrapped up in his non-regulation black fur coat, thanked the French General, and turned to us and said, 'Gentlemen, you have heard the suggestions of the General. Please give them your due consideration and act accordingly.'"

The next day, flamethrowers were added to the rehearsal, and a French soldier demonstrated the scorching reach of a flamethrower for the watching doughboys. "This demonstration was quite impressive," twenty-five-year-old Lt. Welcome Waltz observed, "as the red flame, with a great roar and accompanied with a big cloud of very black smoke, shot out of the high pressure tank, which was strapped on the back of the soldier." Five infantry companies designated to sweep through the village would each have two of these flamethrower teams attached to follow the platoons of their second wave, and here the soldiers practiced covering the crews as they simulated "mopping up" the village cellars of the enemy.

Most novel to these wide-eyed doughboys at the rehearsal were tanks, a new weapon most American troops had never seen in person. Top heavy with a pointed front and narrow, rectangular bodies, French Schneider tanks resembled tall, armored transport boats carried slowly atop caterpillar tracks. Armed with Hotchkiss machine guns that poked out from both sides in swivels, and a 75mm gun that rotated out the right in a ball-mount, Schneiders had been employed in the previous summer's French offensive and recent counterattacks mainly to overcome Maxim nests and enemy strongpoints. The soldiers who would be advancing up the middle of the attack with the tanks learned how to advance in waves with the twelve Schneiders of the 5th French Tank Battalion, and a French officer gave instructions while General Bullard translated.

For the final run-through, a handful of war correspondents—all sworn to secrecy until after the battle—were invited to observe. "French machine gunners played the role of Germans," Fred Ferguson of the UPI later reported. "They had their machine guns hidden in pits and elsewhere in the field." The three waves of infantry and machine-gun teams ran through the assault in tandem with flamethrowers and tanks. "They were kept at it until they were letter perfect on every detail," another reporter, Herbert Corey, noted. "They knew where they were to jump off from and where they were to go to. They knew the compass bearings of their prospective routes, and each had marked down a landmark to follow."

"In the last day's practice the entire Regiment, with flamethrowers, were used and was fairly satisfactory," Colonel Ely approvingly noted. He understood the great weight placed on the soldiers of his unit, later recounting that "General Pershing said that 'no inch was to be given up' when we attacked the place." Ely later complained that he would have preferred a day or two more slated for this training, so "a few rough edges could have been better smoothed off." But satisfied they were as prepared for the battle as time would allow, he gathered his officers for a pre-battle pep speech, which Lieutenant Waltz later described: "In his characteristic, forceful way, he impressed upon us the necessity of driving hard and allowing no opposition to hinder us from reaching our objective."

On Sunday, the troops of the 28th were given a day off. All were treated to a warm meal and, as Lt. George Haydock relished, "a big batch of mail." Three days prior, the call to arms had fired in the doughboys emotions that were soon crowded out by the long hours spent on the battle rehearsal. Now the rare moments of quiet prompted the men to take inventory of their sentiments, and their disparate psychological approaches to impending battle—some fighting the anguish of uncertainty and others daydreaming of glory to come—incited a flurry of letters to loved ones.

"This isn't the eve of battle but it is so close to it that if I don't write now I won't get another chance," Lieutenant Newhall wrote his mother, Elizabeth, adding, "[p]erhaps my next letter can describe a battle." Eighteen-year-old Pvt. Carl Fey wrote his mom back in Schuylkill Haven, Pennsylvania: "Mother I will stay with you if I ever get back." Telling her he was headed back into the trenches again, he added a closing assurance: "I am under the lucky star. Don't worry."

Lt. Dan Birmingham tap-danced near the edge of his officer duty of self-censorship, writing his father: "Watch the papers and magazines for the efforts of the 28th Infantry." Of the imminent battle, Lt. Vinton Dearing was not so candid with his sister Peggy, telling her simply, "Things are very different this time." He wrote of the war-torn French villages he had seen, describing "roofless walls" and streets "ripped up with shells," and revealed the higher cause he had applied to his role in the coming action: "I am here in France to save our own homes and parks from being ruined as they are ruined over here."

Back up in the trenches facing Cantigny, the men of the 18th Infantry and 1st Engineers had been working at a fiendish pace adding the duplicate trench lines and supply points needed by J-Day. Because German artillery already had guns registered on the existing division front lines, and because, at Zero Hour, seventeen companies of riflemen would be packed into the length of a front normally held by only four, new lines had to be dug for jumping-off trenches. The labor of these troops—who still knew nothing of the planned attack their comrades in the 28th were rehearsing—was evidenced in the 18th Infantry Daily Reports: on May 25 alone, 265 men from two companies dug 450 yards of trenches, and 131 men from a single company dug 400 yards to a depth of four feet. One engineer recounted how he was sent forward "to help out on some rush trench digging . . . The trench I had to tape out was in a clover field on top of a flat hill and I was told a [German] machine-gun opened across it occasionally for luck and that my tape had to laid, while crawling, after dusk."

But in the midst of this work, one incident threatened to derail the entire operation. Around eleven p.m., Saturday, May 25, a detail carrying sacks of heavy entrenching tools and led by twenty-nine-year-old Lt. Oliver "Judd" Kendall was up near the front lines when it came under artillery fire that scattered a few of its members into nearby trenches for cover. When the shelling ceased, Lieutenant Kendall tried to reassemble his men, but noting half were still missing, he ordered a member of the party to find them. Hearing a noise, Kendall told his sergeant to wait for his return and disappeared into the darkness of no-man's-land. Only a single sound of shovels being dropped broke the silence that followed. As anxious minutes passed without Kendall's return, the sergeant and another officer went forward, falling into a trench that, after being instantly fired on and seeing outlines of Germans in coal-scuttle helmets, they realized was an enemy outpost. They climbed out and ran back, and the officer returned fire with his pistol. But Lieutenant Kendall was missing, likely in the enemy's hands.

Lieutenant Kendall did not know the specifics of the planned attack, but he knew one was imminent, and he was carrying a detailed map of the jumping-off trenches and newly constructed supply and ammunition points—enough to make high command "deeply concerned" about his likely capture. George Marshall and others at Division Headquarters feared the maps and entrenching tools "would disclose to the enemy our intentions, with the inevitable disastrous result." The fear of losing surprise, the most vital of all fragile elements essential to success, was now immeasurably heightened—so much so that, according to one officer, they "considered suspending the operation." But in another calculated risk, General Bullard decided to proceed.

Twelve miles away, where Colonel Ely's doughboys were spending the contemplative stillness of Sunday writing letters or enjoying the quiet of the French countryside, a memorandum arrived from the division chief of staff: "J day will be May 28." Thus Sunday became J minus 2, and by the schedule of Field Order No. 18, the countdown would begin with the middle of the attack force—the four infantry companies of 2nd Battalion and its attached machine-gun company—moving into the front lines after dark that night. The rest of the troops were to move up Monday night, just hours prior to the attack. Nighttime relief of troops in the trenches was a difficult task under normal conditions, and the movement of an entire infantry regiment, three machine-gun companies, a company of engineers, and a French flamethrower section into their specific jumping-off positions would create a trial of logistics the planners felt was better spread over two nights instead of one.

But many questioned the wisdom of the two-night move. "This was the subject of careful consideration beforehand," wrote Colonel Ely, who later disagreed with the final plan: "it is believed that it was better to put it in on night of J-1 . . . rather than on J-2." Lieutenant Waltz, whose machine-gun company was part of the early move, agreed: "This was wrong because it is the same as bringing a football team out on the field twenty-four hours before the game. Assault troops are dead on their feet, if they are required to wait this long." But the planners disagreed and the orders were set, a decision that was to carry deadly consequences.

So as shadows lengthened with the setting sun, the soldiers of Companies E, F, G, and H of the 28th Infantry and Company C of the 3rd Machine-Gun Battalion packed their gear and lined up to fill wooden benches in the canvas-topped truck beds for the clattering twelve-mile ride back to the front. Young Capt. Edward Johnston rode "the dim white roads to the front" with his men of Company E. The drive was eerily quiet, and his troops said not a word. "[T]heir minds," Johnston estimated, "were intent on their own problems, they were brooding on the probable events of the next few days in the troubled eddies of Cantigny."

On the way, townspeople in each village through which the dusty convoy passed lined the roads to cheer on the American troops with shouts of *"bon chance! [sic]"* "All the French peasants in the nearby villages, through which we passed," Lieutenant Waltz observed, "seemed to know of our attack and were lined up on the road as our trucks passed towards the front, to give us farewell. It made one think twice."

All traces of dusk's light had disappeared by the time the trucks arrived in the rear of the sector, and in the night's pitch-black, the soldiers detrucked and began trooping forward in long lines by squad, toward Death Valley and the trenches. "All nights near the front lines were very dark, and certainly this was no exception," Lieutenant Waltz later recounted. "One just had to feel his way along. I have often wondered whether the nights in France get black or whether they just appeared that way to us."

Joining them on their trek forward was one officer and a dozen-man reconnaissance team from each of the companies of the other two battalions, tasked by Marshall's plan with measuring out space in the new jumping-off trenches for each platoon of their companies "to avoid all possibility of error on the following night." For Company L, the designated officer was Lieutenant Newhall, who led his small advance team forward "in the dark," he would recount, "mostly cross country, because the roads were shelled." Captain Johnston, leading not only the four platoons of his company but six machine-gun teams attached for the operation, also took note of the inky darkness: "There was no moon at all at this late hour, or mist and clouds hid it from view." His own move to the front lines was painfully slow, because "the guns had to be carried forward by hand" a distance of three miles.

Johnston and his company and machine-gun teams lugged their guns, tripods, spare barrels, and ammunition boxes, snaking down "narrow trails winding through the wheat," and as they moved closer to the front, skirting the edges of Death Valley, the boom of distant German batteries grew louder. "Now and then," Johnston noted, "a crashing shock marked the use of a proportion of high-explosive shell." The march to the front, in his mind, "seemed to go on interminably" as the "machine-gunners, overloaded, toiled ahead, burdened with guns and ammunition," a journey broken only by rest breaks and frequent dives into the dirt at the sound of incoming shells.

After midnight, the soldiers of Companies E and H filed into the communication trench, relieving two companies of the 18th and taking over the front lines facing no-man's-land. "The moon was veiled and the stars were hidden," Johnston noted, as his Company E platoons "settled down for the remainder of the night." Once relief was completed, around three thirty a.m., he and his number two, Lt. Irving Wood, climbed into a dirt bunker on the rim of Death Valley a few hundred yards behind the trenches and tried to find sleep on their canvas cots.

Behind the front lines, advance teams from 1st and 3rd Battalions worked through the night measuring and taping boundaries in the new jumping-off trenches for each of their platoons to use as guides when they moved into position the next night. Lieutenant Newhall and his team finally finished after four thirty a.m., at which point he curled up in a corner of a communication trench "with a view to getting a little sleep." Back in a patch of woods behind the trenches, under tree trunks stripped of foliage and chewed yellow by shellfire, Lieutenant Waltz and his "quite fatigued" men slept on the dirt where they could find space to sprawl out among dropped guns and strewn equipment.

Dawn struggled to break through a morning fog. Around four thirty a.m., Lieutenant Waltz, grabbing some fitful sleep on the cold ground near his men, was awoken by "a real drum fire barrage of 77-mm shells" just in front of the woods. A few mortar shells whistled into the skeletal tree canopy above, but as Waltz noted, "they didn't put them on us thick enough to do any damage." Sporadic bombardments near the front lines were not uncommon, so at first Waltz and his men, now being stirred awake one by one, "thought little of it . . . but as it kept dragging on, we began to wonder whether it didn't amount to more."

Like a snowball rolling, the bombardment intensified. Still curled up in the communication trench, Lieutenant Newhall gave up on sleep: "At five fifteen, the Germans opened bombardment on that part of our line, and for an hour and three quarters I had more shell fire than I ever had before." Hunkered not far from him was Lt. Si Parker, leading the advance team for Company K, and one of the blasts sliced a shard of hot metal across him as he dove for cover. "I got a little scratch on my left arm," he noted. "It cut quite a slit in the sleeves of my coat and shirt, but only grazed the flesh."

Two miles away, Sitting Bull's gunners, always on standby to support their front-line infantry, were monitoring their phones while battery commanders squinted through field glasses, scanning the gray, foggy sky above the front lines for flares. They had just the night before been handed charts showing the new jumping-off trenches to be seventy-five to one hundred yards behind the existing front lines, along with a report that the troops would be moved back to these new lines at "H-1" (H minus 1 hour). But someone—exactly who is unknown—misread "H-1" to read "J-1." So when Lt. Charles Avery's flares signaled for a barrage out in no-man's-land, the gunners, thinking Avery and his men had moved back in the jumping-off trenches, fired directly on his position. The fratricide that resulted from this misreading of a single letter threw into stark relief the exacting attention to detail required for the successful coordination of combined arms in the battle to come.

Over the front, the German bombardment shifted, forming a box barrage that surrounded a portion of the front trench and began pulverizing the rear trenches. Lt. Gerald Tyler and the advance team for Company M, resting in a communication trench, were lashed by the blasts. Sprinting with another officer between plumes of dirt and sprays of hot shrapnel, Tyler dove to the trench floor and looked back to see "a 105 hit the place we had just left and blew it off the map." He and his comrade—their faces "blackened with smoke"—tried to escape the vortex by scrambling up to the front lines. "This minute I do not know how on earth we ever got there falling down over picks and shovels, knocking off corners of traverses and firebags."

Lieutenant Tyler reached the front lines with his Colt .45 drawn, but immediately "huddled . . . in the bottom of the trench" to avoid "a steady hail of machine-gun bullets which combed our parapet." Frantic word reached the troops near him that the "Germans were coming across just to our left." It was the German raid. From his left, Tyler could hear the unmistakable crackle of Springfields and the violent chatter of a Hotchkiss, a medley of fire from Capt. Edward Johnston's soldiers—among them the riflemen of Lieutenant Curry's and Avery's platoons and Cpl. Dickie Conover's machine-gun crew—repulsing the fifty enemy raiders.

Back in their woods down the slope, Lieutenant Waltz and his men knew only what they could hear, that "[o]ver an hour had gone by and still the 77's were pounding our lines just above us." Waltz walked forward to investigate, when an excited private came running out of the fog from the front, yelling, "Retreat, they have broken through!" Panic spread like a wind-fed fire, and the machine-gun crews scattered in sprints down into Death Valley. Waltz chased after them waving his pistol, suddenly finding himself under the iron rain of another bombardment. As he rushed to reassemble his troops, he "took one look at those huge geysers of dirt going up all over the floor of that valley and just knew that [he] was ready for [his] last run."

Adding to the mayhem, a shell hit the ammunition supply point on the edge of the woods, detonating stacks of grenades, mortars, and flares. "It made quite a show as the smoke and flames shot skyward," Waltz observed. Lt. Dick Dacus, leading the advance team for Company I, had just sought cover by dropping into a trench beside the ammo point. "We were," he would later recount, "in the midst of the biggest 4th of July fireworks I ever saw, with shells, ammo of all kinds and rockets of all colors around us." The eruption, one officer later noted, sent men "scurrying to escape the grenade fragments and pyrotechnic flames." But after getting far enough away to avoid the danger, as one company commander noted, all the soldiers "promptly reformed in order."

The popping of rifle and pistol fire trickling from the front lines faded, and after a final few scattered artillery thuds, the air fell silent. As the rising sun finally burned through the fog, adding some color to the gray morning, news of the German raid spread at viral speed. Medics and reserve troops rushed to the front with stretchers against a tide of limping, injured, and shell-shocked men flooding out of the communication trenches down the slope. Field Hospital No. 12, set up behind the lines on the far edge of the valley, received three dozen patients, with injuries ranging from machine-gun wounds to shrapnel gashes. Among them was the jittery Lieutenant Avery, listed on his chart as "buried and shell shocked," still drawing on a cigarette to calm nerves frayed from partial paralysis and near suffocation after three hours buried in a trench collapse.

Also arriving on a bloody stretcher was twenty-year-old Pvt. Clifford Ledford of Cincinnati, Ohio, a member of Lieutenant Dacus's advance team. His entire left side had been flayed open by shrapnel, and his leg was dangling at the thigh by a few strands of flesh. He was given morphine and trucked to a French field hospital, where his leg was amputated and his arm stitched up and bandaged. Young Clifford clung to life the rest of the day and through the night, finally letting go the next morning, becoming the thirtieth doughboy killed in the enemy raid.

The raid on the American trenches facing Cantigny had been planned by the German 18th Army command a few days earlier. The operation was code named "Tarnopol," and had been well coordinated, with a swift, destructive artillery bombardment (two hours of high-explosive rounds) followed by an infantry assault protected by a creeping barrage. The raiding force was a team of fifty *Jagdkommando* (hunting command), who like *Stoßtruppen* were handpicked, volunteer troops in their physical prime who received additional training and double rations. For the assault, they were well armed, each man carrying a Mauser with fixed-bayonet, eight potato-masher grenades, and four egg grenades. Their mission had been to cross no-man's-land, enter the American trenches, gather any materiel they could find, capture one or more prisoners cut off from retreat or reinforcement by an accurate box barrage, and return to their own lines.

That the Germans targeted a stretch of trench taken over just hours earlier by doughboys who knew every detail of the next day's planned attack was pure chance, but it added incalculable weight to the actions of Captain Johnston's men. Had a single prisoner been captured—had Lieutenant Avery not recognized the signs of impending attack and prepared his platoon to defend their line; had Lieutenant Curry and his men not made the awful but unavoidable decision to kill one of their own who had surrendered to the enemy; and had Corporal Conover not climbed over the parapet and sniped German captors to free his comrades—surprise might have been lost and the entire operation placed in jeopardy.

"Raid was repulsed with heavy casualties," Captain Johnston matter-of-factly reported of the morning his company saved the Cantigny operation. But a fellow company commander, Capt. Charles Senay of Company C, would later give praise where it was due: "I do not believe that the Second Battalion, 28th Infantry, and E Company in particular, has been given full credit for the magnificent manner in which they annihilated a group of fifty German troops." Still, although the dogged resilience of the soldiers up in the front line had thwarted the enemy's assault and prevented the worst—the capture of any Americans—more than sixty casualties had been suffered—manpower that would not be replaced before Zero Hour.

Those given the luxury of hindsight can easily call the decision to bring up one-third of the attack force one night early a mistake. But perhaps Lieutenant Parker, bandaging his own bloody arm, assessed the most lasting effect of the German raid accurately: "Their efforts failed, and worse than that, it put more red blood in the boys' eye for the next day."

CHAPTER 7

A Hellish Clamor

By midmorning, onto the sun-drenched fields surrounding the villages in the rear of the sector came the French guns, more than three hundred of them, drawn by horses and surrounded by teams of French artillerymen frantically digging emplacements, throwing up branches and camo netting, and stockpiling shells for the next day's work. To make space and avoid German counter-battery fire during the battle, most of Summerall's artillery batteries had moved the night before into new positions.

After dark the previous night, twenty-nine-year-old Lt. Daniel Sargent of Massachusetts, an officer with Battery F of the 5th Field Artillery, had helped his crews haul their 155s a half mile closer to Cantigny. For the three weeks prior, he and his gunners had enjoyed "beautiful dug-outs" in their positions near Sérévillers. But on the night of May 26, up on the edge of some woods, they "had no dug-outs and had slept on the ground."

In the morning, a messenger came by motorcycle from General Summerall's headquarters to retrieve Sargent for a special mission. Riding by sidecar on roads back to Mesnil-Saint-Firmin, Sargent peered through passing corridors of open fields stretching to the horizon and noticed "an unfamiliar sight—an endless row of heavy French artillery: howitzers that looked to be 210's, and huge mortars that I estimated to be 240's. . . . There had been none of these batteries here yesterday."

The messenger drove Lieutenant Sargent into the paved streets of town and up to Division Headquarters, "a grandiose nineteenth century chateau of brick, with a park beside it." He was ushered downstairs into the headquarters of Generals Bullard and Summerall, a "rather ornate basement" with sandbags stacked against its brick walls and housing a bustling command center that reeked of scorched coffee and smoldering Chesterfields. George Marshall was seated, scratching out last-minute directives, his foot in a cast and propped up on a wooden chair after a spill from his horse had snapped his ankle the day before.

Puffing on a cigarette, a gray-haired French officer in an unbuttoned, threadbare tunic asked Sargent if he could speak French. He answered "a little bit," and was told his assignment in the next day's battle was to help liaison between the 1st Division and the French artillery. On a sector map draped over a table, a young French lieutenant pointed to a mark depicting an observation post up at the front lines where Sargent was to station himself by 5:45 a.m., and showed with a penciled line the path he was to take there. The French officer folded the map, gave it to Sargent, and sent him on his way with a final reminder: "Don't be late."

But as Lieutenant Sargent left, disturbing news began trickling into headquarters by telegram and by phone. That morning, thirty divisions of the German 1st and 7th Armies had attacked seven French and British divisions along a quiet front on the Chemin des Dames, and all reports indicated the enemy was, in Pershing's words, "making dangerous headway." The raid that morning against the 28th had been one of many matching "feint attacks" launched against the Allied front, all intended to distract from the renewed offensive, the third stage of Kaiserschlacht. This one was aimed directly toward Paris, and as General Ludendorff noted proudly: "Once more it proved a brilliant success."

To halt the enemy's alarming progress, forty-one French divisions were hustled into the breach, but still more were needed. By late afternoon, General Bullard and his staff learned this would include the French Corps artillery that had been designated to reinforce the next day's attack. The big French guns—the only ones with sufficient range to reach all enemy batteries—would still support the initial bombardment and infantry assault, but would withdraw after the objective was reached. "This was a heavy blow," Marshall noted, "as we were to depend on these guns to suppress the enemy's artillery fire, which would undoubtedly be directed at our infantry in their unsheltered positions on the final objectives."

Although this was the most devastating setback to the planned operation yet, General Bullard was confident his infantry could still hold. No obstacle—not an engineer officer and his map falling into enemy hands, not an enemy raid causing five dozen casualties to the attack's first wave, and not even this loss of critical counter-battery support—nothing was standing in the 1st Division's way. The battle was, as ever, still a go.

As the day slid toward dusk and late-afternoon shadows stretched, legions of khaki poured out of trucks and streamed across the plains toward the front lines. "As we left the trucks we heard the big naval guns barking for the first time," Pvt. John Johnston later recounted. "We were headed for the first all-American fight—for Cantigny." Each company was met by a guide from their advance team and, in the failing light, shepherded through paths to avoid shelled areas. "That night everything seemed quiet," one officer noted, "yet on the roads and on every path leading down to the front went constant files of infantry, machine-gunners, engineers, and carrying parties."

The night was, as one artillery officer described, "as black as hell itself," and as the lead column of doughboys loaded down in full gear felt their way forward through Death Valley, gas shells pinged into the darkness. Helmets and rifles and ammo boxes fell to the ground as men scrambled to yank their masks from canvas bags and strap them on. Leading a squad in the long column, nineteen-year-old Cpl. Charles Simmons Jr. had been fiddling on the dark march with a loose rifle grenade strapped to the shoulder strap of his pack. In his fogged mask, as he threw his gear back on, the grenade blew. His helmet was blown off and he fell in a heap to the dirt, with his shredded gas mask revealing a mass of blood. Simmons was unconscious but still breathing when his men loaded him on a stretcher, but by the time he reached the field hospital, he was dead. When his widower father, Charles Sr., received word by telegram from the War Department that his only son had been killed in action, he asked that his remains be returned home. After the Armistice, Charles Simmons Jr. was buried in a family plot in Whitewright, Texas.

It was 11:00 p.m. when Maj. Raymond Austin, in his dugout on a hilltop near his batteries of 75s, was handed a folded piece of paper by a motorcycle courier, who motored off to the next command post with a satchel filled with more of the same. Austin held the sheet up to his beacon light: "Very Secret. H hour will be 6:45 a.m. By command of Major General Bullard." Austin notified his crews, who would be firing the creeping barrage, and they "prepared schedules for each gun," he later recounted. They taped lined charts of coordinates to their gun barrels, "each line covering one minute of firing," which would, the next morning, be "torn off as the firing for each minute was completed." Battery commanders all across the sector received the same message by messengers dispatched from Division Headquarters with strict orders to deliver the H-hour notice "in person," not by telephone.

With H-hour set, timing—precise and to the microsecond—was paramount. Back in the afternoon, two "reliable watches" had been synchronized by Bullard's staff with the division clock and sent by runner up to Colonel Ely's bunker. More watches were then set with those, and so the process had continued through the afternoon and into the evening until every battery officer, machine-gun crew, and platoon leader was synchronized. Phone calls were then made to each command post and artillery battery from Division Headquarters to double-check that all were running in tandem.

Around midnight, the companies arrived at the front and entered communication trenches single-file, company by company, platoon by platoon, and man by man. Lt. Richard Newhall met his platoon and guided them into their lines on the far left; then with remaining columns still scattered after the gas attack "came a wait of perhaps an hour before the first platoon with Haydock leading appeared out of the dark."

Into the freshly dug jumping-off trenches the doughboys crammed. Man after man, clutching Springfields and top-heavy with full packs and crowded web belts, dropped with exhausted sighs against the rear trench wall, each trying to stake a claim on a precious plot of dirt. Troops kept shuffling in, forcing the rows to slide closer and closer until they were shoulder to shoulder. Platoon leaders urged their soldiers to try to rest, and some caught catnaps wedging their heads back into soft parts of the trench wall. But in the tight space, the bustle of activity was unending, and seated troops were constantly pulling their legs up to clear paths for strangers from other units, all in hunched shuffles, carrying machine guns and tripods and ammo boxes and barbed-wire coils into position.

Three miles away, Division Headquarters was under sporadic fire from the long-range German guns when General Pershing arrived to confer with General Bullard one last time about the attack. On the drive in, shell fragments had pinged like hailstones off the metal roof of his command car. His driver, Sgt. Cesar Santini, parked under the cover of some trees and, as he would later recall, "[I] tried my best to take a little snooze on the seat. More than once the shells fell too close to the machine to make me feel comfortable." He even watched as a mortar round hit the headquarters directly, destroying a chimney.

Downstairs, in the cellar command center, Pershing talked over the attack with Bullard, then spoke with the French artillery liaison, Col. Jacques de Chambrun, who assured the Big Chief, between puffs on a pipe, of the division's readiness. Pershing departed to spend the night at his forward headquarters north of Paris, leaving the patchwork of infantry and artillery staff and engineers and signalmen and French liaison officers to toil by lamplight, each focused on indispensable cogs in their respective gears of the large machine. In the small hours of morning, the phone rang with a message from the front: "5440," code for "every element in position for attack."

Lt. Daniel Sargent again spent the night sleeping on the cold, hard ground near his artillery battery, and was jolted awake by a nightmare that he had overslept. "Don't be late"—the parting words of the French lieutenant back at Division Headquarters kept replaying in Sargent's head, a ringing reminder of this morning's mission. Scanning the dark night sky, he was reassured of the early hour as he found no hint of morning light. "I could see the stars above the trees and also I could read my watch," he observed.

It was not yet 4:00 a.m., the assigned hour for the guard to wake him, but with thoughts of his assignment clogging his mind, more sleep for Lieutenant Sargent would be impossible. The artillery was scheduled to begin its bombardment of German positions at 5:45 a.m. precisely, and it was imperative that he make it to his observation post up at the front lines by then. Although a few minutes ahead of schedule, he worried there was "still a chance of being late," so he stashed his folded map, a canteen of water, and a slice of bread into his pack and set off for the front.

Sargent noticed, as he came out of a patch of dark woods and into the open, that the night was clear and the fields leading toward the front "seemed to be luminous. There were only the stars to light me from the sky, but there was no haze." These conditions would aid his task of observation, but they would also make obvious artillery targets of any doughboys clustered out in the open without cover should they be spotted by German observation pilots. By a few minutes past 4:00 a.m., as Sargent continued his starlit walk through his carefully planned route toward his observation post, most of the men at the front were still resting, either huddled in trenches or assembled under the tree cover of woods behind the front lines.

But the 150 members of Company D, 1st Engineers, were resting in the open, bunched together in an old chalk quarry two hundred yards behind the front line. On the east side of the quarry was a thirty-foot-tall cliff wall that cut into the landscape that ascended toward the front lines. Though it provided a comforting bit of cover from enemy shells, the resting men could be seen clearly from overhead. They had been there for about two hours, and aside from a single German plane that had circled over their position earlier, their time in the quarry was passing uneventfully. Most had dropped their packs and cartridge belts and were lying down, their rifles and gas masks at their side, attempting to catch a bit of sleep in the final moments before the bombardment began.

Serene moments near the front were rare, but this morning was so quiet that twenty-six year-old Cpl. Boleslaw Suchocki, a Polish immigrant who worked as a cabinetmaker back in Worcester, Massachusetts, before volunteering to serve his adopted country as an Army engineer, "could hear a fly buzzing in the air" around him. The dead calm was charged with an awareness of the coming battle, and it shrouded a scene that mixed anxious expectation and calm brooding. Some men were sleeping wherever they could make space, either flat on the rocky ground or leaned back against the cliff wall. Others were sitting up smoking cigarettes, prepared to extinguish them at any more signs of an enemy spotter plane. For his part, Corporal Suchocki paced in full gear, working off nervous energy. The company first sergeant implored him: "Suchocki, why don't you rest. We have a big job tomorrow."

Many were kept awake by nerves and fear, and others by the chill carried in the twilight air. Lt. John McClure later remembered stretching out with two other lieutenants and trying to sleep, "but after one had slept for a while, he would wake up from the cold, aching all over." Clothed and equipped only with what they needed for battle, none had blankets or overcoats. "I was colder than I had been in a long time and several times walked up and down the valley toward Colonel Ely's bunker to get the blood to flowing again," McClure noted.

As the pitch-black darkness began to give way to the first glimmers of faint light, McClure was with fellow lieutenants Boyd Crawford and Hamlet Jones near the road at the opening of the quarry, and the three were "all awake, half sitting up." Standing nearby, Corporal Suchocki could hear the three of them "carrying on a very interesting conversation." Recounting the moment later, McClure relayed, "I remarked to Jones on my right that we should get the men up the hill under the trees there, so any early planes would not spot them." Lieutenant Jones agreed, but thought there was still sufficient darkness to allow the men to rest a few minutes more, so they waited.

It was 4:20 a.m. In just twenty-five more minutes the artillery would fire at assigned targets to register the guns and gauge the wind and range for the opening bombardment. Platoon and section leaders would then get their men geared up and moved to their assigned starting positions for the attack. All was set to move like clockwork, but as the previous morning's enemy raid had grimly demonstrated, the best-laid plans hold no control over the crush of events. That morning, fate again threatened to disrupt the planned attack as the stillness in the quarry was broken by the whistling of an incoming shell. The sound sailed over the resting men and hit with an explosion a few yards behind them, where the ground descended into Death Valley.

"It burst with a thunderous roar," Corporal Suchocki observed. As he dropped to the ground, he could hear lead shrapnel "go way up in the air with [a] buzzing sound like [a] swarm of bees." Men scrambled to grab their packs and rifles. Those who were sleeping were jarred awake, their stunned eyes adjusting to the mayhem. As the engineers scattered, Suchocki told them there "is no need to run around because we don't know where the next shell will fall." Lieutenant McClure saw two men rush toward the cliff wall for better cover, and had to laugh when he saw one of them fall over a pile of empty artillery shell casings in a clattering panic. He tried to calm the men, assuring them it was "an impossibility for a shell to hit in there on account of the hill and cliff."

McClure's fellow lieutenants Crawford and Jones had each sat up at the sound of the explosion, and it was only a few moments before another whistle sounded from above. "We heard another one coming," McClure noted, and he and the others thought "it was going over" like the first shell. But abruptly the whistling stopped, the air went silent, and it hit. "I saw lighting," McClure later recounted. He only heard the beginning of the explosion before he was struck with "an awful wallop." Corporal Suchocki later summoned the moment from his memory with grisly clarity: "At once a tremendous explosion shocked the air, the quarry was filled with thick dust, blood, and terrible sights, some of the men [were] tore into pieces."

Fatal sprays of horseshoe-sized shell fragments lashed the cluster of men in the quarry. Lieutenant McClure was hit by shrapnel and struck by the blast concussion but was somehow still conscious. "I had a random thought, real quick, that a stray chunk of that one hit me in the head coming down." He asked Jones if he was hurt, but got no response. He asked the same of Crawford and was met with the same silence. The outlines of figures were only barely discernible in the faint predawn light, and McClure thought

Jones had only been knocked unconscious. McClure called two men over to help pick him up to drag him to the first-aid station dug into the face of the cliff.

Corporal Suchocki rushed to get Lieutenant Crawford and noticed that "as soon as I put my arms under his shoulders there was no bone at all." He and another man carried Crawford, whose body felt "as soft as a pillow," over to first aid while Lieutenant McClure and two others carried Jones. As Suchocki lowered Crawford onto a stretcher, he heard a "deep sigh," which he knew "was the last signs of his life." Crawford was dead. Jones, who had shown no signs of life since the blast, was dead also. In all likelihood he had been killed instantly, as one officer nearby estimated: "Jones never knew what hit him."

Corporal Suchocki looked back at the area near where the officers had been and saw only "a small hole and . . . nothing but a mess of human bodies." One lifeless figure was eighteen-year-old PFC Albert MacDougall from Cleveland, Ohio. Just moments before, MacDougall had been seen "sitting on a stone pile in the center of the quarry," but the blast of shrapnel had killed him as well. With no dirt or soft ground to absorb any of the shell's fragments or concussion, the stone floor and rock wall of the quarry served as an unforgiving backdrop for the explosion. Many who managed to survive were badly injured. The right side of Suchocki's face felt numb, and he noticed his neck "was hot as fire and a little bleeding." And after helping carry Jones's lifeless body, adrenaline loosened its numbing grip on Lieutenant McClure, who realized he had been hit in the face and knee and was getting dizzy from loss of blood. The dimly lit first-aid station in the cliffside was a hive of activity. "That was a busy bunch in there," McClure observed of the medics, working beyond their capacity as injured men kept appearing. Section leader Sgt. Carl Thoete (pronounced "Thotty") appeared with chunks of lead in his neck and back and asked a medic to cover the wounds with iodine. Another arrived with his neck gushing blood.

In all, the single blast had killed four and injured two dozen. A fifth of the company's men and three of its seven officers were casualties. Their position was likely exposed by the airplane observer, and a German howitzer had found its mark with devastating effect only two hours before H-Hour. These engineers were an indispensable piece of Marshall's operations plan, assigned to assist the infantry with building new trenches once the objective had been gained, as well as constructing and equipping three separate strongpoints. Capt. Horace Smith, the company commander, noted that the shelling "caused an immediate change in plans at the last minute, as each officer had a definitely assigned task." Lt. Moses Cox remarked that the surprise shelling "made the work very hard for the rest of us as each officer had a well-defined piece of work to do, and it had to be taken care of by the other officers."

But these engineers had passed their initial test of strength, and the attack served only to fortify their will. Had they allowed the decimation of their company to hamper their mission, the implications for the morning's planned operation would be demoralizing if not ruinous. Much like Company E after the previous morning's deadly raid, they suffered no failure of nerve, swiftly regrouped, and prepared themselves for the attack. With the quarry now registered in by the German guns and no longer safe, the engineers sought security down the valley in the edge of the wood line closer to Colonel Ely's command bunker. Many of those injured in the shell explosion, such as Corporal Suchocki and Sergeant Thoete, refused evacuation for medical treatment and insisted on remaining with their company. By Zero Hour, they would be prepared with the others to go over the top.

The night's darkness was giving way to the first faint light of dawn when Lieutenant Sargent arrived at his observation post, a foxhole three feet deep with a single field telephone "which glinted in the starlight." As he lay on his stomach, concealed by a clump of trees jutting out from the American lines, he scanned across the calm, quiet no-man's-land and noticed that Cantigny, three hundred yards away, "was a black silhouette against the not-as-dark sky. Not a spark of light in it." He lay in silence, and as dawn broke, he kept his gaze fixed on the village that stared silently back at him.

After receiving his assignment the day before, Sargent had walked up to the front lines to find his observation post and get his first close look at Cantigny. He had been struck by "how small the village was," and in the afternoon sun, it "looked peaceful enough" to him. Now, as he surveyed the village in its final moments before destruction, it "blanched white" as the sunlight began to drape over the ragged rooftops. Like a motionless beehive inwardly heaving with hidden Germans, "[t]he buildings of the village remained as silent as if no one was living in them."

In the two lines of trenches nearby, stretching to his north and south the distance of a mile, the infantry platoons waited. For these soldiers, crouched or propped up shoulder to shoulder against the cold, hard dirt walls of the trench in full gear, fighting a mixture of fear and anxiety and impatience and chilly air, the past few hours had been a tortured stretch of slow time. Officers and NCOs scampered up and down the line ensuring each man had his pack and sufficient ammunition and water. Lieutenant Newhall surmised the men in his platoon, just two hours from going over the top in the first wave, were "seriously subdued" with thoughts that soon "they would be under fire in the open." But he still spotted nothing in them "which looked like fear, only eagerness to get into the big game."

Nearly three miles behind the front lines, Maj. Raymond Austin was at his observation point with his binoculars prepared to watch the registration fire of the two dozen 75s of his 6th Field Artillery, scheduled to begin at 4:45 a.m. The hour was selected, as George Marshall noted, because it was "the first moment the light would permit the proper observation of results" yet still late enough to accomplish "without forewarning the enemy of a possible attack." The step was important to ensure that all guns, particularly the newly placed French guns supporting the attack, were zeroed accurately on their assigned targets for the bombardment. For these purposes, the morning weather was fully cooperating. In stark contrast to the thick morning fog the day before, J-Day was noted in the field artillery brigade journal as "quite clear. More so than usual." A battery logbook noted the dawn weather as "bright and warm," as temperatures began to rise comfortably into the sixties.

At 4:45 a.m. precisely, a few gun batteries erupted with single shots. Artillery observers squinting through binoculars from elevated perches up in trees or hilltops waited through the silence as the shells sailed through the air, then scanned target areas for the location of explosions. Adjustments were made over field telephones connected with specific batteries—to shorten the range, adjust elevation, or shift right or left—and this process repeated with more single shots until every gun was dialed in. A French airplane observer aided in this as well, sending back wireless reports to the French liaison officers at Division Headquarters to relay corrections to artillery groups. Each group of gun batteries was allotted fifteen minutes for this until at hour's end, they were prepared to unleash the critical preparatory bombardment with devastating precision.

These staccato salvos sailed over the heads of the men waiting in the trenches and lifted their spirits. Though tentative and not sustained, the singular and scattered boom of guns behind their lines broke the silence and finally, as one officer noted, "there was plenty to occupy one's attention."

Back with the artillery, Major Austin noted "at the first shots the Boches' sausages [observation balloons] went up in a hurry to see what was going on." The artillery brigade journal noted "[t]hree enemy balloons up" at 5:08 a.m., and by 5:15 there were at least six. These German observers relayed information to their own artillery batteries, and by 5:40 a.m. German shells were falling in the Saint-Éloi Woods behind the American front lines, where the reserve companies and French support tanks were waiting. Captain Noscereau, the French tank commander, reassured the American soldiers around him: "*Tout le artillerie est comme ça. C'est la guerre.*" (All artillery is like that. Such is war.) In five more minutes, as the American and French artillery began the planned bombardment on enemy positions, this German shelling would cease.

General Summerall monitored reports from the front with General Bullard down in their wine-cellar headquarters back in Mesnil-Saint-Firmin. Phone lines connected Summerall with each of his three artillery regimental commanders, French liaison officers with the French artillery group commanders, and Bullard with his two brigade commanders as well as a direct line with Colonel Ely in his bunker up near the front. Spread over the three miles of countryside leading from Division Headquarters to the front lines were 386 artillery pieces. Standing by his battery with the 7th Field Artillery, Lt. "Doc" Bedsole of Alabama was amazed as dawn revealed the amount of artillery packed into the area. "How many guns there were in this sector, I don't know. I counted sixty-four that were in a few hundred yards of my battery." Every gun had a specific target and rate of fire to last for the next hour until the infantry was to go over the top, and as the final seconds ticked away to 5:45 a.m., each was loaded with a round, and the crews stood by as officers eyed their watches.

With a thunder that shook the earth, sheets of white flame flew out of nearly four hundred American and French gun pits at 5:45 a.m. precisely, lighting the sky and hurling steel toward German positions at the speed of a half mile per second. The roar shocked even the veteran artillerymen at the guns. "Mother of God!" Lieutenant Bedsole later recounted, "I have never heard such a hellish clamor!" Major Austin noted "at 5:45 all batteries began a heavy raking fire throughout the zone to be covered by our advance . . . We had guns of all sizes working—up to 10 inch."

Back deep in the Division Headquarters, brick cellar walls telegraphed the vibrations marking the beginning of the bombardment. No phone call from the front was needed to confirm what was evident, and a staff officer jotted in the artillery brigade journal: "5:45: Fire for destruction starts." Only four minutes into the loud, sustained rumble the phone rang from one of the observation posts, reporting, "you cannot see Cantigny on account of the smoke." Outside near his 75s, Major Austin watched the thrashing of the village through binoculars: "The ground was pounded to dust by our shells—all that was visible was the heavy smoke hanging over Cantigny and the ridge."

To the men at the front lines, the scene was overwhelming. Out at his observation post, Lieutenant Sargent had counted down on his watch the scheduled beginning for the bombardment but was still startled by its eruption. "[A]t 5:45 a.m., the world turned into thunder . . . I would not know how to exaggerate its roar." The artillery officer was accustomed to the boom of batteries firing barrages, but he was unable to find adequate words to paint the scene. Having seen the French batteries arrive the day before to supplement the three regiments of American division artillery, he knew the total number of guns was high but noted that "statistics can give no idea of how earthshaking was the sound."

Up in the far north end of the jumping-off trenches, the confidence of Lieutenant Newhall's men had been lifted by the registration fire over the previous hour, but the sustained hail of shells that were shrieking over their heads into the German lines boosted morale higher still. "If the men felt confident before, they were doubly so as they watched the 'big ones' dropping on the enemy position," Newhall observed, adding that the Germans "over there, they certainly were getting theirs." Behind the lines, Lieutenant Waltz noted that the bombardment gave the same lift to the spirits of his six machine-gun crews assembled in the woods around him. "Every one of us came to life, so to speak, and things began to brighten up," he later recalled. "All of us, at once, sensed the power of our own artillery and knew with that kind of protection the enemy would be helpless."

Fire filled the sky, and over the village the smoke lay thick and heavy. Pvt. Sam Ervin, newly reinstated and in charge of a dozen-man carrying party of Company I, stood on the crest of a hill behind the front lines and watched the village "practically melt down." Nearby on crutches, Lieutenant Colonel Marshall hobbled out of Colonel Ely's bunker to see the bombardment, and later relayed the scene before him: "Cantigny itself took on the appearance of an active volcano, with great clouds of smoke and dust and flying dirt and debris, which was blasted high in the air."

Seeing the results of such unleashed fury must certainly have satisfied Marshall that all was going according to his plan. This preparatory fire was the critical first step, designed in his words, "to destroy the enemy's trenches and gun positions, and to demoralize the garrison." What that left conspicuously unsaid was a necessary consequence of such shelling: destruction of as much of the German garrison as possible. More German soldiers killed or rendered incapable by the opening hour of shellfire would mean quicker and easier success for the American infantry in capturing the objective. And with Germans occupying the village's deep brick cellars and stone-walled dugouts, this employment of large caliber high-explosive shells was necessary. The artillery onslaught was thus far exceeding expectations, and it was providing an unprecedented show of force for the watching doughboys.

Calibers of 220mm, 240mm, and 280mm—all the big French guns added to the sector the previous day—were firing simultaneously into concentrated areas and transforming empty homes and barns into twisted masses of flame and matchsticks. "The shells kept on going overhead in one steady screeching yowl," one soldier later recounted, adding that "Cantigny just began to boil up . . . The air was full of trees, stones, timber, equipment, bodies, everything you can imagine, all smashed up and whirling around with the dirt." In the front-line trenches with his platoon, Lt. Gerald Tyler observed: "One could see half a building rise a hundred feet in the air, then spread out in all directions." An officer with a reserve company in the Cantigny Woods watched "a sight never to be forgotten." The village "was going skyward, large pieces of stone, shell and brick were thrown into our position by the force of the explosion of the larger shells." That his position was in the southwest corner of the salient over five hundred yards from the nearest village structures gives some idea of the power released by each of the high-explosive shells.

Across no-man's-land, there was no perceptible reaction from either the German artillery or the garrison in the village. Lieutenant Sargent "could not hear any response from the Germans" up at his observation post and guessed that "[t]he Germans had all been killed." Lieutenant Newhall noted confidently: "Our artillery was pounding the German lines in such a way as to make it seem probable that we would merely walk over and occupy them." Lieutenant Waltz shared this optimism, observing that the force of destruction let loose by the heavy artillery "brought the awaiting troops to their feet" in the woods around him. "The results were inspiring."

The pervading confidence in the American lines was not misplaced, and unforeseen circumstances were intersecting to give even more effect to this hour of destructive fire. In a stroke of bad fortune for the Germans, the previous night was a scheduled relief of the battalion of the 272nd Reserve Infantry Regiment holding the north half of the village, and the bombardment hit just hours after these men had first arrived at their positions. In fact, many of the soldiers, having marched in full equipment through the dark of night from their reserve positions, had still not yet fully situated themselves before the shelling began. As their regimental commander, Maj. Hans von Grothe, later explained, the bombardment began while they were "still in the act of installing themselves and not sufficiently prepared." This was the first time this battalion had ever held the front lines, and its members were entirely unfamiliar with the locations of dugouts, fields of fire, observation points, and most things necessary for effective defense. In von Grothe's words, they "had not yet become fully acquainted with all the details."

Two German companies held the village of Cantigny itself—the two officers and fifty-five men of the newly arrived 12th Company of the 272nd Reserve Infantry Regiment held the northern half, and the 1st Company of the 271st (a regiment that had been in place for six days) held the southern half. Caught in the vortex of a storm of fire and steel, the men of both companies were driven down into a subterranean web of deep cellars and dugouts where many were either instantly killed by the concussion of explosions or buried alive. Any who had remained above in observation posts were dead. Lieutenant Kuntze, second in command of 12th company, went up to observe the American line during the bombardment but was fatally struck in the head by shrapnel.

The German company held in combat reserve behind the village was 1st Company, led by Lieutenant Schreiber, who ordered his men down into dugouts as the shelling began. He attempted to sound the alarm for artillery support, but was seriously wounded by shrapnel. Sergeant Major Kunnt assumed command and kept the men belowground as the bombing continued. The shelling had severed all phone lines to the rear, thwarting the few attempts made from command posts within the village to call for support, and with runners unable to make it more than a few steps without being blown to bits, all communication with those outside the village was cut off. Signal flares fired by the few survivors aboveground went unseen for all the smoke hanging over the village. The commander of 3rd Company of the 271st, manning the trenches on the south side of the village, believed the shelling to be only retaliation for the previous morning's raid and did not order flares sent up.

The timing of that previous morning's raid was now proving fortuitous, as the mistaken belief that this heavy bombardment was merely retaliation also invaded the minds of the German commanders at the battalion and regimental levels, preserving for the Americans the crucial element of surprise for the impending attack. Even without communication from the front, the scale of the bombardment was obvious to the commanders of the German reserve battalions and at regimental headquarters. But presently the smoke hanging over the village concealed the massed American infantry waiting to attack, and guided by a miscalculation of its true purpose in their ground level positions, the German command took no action. If there were any way to discover this bombardment was actually preparatory fire for an attack, it would be by aerial observation.

At that very time, about 6:30 a.m., a German plane was in fact flying high above the American lines. The pilot, Lieutenant Geh, had been tapping out frantic wireless messages over the past half hour trying to warn of what he could see was a planned attack, but with no response. He had taken off an hour earlier with the mission of locating the range for a gun battery from the unit holding the sector to the immediate south, the 25th Reserve Division. Immediately upon gaining altitude, the clear morning light had revealed to him the beginning of the bombardment and, behind it, thousands of American riflemen huddled in trenches and massed in the woods. Geh sent a wireless message at 5:57 but received no response. Circling overhead, he sent another: "Enemy preparing attack against 82nd reserve Division in sectors b and c [north and south sides of Cantigny]." Again he got no response. Between 6:13 and 6:42, he would send four requests for artillery support fire against the American lines across from Cantigny and receive no reply.

Because Lieutenant Geh had taken off as an artillery observer, the German wireless stations set up to receive aviator messages were not notified of his flight. Regardless, five of the six wireless aerials in that sector had already been destroyed by the morning shellfire. Back down south in the sector from where he took off, a lone operator at one wireless station, Private Lehman, did in fact receive Geh's reports of the impending attack and requests for targeted artillery fire. But due to a "special understanding" that "no attention should be paid to reports of the aviator not connected to range finding," Lehman sat on them. It was inaction that the division commander, Gen. Oskar von Watter, would later say "cannot be justified," and that would carry deadly consequences for the Germans.

Back in Division Headquarters, Generals Bullard and Summerall and their staffs monitored the jangling telephones for reports from the front, particularly any news of enemy artillery firing on the American jumping-off trenches. Twelve minutes into the bombardment, all signs had been good with the report, "Enemy artillery very quiet," but in the same minute came word of American shells "falling short" into the corner of the Cantigny Woods, where the men of Captain Stuart Campbell's reserve company from the 18th were waiting. By 6:07 a.m., another call from the front reported more "shorts" with the sighting of a "[s]ix star white rocket" flare fired in the Saint-Éloi Woods, a signal to the artillery to "lengthen the range." Artillery "shorts" were a tragic and rare occurrence typically caused by a bad charge or defective ammunition, and given the unprecedented number of shells being fired that morning, the possibility was a risk that had been calculated and accepted by the planners. Still, although a 6:16 a.m. entry in the brigade artillery journal noted "[a]nother report that 75's are falling short" in the Saint-Éloi Woods, not a single American casualty was reported through the hour-long bombardment.

That these "friendly" shorts were the only few desultory shells reported falling in the American front lines and wooded reserve positions is itself proof of the bombardment's success in keeping the German artillery fire suppressed. The big guns of the French Corps artillery not devoted to pulverizing the village were tasked with counter-battery work—firing gas and high-explosive shells around every known enemy gun emplacement, destroying or rendering incapable each gun crew. By all accounts this was thus far successful. Two French pilots were in the sky far on the other side of the village watching German artillery positions carefully for any signs of activity, and by 6:35 a.m., only four of the ninety known German guns were reported "in action." By H-Hour, they too would be silenced.

By 6:40 a.m., one artillery officer estimated that "any Germans who were not in deep dugouts must have been dead." With five minutes remaining until H-hour, the preparatory bombardment had lasted its scheduled fifty-five minutes and succeeded in all its aims, proving lethally effective in destroying German positions, cutting off communications, and suppressing all means of retaliatory fire. Pvt. John Johnston of La Crosse, Wisconsin, one of thousands of men filling two sets of mile-long trenches and buoyed by the previous hour's stunning display of firepower preparing their pathway into battle, called it "a million dollar barrage." Like those on either side of him, John readied himself mentally to go over the top and attack, and his simple recollection of the moment seems the most universal depiction of the mixed emotions of thousands of men, young and old, facing their first daring encounter with history: "I can truthfully say that every man had a prayer on his lips."

CHAPTER 8

Zero Hour

No matter how he tried to situate himself, twenty-five-year-old Pvt. Arthur Hansen of Sparks, Nevada, could not find a comfortable seated position in the trench while enveloped in full battle gear. If he tightened the shoulder straps on his pack, his arms lost circulation; if he leaned forward, his legs went numb and his stiff, high-neck collar choked him; and if he leaned back his steel canteens cut into his lower back. Like every other rifleman packed into the trenches shoulder to shoulder on either side of him, Hansen was the picture of cumbersome immobility—an overburdened warrior topped off with a soup-bowl helmet. Two canteens full of water dangled from the back of his equipment belt, and in front his canvas ammunition pouches and cloth bandoliers bulged with forty-five five-round clips of .30-caliber rifle ammunition. The bulky case carrying his gas mask was slung across his chest, and on his back was a tall pack stuffed with two days' rations, a shelter half, four sandbags, and a flare. The blade end of a full-length shovel stuck out the top, prompting thoughts of his days as a coal shoveler on the Southern Pacific Railroad. And around his crowded waist he carried two hand grenades, a rifle grenade, and a sheath for the bayonet that stood affixed to his Springfield rifle.

A few of the soldiers in the trenches with Private Hansen already knew the sensation of going "over the top," mostly on patrols under the cover of darkness. Hansen, who had enlisted for Army service the day after America declared war, recently became one of the select few to experience the brief and sudden combat of a raid on the German trenches. "It is a queer sensation when you climb over your trench parapet and wonder if you are ever coming back," he observed. As he readied himself to enter battle with the first wave, thoughts of that raid helped to bolster his confidence for this morning's attack as he remembered, "[A]fter you get started you are all right."

But for many, this would be their first venture into no-man's-land, and for all this would be their first battle. Lt. George Butler, who just one year before was an Indianapolis attorney, described the emotions churning in his breast just before Zero Hour as "not fear, but a sort of excitement." Lt. Harry Martin from Kansas felt much the same, later writing in a letter home: "I honestly was nervous and rather excited." Pvt. Billie McCombs of New Castle, Pennsylvania, who had volunteered the very day his hometown paper published news of the Zimmermann Telegram, struggled to articulate what he felt in these moments before battle: "I can only tell of my feeling and I suppose others had the same. It wasn't the fear of going 'Over the Top'—it was the fear of losing our nerve. I would rather be hit—as would others—than to lose my nerve."

Waiting men each calmed their own nerves in their own way, some in silent prayer, some by smoking cigarettes as if their last, and some by nipping at rum rations or cognac they had managed to finagle from the French. Many found a measure of encouragement in the thoroughness of their training and the detailed battle rehearsal two days earlier. "We had practiced it until each man knew just what he was going to do," Lieutenant Newhall remembered confidently. For his part, there was no "tense excitement" in the time waiting to jump off, but a feeling that he and the troops in the platoon he led were merely "getting ready to pull off a big demonstration."

The well-oiled mechanics of the 4,000-man machine were wound tight, and their unspooling was no longer in the hands of the top commanders—Zero Hour would launch them automatically. This would be a platoon-leader's battle, and with every second planned and every detail rehearsed, Generals Bullard and Summerall and Colonel Ely were reduced to observers as the launching of the infantry into the breach fell into the hands of the young lieutenants and captains in the front trench. Responsible for leading their platoons over the top at 6:45 a.m. precisely, most of these junior officers had their eyes fixed on their synchronized wristwatches. As minute hands reached 6:40 a.m., the ear-splitting bombardment ended, cueing the 75s to begin the protective barrage.

Staccato slams broke the fleeting silence, sending shells whirring over the waiting doughboys and detonating in a choreographed curtain of explosions out in no-man's-land. These first shots of the protective barrage signaled that the jump-off was five minutes away. Each of seventy-two guns fired three shots in the first minute, six in the second, then finally twelve shots per gun per minute. The ascending intensity culminated in more than a dozen blasts per second for the remainder of the barrage, scheduled to last until after the Americans had captured the village. As one artillery officer described it: "One by one the batteries dropped their fire into the line, one here and another there, then others would drop in between and link up until along the whole front of the attack there was a perfect, even line of bursting shells a mile long."

A watching correspondent described the scene out in no-man's-land caused by such concentrated firepower as "a wall of heavy smoke within which, continuously, burst new geysers of smoke, black or gray or sulphurous yellow." Even for men accustomed to the incessant clamor of artillery, the sound was staggering. By the final seconds before H-Hour, what had begun minutes before as loud, successive crashes had merged into one continuous roar, which along some parts of the line was constant and deafening. "Our guns made so much racket it was impossible to shout orders," noted Lieutenant Butler.

The barrage churned two hundred yards in front of the trenches, and beneath the resounding thunder, in the center of the line where 2nd Battalion faced Cantigny head-on, French tanks slowly rumbled forward across the trenches through paths marked by stakes, their engines barely audible above the boom of the barrage. The handful of supporting French infantry and their diminutive tank commander, armed only with a walking stick, led the way on foot, standing out in pale-blue uniforms. Apace with them, ten Schneiders lumbered out into no-man's-land and stopped, their engines idling and billowing smoke, waiting for the line of explosions to leap forward.*

Hunkered in a trench behind the tanks, Lieutenant Martin did his best to mind the countdown: "I would look at my watch and when it read five minutes more, every minute after that seemed an hour." Waiting in the second parallel with the men of his machine-gun company, Capt. Adelbert Stewart noted the silence in the trenches around him: "While waiting for H-hour the men never seemed quieter or more collected." In the northern stretch of trenches with 3rd Battalion, Lt. Si Parker's attention was on his men, squatted in a long line beside him: "This was our first real attack and naturally everyone was not chatting as if at a dinner party; however, everyone

---

*One of the original twelve had burned its clutch at the rear rally point, and another sat stalled back in the woods behind the lines.

was in good spirits and waited anxiously for the minute to hop over the parapet."

All was set. Zero Hour would be marked by the barrage wall advancing and the shouts and whistles of platoon leaders signaling their troops to jump off. Senses were plainly heightened, but waiting for battle induced no inner philosophers or poets. If men counting down these last few seconds were compelled into any mortal contemplation, words mostly failed them. Pre-occupied with grave thoughts, twenty-four-year-old Pvt. Frank Last, a for-mer mail carrier from North Dakota, spilled his own mixed feelings into his diary: "Everybody seemed to be more or less excited or anxious . . . or something. I don't know if one can exactly explain the sensation." He noted that "[e]verybody seemed jolly enough, but we all did a lot of thinking." Pri-vate Last recalled a veteran French soldier once remarking that explaining one's feelings while waiting in the trench for Zero Hour "would be like a young man trying to express his feelings when he proposed to a young lady."

Nearly three miles behind the front lines, twenty-eight-year-old Maj. Ray-mond Austin stood on a leafy hilltop among two dozen 75s of the 6th Field Artillery which were, along with the 7th Field Artillery and two French artillery regiments, firing the protective barrage. With cotton stuffed in their ears and rumpled soft caps atop their heads, the three-man team at each gun—like all the guns of each battery and all batteries of the group—worked as one, a display of united action that was causing devastatingly impressive results.

Once a shell was fired, the gunner pulled open the breech hatch and with a hollow clink the empty white-hot shell casing would fall atop the grow-ing pile. The loader would slide another shell in the breech and the gunner would quickly close it as the loader rechecked the gun's elevation while both stepped clear of the recoil. Eyeing his pocket watch—his head bobbing sharply as he counted the seconds off to himself—the leader would again signal to fire, the gunner would pull back the sprung lanyard and release it, and with a loud slam another shell was on its way. Then over again the pro-cess repeated every five seconds—nonstop—at each of the seventy-two guns.

Gusts of white flame shot from each gun barrel, lighting the gray clouds of acrid smoke that more and more shrouded the hilltop. A choking scent of cordite carried on the morning air. Major Austin eyed his wristwatch, and as the second hand clicked onto 6:45 a.m., he watched with wonder as the crews manning the separate guns of the barrage groups simultaneously stopped, quickly adjusted the elevation wheels of their 75s in precise unison, and resumed firing, moving the protective barrage one hundred yards forward and inviting the infantry over the top. In an age before instant wireless communication or digital solar clocks, the impressiveness of such celestial precision cannot be overstated. Major Austin recounted the scene with no small amount of awe: "[A]t 6:45, as though by the command of a single officer, although in reality each battery worked independently by prearranged schedule and synchronized watches, the barrage moved forward." The moment was now—Zero Hour had arrived.

His elevated position near Rocquencourt afforded Major Austin an Olympian view of the launching of the attack, and he watched through his binoculars as the first wave of men brandishing Springfields with fixed bayonets climbed out of the trenches and began the advance. "At the same time as the barrage left the line of departure (our first line trenches) the infantry suddenly appeared on the slope of the ridge close behind our barrage." From nearly three miles away, they appeared to him as "a long brown line with bayonets glistening in the sun" that "seemed to have sprung from the earth."

By this moment, Colonel Ely had left his command bunker and positioned himself closer to the front to observe his men emerging from the trenches. He could not but be impressed with the scale and coordination of the scene before him. "The jump-off at dawn," he would later recall proudly, "was the most dramatic thing I have ever seen. I stood in a position to see my men go over and the French, very much impressed by the attack, took pictures from our vantage point."

In the face of a rising sun on such a clear morning, the first wave of the American attack must have offered a splendid spectacle. What Major Austin and Colonel Ely could each see on the plateau before Cantigny was a horizon-filling tide of khaki-clad American soldiers, advancing side by side with three to four feet between them, stretching to a width of over a mile. Just as with the synchronized firing of the artillery, the dozens of individual infantry platoons making up the whole emerged from the trenches and moved forward as one. As one staff officer observed, the soldiers all at once simply "started up from the earth and began their advance."

The direction of the attack was due east, and the morning sun was shining directly in the face of the attackers, though its harshest light was still shrouded by a dissipating wall of white smoke, the fading remains of the first barrage wall. As the smoke cleared, it revealed the new curtain of flame now roiling one hundred yards beyond the first. Toward it, the men "walked steadily along behind our barrage," Major Austin noted, as they followed the "tanks which buzzed along with smoke coming out from their exhausts and their guns."

Between this line of attackers and the protective barrage lay a vast, open plateau that ascended uphill toward the village. Its fields of knee-deep wheat were still largely untouched, save for clustered craters caused by the bombardment. One correspondent present on the morning's attack described it as a "beautiful plateau . . . a clean and virgin No Man's Land untainted yet of the terrible stench of mortal man, carpeted with flowers, with grass, with wheat, with red poppies, yellow buttercups, and purple thistles—the ideal battlefield of an ideal battle." Combining such a setting with the sight of the Americans advancing, he declared himself unable to "give with words even one millionth of the splendor of the spectacle."

One officer in the front lines shared this view, effusing over the sight of the initial advance: "It was a wonderful sight—really the most wonderful sight I have ever seen." Pvt. Ralph Loucks from Indiana watched the first minutes of the attack from the right in the Cantigny Woods, where he and his platoon from Company A waited to swing out and join the first wave. "I will never forget it as long as I live," he soon wrote home. "It was a great sight to see all those bayonets shining." Twenty-three-year-old Pvt. Chester Hinner of Sidell, Illinois, would paint the image of the morning attack in a letter home: "It was a wonderful picture when we went over the top at Cantigny. We went over in two waves just as the sun was coming up over a misty, dew-laden No Man's Land."

But up on the far northern end of the assault line, leading his platoon slowly into the attack, Lieutenant Newhall took a less romantic view of the moment. "Zero Hour itself consists merely of blowing your whistle, climbing up on the parapet, and calling out 'Come on second platoon' and they all came," he remembered dryly. To his right was his good friend Lt. George Haydock leading 1st Platoon. Together they comprised the first wave of Company L, the far left side of the attack.

Company L's task, as its commander, Capt. Francis van Natter, explained, was "to act as a sort of pivoting unit swinging out from the recently constructed trench system." The ground over which Newhall and Haydock led their first-wave platoons was flat, slightly inclining up toward the Cantigny Road and opening into a wider plateau beyond, ascending to the horizon's dark wood lines of the l'Alval and Framicourt Woods. The Germans occupied trenches before and after the Cantigny Road, and Company L's first-wave platoons were to conquer both. Their mission, in Newhall's words, was "to reach the German trenches and hold them, while the other two platoons [of the second wave] were to dig in on the new line to be established." They had what he called, in his customary understatement, "a plain ordinary frontal attack to make."

As 6:45 a.m. came and the barrage moved forward, Lieutenant Newhall stepped up on the dirt and signaled for his men to follow, and he could see that "the whole 1st line down toward the right came on too, and moved forward at a walk." For a brief moment, as he looked to his right and watched the line of soldiers "as far as the eyes can reach" topped off with "the gleam of the bayonets," the Army officer gave way to the history PhD, unable to ignore the historic significance of the moment: "It is impossible to imagine a sight more thrilling, an impression of power more imposing, a feeling of more intense, exultant, enthusiastic excitement. It is America going into battle."

To his right, beyond Haydock's platoon, the first wave of Company K was being led from the front by the commander, Capt. Henry Mosher of Falconer, New York, sporting a pistol in one hand and walking cane in the other. A West Point dropout, Mosher had earned his officer's commission as a civilian two years earlier, and took charge of the company in the cold mud of the Seicheprey sector. Beside him was Lieutenant Parker, who noted of his platoon: "Everyone was on his toes and when the second came around to go 'over the top' every man sprang out of the trenches." The men immediately spread into a line and moved toward the barrage as they had practiced in rehearsal. "Attack formation was quickly taken up and we began moving off in proper order," Parker observed.

Also with Company K was Pvt. Emory Smith, one of the "Three Musketeers" from Denton, Texas. Like the others described by Lieutenant Parker, Smith was on his toes in the seconds leading to Zero Hour, fortified by a shot of cognac he had downed at first light. "[W]e went over the top cheering at the top of our voices," he later wrote, remembering with relish the eagerness of the men who jumped off with him.

As this first wave of doughboys began the attack, unbridled enthusiasm swept from one end of the American front to another, and the air itself seemed charged with excitement. If the men bore any fear or anxiety, they cloaked it, whether from themselves or the men to their right and left.

A private jumping off with the first wave remembered going over the top with a cigarette in his mouth, but after his swift thrust into the fighting that followed, he admitted, "after that—well, I thought a little more about it."

But the eagerness of the day was not all naïve bravado or juvenile fantasy of illustrious death in battle, especially given the equally enthusiastic attitude of the men of Company E, already baptized in the carnage of war in the previous day's raid. They had seen a platoon leader buried alive, a sergeant ripped in half by shell fire, and over two dozen of their comrades killed, yet they still attacked with fervor equal to the rest of the regiment. "They went over into the fighting singing, laughing, joking, absolutely unafraid, uncaring," Lt. Irving Wood later wrote. "They couldn't move forward fast enough, and some who were wounded struggled to their feet with smiles on their faces and kept going."

Lt. Harry Martin, leading a platoon in the first wave of Company H's attack, was gripped by the same unbounded confidence at Zero Hour: "I took my men, for the first time, over the top, all smiling and with the determination that all Heaven and hell couldn't beat us." Martin's platoon formed the right side of 2nd Battalion, the center of the attack line. Jumping off from lines back in the deepest part of the salient and having an objective beyond the village, this battalion had the farthest to go—parts faced an advance of a mile. Martin's men, together with the remainder of the platoon on their left (at half strength and led by a sergeant after the raid the day before), were to follow the tanks across the field to the edge of town, and then proceed into the remains of the northern half of Cantigny itself.

The first wave of 2nd Battalion moved forward slowly behind the ambling Schneiders. From his observation post, Lt. Daniel Sargent observed, "The tanks looked like haycarts (horseless)," noting that the wave of riflemen trailing behind "looked like haymakers that carried rifles instead of pitchforks." A few of the men, as a correspondent observing the advance later described, "followed the tanks over, and ran ahead of them in their enthusiasm."

Even in their zeal the soldiers labored to keep their line straight, maintaining flanks with the man on either side just as they had during the battle rehearsal. "The formations were the same as those of the practice maneuvers," one officer noted, "and the movement was equally precise as it kept to the time-table of the barrage." The straightness of the line continued through the segment of 1st Battalion advancing on the far right. One officer observing the advance noted, "Their line was perfect and they looked as if they were taking part in the drill movement."

All along the length of marching khaki, lieutenants kept a step or two ahead of their men, setting a constant pace toward the barrage wall, now and then waving their Colt .45s to urge the line ever onward. Their forward movement was steady but not hurried. The "creeping" protective barrage was actually staggered, sitting stationary for two minutes before advancing a hundred yards, then again loitering for another two minutes, then advancing, and so on. "The barrage proceeded as we went ahead in waves," one private later remembered. "It is a slow process working with a barrage and there is not the real charge that one imagines. You simply run ahead a few yards and lie down waiting for the barrage fire to lift, and can only go as fast as it does."

Advancing a few steps ahead of his platoon, Lieutenant Martin could see the doughboys working to keep a forward pace to his right and left. "All the men were walking with a firm step, rifles with bayonets fixed and at a high port, walking over no-man's-land with worlds of artillery fire over our heads," he wrote just days later in a letter home. In places where the green brush or wheat had grown especially high, soldiers struggled to maintain the line. One correspondent observed them "trampling with high steps, tearing themselves loose with vigorous twisting movements, their rifles held high above their heads as though they were wading a stream with water up to their necks."

The barrage wall between the Americans and Cantigny stood tall and thick, impenetrable in some places even by the bright morning sun. Facing the soldiers in no-man's-land was not a waiting enemy but a roiling blend of fire and smoke, a protective curtain of mayhem produced by their own artillery. At that moment, it concealed a village reduced to rubble and ruins, smoldering piles of twisted timber and stone filling space once occupied by Cantigny's homes, a grim testament to the effectiveness of the preparatory bombardment.

Most of the Germans in the two companies holding the village itself who had managed to survive the hour-long bombardment remained underground. And as the creeping barrage passed, many stayed below to ride it out rather than ascend to man observation and machine-gun positions. "The rolling barrage was extremely accurate," Colonel Ely observed, adding that beyond concealing the infantry attack, it kept "practically all elements of the defense under cover and deprive[d] them of all aggressive action." As his counterpart, the German regimental commander Maj. Hans von Grothe later complained of his own men: "[T]he commanders, as well as the men . . . lost their heads somewhat and in any case forgot all about observation during the brief but intense bombardment."

Many of the Germans in 12th Company in the northern half of the village attempted to go up and monitor to effectively defend their position, but they were prevented from doing so by collapsed stairwells and entrances. One of the three officers in the company, Lieutenant Kuntze, had already attempted to observe the American line during the bombardment but was killed by shrapnel. A crew was sent out to man a machine gun, but there was zero visibility for the thick dust and smoke. As the company commander, Lieutenant Kokok later complained, these impossibly difficult conditions combined so that "[a] defense could not be undertaken against the enemy at the proper time." In the southern half of Cantigny, if any part of the 1st Company of the 271st Regiment emerged to defend, there is no record of it. In the German combat-strength report the next day, it was reported "destroyed."

But if the Germans hiding or trapped in the remains of Cantigny offered little resistance to the attacking American infantry, those defending the lines to the north and south of the village gave plenty. Because the hour-long preparatory bombardment focused primarily on Cantigny and the woods concealing the reserve units to the northeast, east, and southeast, the Germans defending the trenches extending north of the village facing the left flank of the American assault were still fully capable of observation and effective defense.

Tenth Company of the 272nd Reserve Infantry Regiment was the northernmost unit in the German sector and occupied the two lines of trenches the doughboys of Company L were to conquer. At Zero Hour, Lieutenant von Vegesack, an officer with the company, noticed "a heavy barrage" in no-man's-land (the American creeping barrage which he mistook for a defensive bombardment fired by German artillery) and the bombardment of the woods to his rear. "At the same moment," he later reported, he could peek through the barrage smoke sufficiently to see when "American troops came out of their trenches in dense successive waves."

The khaki figures Lieutenant von Vegesack spotted walking through the wheat toward his company's position were the doughboys of Company L's first wave—the platoons led by Lieutenants Newhall and Haydock. Up to this point, the whole length of 3rd Battalion had moved forward with what the commander would call "an utter absence of confusion" as "every detail had been worked out." But the defiant Germans of 10th Company were soon to add mortal reinforcement to the earthly proverb "No battle plan survives contact with the enemy."

On Lieutenant von Vegesack's order, German riflemen and Maxim crews fired blindly through the barrage wall, dosing the Company L doughboys with a "heavy infantry and machine-gun fire" and inflicting on the Americans their first casualties of the battle. The one to first suffer "contact with the enemy" was twenty-year-old PFC Anton Jurach of Texas. Wading through waist-high wheat, Company L's first wave had not made it very far from the trenches when Jurach was struck by a machine-gun bullet and collapsed beneath the soft cover of grain, dead. The rattle of the Maxim quickened the pace of the men beside him, and Jurach was left where he fell. Exposed to the hours and days of enemy shell fire that followed, his body was never seen again. PFC Anton L. Jurach is honored on the tablets of the missing at the Somme American Cemetery, his chiseled name undistinguishable as likely the first American soldier killed in the attack.

With a tempo hastened by enemy fire, Sgt. Harry Klein of New Jersey rushed ahead, urging his squad to keep up, but was struck by the same machine-gun fire and killed instantly. The bullet tore through his chest, cut through the contents of the pack he was carrying, and spun out the back in a grisly display of blood and sparks as he slumped forward. A private about fifteen feet behind Klein "saw flame come out of his back when he fell." Another bullet knocked Pvt. Herbert Smith of Milwaukee out of the column and to the ground. He lay unconscious and bleeding for hours, hidden in the wheat. He was finally found and evacuated by stretcher-bearers back to a field hospital, but died midafternoon.

As if the wheat itself was tugging men down, one by one the doughboys dropped out of sight, each with the gut-punching sound of a bullet hitting flesh. Newhall and Haydock, with pistols drawn, could only urge those still afloat to keep moving forward. There was no target at which they could return fire—the bullets were cutting through a faceless wall of smoke. And there was no way out but forward, closer to the barrage. Each demented "tat-tat-tat" of the Maxims, sharply audible over the thunder of the artillery, meant the spray of bullets was still coming. An occasional echoing "ding" evidenced a round hitting the steel of a shovel or pick on someone's back; a dull "plink" meant a hole through another helmet. Some men were shot mid-stride in the knee or foot, falling and writhing in pain. Many dropped where they were and a few kneeled, gingerly straining for a line of sight above the wheat tops to find a target through the smoke: a muzzle flash from the German lines, something—anything—to shoot at and make it stop. Some who were shot were able to roll into nearby shell craters for cover, and others found the strength to crawl back under fire, a long and slow hundred-plus-yard journey to the safety of their former trenches. Many of the injured and dying lay helpless, left to yell desperately for medics to find them and pull them back behind the lines for first aid. Most of those not felled by bullets ran forward closer to the barrage wall and lay flat, hugging the dirt tightly and waiting for the barrage to move forward again, where they might finally see the German trenches and return fire.

A half mile away, in the center of the attack directly in front of Cantigny, the scene was starkly different. With the two companies of Germans in the village either killed or still taking cover belowground, the response from the defenders during the advance there was, one officer noticed, "very feeble." It was, in fact, so "feeble" that 2nd Battalion had yet to suffer a single casualty. Two minutes of steady, adrenaline-filled walking had brought the platoons in the first wave to within about forty yards of the barrage wall, where they waited, some kneeling and others lying flat in the grass. Abruptly, with the same coordinated timing as before, the explosions stopped. Before the echo of the final blasts faded, the barrage erupted another hundred yards forward. Tanks popped into gear and began edging ahead once more, and the men stood and resumed their steady walk onward.

This exposed the soldiers in the first wave to the enemy outposts and trenches skirting the village, and it gave the German defenders their first unobstructed view of the attackers. If the spectacle of the mile-wide attack wave of rifle-wielding Americans didn't give them pause, the slowly stampeding Schneiders outright panicked them. It was the first time soldiers of the kaiser's 18th Army had ever seen these new tools of warfare on the battlefield. As General von Watter later admitted, the surprise of the American attack was "enhanced by tanks, which our men had never seen before."

Second Battalion moved forward at a quickened pace to overtake the surprised and shell-shocked enemy. Lt. Welcome Waltz, advancing with his machine-gun company directly toward the village, had seen "one big howitzer shell after another" roar into the German trenches before Zero Hour and didn't expect much effective defense from the survivors. As he and the rest of the line neared the enemy trenches, the sound of enemy fire, clearly audible before the bombardment, diminished "until all one could hear was a feeble burst now and then."

Twenty-one-year-old Pvt. Earl Simons of Altoona, Pennsylvania, advancing behind the tanks with Company F toward the north end of the village, described 2nd Battalion's advance as "a complete surprise to the Huns." The Schneiders lumbered forward steadily as sporadic Mauser rounds pinged like marbles off the armored hulls. Enemy crews manning two Maxims "surrendered immediately," spooked after being fired on by a 75 from one of the tanks. Another Maxim crew, perched in the broken remains of a house out near the German trenches, was shut down quickly by another approaching tank's machine gun. On reaching the German trenches, Private Simons recalled, "We captured about all of them. I did not see one German infantryman fire." When Lieutenant Waltz reached the trenches, he noted that the preparatory bombardment "had erased them from the terrain," and he could only make out where the line was in some places from the bodies of the German dead: "I noticed an arm here and a leg there protruding from the churned up ground."

Back up in the far northern end of the first wave, Lieutenant Newhall resumed leading the forward pace of his platoon as the barrage advanced beyond the Cantigny Road, exposing him and his surviving troops to the first line of German trenches, manned by the stubborn defenders of 10th Company. The Maxim's menacing rattle continued, punctuated more and more by the pops of aimed Mauser fire from the German trench. Waving his men forward with his pistol, Newhall was shot through his right armpit. "The force of the blow knocked me over," Newhall noted. "My first reaction was astonishment that it hit as hard, but the next and immediate reaction was rage which, being accompanied with the realization that I wasn't really hurt and not at all disabled put me into violent action."

Although hit, Newhall "jumped up and resumed the advance" with his platoon. Bullets zipped through the air past him and his men, and he managed only a few steps more before he was struck again, this time in the left arm. "That knocked me over again," he later remembered. "I think there was a sniper in front of us picking off the officers." This one drilled through his upper arm, breaking the bone above the elbow. As Newhall lay stunned in a clearing of shallow wheat, he made an easy target on the open ground, and he was hit again. This third shot "dazed" him, and he later described the resulting wound in painful detail: "The bullet struck my left arm at an angle, broke the bone again, flattened, and tore its way out through the muscles of the upper arm leaving a wound about seven inches long and two wide."

With his arm torn to shreds, Newhall lay on his back with his helmet over his face. "[W]hat went on after that I only know by sound," he later wrote of the moment. Yells of his men and the crisp sounds of their boots trampling onward through the cracking wheat grew more distant, leaving him alone with only unsettling bursts of gunfire to break the loud and sustained din of the barrage. "I never lost consciousness," he later remembered, "but it was some time before I began to take an interest in things."

The men of his platoon tried to keep advancing without their leader, but with every step forward, enemy fire grew more severe. The charge was spearheaded by eighteen-year-old Pvt. Carl Fey of Schuylkill Haven, Pennsylvania. Thirteen months prior, Fey had secured his mom's permission to leave his job as an ironworker on the Reading Railroad and enlist just days after turning seventeen. Now, after a long year of service, the teenage private was out front, leading by a few firm paces the first wave of his country's first attack. Bullets had been hissing past his ears, dropping his buddies into the wheat behind him, and his own luck ended just a few yards from the German lines. With a jarring pop, his head snapped back and he tumbled forward. Dazed, seized with fear and gripped by numbing adrenaline, he moved his hand up to his face and felt warm, oozing blood. With his tongue, he sensed through the copper taste of blood only a gaping hole where his right upper molars once were. The bullet had torn through his cheek and shattered his upper jaw, knocking several teeth out. "I got shot in the right jaw," he later wrote to his mom, adding, "I got a hole through my right cheek." A comrade behind him saw him get "[s]hot in [the] head by rifle or machine-gun bullet" and believed him dead. In shock but alive, facedown in a pool of blood and teeth, Fey was too close to the German lines to be evacuated even had the men of his platoon not already given him up for dead.

Lacking Lieutenant Newhall's guiding hand and under increasingly deadly and accurate enemy fire, the soldiers of 2nd Platoon began to splinter off in search of cover or a way through. Fear and courage were in play, indistinguishable. A few, paralyzed by a sense of helplessness, flattened themselves in the dirt. One small group of three or four fell back beside their broken and semiconscious lieutenant and began digging in. Some fired single shots with their Springfields aimlessly toward the sounds of enemy fire in small acts of defiance. Others escaped the killing zone by wading blindly in a hunched scamper through the wheat chaff to the right, parallel with the German lines. There they linked up with Lieutenant Haydock and his men, who had reached, cleared, and entered the loosely held first parallel of enemy trenches in their path after flicking grenades over the parapet. Looking out from the German lines, Lieutenant von Vegesack could see that his company's rifle and machine-gun fire had pinned a part of Newhall's platoon down in the wheat directly in front of him, and he watched as "a part ran back to the trenches, while another part evaded our barrage and invaded the adjoining company (9th) to the left."

These invaders to the south were the men of Haydock's platoon and beyond them the Company K platoons led by lieutenants Si Parker and Clarence Milton "Milt" Drumm. The enemy lines in their pathway were manned by the Germans of 9th Company, and unlike 10th Company on the northern end, its soldiers had sustained heavy casualties during the preparatory bombardment and were offering only sporadic resistance. On the approach, Company K was able to move swiftly and suffered no men killed—Lieutenant Parker later reported that his platoon only "lost one or two men wounded by the advance by machine-gun fire." He and his men had not advanced far before they noticed that the Germans manning outposts "began jumping out of shell holes and beating it for the rear." A few of Parker's soldiers paused mid-stride, raised their rifles, "let out a terrible 'rabbit-hunting' yell and began cutting them down." In this manner, Parker reported, "many of the enemy were killed." The Americans swarmed, and the Germans in the first line of trenches offered no more fight. One later recalled, "I saw your infantry coming, I knew it was all over."

Lieutenant Parker and his troops rushed to the edge of the enemy trench and began pouring in rifle fire. A dozen survivors who hadn't run back to escape death or capture dropped their Mausers and raised their arms in surrender, wearing looks of submissive fright and shouting "*Kamerad!*" repeatedly to avoid being shot. Parker ordered them taken under guard back across no-man's-land to the American trenches. Together with three more captured by Lieutenant Drumm's adjacent platoon, these would be the first 15 Germans marched back to the American lines as prisoners—a number that would climb past 250 through the course of the next two and a half days of battle.

Leading the platoon directly to Company K's right was twenty-five-year-old Lt. Wayne Schmidt from Martinsville, Indiana, where his father was mayor. He had served four years in the Indiana National Guard, and when America entered the war, he left his studies at Indiana University and volunteered for officer training. Leading the platoon to his right was twenty-three-year-old Lt. Gerald Tyler, who had been a draftsman and a student at Clemson College in his native South Carolina when he volunteered for officer training, like Schmidt, during the first month of the war. Together, their platoons formed the first wave of Company M's attack.

Like Company K, their initial advance after jumping out of the trenches had been smooth and swift, aided by the French tanks advancing with 2nd Battalion to their right. "The French tanks were right along with us," Lieutenant Tyler noted as his platoon and Schmidt's "moved forward encountering little resistance." About halfway to the objective, Lieutenant Schmidt, leading his men with his pistol drawn in one hand and his compass in the other, was shot through the right thigh. Two of his men carried him back across no-man's-land to a first-aid station, and the rest halted, adrift and unsure about the direction of advance or even whether they had yet reached the objective.

When word of Schmidt's evacuation made its way over to Lieutenant Tyler, he left his men under the command of his platoon sergeant and ran to check on Schmidt's platoon. "I went over there and could see no connecting troops on the left of that platoon, but saw that its left flank was exposed," he noted, thinking that Company K "had not moved forward or had not kept up." In fact, Captain Mosher's men had made it to the German front line, which in their assigned path was only about two hundred yards from where they jumped off. They were now still clearing the trenches and sending back prisoners, a process that held up their further advance, creating open ground a hundred yards or so ahead of them when Schmidt's platoon came to a halt, distracted into disorder by his shooting.

Realizing he was now in charge of Company M's entire vanguard, Lieutenant Tyler ordered the men to fan out to the left into the open flank and move forward again as he ran back to the right to catch up with his own platoon still being led forward by Sgt. Carl R. Sohncke. It was at this moment that German lieutenant von Vegesack, up in the trenches on the far northern end and facing no more threat from Lieutenant Newhall's troops pinned down to his front, ordered his men to turn their rifles and machine guns south and open fire on Company M's flank. The doughboys between von Vegesack's position and Company M—those platoons led by Haydock and Parker and Drumm—were down in the subterranean cover of the German trenches, safe from the enfilading fire. But the upright khaki figures of Company M—particularly Schmidt's men still slowed by confusion—formed a distant but easy target for von Vegesack's gunners, and as the German lieutenant later reported of his American adversaries, they "suffered heavy losses" as a result.

The flurry of bullets came all at once, one slicing through the neck of PFC Harvey Fahnenstalk of Michigan. With a pop and a spray of blood, Fahnenstalk collapsed to the dirt and, a nearby sergeant would note, "died instantly." The ragged line of riflemen advanced quicker as the Maxim chattered loudly from the left. With a dull thud, Pvt. Thomas Larsen was struck in the stomach in full stride. Falling forward, he also died "instantly." Remaining doughboys lunged forward in a mad dash to the cover of German front lines, which in this stretch had been largely abandoned by the enemy for the bombardment and the sight of approaching tanks.

Running and within sight of the defilade of the trenches, Pvt. James Caskey of Loveland, Kentucky, was hit. Two men ran back and drug him into the trench to give him first aid, but he never regained consciousness. Although evacuated to the field hospital, he died the next day, one week after his twenty-seventh birthday. Two years later, at his mother's request, Private Caskey's body was shipped back home to Kentucky to rest in the Caskey family plot.* But like the fate of so many whose bodies were left out in no-man's-land where they fell, the remains of PFC Fahnenstalk and Private Larsen were never found. Their carved names on the tablets of the missing at the Somme American Cemetery serve as their single memorial.

Down in the unfamiliar surroundings of the hastily abandoned German trenches, freshly churned up by the barrage and littered with dropped Mausers, dirt-covered blankets, and ration tins, Lieutenant Tyler and the wide-eyed soldiers under his charge were finally safe from the unrelenting Maxim fire. A few peeked over ragged parapets while others hugged the dirt floor, waiting for the barrage beyond the enemy lines to leap forward again, the signal for the start of the second wave's advance behind them. Likewise, in the lines to the north and south the fighting remains of the first wave waited.

Its shape now formed by action in the fog of war, dented here and there

---

* Private Caskey's name is inscribed on the Somme American Cemetery chapel's tablets of the missing in error.

where German resistance was the stiffest, the straight line that had reminded a watching officer of the perfection of a "drill movement" was no more. In the five minutes since Zero Hour, the thousand-odd men along its length had been thrust abruptly into manhood. Some like Lieutenant Newhall and Private Fey lay bleeding, flat in the dirt in painful submission to gunshot wounds, hoping for a medic or comrade to drag them out. Many hunkered down in captured enemy trenches filled with a fresh confidence found somewhere in their journey across no-man's-land. Others lay in shallow shell holes, seeking sanctuary from the death around them, waiting for a pause in the volleys of rifle and machine-gun fire to sprint forward and join their platoons. And still others kneeled between idling tanks at the edge of the charred, skeletal remains of the village, ready for the barrage to move again and open a pathway into more unknown peril.

Thus, in the glorious early sunshine of spring, the first American attack of the World War was successfully launched. Up near the front in Colonel Ely's bunker, Lieutenant Colonel Marshall noted that "everyone was enthusiastic and delighted" with the progress. Tanks and infantry had disappeared up the incline into the dust and smoke shrouding the village, and with clusters of frightened German prisoners with arms held high led back across no-man's-land at the bayonet tips of rifles held like cattle prods by doughboys, the success of the first wave of the attack was apparent.

Generals Bullard and Summerall and their staff back in Division Headquarters hung on every piece of news dribbling in from the front. The battle was just five minutes old, but so far the few broken bits of scattered reports indicated that all was progressing as planned. One minute into the attack, a phone call from Colonel Ely's command bunker had reported that "the infantry has gone over the top and that the barrage looks fine." Another minute later, a call from a watching artillery captain reported "very little enemy fire." Now five minutes into the fighting and for the first time in history, United States Army riflemen were successfully sweeping into German positions, step by step, reclaiming for the Allies territory held by the enemy.

With the gears of the division machine turning successfully, there was nothing for Bullard to do but wait. He silently grabbed his gas mask, climbed the steps from his basement lair, exited the manor house and walked down the cobbled street to a nearby orchard. There he paced for nearly an hour, strolling among the lined trees and puffing on Lucky Strikes in solitary thought as the distant, sustained din of artillery evidenced his men giving battle. Even for a man already accustomed to the isolated, brooding moments of command, these must have been his loneliest.

As Bullard paced outside, the phone down in his headquarters rang with a message from brigade: "First line went over led by tanks . . . 2nd and 3rd line appear ready to jump." These were the infantry and machine-gun teams of the second wave and the engineers and carrying parties in the third wave. The crews at each of the 75s spread over the countryside toward the front were still burning through shells—one shot from each gun every five seconds—laying down the creeping barrage. Battery officers eyed their watches waiting for 6:51 a.m., Zero Hour for the second wave. The attack was far from over and the final objective still unreached, but the Rubicon had been crossed.

CHAPTER 9

Second Wave

"The worst part was the minutes approaching the time to go into action," noted twenty-five-year-old Lt. George Butler, who stood six-feet-four when not hunched in a four-foot-deep trench. At Zero Hour, the former Indianapolis attorney and semipro football player had, like other platoon leaders in the second wave, led his fifty men in a hundred-yard scamper from their rear line up into the jumping-off trench that had just emptied of the first wave. Here he and his troops waited for five dragging minutes, watching the first wave disappear across no-man's-land toward the creeping barrage and into the smoke and dust shrouding the southern end of the village. "We were," he later recounted, "anxious to have it over with."

Three miles behind the lines, standing among his 75s and squinting through binoculars into the increasingly bright glare of dawn, Maj. Raymond Austin eyed the first wave of infantry advancing up to the hilltop horizon. "As the line reached the crest and was silhouetted in the morning sun (we face well toward the east here) it looked like a long picket fence." He watched as the "fence" of doughboys "disappeared over the crest, having crossed the first enemy lines" as Zero Hour for the second wave approached.

At 6:51 a.m., "H+6 minutes," the scattered 75mm crews stopped firing, elevation gauges were rolled to the next coordinate, and the firing resumed, inviting the second wave of infantry over the top. By the preplanned artillery schedule, the protective barrage that had been advancing at a rate of one hundred yards every two minutes would now slow and advance only every four minutes, allowing the second and third waves to catch up with the first.

As the barrage moved, Company K's Captain Mosher sent his first-wave platoons led by Lieutenants Parker and Drumm out of the first enemy trench, and with the clomping of hobnail boots on rock-hard dirt, they crossed the shell-scarred Cantigny Road. Behind them, the second wave—which included Pvt. Emory Smith, one of the "Three Musketeers" from Denton, Texas—sprinted to close distance with the first. Mosher urged them forward, and unslowed by the creeping barrage, their "advance was swift and unchecked," one platoon leader reported. Seeing Parker's and Drumm's platoons pass the road and charge toward the enemy's second-line trenches, where Germans could be seen breaking in retreat, Private Smith broke ranks and rushed ahead of his wave, Springfield held ready, eager to enter the action. "The Germans just threw up their hands and ran back," he later wrote of what he could see up ahead, "some of them firing."

Private Smith passed over the first trench, still filled with German dead and a few hiding survivors, and sprinted to catch up with the first wave. "I was between the first and second waves and so could not fire," he noted, "[b]ut then presently I caught up with the first wave and had plenty of chances to shoot and did so." His platoon leader, Lt. John Mays, a tall, slender thirty-year-old from Georgia, noted, "[I]t was our duty to clean out ('mop up' we call it) the German trenches when the first wave had passed over," but he had to work to hold his soldiers—like Smith—back from joining the fighting up ahead. "When our second wave sighted the Boche running out of their trenches they closed up into the front wave, so as to get a better shot at the enemy," Mays noted in frustration. "I had to drive the men back at the point of my pistol."

Parker's and Drumm's men had swept through the first enemy line in a hurry, per their assignment, but the platoons of the second wave were equipped with Chauchats to "mop up" the trench of remaining Germans. "Two squads of automatic riflemen ran up and down the parapet," Lieutenant Mays reported, "pouring their fire into the trench, and at least 50 of the dead were left there." Mays's soldiers jumped in and methodically snaked up and down the trench, mopping up the sleep holes and dugouts of hiding Germans. "I myself killed two Boches and took three prisoners," he later recounted. "[P]erhaps I should have killed them, too, but when they came toward me with their hands up crying 'Kamerad, Kamerad,' I just couldn't do it."

On the far left flank, Lt. Howard Hawkinson stepped up on the parapet where Lieutenant Newhall had stepped six minutes before and signaled for the men of Company L's 4th Platoon to follow. To his right, leading 3rd Platoon forward in the path blazed by Lieutenant Haydock was Lt. Frank Croak. Because the flat plateau before him was, as one officer described, "covered with growing crops, largely grain, which shortened observation from trenches and hid entrenched men from each other," he could not see the action up ahead, or the expanse of dirt littered with the khaki heaps of crawling injured and motionless dead. The grain obscured Pvt. Carl Fey, still facedown to keep from choking on the blood filling his mouth from his broken jaw, and Lieutenant Newhall, lying on his back half-conscious, bleeding from his shredded arm, and growing ever weaker.

Lieutenant Croak, twenty-seven and a graduate of St. Louis University, who worked at his father's retail clothing business until America's entry into the war, was in only his second month as platoon leader. Gripping his pistol and walking ahead of his men, the hot churn of fear and pump of adrenaline drove him forward, his senses stirred by a scene far more imposing than that facing Haydock only minutes before. The protective smoke curtain and reassuring roar of the creeping barrage had moved off uncomfortably beyond reach, and carrying back over the wheat surface were the ominous sounds of pitched battle. Every step toward the German trenches drew the chorus of rifle pops and Maxim chatter louder, nearer. With no pace to set, he and Lieutenant Hawkinson to his left began a slow run, urging their second-wave platoons forward faster and faster. "The 2nd lines rapidly closed on the 1st," Colonel Ely would later report.

The racket of small-arms fire echoing from four hundred yards ahead was the sound of Lieutenant Haydock and his platoon fighting their way to the second German line. They had cleared the length of the first enemy trench in their path, killing a Maxim gunner with rifle fire and the rest with grenades and automatic rifles. With the barrage having advanced past the Cantigny Road, Haydock led his doughboys sprinting over the dirt road and into the tall grass of the plateau beyond.

As his men ran to the edge of the second trench and began clearing it with grenades, Lieutenant Haydock noticed an enemy machine gun about fifty yards to his left firing across his front. This was the nettlesome Maxim from Lieutenant von Vegesack's 10th Company that had wreaked so much havoc on Company M's first wave to the south. Its muzzle flashed a strobe of white flame from behind a rotted pile of harvested beets, and Haydock ordered his men down while, as one of his privates would later recount, "[t]he Lieutenant walked from one end of the platoon to the other cautioning repeatedly, 'Men keep lower for your own sakes.'" They implored him to take cover as he stood, pistol in hand, straining for an angle on the gun and devising a plan to direct his platoon's fire and overtake it. "Lieutenant you keep low," one of his soldiers yelled; "they will get you."

"They can't kill me," Haydock responded. The sweep of the gun's typewriter stutter shifted, and with a gut-punching thump, Haydock fell flat. "He was hit by a machine-gun bullet and died instantly," the same private later recalled.

For his men, the loss of their leader was a heavy blow. He had led them since the Seicheprey sector, where "he won the highest respect of every man in the platoon," one of them recounted, and "never asked a man to do a thing or take a chance that he wouldn't do or take himself." For his actions, George Guest Haydock, the first American officer killed in the battle, would be posthumously awarded the Silver Star. In the words of the citation, he "displayed qualities of coolness and gallantry which inspired his entire platoon; he was killed while attempting, almost single-handed, to take a machine-gun."

With their leader now lifeless on the edge of the enemy trench, the platoon was, as *Five Lieutenants* author James Carl Nelson explains, "rudderless." Twenty-seven-year-old Sgt. Eller Fletcher of Ohio reorganized the troops, directing them to enter and organize their newly won trench line. But the enemy machine gun, defiantly unconquered, traced their movements, and before Sergeant Fletcher could take cover he was shot in the head, falling on the dirt floor. The bullet had grazed him, wounding him severely but not fatally. He would survive, later awarded the Silver Star for "gallantry in action . . . while supervising the consolidation of his position until wounded." While a few soldiers tended to him, others moved up the trench, rustling Germans from dugouts and sleep holes, and the rest set up their Chauchats along the rear trench wall to cover the plateau and thick wood line beyond. Another sergeant found a corner of the parapet to angle fire on the stubborn Maxim that had felled his lieutenant, but without success.

Behind the German lines, five or six hundred yards up the plateau to the east, machine-gun teams from two support companies in the dark cover of the l'Alval Woods had a clear angle on the second and third waves of the American infantry rushing up the wheat field. These were some of the "[m]any machine-gun positions" that 3rd Battalion commander Lt. Col. Jesse Cullison noted "had not been touched by our artillery." One by one, the German gunners angled their Maxims up to dial in the distant targets and opened fire, their aim adjusted by binocular observation. Lieutenants Croak and Hawkinson were unknowingly rushing their platoons into a buzz saw—the interlocking fire of more than a half dozen enemy machine guns.

Lt. Frank Croak had made it two hundred yards into no-man's-land and toward the sounds of battle when the hail of bullets chopped him down, killing him instantly. His slide beneath the grain surface was so abrupt it went unnoticed by most of his men, who kept rushing forward until they too were bowled down, one by one, by the sweep of machine-gun fire. Twenty-seven-year-old James Coleman, a short, red-haired private from Philadelphia. Twenty-eight-year-old PFC Patrick Fox, a two-year veteran from Brooklyn. Twenty-three-year-old Pvt. Joseph Boyland of San Francisco. Twenty-year-old PFC William Mitchell of Portland. Like their lieutenant, all slipped beneath the wheat and into eternity, their bodies never seen again. All are honored on the Somme American Cemetery's tablets of the missing.

On the far left, Lieutenant Hawkinson's 4th Platoon soldiers pushed forward as the spray of bullets slued side to side, mowing down more men with every pass. Pvt. Nick Beltman of South Dakota, struck square in the face, was killed instantly, thrown back flat in the dirt as if punched. A few more steps, and Pvt. Michael Sprangers dropped. More steps, then Cpl. George Davidson. Then PFC Wesley Keller. Every stride forward brought another friend's final moment, death that came too easy at the hands of the maniacal "tat-tat-tat." Finally, the Maxim fire drove the entire platoon into cover in the wheat. Still in the lead, Hawkinson crawled forward on his elbows beneath the invisible canopy of zipping rounds, gripping his pistol and keeping his compass heading while yelling for his surviving men to follow his voice.

At least a hundred yards behind him, the four machine-gun teams and carrying party in the third wave, heaving gun tripods, ammo boxes, and coiled barbed wire, proved easy targets for the enemy fire. PFC Edward Lutz of Buffalo, lugging a sixty-pound Hotchkiss, "advanced 20 yards when he was seen to fall," a nearby private would report. "Mechanic Lockwood ran over to him and picked the machine-gun out of his arms," carrying it forward, believing Lutz to be dead. The bloodletting continued for the ragged line of doughboys still upright, their pace slowed by heavy loads, here and there falling midstride into the wheat as if taken down by some invisible force. Twenty-year-old Pvt. Meyer Sereysky, an immigrant from Poland who had volunteered the previous summer, dropped forward dead. Pvt. Noel

Troncy, in just his fifth day with the unit, fell dead. Pvt. Julius Kahn and PFC Lazard Landry, hauling an ammo box together, simultaneously dropped the box and fell in a heap, neither to be seen again.

Sprinting to catch up with the survivors of the second wave, Pvt. Joseph Belanger of Lowell, Massachusetts, was shot through his right knee, sending him to the dirt in screaming agony. He was carried out of the killing field and back across the trenches to a field hospital, where the doctor was forced to amputate his leg. For the next forty-eight hours, Private Belanger lay on a cot in misery soothed only by morphine until growing feverish from infection. On May 30, he lapsed into septic shock and died. He was buried in a makeshift cemetery, but after the war, due to loss of accurate burial records, his remains could never be found. Together with PFC Lutz, whose body was never seen after his machine gun was pulled from his limp arms, Belanger, Troncy, Kahn, and Landry are all honored on the tablets of the missing.

Up ahead, Lieutenant Hawkinson kept low-crawling until the wheat cover shortened into a clearing, affording him a good view of the Cantigny Road and the German lines still manned by Lieutenant von Vegesack and the stubborn defenders of 10th Company, who had not yet spotted him. To his right, there was no sign of Lieutenant Croak's platoon, or any Americans at all. Crackling through the grain stalks behind him came a dozen of his men, clutching rifles and hunching to keep their helmets down below the wheat tops. Hawkinson organized a small patrol to run to the right to find and link up with the rest of the company, and asked for a volunteer to run word of their position back to the company commander, Captain Van Natter. An advance forward into the open would be suicide, so Hawkinson ordered the rest to drop their packs and start digging where they were, pinned down short of their objective on the far left flank, where they might at long last find some small refuge from the onslaught.

On the left flank, Marshall's battle plan was dead, a casualty of the proverbial contact with the enemy. Although Company L's commander, Captain Van Natter, would later report "the company reached its assigned objective and consolidation commenced," this was untrue. Lieutenant Haydock's platoon had indeed reached and occupied the German lines in their path, but they never reached their objective line beyond. And neither Lieutenant Newhall's platoon nor Hawkinson's that followed reached even the first German trench facing them.

After just ten minutes of fighting, over fifty men from the three waves of

Company L and its attached machine-gun teams lay wounded or dead in no-man's-land, every one of them felled by Maxim bullets. The scene framed a grim contrast to the other companies of 3rd Battalion and all of 2nd Battalion in the middle, where the second and third waves were now traversing the plateau to catch up with the first. "The advance was made at schedule rate of march, and experienced no difficulty," an officer in 2nd Battalion noted, where all was clicking with the battle plan just as in rehearsal, and where not a single soldier would be killed by enemy fire while crossing no-man's-land.

In the center of 2nd Battalion, leading Company E's second wave toward the northern end of Cantigny, was young Capt. Edward Johnston, only a day removed from the previous morning's deadly raid. He could see his first-wave platoons up ahead trudging along with the ambling tanks, led on the left by Lieutenant Curry and, with Charles Avery still recovering back at a field hospital, on the right by a sergeant with only "skeleton squads." They "followed the barrage through Cantigny," Johnston reported, "moving competently and cannily from hole to hole about 30–60 yards behind the inner wall of explosions." His second-in-command, Lt. Irving Wood, likened the advance of the second wave to "a football rush, only less rough." The progress of Company H on their right flank directly toward the village was just as trouble-free, as the company commander would report: "From the time we left our jumping off trenches everything seemed to go along smoothly, without incident."

Following closely behind was the third wave, which in the middle comprised all of Company G along with a blend of machine-gun teams, engineers, French infantry strapped with flamethrowers, a large carrying party, and signalmen unspooling phone lines from Colonel Ely's bunker. Also sprinkled in were a handful of war correspondents wearing khaki with white armbands and armed only with pencils and notepads. At General Bullard's specific invitation, these reporters had gathered at Division Headquarters the night before and, in George Marshall's words, "were given the complete plan and full liberty as to their own movements" on the condition of strict secrecy.

Among them was James Hopper of *Collier's,* who had won renown for his eyewitness account of the 1906 San Francisco earthquake. The night before, he had pressed Marshall for the exact limits of "full liberty," to which Marshall responded that Bullard's only rule was correspondents "should not precede the first infantry wave into Cantigny." Now, following the third wave across no-man's-land, Hopper's pencil described the scene: "The sun, which had risen above the barrage smoke, beat down on us hard, and under our feet were plowed fields, sudden shell holes, and high grass in which the telephone wires, run quickly behind the attack, lurked like traps."

Out front, a single, tall, commanding figure led the second and third waves toward the village, clutching a Colt .45 and walking with a square-shouldered, upright sureness that bristled with military virility. This digni-fied, dark-haired figure with a perfectly groomed wax-tip mustache was the highest-ranking officer—and the only battalion commander—to personally participate in the attack, Lt. Col. Robert Jayne Maxey. A forty-five-year-old West Pointer from Montana, Maxey was a veteran of the Philippines and Mexico, and had instructed at Fort Leavenworth and officer-training camps in France. Though only in his third week commanding 2nd Battalion, he had hurled himself wholeheartedly into preparations for the attack, study-ing on his map every enemy trench, bunker, and machine-gun position, then plotting not only the most effective location for a strongpoint, but also the best avenues of approach for the French tanks and four infantry companies of his battalion to sweep through the village. If the right and left flanks of the operation were platoon leaders' battles, then the middle would be Maxey's, and for the doughboys marching apace toward Cantigny, his was an affirming presence through such a trying passage.

Before Maxey, the Schneiders and first wave of his battalion had slipped past the smeared remnants of the enemy front lines, in many places with-out firing a shot. "Nobody was running," Lieutenant Sargent witnessed from his observation post; "or I should say no American soldier was running, for some Germans had come running out of Cantigny toward the tanks with their arms raised in surrender." On reaching the steep edge of the village, the Schneiders turned left to skirt around the town's northern end through the orchard, as riflemen drove straight forward "climbing equally steadily up the slope" when the barrage jumped ahead once more, exposing the ab-solute destruction of Cantigny. "And our soldiers were entering Cantigny," Sargent observed, stunned to see that "the smoke was drifting away from Cantigny and revealing that its buildings were no more."

"Cantigny had not a wall left standing when we went through," one pri-vate soon told his diary. The hour-long bombardment had reduced orderly rows of homes to mounds of smoldering ruins. Stone buildings—to include the church—had been smashed into unstately piles of bricks and masonry chunks; wooden dwellings into unrecognizable twists of matchsticks. "Cantigny is completely wrecked," a war correspondent noted. "Only the skeletons of buildings remain." Every pile of splintered timbers masked another cellar or basement, each one a possible bunker filled with Germans, presenting terrain congenial to defense and ambush.

Through streets clogged with rubble and German dead, Lt. Harry Martin led his platoon, their senses amplified by a labyrinth of brick caves filled with a hiding enemy. "I tell you, you can't tell when you are going to get yours and it is one mean sensation, too," he soon wrote home. Fingering triggers of their Springfields, the doughboys darted through town, flicking grenades into any cavern or opening that might conceal lurking Germans. Walking with his pistol drawn through Cantigny's pinched streets, Martin spotted a German soldier walking toward him. "I raised my pistol on him and with his left hand in the air yelling 'Kamerad,' I saw him reach with his right for his gun," Martin soon wrote home. "Fortunately I was a trifle too quick for him and I gave him two bullets."

Martin's men and the other three platoons of Company H swept through the left half of Cantigny and into the open plateau on the far side, where they were to establish a new line facing the German-filled wood lines on the distant horizon. "The town was hit at the correct places," their captain reported, "and my company went through the town with as little delay as possible throwing grenades in any places that by any chance there might be some enemy and went on to the consolidation line."

Amid the engine thrum and exhaust fumes of ambling tanks, the troops of Companies E and F trooped around the left side of Cantigny, a track of advance over the flattened remains of isolated houses, then into an orchard lined by trees and hedgerows, believed by division intelligence to be a haven for snipers and machine-gun nests. Escorted closely by squads of riflemen, two lines of Schneiders edged forward like floats parading into town. Their armor-plated noses angled up and over the piled spoil of enemy parapets and their metal treads crunched over barbed wire and broken timbers of destroyed dwellings before leveling off to cross the Cantigny Road and flat orchard beyond. The short French tank commander, in his Adrian helmet and pale-blue tunic, led the way on foot, described by Lt. Welcome Waltz as "strutting among them and displaying a shining bamboo walking stick as his only weapon."

Collier's correspondent James Hopper wrote that Schneiders "charged in a straight rhinoceros line; then, now and then went waddling off to one side or the other, meticulously fast, in some strong nest of boche resistance." Lieutenant Waltz reported that "these tanks got in some good work by firing on enemy groups, mostly machine-guns, which were maneuvering for position." Inside the cramped, noisy steel boxes that reeked of gas fumes, seven-man crews worked practically blind, eyeing the battlefield through fogged periscopes and slit peepholes. Gun barrels angled and twirled out the sides of each tank like awkward appendages, flushing frightened Germans out of hiding, where they were shot or taken prisoner by the American infantry.

Lieutenant Colonel Maxey strode surely among the platoons of his battalion, his eager men rushing up ahead of the tanks closer to the barrage wall. Along the way, narrow corridors formed by the town's rubble hosted a few instances of hand-to-hand fighting. A bayonet duel between an undersized doughboy and hefty German caught Lieutenant Waltz's eye: "They seemed to be off to themselves and it was almost funny to see that small doughboy jumping around the big, slow German, playing for an opening. But very shortly the smaller one saw his opening and I saw him give a quick lunge forward, dropping his opponent with a jab to the stomach." Perhaps this was Pvt. Levy Wilson of Company E, the smallest of the "Three Musketeers" from Denton, Texas, who wrote his sister two days later: "Tell Ruth Uncle Levy killed her a big fat one; tell her I surely greased my bayonet good on him."

The barrage wall slowed the parade of tanks and infantry to a stop, with second and third waves bunching up on the leaders like a traffic jam. An off-pitch whistle sounded—the telltale sign of a shell falling short—but before any of the men could duck, it hit with a whiz and a bang and a hiss of spraying shrapnel. One soldier, just a step from the blast, collapsed. Rifles dropped as men grabbed arms and legs and fell to the dirt. Nearby was Corporal Suchocki, the combat engineer with a bandage still wrapped around his arm's shrapnel gash from the quarry blast three hours earlier, who noticed doughboys all around him "falling down."

More incoming shorts added whistles to the din of the creeping barrage. Maxey ordered the rest of his troops down, but the fratricide continued. "[A] shell burst about ten feet in front of me and exploded," Suchocki would recall, adding that a "lump of dirt or chunk of rock struck me square in the chest knock me down on my back." Shrieks of pain and burning whiffs of cordite carried through the wild confusion and swirling clouds of dust and smoke. "I could not see farther than 100 feet around me," Suchocki noted. Lieutenant Colonel Maxey ordered a white flare shot up, the signal for the artillery to "lengthen the range."

Lying motionless in the dirt was the man nearest the first blast, twenty-three-year-old PFC Willford Wethington of Kentucky, the middle of three sons who had volunteered the day after President Wilson's speech to Congress the previous April. His corporal would report: "[T]he shell exploded directly in front of him, he died instantly." When his family received word of his death one week later, both of his brothers would leave their civilian jobs and enlist, and each would serve in France before the Armistice. After the war, at his widowed mother's request, PFC Wethington's body was shipped back for burial in Arlington National Cemetery.

Litter-bearers ran forward, throwing limp men onto stretchers and disappearing in hunched sprints back into the smoke of no-man's-land, leaving comrades to gather dropped rifles and fallen helmets from the crimson-splattered dirt. Field Hospital No. 12 received the wounded—improbably casualties of their own artillery. Most survived, but Pvt. Frank Malone—his left hand, right forearm, and right leg flayed open by shrapnel—did not, passing the next afternoon.

Finally, the barrage moved again, and Maxey yelled, "Forward!" Following only three men away, Corporal Suchocki could not miss the "tall man" so clearly in command, "with a revolver in right hand and stretching arms leading the 1st Division into victory." About two hundred yards of orchard, lined with a few scraggly trees, opened up before them, bordered to the left and front by a tall, thick hawthorn hedge. Stepping over a barbed-wire fence, Corporal Suchocki jumped as the fencepost beside him splintered with an enemy bullet. Before him, enemy Maxims concealed behind the hedgerow opened fire, and in what was becoming a tragically familiar sight of the morning, doughboys fell in heaps as they were raked with machine-gun bullets.

Twenty-year-old Pvt. Earl Simons of Altoona, Pennsylvania, advancing in Company F's first wave on the far left of the battalion, who had been surprised by the lack of enemy fire in his crossing of no-man's-land, was stunned at the "violent machine-gun fire" that stopped his platoon's charge into the orchard: "The only ones in action were the machine-gunners. There was some hard fighting in the wood to the right of me the Germans concealing their machine-guns about 200 yards above us." In his best English, Corporal Suchocki noted, "there stop us of some kind [of] unknown power, many boys fell on both sides of me."

German Maxim fire perforated the tide of khaki surging through the open ground of the orchard. In a hunkered charge toward the hedge, PFC Eddy Sledge's head snapped back from a bullet to his skull, and the twenty-five-year-old fell on his back, instantly killed. Back home in Asheboro, North Carolina, his mother, Martha, widowed when Eddy was only eight, would ask that Eddy's remains be buried in Arlington.

Comprehending almost at a glance that his infantry alone could not overcome the well-positioned German machine-gun nests, Maxey dropped to one knee, calmly signaled the tanks toward the hedge, and yelled for the troops surrounding him to "lay down." Pvt. Bernard Kavanagh of Sandwich, Illinois, was one of many who dropped for cover in the same instant. Collapsing dead beside him was eighteen-year-old Pvt. Joseph Leiter from New York City, "the first man in Co. F that was killed," Kavanagh noted. Shot in the shoulder, Pvt. Frank Moran began walking back for help before feeling faint from loss of blood. A comrade helped him back to the field hospital. Pvt. William Hall and PFC Ralph Carpenter both squirmed on the dirt in pain, Hall grabbing his leg and Carpenter clutching his right biceps tightly in a futile effort to stop the spurting blood. With the help of a comrade, Private Hall made it back across no-man's-land, where he was carried by stretcher to the field hospital. Two soldiers tied PFC Carpenter's arm up in field dressing and carried him back to the same hospital as Moran and Hall. Private Moran would die of blood loss midafternoon. Both Hall and Carpenter would succumb to their wounds the next day.

Finally, two of the chugging Schneiders reached the hedgerow and slammed a few 75mm rounds into the foliage while their machine-gun barrels swept its length until the enemy Maxims fell silent. Surveying the carnage in the orchard, Corporal Suchocki could see "only six of us left, the rest killed or wounded."

The left flank of 2nd Battalion kept adjusting rightward with the tanks on a heading that hugged the north side of the village, widening the gap Lt. Gerald Tyler was trying to cover with his two Company M platoons forming 3rd Battalion's right side. When the barrage moved, Tyler had led his hundred-odd men forward from the torn-up German trench line that had given them welcome refuge from machine-gun fire. Still unable to spot Company K to his left, Tyler continued to spread his men out as they advanced, then he shuffled to the right through the advancing column to link back up with his platoon sergeant, Carl Sohncke.

Minutes before, Lieutenant Tyler had left Sohncke, a three-year Regular Army veteran from Long Island, with instructions "to watch closely the compass reading as he advanced" and act as a "right guide" for the company while Tyler checked on Schmidt's platoon to his left. Now Tyler discovered that Sergeant Sohncke, one week shy of his twenty-fourth birthday, "had been killed by shell fire" when crossing no-man's-land, likely by another artillery short. As with most who died in the battle, Sohncke was the first from his hometown killed in the World War, and at his father's request his remains would be shipped back home for burial nearly three years later. In his hometown of Woodside in Queens, the small, enclosed park where Roosevelt and Woodside Avenues meet Fifty-Eighth Street is called "Sohncke Square" to this day.

Unable to see either 2nd Battalion to his right or Company K to his left, Lieutenant Tyler ordered his two platoons to continue spreading into what he called "a fan shaped forward movement," an unplanned adjustment that he later admitted caused him "great alarm" as "they were now occupying a frontage ordinarily held by two or more companies." They had not yet passed the Cantigny Road, but Tyler, somewhat wary of his thinly spread front, ordered his men to stop and "dig in" where they were.

Back in his command bunker, Colonel Ely sat on his horse saddle sifting through phone calls from observation posts and messages from platoon leaders and company commanders brought back by frantic, wide-eyed runners. Trying to piece together the status of a battle he could hear but not see, Ely had no way of knowing his regiment's left flank was wide open, and though he had heard his artillery liaisons mentioning "shorts" falling on his men, he was encouraged by the growing clutches of enemy prisoners being ushered back by his proud troops. Finally, a few minutes delayed, came the report he had waited to hear: "Our men have entered Cantigny."

CHAPTER 10

We Took the Hill

By 7:00 a.m., the center thrust of the American attack, 2nd Battalion, was successfully sweeping through the orchard and the left half of Cantigny, dislodging Maxim nests hedge by hedge and evicting German soldiers house by house. But the battle's bloodiest fighting was unfolding on the flanks. In 3rd Battalion, Company K was still driving forward, but Company M was spread ineffectively thin and on the far left, three of Company L's four platoons had not even reached the enemy lines, leaving an entire German company firmly ensconced to rake the khaki-littered wheat fields with more machine-gun fire and survey the remaining battlefield for new targets. On the right flank, facing the longest open stretch of no-man's-land the length of the attack, the three waves of 1st Battalion were still only halfway to their objective, and German defenders there were to prove just as stubborn as on the left.

Lieutenant Schuster of 1st Platoon, 3rd Company of the German 271st Reserve Infantry Regiment, had ridden out the hour-long bombardment huddled with his two dozen soldiers in the company command post, a dark, stone cellar on the southeast end of the village. Sprawled on a wooden table were maps of their positions in the village and aerial photographs of the American trenches. From down in their small eye of the steel hurricane, Schuster and his men had heard the remains of Cantigny pounded to rubble above them in concussive crashes of timbers and masonry. When the roaring drumfire finally lessened, fading into the sustained rumble of the creeping barrage denoting the American Zero Hour, Schuster led his platoon out of their cellar up into the hanging swirl of ash and smoke. There he and his men, badly shaken and doubtless shocked at the sight of the flattened village, took refuge in a fresh shell hole as the American barrage crept nearer.

"Nothing was seen any more of the other platoons located in other cellars," the German War Diary would report. Third Company's effective strength had been reduced by at least half, and there was no sign at all of 1st Company, crushed or entombed belowground. From their shell crater on the village edge, Lieutenant Schuster and his platoon could not yet see any approaching doughboys, but at the sound of machine-gun fire to their right rear—likely from the tanks rolling into the orchard with the American 2nd Battalion on the north side of the village—they fled east across the rising plateau to the cover of the distant wood lines.

The open ground south of the village fell off steeply into a pronounced ravine, ascending again to the Cantigny Woods, a long patch of trees that formed the southern boundary of the American salient. The low ground ran almost parallel with the wood line and ended suddenly at swiftly rising ground that led up to a ridge, along which a dirt road stretched southeast from the rear of Cantigny and on to the village of Fontaine, two miles deep into German territory. German trenches followed the road along the ridge and connected with troop positions back in the Fontaine Woods.

This stretch of German lines, manned by 2nd Company, was mostly untouched by the preparatory bombardment. Peering over parapets down into the ravine, Germans there had a commanding view of the Americans attacking "in dense masses." Their lieutenant ordered up green flares, one after another as the rifle-wielding doughboys swept closer. "*No* artillery fire followed these signals," the Regimental War Diary would later report. "More than likely, these signals were not seen due to heavy smoke and mist." Cut off from artillery support, Maxim crews opened their ammunition boxes, fed canvas ammo belts into the receivers, and prepared to defend their lines.

In a shallow trench furrowed out through the web of healthy roots connecting the elms and tall oaks of the Cantigny Woods, Lt. Robert Banks Anderson stood to get a line of sight over the thick undergrowth and surveyed the smoking remains of the village through binoculars. The Wilson, North Carolina, native was only four years removed from his time as captain of the baseball team at Trinity College (present-day Duke University). One of five sons to a physician and Confederate Army veteran, Robert and his four brothers had all volunteered for Army service when America entered the war. In October, after attending officer training at Fort Oglethorpe with Sam Ervin and Si Parker, the newly minted lieutenant had walked the gangplank from his transport onto French soil on his twenty-fifth birthday.

Anderson had become a platoon leader in Company A down in the

Seicheprey sector, after which he attended a British Corps combat school, graduating with honors in time to rejoin the company for the battle rehearsal days earlier. But a scourge of Spanish influenza had incapacitated his captain and two fellow lieutenants, and despite the fact that at the crucial hour Anderson was also feeling early signs of its symptoms, he took the reins as acting company commander for the battle. "Tomorrow we are going to attack," he had written his mother on J-1. "I will be in command of my company, but we'll be miserably handicapped with so many men, non-commissioned officers and three officers sick."

Squinting through his binoculars, Lieutenant Anderson could see the deep ravine cutting through the open ground between him and the village, and to his right, up on the commanding high ground behind a staked strand of barbed wire lining the dirt road, he could make out the coal-scuttle helmets of 2nd Company's field-gray infantry waiting on the far sides of their Maxims, the bright morning sun rising behind them. To his left, he could see the churning wall of the barrage, behind which the khaki waves of Company B followed on a path that would take them through the ravine before him and up to the German lines crowning the ridge.

Anderson and his four platoons of Company A were the only portion of the attack force to not jump off at Zero Hour and join the waves marching across no-man's-land. This wrinkle in the operations plan had formed only after George Marshall's personal reconnaissance of the front lines had thrown the contours of the ravine into steep relief. To Marshall and the planners, this long strip of vulnerable low ground covered by the overlapping fire of German Maxims presented a deadly gauntlet for infantry, even behind the cover of a rolling barrage. The risk and its attendant casualties were believed avoidable by simply stationing the right wing, Company A, forward in the cover of the Cantigny Woods, where two of its platoons would swing out at H+14 minutes and join 1st Battalion's assault waves nearer the objective.

Forty minutes prior, Lieutenant Anderson had sent his other two platoons to his right into the easternmost finger of the woods, where they were to dig new lines facing the Germans infesting the nearby Fontaine Woods. One platoon was led by a sergeant and the other by Lt. Jim Hartney, whose correspondence with his "beloved Margaret" back in Minnesota had not cooled a bit since his New Year's profession of love. There they would, in their battalion commander's words, "prevent the right flank being turned," and act as the southern anchor of the new American lines. "The digging in woods was very difficult," Hartney would later report of the thick under-growth, one of the sector's only patches of countryside still untouched by shell fire. Covered by three attached machine-gun teams, his men cut "about 50 yards of trench, 2 ½ feet wide and 4 feet deep" through the hardpan and a network of stubborn roots—a task that would occupy them past night-fall.

Out in no-man's-land, leading a platoon in Company B's second wave behind the barrage down into the ravine, was Lt. Neilson Poe of Baltimore, Maryland. At forty-one, he was the oldest platoon leader in the entire at-tack, though with his dark-brown hair still showing no hint of gray, his men all presumed him to be far younger. Known as "Net" to his friends, the for-mer Princeton football player compared jumping off at Zero Hour to rush-ing "down the field under the kick-off of a Princeton-Yale game." Between the Cantigny Woods to his right and the village to his left, Poe—together with his platoon and the rest of Company B—had so far advanced more than six hundred yards without a casualty. "The artillery laid a beautiful barrage in front of us as we advanced," he later recalled, "and all we had to do was to follow it, keeping about 50 yards behind it."

"We were to take a hill to the right of Cantigny," one private would later recount. "We had a creeping barrage which throws a curtain of shell fire 50 yards continuously in front of the advancing forces." As the waves of ri-flemen edged forward, the occasional off-pitch whistle signaled an incom-ing short, prompting men to brace or duck in futility. "Sometimes you would hear shells coming from behind and know they were going to fall short," Poe later described, "but you have to look out for a few 'shorts' and be ready to drop." To his left, one short blew a hole in the soldiers of Company D's second wave just before they climbed into the village, seriously injuring two and blowing Pvt. George Dust of Chicago, Illinois, to unrecognizable pieces.

As part of Company D's dash through the south side of Cantigny, Lt. George Butler led his platoon into the rubble-filled streets. "When we reached Cantigny it was only a pile of bricks and stones," he soon described in a letter home. "The German machine-gun bullets were buzzing about like bumble bees, but our fellows did not pay any more attention to them than if they had been confetti." Like Maxey's 2nd Battalion to their left, sweeping through the orchard and northern half of the village, Company D's infantry were closely followed by a third wave of French flamethrower teams assigned to "mop up" any lingering pockets of Germans in the village ruins. "It was the finest example of teamwork I ever saw," Butler would add. "There was not a hitch anywhere."

Walking in loose tandem over the jumbles of broken beams and smoking rubble, Company D's riflemen moved steadily through town, squads stopping here and there at debris piles covering cellars and lobbing grenades into any dark cavity where Germans might be hiding or entombed. "Our fellows threw grenades like baseballs and captured machine-guns," Lieutenant Butler would recount. A few soldiers in the company's first wave came upon an opening through which stone stairs could be seen leading down into a cellar. "Huns were called upon to come out," an officer would later report, but from inside echoed only yells in German and the loud, brisk notes of a Maxim opening fire. The doughboys jumped back, sent grenades clattering deep inside, waited for the muffled detonations, then rushed down into the hanging smoke. A few pops of Springfield fire sounded, followed only by silence. "[A] general clean up took place—about 70 killed, no prisoners taken," the report would continue. Combing through the dark cellar full of German dead, the soldiers retrieved the Maxim and lugged it out, carrying it forward through the narrow street like a war trophy.

Following with his platoon in the second wave, Lieutenant Butler noted most German soldiers put up no fight: "The enemy ran out of caves and dugouts very much scared. They held up their hands shouting 'kamerad.' It was a tough looking bunch of youngsters and old men. There was no fight in them." Up in the first wave, troops found a cellar buried under the remains of the last house on the back edge of town—the command post abandoned by Lieutenant Schuster and his platoon just minutes before. Inside, as 1st Battalion's intelligence officer would later report, Company D soldiers snatched the following gems: "Map of enemy's positions of rear area's found here with other company records and 5 aerial photos of our old positions."

Down in the ravine, the barrage curtain again moved forward, sending Company B nearer the German lines and luring Company A's two platoons out of the woods. "The men were rolling cigarettes as they took the level ground," Pvt. John Johnston later recounted of the moment he casually crawled out of his tree-shaded trench, twisted through the undergrowth, and stepped into sun of the open field. Lt. Robert Anderson, pistol in hand and dangerously ill, led his two fifty-man platoons and attached machine-gun teams out of the woods and fell in line with Company B's waves in the low ground of the ravine. Before them rose a sun-drenched carpet of tall green grass sprinkled with yellow buttercups and red poppies, climbing steeply to steel barbed wire and stacked sandbags lining a ridge dug with German trenches, an incongruous blend of nature and war.

"It was a great sight to see all those bayonets shining," twenty-four-year-old Pvt. Ralph Loucks, advancing with Company A's front platoon, would write his mom back in Janesville, Wisconsin, "but the further we advanced over No Man's Land the smoke got so thick sometimes that you could hardly see." The creeping barrage had scarred the field with shell craters, "big enough nearly to put a threshing machine into," Loucks noted. Four more minutes passed and the barrage wall jumped forward again, this time beyond the German lines, and before the lingering smoke lifted from the ravine, the Maxims opened fire.

Bullets lashed the first wave, mowing through the doughboys headed up the steep ground from the ravine. "The platoon I was in was nearly up to the German trenches when the Germans started firing on us with machineguns," Private Loucks would write. "I heard something go through my arm like a red-hot iron. The bullet went through the upper part of my left arm through the muscle." The soldier to Loucks's left, twenty-one-year-old Pvt. Walter Daetwiler, also from Janesville, Wisconsin, fell in the same moment. Loucks grabbed his arm and checked on Daetwiler, who had multiple shots in the chest and faded quickly. "I guess he never knew what hit him: he died a few moments later," Loucks noted. "The two of us were hit the same second and both fell together."

Those not hit dropped into the short weeds. Desperate for cover, one handful of doughboys took refuge in a large shell hole. With Maxim and sniper rounds zipping overhead, they sought out comrades lying in the open ground nearby, pulling them into the safety of the dirt crater. They dragged in twenty-four-year-old Pvt. Andy Siler of Eagan, Tennessee, and found him lifeless, riddled with bullets. They also pulled in Private Daetwiler's limp body, not yet stiff with death. Private Loucks, gripping his shot arm, spotted the crater and low-crawled to its edge. "I crawled into a shell hole and just barely had enough strength to get to it," he noted; "the blood was pouring out of my arm like a fountain. Some of the boys pulled me in the shell hole and cut my pack off my back and my coat and put the first-aid bandage around my arm."

To their left, a machine-gun team jumped up from where they had dropped for cover, grabbed their equipment and ammo boxes, and pushed defiantly through the gunfire. Left behind was Pvt. Jacob Ciezielczyk of

Milwaukee, thrown into the weeds by the first sweep of Maxim bullets. "He was hit several times, by machine-gun fire, but was not killed instantly," a fellow soldier would report. "When he was offered first aid, he said: 'I am done for, save it for someone who needs it.'" The rest of the crew pressed forward, making it up to a shell crater nearer the German trenches, where the sergeant decided they could set up the gun and lay down covering fire for the infantry. But their corporal, Thomas McCracken, and gun tripod he was carrying, were missing. The crew looked back down the slope and noticed him lying facedown in the weeds beside the dropped tripod a few dozen yards behind them. Twenty-four-year-old Pvt. Russell Goodwin dropped his rifle, ran back through the gunfire and found McCracken dead, a bullet through his head. Goodwin heaved the fifty-pound tripod over his shoulder and ran it forward through the flurry of bullets, somehow unscathed.

Flattened in the weeds, riflemen glancing up the endless field caught fleeting outlines of German helmets behind the barbed wire as the white muzzle flashes of Maxim barrels swung right and left above sandbagged earthworks. Goodwin's crew finally got their Hotchkiss set up and added its reassuring chatter to the enemy's incessant typing, giving the infantry enough cover to jump up and resume the charge up the hill.

A second crew, led by twenty-three-year-old Cpl. Walter Christenson, still another who was weak and feverish with the flu, trooped forward and began to set up their gun in another shell hole just seventy-five yards from the German lines. But an enemy sniper traced their movements, and while PFC Frank Caralunas was locking the gun on its tripod, he was shot through the neck and fell over the front edge of the crater. Pvt. John Eaves crawled forward to check on Caralunas, but the sniper shot Eaves in the head, killing him instantly. Corporal Christenson and other crew members pulled Caralunas back in. Fading swiftly, his eyes closing, he muttered quietly, "I am going to die." The crew dressed his wound, but he died forty-five minutes later, never uttering another word.

Christenson, sweating profusely and flushed red with fever, kept working, leading his crew in getting their gun set up and putting more fire on the ridge, but the two German machine guns continued sweeping the hillside with bullets, only stalling here and there as the nettlesome fire of the two American Hotchkiss crews proved too heavy. Doughboys struggled to reach the high ground in episodic sprints between the deadly Maxim bursts, dropping for cover again at each recurring sight of more men shot down, leaving a grim trail of overturned helmets, dropped rifles, and bodies. Among the dead was tall, blond-haired, blue-eyed Pvt. Howard Stevens, who, until enlisting at twenty-two had worked on his father's farm in Mill Shoals, Illinois; twenty-nine-year-old PFC Charles Digelman of Coshocton, Ohio, who enlisted two weeks after America declared war; and twenty-one-year-old Mech. Cecil Abels of Jackson, West Virginia, shot directly through the heart. And in a battle that would see only five fathers killed, two of them fell here, side by side: twenty-nine-year-old PFC Ray Brandow of Michigan, who left behind two small children, and nineteen-year-old PFC Paul Eskew of Kentucky, who left a seventeen-year-old wife, Zida, and their son, Paul Jr., not yet a year old.

As surviving doughboys in the first wave dove and hugged the steep ground for cover, the German Maxim crews cut through the second and third waves still exposed in the ravine's low ground. Twenty-two-year-old PFC Clifton Eby of Detroit—big, husky, and popular in Company B's Chauchat squad—was shot in the chest and thrown back. His buddy from Detroit, Pvt. Joseph Lukachonski, dropped to check on him. Shot through the lung, Clifton struggled with his final breaths, forcing out only: "Tell my mother I died like a man."

Advancing along the edge of the woods in Company A's rear platoon, Pvt. John Johnston noted the enemy fusillade reaching him was so heavy that "the bark could be seen peeling off the trees, and then I and some other fellows found a shell hole and we dropped into it." Hugging the ground nearer the wood line, he and his platoon dug in where they were. The other Company A platoon did the same about fifty yards in front of them, stuck in the vulnerable low ground of the ravine near the northeastern edge of the woods, leaving a two-hundred-yard gap between them and Company B, then charging up the ridge.

Nearly one mile north, with Company M digging in shy of the Cantigny Road and three of Company L's four platoons strewn throughout no-man's-land far short of their objective, Company K was the only part of 3rd Battalion still pressing forward. Having already passed the first and second line of enemy trenches and taken more than a dozen prisoners, Lieutenants Parker and Drumm and their men arrived at a series of shell holes left by the creeping barrage, forming ragged starting points for the new line they were to dig. Captain Mosher directed two teams forward to establish automatic-rifle outposts and ordered the rest to start digging. "On reaching the objective," Parker would report, "outposts were immediately put forward and the platoon began to dig in."

But they came under fire from an enemy machine-gun nest hidden behind a haystack about fifty yards to their front. Automatic riflemen provided covering fire while Lieutenant Parker, his platoon sergeant, and about a dozen men from his platoon rushed the strongpoint. "The enemy saw me rush-in," Parker would recall. "One big burley cuss, with whiskers, thought he would stay us off. He threw a grenade between my sergeant and me, but it did not explode until we had rushed past." As Parker led the charge toward the gun pit, the husky German jumped up with his hands raised yelling, "*Kamerad*" repeatedly. Parker's platoon sergeant said, "Yes, a Hell of a Kamerad," and, as Parker described, "shot his bayonet clear through him." Fifteen more gray-clad soldiers climbed from the slit trench, hands up in surrender. Parker added: "I will never forget the expression of one of them. He was scared plum to death. His hands were just about as near to heaven as he could get them. He cried out in English, 'I have a wife and five children.' I took him prisoner. Didn't have the heart to shoot him."

Following Captain Mosher's directive, Parker and these dozen-odd soldiers began establishing an outpost at the haystack for one of the attached Hotchkiss crews, and Lieutenant Drumm began establishing another. Their work was protected by helpful covering fire laid down by 4th Platoon doughboys with a captured German Maxim. The platoon leader, twenty-six-year-old Lt. Irwin Morris of Lexington, Missouri, had captured the gun with his sergeant and three privates. "The gun was then slewed around and we commenced firing at the enemy who could be seen on the reverse slope of the hill, just in the edge of the woods," Morris noted. The team he left on the gun fired at Maxim positions in the l'Alval Woods as well as fleeing Germans, providing valuable but brief cover for the company until the ammunition was exhausted. "The enemy," Morris would report, "left about 300 dead and wounded in front of us."

Beyond the smoke-filled gap on Company K's right, Pvt. Sam Ervin and his dozen-man carrying team had paused in their advance, kneeling in no-man's-land, trying to match the shelled and tangled landscape to Ervin's map. Their objective was a small cemetery to the left of the orchard, where they were to help an infantry platoon and six Hotchkiss teams construct a strongpoint, but there was no sign of the platoon or gun teams—or the cemetery, for that matter. Then out of the hanging smoke walked the one man who knew this ground better than anyone, the 3rd Battalion intelligence officer and Ervin's good friend, Lt. George Redwood.

Redwood, as Ervin would later recall, "directed me to the exact location—the ground being so torn by shell fire as to render it exceedingly difficult to ascertain the same." With bursts of Maxim fire sweeping the ground, Ervin and his soldiers kept low as they scampered to the cemetery. But heedless of his own safety, Redwood walked upright, scribbling in his patrol notebook and ignoring the bullets. "I remarked to him that he was somewhat recklessly exposing himself to machine-gun fire," Ervin would recount. "He merely smiled in his quiet, cool way and said he had already been 'slightly wounded.'"

Redwood had indeed been injured, shot in his right shoulder by an enemy bullet sometime in the attack's first minutes. As the platoon and machine-gun teams arrived at the cemetery, led by tall, twenty-two-year-old Lt. Charles McKnolly of Missouri, Redwood allowed them to bandage his wound but demurred at advice to go to the first-aid station. "Instead of doing what is ordinarily expected of a wounded soldier," Ervin noted, "he gallantly continued to gather information as Intelligence Officer."

Within sight of the cemetery, Company M's Lt. Gerald Tyler and his two-platoon front continued digging a new line, short of their objective. They had been at it for a few minutes when a French tank officer approached and suggested they move forward a couple hundred yards for a better field of fire. "I told him I thought it inadvisable, because my front had been extended so much that the line was now very thinly held," Tyler noted, "and that I had not the slightest idea where the Companies on my right and left were, also that we would certainly be isolated from the rest of our troops and would probably come under their fire." But the French officer kept pressing, and seeing Lieutenant McKnolly and Private Ervin and their men digging in the cemetery ruins to his right front, Tyler "decided to follow his advice" and ordered his platoons "to stop digging and to move forward again."

After lugging their packs and rifles and picks and shovels forward another two hundred yards through machine-gun fire, Tyler's surviving men dropped into a series of shell holes for cover, squirmed out of their packs, grabbed their shovels, and on hands and knees began connecting the craters into a new line. With enemy Maxims still rattling, a newly bandaged Lieutenant Redwood appeared at Tyler's shell crater and asked for an update. "I gave him what information I could," Tyler would recall, "and advised him to get under cover because the area was being subjected to heavy machine-gun fire." Noticing Redwood clutching his wound, Tyler inquired if he was OK, to which Redwood "replied that he had already been wounded and intended to proceed at once to Bn. Headquarters to make his report." With that, the intrepid Lieutenant Redwood disappeared back into the smoke hanging over no-man's-land, and Tyler and his men, still under fire but finally at their objective, dug in.

Back down south of the village, in Company B's first wave, twenty-six-year-old Lt. James Lawrence of Atlanta led his platoon in a pell-mell rush out of the ravine and up to the ridge of the German trench. "I had nearly reached it when things began to get too warm for comfort," he soon recounted. "A bullet chewed up my right ear." But it slowed him only slightly, and he jumped up and led the charge over the crest of the hilltop. With Springfields leveled, doughboys slipped through the piled scraps of barbed wire left cut up by the creeping barrage and finally the Maxim's fire stopped. Its last burst got twenty-two-year-old Pvt. Otto Hanson through the ankle. His hometown buddy from Wisconsin, Pvt. Harry Gums, pulled him forward into a shell hole at the top of the hill, and began bandaging his wound.

The nine-man Maxim crew of skinny teenagers and scrawny older men in ill-fitting gray tunics and oversized helmets stood with arms held high and yelled "*Kamerad*" in surrender, their eyes filled with fright. Nineteen-year-old Pvt. Ralph Amundson was nearest them, but just as he relaxed his grip on his rifle to take them prisoner, the German in the rear shot him dead. "Then I saw red," one of Amundson's buddies soon recounted. "I took my knife and tried it first on a wounded German and found out it worked and then I tried it on four live ones." Other doughboys leveled their rifles and shot the survivors into a heap of field gray. Pvt. Charles Basel of Illinois began to take the surrender of three more Germans climbing from their trench, but one of them shot him in the head, killing him instantly. "These men were also killed," Basel's commander, Capt. Clarence Oliver, would dryly report.

With a pistol in one hand and map in the other, Captain Oliver supervised his company's takeover of the enemy lines. Twenty-nine and the eldest of four sons, Oliver hailed from the small town of Chemung, New York, just above the Pennsylvania border, where he had worked as a bridge layer before volunteering for the first round of officer school. He had taken command of Company B down in Seicheprey, and whether on patrol, in a raid, or with the first wave of this morning's attack, he always led from the front.

As Oliver's troops began clearing the newly captured trench, another Maxim opened up and raked the ridgeline with enfilading fire, dropping every doughboy flat or into the trench for cover. Flopping next to Captain Oliver was Cpl. Lewis Kowaski, who immediately began unclipping a small grenade—or "lemon" as soldiers called it—from his pack strap, took to one knee, and threw it toward the machine gun. "I was a pretty good baseball pitcher before I went in the army," Kowaski would soon explain, "and I seemed to have a knack of putting the lemons over the plate." At the sound of the lemon's detonation, Corporal Kowaski grabbed his Chauchat, and he and Captain Oliver jumped up and charged the machine-gun nest. "The 'lemon' did so much damage," Kowaski would recall, "that I figured the chance of getting the whole bunch was too good to miss so I pulled out an automatic and aimed for them."

The grenade blast had killed a few and left nine dazed survivors. Kowaski "banged away" with his automatic rifle, killing a few before Captain Oliver stopped him. Inside were two fully operational Maxims and a supply of ammunition. Another soldier from Kowaski's squad arrived to help capture the guns. "[H]e covered the Fritzes and I swung the two machine-guns around," Kowaski noted. "We didn't know how to operate the things, but we made the Germans show us how at the point of our pistols." For his actions in conquering the strongpoint and capturing the Maxims, Corporal Kowaski would be awarded the Distinguished Service Cross.

At 7:30 a.m., Captain Oliver dispatched a runner to tell the 1st Battalion commander that the objective was reached. To their left, trickling through the village ruins and entering the open fields east of Cantigny were the first waves of Companies D and H, who had dropped their packs and were digging with picks and shovels into the flinty soil. The scene repeated in gathering waves to the north beyond them, as Companies E and F finally punched through the orchard and stopped at clusters of shell holes to drop their equipment and start digging new lines. "We took Cantigny on schedule time, thirty four minutes," Lt. Irving Wood reported, "and then dug in quickly to meet the Germans' counter attacks." Before them, beyond the protective barrage that now stood stationary in the open plateau, the heartening detonations of high-explosive shells hurled by those big French guns was keeping the German Maxim nests and artillery batteries under a rain of steel and out of the fight, giving doughboys much needed protection as they began to dig trenches out in the wide open.

Still at his observation post, Lt. Daniel Sargent surveyed the scene before him. With doughboys and French tanks infesting every corner of the battlefield visible from his position, he felt secure enough to stand. "And now our men were walking through what had once been Cantigny and now they were beyond it. They had taken Cantigny," he would later recount. "How easy it had been!"

In Colonel Ely's command bunker, with German prisoners filing past in a growing stream, and with a flurry of "Objective reached" messages from companies at the front, the mood was exultant. But the battle map was not yet clear, and the officers crammed into Ely's dugout had no way of knowing that the left flank was wide open and a large gap jeopardized the right flank between the Cantigny Woods and Company B's new position. Leaning on his crutches and the only information he had, George Marshall trusted that the "bite" phase of his bite-and-hold operation had been realized. "The success of this phase of the operation was so complete and the list of casualties so small that everyone was enthusiastic and delighted," he would later write.

Over three miles away, General Bullard returned from his brooding stroll back down in his cellar headquarters at 8:00 a.m., in time to get a phone report from Colonel Ely relayed through Brigade: "Over 100 prisoners from two different regiments being sent back. Everything going fine according to schedule. All objectives taken. Very little loss." General Pershing arrived for his scheduled visit anxious for an update, and Bullard buoyantly reported the attack was "most successful." The ever-stoic Big Chief seemed satisfied but exhibited no excitement "with the wonder of the performance," in Bullard's estimation. "He seemed to take the capture, as I took it, as a simple affair."

Perhaps. But most likely Pershing was apprehensive about the coming challenge—holding the conquered ground. As a close follower of the frequent ebbs and flows along the Western Front, Pershing understood that holding newly captured territory had proven the toughest part of all operations for veteran armies over the past three years of fighting. And with the vital French artillery now scheduled to exit the sector to help repel the renewed German offensive down south, victory at Cantigny was not at all inevitable. Pershing lingered long enough to see 140 German prisoners brought in, and though still anxious, he nevertheless extracted himself—and his unavoidably distracting presence—from the scene, leaving the battle's outcome in the capable hands of Bullard, Sitting Bull, and the Fighting First.

"We took the hill—and held it," Company A's Pvt. Billie McCombs would write home. At Zero Hour, McCombs had been consumed with fear over "losing our nerve." But forty-five minutes into the battle, Billie's nerve had held, as had the nerve of all who found themselves back at a field hospital having their combat wounds treated, or lying in tall wheat still calling out desperately for a medic, or digging in at their objective, having pushed their small corner of the Western Front east, forcing the kaiser's soldiers of the 82nd Reserve Division a mile closer to Germany.

CHAPTER 11

A Pack of Bumblebees

Though hundreds of German soldiers were still hiding or trapped beneath Cantigny's ghostly ruins, the village was once again in Allied hands. For the 1st Division, the heft of numbers, speed, and metal had won the hour. Though stymied on the flanks, seven of the nine infantry companies forming the attack vanguard had reached their objectives, and among doughboys in the process of furrowing out fresh trenches and remapping their small stretch of the Allied lines, a new confidence took root. With Cantigny in their tenuous grip, overall victory in the battle felt within reach.

But the day's drama was still unfolding, and this was only the first act. Biting off a chunk of enemy territory gave no assurance of success, no promise that it could be held. Armies up and down the Western Front had tried and tried again, and most had failed. For the Americans, the advantage of surprise was quickly evaporating, and with French artillery batteries exiting the battle, the weight of steel was about to tilt decidedly in the Germans' favor.

"The pick or the shovel, when the objective is reached, is mightier than the gun," one officer would later remark. More than three dozen platoon leaders along a fragile new mile-and-a-half-long front plotted imaginary lines on the ground where their men were to establish trenches in the shell-cratered dirt. Troops shed packs and ammo bandoliers, grabbed picks and shovels, and commenced the big dig. As with the initial attack, the two flanks saw the heaviest fighting. For the doughboys Company K, the immediate danger was their open left flank.

"Just as the digging began, a machine-gun barrage was put down," Lt. Si Parker, establishing his outpost up near the haystack, would report. Maxim fire came in torrents from Germans on the left flank and the distant l'Alval Woods. Pvt. Emory Smith, chasing a German he had spotted out in front of him "dodging from one shell hole to another," leveled his Springfield and fired just as the wall of machine-gun fire knocked him back. "Just as I fired at the Dutchman [*sic*], being in an erect position, I was shot in the breast and for a moment everything was black," he would recall. Smith fell into a shell crater and lay dazed while the company dug in behind him. Though Smith was far forward in a position raked by automatic fire, Captain Mosher made his way up to the crater, kneeled to check on him, gave him an aspirin, and told him to hang on until dark, when he would send a stretcher forward to evacuate him.

All along the line, upright, digging doughboys proved easy targets. Pvt. Amedeo Gialanella was "taking an entrenching tool from comrade's pack when shot thru [his] head with a machine-gun bullet, killing him instantly." Digging an outpost with his squad, twenty-year-old PFC Charles Harsch, "a quiet fellow" from Brockport, New York, was shot in the forehead. When hit, "he fell backwards and said, 'My God Mother,'" then died, a watching corporal would later relay.

Twenty-year-old Pvt. Eugene Griepentrog of Milwaukee "made a step for a shell hole to start digging in when a machine-gun bullet penetrated his heart, killing him instantly," Pvt. Harry Langley of Indiana noted. "When he was shot, he fell on his face." Also from Milwaukee, seventeen-year-old Pvt. August Beckman Jr., the youngest of five children to German immigrants, was shot through the right leg and fell, but was able to low-crawl to Private Langley's shell hole. As Langley opened his first-aid pack to bandage the wound, Beckman told him to write his mother if he should die. Before Langley could help him further, Beckman was shot through the heart. Nearby, Cpl. Harry McCredie of New York stood momentarily to dig a connection between two shell craters and was cut down with two bullets through his groin. "As soon as he was injured he became unconscious," Langley would recall, "remaining so until he died" about twenty minutes later.

Machine-gun fire from a half dozen German guns swept side to side and back again, perforating anything exposed above the lips of shell craters and making it impossible for the hunkered survivors to dig any kind of cover. Cpl. Jethers Schoemaker of Georgia poked his head up, "was struck in the left temple with a machine-gun bullet, and died instantly," a comrade would report. PFC Robert Veal, also from Georgia, was shot through the throat and collapsed. Unable to make any statements, he fought the end for an hour before bleeding to death. And eighteen-year-old Pvt. Matthew Rivers, defiantly digging despite the danger, was shot in the chest. He dropped his shovel, said calmly to a fellow private, "I'm shot," then dropped over dead.

The teenage soldier known in his platoon as Matthew Rivers was actually Matthew Juan, a Native American from the Sacaton Indian Community in Arizona. Having shown athletic promise in baseball, rodeos, and calf roping from a young age, Juan was working for the Ringling Brothers Circus to help support his widowed mother when America entered the war, and being too young to register for Army service without parental permission, he registered under the false name "Matthew Rivers." When he shipped out for France in February, his transport, the SS *Tuscania*, was torpedoed and sunk by a U-boat. More than two hundred died, but "Private Rivers" was rescued, making it to France for assignment to the 28th Infantry just before the move to Cantigny. After the war, correspondence between his mother and the War Department would confirm his identity, and his body was shipped home at her request. Today, in a Sacaton park named in his honor, Private Juan is memorialized with a life-size statue and a stone obelisk, on which a plaque reads: "Dedicated to the Memory of Matthew B. Juan, Co K 28th Infantry, First Arizonian Killed in the World War, Battle of Cantigny, May 28th 1918."

A mile south, Lt. Robert Anderson's Company A soldiers worked to dig the anchor for the right wing in the eastern edge of the Cantigny Woods under increasingly irksome machine-gun fire from Germans hidden in the Fontaine Woods. Twenty-nine-year-old Cpl. Robert Finnegan of Pennsylvania led a team out in the open to string barbed wire before their position and was shot in the shoulder blade and rib. But he concealed his wounds, and still under heavy fire, led his team scurrying back to the wood line and into their shallow foxholes. Finnegan fired his Chauchat on the enemy-infested woods across from him for more than an hour, providing covering fire for his digging squad before falling weak from blood loss. He was evacuated on a stretcher to a field hospital, where he would succumb to his wounds midafternoon. For his actions, which "encouraged his men by his example of fortitude," Corporal Finnegan was posthumously awarded both the Distinguished Service Cross and the Silver Star. He is buried in Arlington National Cemetery.

The two platoons that had swung out and joined the assault through the open ground had since become trapped by the heavy Maxim fire in the low ground of the ravine where they dug for cover, unable to connect with Company B's position up on the ridge. "We dug while the sun was coming up," Pvt. John Johnston would describe, "and half of the boys dug, and dug frantically with their helmets." Any standing figure was perforated by the torrent of bullets, so men lay flat on their stomachs scratching out holes with ration tins and helmets, piling dirt and uprooted weeds before them for a few precious inches of defilade. "Some of the men had tough luck, for they ran into rock," Private Johnson would add.

Up on the ridge, after clearing the German trenches lining the dirt road, Captain Oliver moved Company B forward to connect with Company D on the left, a movement covered by the two Hotchkiss teams and men operating the captured Maxim. In the rehearsal, the company commanders had been instructed to establish two trenches for defense-in-depth: a line of surveillance with machine-gun or automatic-rifle outposts out front and a line of resistance fifty yards back. Oliver ordered two platoons to dig the rear trench, two to dig the front trench, and set up three Chauchat outposts—two beyond the front line and one at the road on his right flank to cover the gap between his unit and Company A.

But on schedule, the standing barrage in the wheat field before them stopped, lifting a valuable smokescreen and clearing sight lines for enemy Maxim crews in the Fontaine Woods three hundred yards away. "As soon as we reached the objective we ran into machine-gun fire, and digging a trench under these conditions is not the pleasantest occupation I know," Lieutenant Poe would soon write home. "Most of our losses occurred at this spot and our company was badly cut up as any. I thought the sight of seeing men killed would affect me more. The first to fall was about 10 feet away and I knew he was killed the moment he fell."

While Chauchat and Hotchkiss teams did their best to put down covering fire on the distant wood line, panting doughboys in sweaty tunics dug for their lives. Sweeps of a half-dozen Maxims merged into a nerve-wracking din, and digging soldiers were bowled over dead, life after life extinguished and added to the day's grim tally. Twenty-five-year-old Pvt. Samuel Tunno, an Italian immigrant from Akron, Ohio; eighteen-year-old PFC Abner Cooper, the fourth of eight children from Monticello, Mississippi; Pvt. Roman Dzierzak, a Russian immigrant drafted in only his fifth year in America; Pvt. Harry Heimbach of Pennsylvania; Pvt. Charles Drake of Mississippi; PFC Simon Czech; Pvt. Dewey Beam; Pvt. Joe Kasper.

Men were forced to roll their dead friends out of the way to keep digging, left to wonder if the next sweep of bullets would be the end. Pvt. Harry Gums was still lying in a shell crater bandaging the leg of his Janesville buddy, Pvt. Otto Hanson, when machine-gun fire pelted his position. A bullet hit Gums near his elbow, tearing through the length of his forearm and ripping tendons before exiting his thumb. Having lost all feeling in his hand and use of his arm, he wrapped a bandage around it to stop the bleeding, grabbed his rifle with his good arm, and held his position for another hour before finally being evacuated.

Lt. James Lawrence, whose ear had been "chewed" up by a bullet on his charge out of the ravine, was directing his platoon's digging in the wheat field when, as he would describe, "I tried to stop another bullet, but it was too lively for me; it sideswiped my upper left chest and around under my side and cut through my upper arm." He was evacuated late morning and would recover after a stay in the hospital, calling himself "mighty lucky" but joking that his shot ear would forever be "about a size smaller."

Digging new lines to Company B's left were the men of Company D, led by thirty-five-year-old Lt. Soren Sorensen, a ten-year Army veteran who had been promoted for bravery in the Philippines. He would report that, much like Company B, "most casualties were on reaching objective where we received heavy machine-gun fire from wood on our right." In fact, over their crossing of no-man's-land and sweep through Cantigny, Private Dust—killed by an artillery short—had been the company's only death. After rushing to the objective, twenty-six-year-old PFC Walter Dawe of St. Louis was shot in the back "between the shoulder blades" as he began to dig in. He died instantly, killed by a hidden German machine gun "passed up in the attack" before flamethrower crews could catch up and clear it, a sergeant later recalled.

"When they began digging in, the Boche machine-guns ranged in half a circle began spouting bullets," Lt. George Butler noted. Fortunately, in the rear line of resistance that his platoon was consolidating, the creeping barrage had left a series of deep craters the men used as starting points. "[A]ll possible use was made of shell holes which were deepened and later connected up by the men in the holes digging toward each other," Butler would report. But their position exposed them on a forward-sloping field at the mercy of enemy guns, a topographical handicap that the lines of Marshall's flat map board had not revealed. The company, as Butler later bristled, "found itself on the highest nose of the plateau and was forced to dig in under a fury of machine-gun bullets which inflicted severe pun-ishment on it."

Pvt. William Fishette, an Italian immigrant, was struck before he could make any progress with his shovel. "The bullet hit him in the forehead, and killed him instantly," his corporal reported. His friend and fellow Italian American, Pvt. Antonio Grassi, was shot through the stomach, folding over in pain until stretcher bearers finally evacuated him. He would undergo sur-gery to remove the bullets, hanging on in pain before losing the fight four mornings later.

Trying to cover the consolidation, Cpl. George Anslow of Boston, the company sharpshooter, was sniping Germans along the distant wood line while his fellow doughboys dug. He was peeking over the dirt lip of the parapet when, as his sergeant later recalled, he "[d]ropped his head a little." A couple of men in the trench "asked him why he did not fire" and "if the Germans were coming over," but he was silent. They tugged on him and he collapsed, having been "killed instantly" by a German bullet above his right eye.

Machine-gun fire chewed through Company D's ranks, and it was not long before Lieutenant Butler was struck. "It was like a pack of bumble-bees," he said of the bullet that entered his upper thigh and exited the flesh of his hip. "It felt like being hit with a rock," he noted. "The pain was not much worse." The bullet had not hit any bone, but he was bleeding freely. Butler left his men under the charge of Sgt. Roy Hockenberry and limped the half-mile journey back to a first-aid station, where he was carried to a field hospital. After surgery he made a full recovery, save a slight limp he could never shake. But his platoon sergeant, Roy Hockenberry, a twenty-five-year-old from Pennsylvania, met his end only moments after Butler left. He had just started turning the soil up with his pick when he was shot. "He was hit by at least five bullets, which pierced his chest and stomach," a cor-poral in the platoon reported. Hockenberry fell flat, grabbed at the blood-ied uniform covering his chest, and with his final breaths, he muttered, "I wonder how deep it went in."

Back in Cantigny, flamethrower crews and riflemen of the third wave moved methodically from one pile of rubble to the next, purging cellar after cellar of hiding Germans. Correspondent James Hopper noticed them immedi-ately when he entered the village: "Now I could see into its ruined main street. There was a group of our boys standing there, about a French soldier who held a hose end down into a cellar entrance." Flamethrower operators wore Adrian helmets and long, leather trench coats with bottoms buttoned back at the knees. Strapped to their backs were two metal tanks with hoses extending out arm's length to a nozzle, and slung over their shoulders were sacks full of hand grenades.

Cpl. Daniel Edwards, a machine gunner attached to 2nd Battalion for the attack, watched one in particular, an older man with "a bushy black beard" who calmly puffed on a pipe as he worked. "Placid and methodical, he walked along," Edwards recalled, "smoking his pipe and looking around for dugouts." When the loaded-down Frenchman spotted a cellar, he would lumber to the entrance, yell "*Raus mit ihm!*" down into the darkness, then, as Edwards noted, "trained the nozzle down into the dugout and let her rip. Then he'd take out a grenade, tap it on his tin hat and toss it in."*

Each time, the scorching sound of spraying flames attracted nearby soldiers who would gather around with rifles ready. After the muffled grenade detonation sounded, doughboys waited for survivors to appear. Masses of field gray scurried out with hands up and faces black with soot and smoke. At the tips of bayonets, they were herded into prisoner columns—the captain of the French flamethrower company reported 136 enemy soldiers taken prisoner in this manner. James Hopper rushed to get a close look at the captured enemy. "So many young boys—they looked hardly sixteen," he would write. "So comically bedraggled and piteous, those warriors whom it has been the great care of their masters to make appear dreadful and terrible— they looked so small, their clothes were so wrinkled, their faces so dirty."

Of the prisoners filing back from Cantigny to the American lines, one officer observed "some running but few looking back and all headed for safety, a craven looking lot but they did march well even under such circumstances." One soldier noted, "They were so thin it looked impossible for them to be alive." As American guards escorted the first gray columns back through gun positions of the 6th Field Artillery, Maj. Raymond Austin noticed most "seemed quite young and all were apparently glad to be captured excepting the officers." He gave one German a box of cigarettes, "which seemed to surprise him," and spotted a lieutenant who "couldn't have been more than 17. He must have been a Von-somebody's son. He kept his big helmet down over his forehead and his head bowed."

---

* This phrase translates literally to "Out with him!" If Corporal Edwards recalled the phrase accurately, then the French flamethrower operator was using jumbled German.

But many Germans who had managed to survive the dawn bombardment could not endure the fire bath inflicted by flamethrowers. Cpt. Clarence Huebner watched one German soldier scurry out of a flaming cellar "just as I had seen rabbits in Kansas come out of burning strawstacks [he] ran ten to fifteen yards then fell over singed to death."

Destined to lead the 1st Division in the D-Day landings twenty-six years later, twenty-nine-year-old Clarence R. Huebner commanded Company G, designated the "reserve" company for 2nd Battalion. Two of his platoons were to build a strongpoint out in the orchard while the other two swept forward and back again through the town's rubble-clogged streets with flamethrower teams until all Germans were evicted.

Captain Huebner first learned to shoot as a young boy growing up in Bushton, Kansas, picking off rabbits and squirrels with .22 short ammunition he had acquired by trading in Buffalo bones because, as he would later recall, "We didn't have money in those days." He was educated in a one-room schoolhouse, attended business school in Nebraska, then worked as a stenographer and typist for the Chicago Burlington & Quincy Railroad. But the true course of Huebner's life was not set until he enlisted in the Army at twenty-one. As a soldier in the peacetime military he rapidly bloomed, passing the exam for an officer's commission after six years in the enlisted ranks. Service as a platoon leader south of the border against Pancho Villa's troops filled his absorbent mind and informed his subsequent thinking. America entered the war just as he was completing infantry school at Fort Leavenworth, and he crossed the Atlantic with the division's first convoy as a company commander. Since then, Huebner had displayed an innate capacity to command, and that morning he stood as the battalion's senior company commander—Lieutenant Colonel Maxey's number two.

Maxey was still cleaning out the orchard on the north side of the village, where sporadic firefights continued. The tanks had shut down the German machine-gun nests behind the hedgerow, but the crackle of Mauser shots from a few elusive enemy soldiers continued. Cpl. Boleslaw Suchocki was still lying down on Maxey's order, and through a break in the hedges, Suchocki spotted a figure standing behind a single apple tree about forty yards distant. "I took good aim right through the bushes, fired and saw that something fell to the ground," he would recount.

Tanks plowed through the hedge and Maxey ordered everyone up again and to the other side, where they ran into an enemy fire trench full of dug-outs and scrambling figures in field gray. An automatic-rifleman next to

Suchocki began pouring fire into the trench and was quickly shot down. Most men dropped but Suchocki and a comrade ran toward the trench, and as he would later describe: "I saw that [as] a Dutchman [*sic*] stick his head out over the parapet I shot at him and he rolled into the trench." Overwhelmed, two dozen Germans stood, dropped their weapons, and raised their hands in surrender. Angry doughboys swarmed, shooting and bayoneting them until Maxey ran over and put a stop to the killing. As Suchocki would recall, "[H]e raised his hand and said, 'boys, spare them, take prisoners.'" For "alone killing four enemy snipers under heavy machine-gun and rifle fire," Corporal Suchocki was later awarded the Silver Star.

While machine-gun fire was shredding exposed riflemen as they tried to dig new lines, the big guns of the French artillery were so far keeping German artillery silent. "During this time the counter-battery work of the 10th Corps Artillery," a division artillery officer would note, "was excellent." In just the first hour of the attack, a French battery of 240s had sent a hundred five-hundred-pound shells sailing into enemy gun emplacements, and a single battery of trench mortars had lobbed nearly eight hundred shells into reserve positions to thwart counterattacks.

But as each French gun crew fired their last allotted shells, they pulled down camo netting, yanked up wheel blocks, hitched guns to horses and tractors, and trooped out for a day's journey south to jump into the larger fight brewing near Champagne. "Orders for the withdrawal of more French artillery arrived before the advance had been completed," fretted George Marshall of news that soured the mood in Colonel Ely's command post. The keystone of the second phase of Marshall's plan—holding the position—was counter-battery fire. Every new draft of the attack plan had elevated more and more the role of the supporting French artillery, finally charging it with "neutralization of enemy batteries . . . with all the intensity possible," a job for which the largest remaining guns—the 155s of Sitting Bull's artillery—lacked the reach.

Since Zero Hour, not a single German shell had yet caused an American casualty, but reports quickly poured into Ely's bunker of soldiers up in shallow, exposed, half-dug trenches coming under increasingly crushing shellfire. "The German guns, unsuppressed by our lack of counter-battery fire," Marshall noted, "opened a violent bombardment on the newly captured positions," and, he added, "troubles were coming thick and fast."

———

Up in his observation post, Lt. Daniel Sargent noticed that "everything changed. Our artillery fire had pretty much ceased, but a German artillery fire took its place." In the village ruins and all along new lines being dug by American riflemen, enemy shells "raised a cloud of yellow smoke, similar to that which we had seen raised by the bombardment a few minutes ago."

On the right flank, Lieutenant Sorensen's digging men of Company D, already under punishing machine-gun fire, faced a storm of fire and lead and steel from above. Pvt. Isadore Czarniewski was digging to deepen a shell-crater when a 77mm shell "made a direct hit and mangle[d] up his body," his corporal would report. Fragments tore into the back and both legs of Pvt. James Papineau of Saginaw, Michigan, who was pulled from the scorched dirt and carried to the field hospital, where his wounds would prove mortal three days later.

Another fragment tore into tall, lanky Paul Davis just as he "had started to dig in." His sergeant would report that the twenty-two-year-old private was "instantly killed," and shellfire that followed left no trace of Private Davis's body. Back in Idaho, his mother Eliza's grief over his loss would only deepen with news that his remains could not be found. She found little comfort in learning his name was inscribed in the chapel of the missing, and declined the government's offer to send her on a gold-star mother's trip to France. She preferred them to send her the equivalent funds "so I can buy a nice stone to put in our cemetery to his memory so he will never be forgotten."

Nine years after the battle, a French hunter pulled two reflective metal disks from a field south of Cantigny. He recognized them as American military ID tags, and another two years later, he passed them to a Marine Corps officer who was visiting the battlefield. On each disk was stamped the following: PAUL DAVIS CO D 28 INF. The Marine mailed them to the US Army's Adjutant General Office, and to this day they remain buried in a manila folder deep within the archives of the National Personnel Records Center in St. Louis, Missouri. Eliza Davis passed away in 1947 at the age of seventy-nine, never knowing these small pieces of the final chapter of her son's life had survived the war.

On the far left flank, it had been more than an hour since Lieutenant Newhall was knocked to the dirt by German bullets. "I had been hit three times more and was lying flat on the ground with my helmet over my face," he would later write. "Four of my men had dug a little trench nearby." A couple dozen yards farther forward, the blood filling Pvt. Carl Fey's mouth was gumming up, and his cheek was swollen and throbbing. Both lay stunned and helpless in the open field of shallow wheat stubble as the sun rose warm and bright overhead. But to the occasional Mauser pops and Maxim bursts was added the mounting crashes of enemy artillery fire, and Newhall and Fey lay helpless.

Back in the deeper wheat cover, rifle and automatic-rifle fire from Lieutenant Hawkinson and his dozen men had drawn scattered soldiers to his position, and his group had grown to about forty. Their digging with long-handled shovels "drew hostile artillery and machine-gun fire," it would be reported, and twenty-two-year-old Cpl. Garner Herring of Mississippi, trying to provide covering fire with his rifle from the shallow hole he had dug, was killed instantly by a Maxim bullet. Short on ammunition, Hawkinson sent men low-crawling into the wheat to gather rifles and ammo from the dead, and he sent his platoon sergeant, Keron Ryan of Waterbury, Connecticut, running back through the shellfire to Colonel Ely's command bunker to fix their position and request support. But an enemy machine gun traced the scrambling target, and somewhere in his hunched sprint back across no-man's-land, Sergeant Ryan was shot in the back. He managed to shuffle back to his captain's position and deliver his message before losing consciousness and dying.

A couple hundred yards to the right, Company K's troops continued to dig in under punishing machine-gun fire. "Within the first five minutes 12 of the platoon were killed and four were wounded," Lieutenant Morris would report. His men were digging the rear trench, still shallow and getting more and more crowded with soldiers leaping in for cover. Pvt. Joseph Zboran climbed from the packed trench onto the parapet. "Just as he got on the parapet he was shot with machine-gun bullets in the chest," PFC James Chastain, still down in the trench, would later describe. Chastain asked Zboran if he was hit, he responded, "Yah," then fell back into Chastain's arms, "dying a few seconds later."

Cpl. August Schmidt was trying to direct his squad to spread out and continue digging despite the torrents of bullets strafing the trench top. "The trench being too crowded he crawled out on the parapet," a private would recall. "I told him he better get down, but he paid no attention to me." Schmidt crawled farther down the line and was shot in his shoulder. "I'm hit," he called out, but kept crawling, instructing his men to keep digging. "He had not gone very far when he was again hit with [a] machine-gun bullet, this time penetrating his left side and came out of his right side," the private recounted. "He died instantly."

Officers stood in the open, coordinating the consolidation of the new lines and directing their digging men, oblivious to the storm of gunfire. Lt. Irwin Morris stood behind the rear trench a few yards from Lt. Paul Derrickson, a tall, slender, twenty-six-year-old from Chicago. Both urged their platoons to keep down while digging. A bullet smacked Derrickson in the chest, and he called out, "Morris come over here and fix me up." Morris, who darted over to him, later recounted: "He laid down with his head in his arms, and when I got to him he had passed away." Paul Waples Derrickson was posthumously awarded both the Distinguished Service Cross and Silver Star. In the words of the accompanying citation, "Fearlessly walking up and down his line, he cheered and directed the work of his men until he was killed."

With a distant low rumble followed by the hum of incoming shells, yet another layer of terror was added to the morning crucible. From his position near his platoon's second-line trench, Lieutenant Morris saw his close friend Lt. Milt Drumm run back from an outpost and resume supervising his troops as they dug their front-line trench, when a shell blast knocked Drumm flat. As he had with Derrickson, Morris rushed to Drumm's side, but saw that a chunk of shrapnel had gashed his head open. Drumm "lived only a moment or two" and "made no statements."

Clarence Milton Drumm, twenty-eight, was a farmer from Bigelow, Kansas, who had filled his spare hours playing amateur baseball before America entered the war. He left his fiancée, twenty-five-year-old Linnie Booth, back home with the promise of a wedding on his return. Upon getting word that her beloved Milt was killed in action, Linnie wrote Lieutenant Morris, requesting the details of Milt's death, filled with hope that "he was captured or is in a hospital wounded." "There is no truth that could hurt any more than I feel now," she explained. Morris doubtless wrote Linnie back, pressed into adding truth's finality to her unbearable grief.

In the shallow trench still being dug by Drumm's platoon, PFC Thomas Fursh tended the bullet wound of Pvt. Virgil Varnado, who had been struck by Maxim fire in his left leg while digging. "I opened my 1st aid packet and applied [the] bandage, but he was bleeding freely," Fursh would recount. Before Fursh could apply a tourniquet, shrapnel from a shell blast struck Varnado in his forehead and arm, killing him instantly. Up in the outpost near the haystack, twenty-three-year-old Pvt. Raymond Branshaw, the company barber and "very well-liked by the boys," was firing his Chauchat across the open plain toward the l'Alval Woods when a shell detonated near him. Lt. Si Parker checked on Branshaw, who was clutching a watch. Branshaw exhaled, "Here's my watch, see that my mother gets it," then died. Parker placed the watch in his pocket, and kept it until after the battle, when he ensured it was sent to Branshaw's mother, Clara, back in Wisconsin. But after days of shellfire, Branshaw's body was never seen again, and he is honored in the chapel of the missing.

Satisfied that the task of "mopping up" Germans from the village ruins was nearly complete, Capt. Clarence Huebner went up to the open ground in the orchard, where two platoons of his company and the machine-gun teams under Lt. Welcome Waltz were digging a slit trench for a strongpoint. His soldiers "immediately began to dig in and wire position, with the wire brought up by 5th Platoon, which was used as a carrying party," Huebner would report.

Enemy artillery had been pounding away for a few minutes now, but most shells seemed to be falling out past the hedgerows and along the new lines being dug. From that direction, Captain Huebner noticed two men carrying a tall figure on a stretcher past his position, attended by more commotion than typically accompanied the evacuation of a casualty. The bearers laid down the stretcher on the dirt, and one of them ran to retrieve Huebner, who rushed over to discover that the wounded man was Lieutenant Colonel Maxey. His neck had been flayed open by a shell fragment, and though losing blood rapidly, he had insisted on being taken to Huebner to pass on detailed plans for the battalion's mission.

"When I reached the colonel I found him upon the litter and helpless," Huebner later recounted, "but he could speak and gave me full and complete instructions as to how to carry on." Maxey directed Huebner to grab his map, and on it he showed him the cellar where his command post was being established, pointed out where he wanted defensive positions, and explained how best to man them. "All this time we were under heavy machine-gun fire with an occasional artillery shot," Huebner noted, adding that the bleeding Maxey "showed utter disregard for his own wound and thought of nothing but the success of the operation."

As Maxey was evacuated from the battlefield, Captain Huebner took the map and two runners back through the village then down into the dark cellar, where signalmen had just connected Maxey's field phone to Colonel

Ely's bunker. Beneath the muffled din of the hostile world above, Huebner sent the runners to the new front lines to bring him back a progress report on consolidation. He then picked up the receiver, cranked the ringer, and intoned: "Maxey seriously wounded. I have assumed command. Am constructing a redoubt at 21.15. One strand wire around entire place. Casualties very slight. Will report complete as soon as messengers arrive from line. After completion will report." The time was 9:08 a.m.

Outside Ely's dugout, just a few minutes after getting Captain Huebner's call, Maxey was carried up on a stretcher. It is unclear whether he was still conscious at this point, though the few surviving witness reports suggest that he was not. He was rushed to the first-aid station and then a field hospital, where all efforts to save him failed, and he died of his wounds by nightfall. Robert Jayne Maxey left behind a wife, Lu, and two sons, twelve-

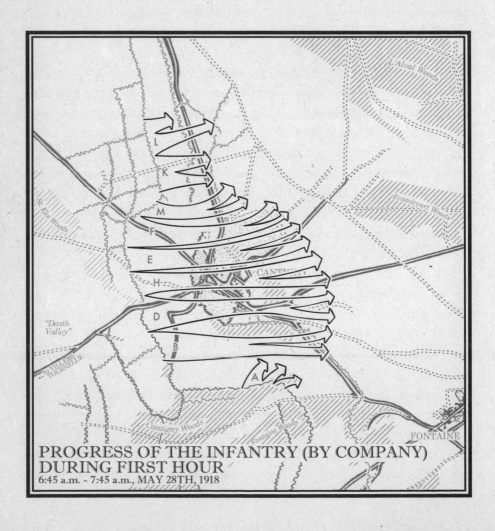

PROGRESS OF THE INFANTRY (BY COMPANY)
DURING FIRST HOUR
6:45 a.m. - 7:45 a.m., MAY 28TH, 1918

year-old Curtis and nine-year-old Ratcliffe. He was posthumously awarded both the Distinguished Service Cross and Silver Star, and after the war he was buried as he wished, in the West Point Cemetery.

On seeing the objectives taken and most enemy strongpoints conquered, the French tank commander, Capt. Emile Noscereau, gave the order to withdraw, and Schneiders lumbered back down the plateau, engines chugging but guns silent. Likewise, their work complete, flamethrower carriers drenched with sweat and blackened with ash and soot trooped out of the village and back through the former no-man's-land. At 9:22 a.m., George Marshall picked up the phone in Ely's bunker and phoned Brigade with a message for Division: "28th Inf. reports everything fine here—all objectives taken—work going on at rapid rate—getting well dug in—strongpoints established. Tanks have returned."

Just over two hours into the battle, with tanks and flamethrower support gone, and with supporting French artillery exiting the sector in a constant stream, the Battle of Cantigny was now America's to win or lose, a cause for which more than one hundred men had so far given their lives. And with the infantry dug in and no longer advancing, dispossessed of the initiative, the longest hours were yet to come.

CHAPTER 12

Ignore the Bullets

In tunics half-unbuttoned and stained with sweat and dirt, the men of Company E's 4th Platoon dug their rear trench at the objective under increasingly heavy shellfire. Having survived the shock of arms in the previous morning's raid, they had launched into this morning's attack wearing the psychological armor of the initiated, and after driving across no-man's-land, over enemy lines and through the village unscathed, many now digging among the hissing bullets and stomping mortar rounds believed themselves immortal.

Their twenty-four-year-old platoon leader, Lt. Wilmer Bodenstab, stood behind them with a Signal Corps photographer who had followed the company through the attack. Bodenstab was "laughing at the photographer who was taking the picture of his men digging in front of him," another officer would report. Abruptly, a shell screamed in and killed them both. The soldiers pulled their limp lieutenant into the trench and laid him gently in the dirt. Bodenstab had died instantly from the concussion, as "there wasn't a mark on his body of any kind."

But most of Capt. Edward Johnston's remaining soldiers still exhibited no fear. Their new trenches sat behind a natural crest of the plateau, giving them some measure of cover from the enemy-infested Framicourt Woods three hundred yards away. With automatic fire and timely flare signals for a supporting barrage, they had repelled a gray mass of enemy infantry that had formed in the wood line just after reaching the objective—an apparent early German counterattack. Now amid heckling Maxim bursts and sporadic shelling, the doughboys worked confidently in the open, digging their trenches deeper, uncoiling barbed wire, and disregarding the danger. "It was nature to ignore the bullets," Lieutenant Wood later recalled, adding that "though many of our men were wounded, dead, or dying, and though the Huns were lying around in heaps, still it seemed more like a dream, a movie show or one of our many practice battles."

Lieutenant Wood's indifference to the peril would cost him a bullet wound to his hip, forcing his evacuation. And this "queer sense of unreality," as he called it, must have also possessed Captain Johnston's only remaining officer, Lt. John Curry. After smoking a cigarette with Johnston while they discussed possible German counterattacks, Curry trotted back over through the wheat chaff to his front-line trench, where his men were connecting shell craters and fortifying their line. As Curry jumped into the trench, immediately his tall, thin figure fell limp against a pile of newly upturned dirt. "I saw his body jerk and then fall back," Captain Johnston would write Curry's sister back in Plains, Pennsylvania. Johnston ran over to him and yelled for a medic, but young Curry stared expressionless at the sky, his blue eyes sparkling cold. "He had been killed instantly and painlessly by a bullet through the brain."

To Company E's left, topography and faulty maps were conspiring to inflict even heavier casualties on Company F. Artillery shorts that had caused so much damage to the company on its push through the orchard continued at the objective, and the commander, thirty-year-old Capt. James Anderson of Summit, Georgia, shot up a fountain of flares and sent runner after runner back through the bombardment to battalion and regimental headquarters imploring division artillery to lengthen the range. But the runners never returned, and given the thick smoke shrouding their position, the flares likely went unseen. High-explosive detonations grew so crushing that the company first sergeant, Samuel Ralston, personally sprinted back through the orchard and across the former no-man's-land to Colonel Ely's dugout. "He was in an exhausted position upon reaching this P.C.," a staff officer noted, "and suffering intense shell shock and exhaustion." Though wounded by a shell fragment, Ralston delivered his message, and the artillery was ordered to "lengthen barrage 200 yards," lifting the shelling off Company F's position.

Back up at the front, the friendly fire on Captain Anderson and his troops was replaced by enemy artillery and machine-gun fire. In contrast to Company E on the right, Company F's new lines sat exposed beyond the crest of the plateau, on ground inclined toward enemy guns with no natural cover. "The slope of the plateau was not where shown on the maps in planning," one officer determined, "and when [the company] tried to move past the geographic crest it came under heavy MG fire and light artillery fire from Bois de L'Alval."

While supervising his platoons as they consolidated their positions, Captain Anderson was knocked down by Maxim fire. Before his men could check on him, a high-explosive shell hit almost directly where he lay, leaving little to bury. Lt. Norborne Gray, a twenty-nine-year-old platoon leader from Louisville, Kentucky, took command of the company, but enemy fire only grew heavier.

Under the zipping bullets and hissing shrapnel, Pvt. Edward White and Cpl. Arthur Wood were both digging their trench deeper "in order to shelter ourselves from shot and shell," White later recounted. A high-explosive round struck and Wood slumped over, "rendered helpless there and then." White checked his corporal, but "did not detect any life in him." Another blast killed both Pvt. Guy Bell and Mech. Arthur Cole. Cole's remains were buried in a shell hole, but nothing remained of Private Bell.

Twenty-year-old Pvt. Earl Simons was also digging when he caught the loudening whistle of an artillery shell. "I heard the shell coming and knew it was going to land somewhere near, if not over me," he later wrote his mom back in Altoona, Pennsylvania. Simons rolled over and braced as the shell exploded and shot fragments into his right thigh, numbing his leg. "It felt like the leg was blown off," he described, "but actually it made only two deep holes." He called for a first-aid man, but none were around. So he lay bleeding in his shallow trench, yelling for a medic and hoping another shell would not find him.

The relentless German guns remained fixated on Company F's exposed lines, and the task of evacuating the wounded was growing unmanageable, testing the limits of decimated ranks of exhausted medics and blister-handed stretcher carriers. "The large number of wounded the first day, and large casualties among the stretcher bearers overtaxed capacity of carrying parties," Colonel Ely would report. And with no way to carry the deadweight of an injured soldier other than aboveground and slowly, it was the most dangerous job on the battlefield. "I had never imagined that carrying a man could be so hard, that a man could be so heavy," noted correspondent James Hopper, who personally pitched in to help. "[I]f medals are given in heaven," he added, "those given stretcher bearers must be wondrously big." One fatigued medic lost both his canteens to the crushing treads of a French tank early in the attack and had to beg other doughboys for sips of water between sprints across the sunny battlefield. "Sure was an awful day," he told his diary that night.

One medical officer, Lt. Eugene Hubbard of Utica, New York, and two privates under his charge, had been busy since Zero Hour removing the wounded from all points of the battlefield. Noticing the heavy shelling and automatic fire strafing Company F's position, Hubbard led his two privates and their stretcher up to the lines just in time to see Lieutenant Gray, the acting company commander, and three members of a Hotchkiss crew get hit by machine-gun fire at an outpost. Hubbard and his team "went to the spot where the wounded men were," one soldier would recount. But as they began to render aid, "another shell exploded in the same place killing all seven men." Only the remains of four could be identified, carried out after dark and buried back near the orchard hedge. But Lieutenant Gray, in just his second hour commanding the company, had disappeared. "There was," one private later reported, "nothing left to bury."

Private Simons, bleeding and slowly draining of strength behind the scant defilade of a shallow trench, decided conditions were getting too hazardous to wait for a stretcher. "[I]n the face of the heavy fire, I crawled out on my hands and knee and made the nearest trench toward the rear," he would write. "As I stopped for a drink from my canteen a shell punched a hole through it and all the water was lost. The canteen saved me from another wound, however." In the trenches nearby, Pvt. Frank Kobin saw a mortar blast flay open the face of his platoon sergeant, Herbert Tobey, and Kobin rushed to carry him back for help. As he lumbered up out of the trench bearing the weight of his sergeant, Kobin felt a wound in his own leg—a shell fragment had torn into his thigh muscle. But he continued, shouldering Tobey all the way back through the orchard, across the plateau, and past the jumping-off trenches.

Arriving at the first-aid station in the side of the chalk cliff past Colonel Ely's bunker, Private Kobin let down his sergeant's body, then limped nearly a mile back up to his company's lines, where he would help evacuate more through the day. For his brave actions, which seem almost routine among the valor of the day, Kobin was awarded the Silver Star. But Sergeant Tobey, forty-six and the longest-serving member of the 28th Infantry to fight in the battle, died of his wounds in the field hospital at 9:15 p.m. that night.

Still crawling on his hands and one good knee, Private Simons also made it to the first-aid station, where medics determined his wound required surgery. "I was taken on a two-wheeled dinky to another station some five hundred yards away," he noted. "Then the ambulance took me. I was operated on at the field hospital and kept there three days." The field hospital, one wounded private later noted, "certainly wasn't a pleasant place that morning." Though set far behind the lines, it was still within range of German artillery, and as one correspondent wrote, "[D]octors work to the noise of bursting shells and exploding shrapnel." One man wounded by rifle fire later described his experience of being evacuated as "a series of more or less painful transfers through first-aid posts, dressing stations and French hospitals, with a Red Cross train and a ninety kilometer ride in an ambulance. I don't think you have ever known the joy of a ninety-K ride on the upper deck of a pitching ambulance. It's an experience. I appreciated the sensations of a pup with a tin can tied to his tail."

German batteries that had begun sounding with a few distant rumbles after the withdrawal of the big French guns now joined in a sustained fusillade, and at 9:45 a.m., George Marshall made his third phone call in fifteen minutes to Brigade reporting enemy shells hitting around Colonel Ely's bunker. Within just a few feet of the dugout, artillery fire killed an artillery liaison sergeant and four privates serving as regimental runners. Nearby, twenty-two-year-old Pvt. Harry Eschbach of Lancaster, Pennsylvania, was "evacuating patients on litters from an advance dressing and aid station to ambulance dressing station" through Death Valley when, a fellow private observed, he "was killed by the explosion of a shell." With mortar rounds whirring into the valley, nobody else risked carrying the dead to the division cemetery back in Villers-Tournelle, so bodies began stacking up under blankets outside the first-aid station near Ely's dugout.

Up at his observation post, Lieutenant Sargent—who just minutes before had felt secure enough to stand—now found the onslaught so overwhelming that he dropped and stretched "as close to the ground as possible." A mortar round hit his foxhole and left him rattled for a few seconds. "A splinter of it tore into my haversack, pierced my canteen of water, causing the water to run out and did not arrive at my ribs only because it was halted by the metal case of my Gillette safety razor on which it made a memorable dent."

In the Saint-Eloi Woods behind the empty jumping-off trenches, twenty-two-year-old Cpl. Clifford Manchester of New Jersey and his four-man team were firing a Hotchkiss at a high angle over the heads of the distant front-line infantry. Their machine gun was one of sixty-four assigned by Marshall to provide "flank protection" for the attack. Crews at each gun had been ripping through box after box of ammo strips since Zero Hour, peppering "probable enemy strong points" in wood lines a mile distant. The machine-gun barrage was appreciated by the riflemen digging up at the objective, especially after the standing artillery barrage had ended. Captain Huebner noted it was "well worthwhile if only for the moral effect it had."

But these machine-gun nests were spotted and relayed back to enemy batteries by enemy pilots, and since the single French observation plane had landed roughly an hour into the attack, the Germans had unopposed dominance of the skies. One officer noted that enemy planes "kept together and travelled in a large circle, first swinging over our position, then back over their own lines," where they transmitted wireless reports and dropped weighted messages—typically scribbled maps of American gun positions. "I would like to state here that there is hardly anything so depressing to troops as to see the sky filled with enemy planes and none of yours in sight," he added. For the doughboys on the ground, the constant buzzing above them was unnerving. One captain later recounted the "very active" enemy planes "flying close to the ground at times," and though some troops fired up at the passing aircraft, "this apparently failed to do them any harm."

Guided by such unobstructed aerial observation, enemy shells stomped closer to the Hotchkiss nests, but crews remained at their guns, firing as they braced at the whistle of each incoming. A single shell hit directly in the shallow fire trench of Corporal Manchester's crew, killing all five in a single blast. Nearby, in charge of another gun, Cpl. Herman Evans was "struck by a shell splinter in the head and back," his sergeant would report. "He died instantly." PFC Ivan Stringer took charge of the crew, but in just fifteen more minutes, he was also killed. "He was holding his watch timing the fire of his gun when struck by fragments of a high-explosive shell and killed instantly." Steel fragments also killed Pvt. Barney Liles as he fed ammunition into his Hotchkiss. Stringer, Evans, and Liles would each posthumously earn the Silver Star. Two dozen more members of their company would live to receive the same medal, each for staying at their guns throughout the day, hour after hour, under punishing shellfire.

Underneath one of the low-flying planes was Lt. George Stein, scampering back and forth among four machine-gun teams under his charge. His German-immigrant parents had died when he was young, and he was taken in by a foster family in Mechanicsburg, Pennsylvania, who taught him to speak English. He had volunteered for the first round of officer training, and after his recent promotion to first lieutenant, Stein wrote his foster father that he prayed "to God that whatever occasion may arise that I—in my position, do not jeopardize one single life of our men." As Stein encouraged his Hotchkiss crews to ignore the buzzing airplane and crashing shellfire, the enemy pilot dipped low and dropped a "grass-cutter" bomb which detonated in Stein's face, fracturing his skull and killing him instantly. Three years after the war, his body was returned to Mechanicsburg for burial, the first of three doughboys who would be killed by enemy planes through the course of the battle.

Back up on a hilltop with the guns of the 7th Field Artillery, Lt. "Doc" Bedsole's battery of 75s had also been spotted by an enemy pilot and shellfire began dicing his crews to pieces. Pvt. Abe Kauffman of Philadelphia lost a finger but still stayed at his gun, earning the Distinguished Service Cross for firing "until so severely wounded as to be unable to assist in serving his piece." The plane returned, circling above and wiring back adjustments for German artillery. Cpl. John Flint ran to a nearby machine gun and took the plane under fire. The rest of the crew took cover, but Flint stayed at the Hotchkiss, shooting up at the circling plane "until severely wounded." Seeing this, Lieutenant Bedsole rushed out from his own trench and into "heavy shell fire" to evacuate Flint to a field hospital, where he would recover.

Back up at the battle's edge, discernable lines now linked shell crater to shell crater, loosely connecting the infantry along a one-and-a-half-mile-long front bulging around the east side of Cantigny. Gaps still existed, and clusters of sweaty troops, exhausted from digging, kneeled against parapets of turned earth under the late-morning sun, bunched in shell holes that provided only scant security from enemy fire. German artillery gunners stalked their prey, hurling shell after shell toward the new American lines, shifting from one cluster of khaki to another and marching the booming footfall back and forth among doughboys helpless to do anything but aim their rifles at the distant, enemy-infested wood lines—sobbing, praying, and cringing with each detonation.

Worried the Germans were due to counterattack, Company K's Captain Mosher wanted another automatic-rifle outpost established, so he sent twenty-six-year-old Pvt. Jesse Gillespie of South Carolina and five others forward from the trenches. "We went forward about seventy-five yards," Gillespie noted, "established ourselves in two adjoining shell holes that offered a measure of protection, and began filling bags with dirt to shield us somewhat from the enemy fire. In an hour or so, two of our men had been picked off by the Germans."

Around 10:00 a.m., enemy shellfire again picked up, this time concentrated mainly on the outposts. Captain Mosher ran out from the trenches to check on the men and, noticing a wounded private in a shell crater, he dragged him "under heavy fire, back to a place of safety," Lt. John Mays observed. As his soldiers hunched for cover, Mosher continued "walking from one place to another cheering his men," Cpl. Marshall Sanderford later recounted. But with a deafening smash and zing of steel, Mosher fell. A shell fragment had sliced through his lower neck, partially severing it from his shoulder. "He was killed instantly," Corporal Sanderford noted. Lieutenant Mays was close enough to catch Mosher when he fell. "I am glad I was there to have my old friend and captain die in my arms," he would write.

Returning to his platoon's trench, Lieutenant Mays could see Lieutenant Parker up at the haystack outpost, still holding his dozen-man team together "with great efficiency and coolness in the face of deadly enfilading fire and machine-gun fire." Captain Mosher, just minutes before he was killed, had commented on Parker's "marked gallantry under the most difficult conditions," conditions that were getting no better.

Near another of Company K's outposts, Pvt. Emory Smith still lay bleeding where he had been wounded over an hour earlier. "I fell where I lay and was bleeding profusely," he later wrote. "I had to lay there all day and they thought I was dying." In the fresh trenches behind him, his fellow doughboys peeked over the parapets between shell blasts, but distant rifle pops and zipping bullets kept them mindful of an invisible but watching enemy. Aiming his rifle over the top, Sgt. Thomas Peden of Gray Court, South Carolina, was "hit in the neck by a sniper's bullet," the company bugler, William Turner of Maine, would report. "He lived about five minutes and told me before dying not to stay around him for fear I might get killed by the same sniper." In his final moments, Sergeant Peden muttered "something about writing," Turner recounted, "but I could not understand him as he was about breathing his last." Another sniper's bullet zipped in and popped Cpl. Nathan Korngold, a nineteen-year-old immigrant from Russia, in the forehead. "He was conscious about thirty seconds," a comrade noted. "His last words were, 'O Mother,' dying immediately afterwards."

Up at the third outpost Captain Mosher had established, Private Gillespie and two surviving soldiers were stacking dirt bags into a higher parapet when a high-explosive mortar round struck beside them, and shell fragments hit Gillespie and one of the others. "A good sized piece of the metal had gone through my right leg breaking it about six inches above the knee," Gillespie later described, adding that his "left leg was slightly injured, and the right hand and wrist were shattered by another fragment of shell that had ploughed its way through." Gillespie used a bootlace to cinch a tourniquet around his leg, and a fellow private bandaged his wrist. But machine-gun and rifle fire continued strafing their position, and in minutes, that private was also killed. Now in the small dirt foxhole, of the six men sent forward by Mosher, only two—Pvt. Jesse Gillespie and his buddy nineteen-year-old Pvt. Willie Drager, also badly wounded—remained alive.

Beyond the gap that remained to the right, the troops of Lt. Gerald Tyler's two-platoon wide front of Company M were digging their second new trench of the morning. The runner Tyler had sent to the right to make contact with Company F returned to tell him "that Captain Anderson and all other officers of the company had been killed and that he could not find anybody in command." Tyler scrambled from one end to the other posting automatic rifles to cover the company's flanks. "By this time machine-gun bullets were filling the air and snipers were active," he wrote home. Running up the edge of the trench, he was shot in his right thigh and knocked down. "It was the sniper's bullet," he noted. "I crawled to the hole a couple of men were digging and not a minute too soon for the Huns played a machine-gun right over the top of it nearly all day."

With the lone officer in Company M's lonely trench now hobbled by an enemy bullet, Cpl. Louis Abend, twenty-three and a four-and-a-half-year Regular Army veteran from Brooklyn, took charge of the platoons even as sniper, machine-gun, and artillery fire pummeled their line. Worried about counterattacks, Abend coaxed the men up to the parapet with rifles pointed over the top, putting fire on the distant Framicourt Woods. One of them was twenty-five-year-old Pvt. Archie Lackshire, a short, blond-haired, mail truck driver from Sturgeon Bay, Wisconsin. Under the overwhelming clamor of shell and Maxim fire, Lackshire's grip on his Springfield loosened, his head drooped, and he slumped back into the trench. He was "hit by a sniper," Corporal Abend noted, and "died about six hours later," one year to the day after enlisting with his brother, who was also serving in

France. His brother would survive the war, after which, at their single mother Birdie's request, Archie's body would be shipped home for burial in his hometown's Bayside Cemetery.

Abend also saw twenty-seven-year-old Pvt. Emery Dean, a two-year Army veteran from West Virginia, "slim, very quiet, dry and very well liked," fall just feet from the trench while running back from an outpost to retrieve more ammunition. Drilled by machine-gun bullets, he "died instantly." With enemy fire too heavy for his fellow soldiers to risk retrieving him, Private Dean lay lifeless in front of the parapet, cruelly tossed and rolled by the stomps of mortar rounds until after nightfall when his comrades finally pulled in his body.

About one hundred yards behind Lieutenant Tyler's two platoons, amid shell-torn rows of broken marble headstone in what was once the small village cemetery, a Company I platoon and six machine-gun teams worked to fortify their strongpoint. Pvt. Sam Ervin had already made two more trips back across no-man's-land with his team, hauling out the wounded and returning with boxes of ammunition and pickets for barbed wire. "The work of this carrying party was particularly commendable due principally to the courage and perseverance of Pvt. Ervin who continued carrying under heavy fire," the company commander would report.

Plastered by shot and shell, Ervin's dozen-man team had been halved by casualties—one killed and six wounded by midmorning. On a third trip back through the open to retrieve more ammo, they entered a patch of tall grass, where one of them tripped on a German soldier, lying flat with a broken arm. "And so I got down and took a pasteboard box or something he had there and a stick and tried to tie his arm up," Ervin noted. The wounded man was babbling nervously, and one of Ervin's men translated. Apparently he thought they were British ("He refused to believe they were Americans because, he said, German submarines would not permit them to get across the Atlantic," Ervin's biographer would explain). A distant German machine gun, apparently having traced their movements into the plateau, opened fire and a bullet speared clear through Ervin's left foot. Embarrassed, the German apologetically muttered, *"Wir sind verdammte Schweine"* (We are damned swine). Ervin hobbled back beyond the old front lines and to the first-aid station, then was taken to a hospital, where he would recover and rejoin his company within the month. For "exceptional courage and perseverance" in making "several trips from the rear to the front until wounded," Sam Ervin was awarded the Silver Star.

For the Germans, every minute that passed without launching a counterattack was another minute the Americans used to dig deeper, position their automatics and strongpoints better, and ensconce themselves firmer. But because their combat battalions in the village had been mostly killed or captured, neither the 271st or 272nd German Reserve Infantry Regiments had sufficient manpower nearby to counterattack in force immediately. Their rest battalions were eight miles away and had just been notified to return to reserve positions—a march that would take them until early afternoon. Until these eight infantry companies arrived and organized a push-back to their old lines, the Germans were leaning on their artillery and automatics to weaken the doughboys in between loosely devised infantry "counterstrokes." Two reserve companies of the 272nd had trooped out of the l'Alval and Framicourt woods about an hour into the attack toward the new lines of Companies E and F, but were driven back handily by the doughboys' small-arms fire and Summerall's guns. Now the reserve battalion of the 271st down in the Fontaine Woods on the south end of the village prepared a "counterstroke" of their own, this one planned with artillery support, and it was Lieutenant Sorensen's Company D that would face the brunt of it.

Sorensen's four platoons had suffered ten killed and twice more wounded to shot and shell in just the first few minutes of digging, but as Sorensen would report, "action had quieted down considerably by ten a.m." Down two officers to machine-gun fire, the remaining platoon leaders still had their troops deepening their ditches. Parts of the trenches, particularly up in the first line, where men under constant fire had been forced most of the morning into deep shell holes for cover, had not yet been completed. Lieutenants John Church and Ross Gahring were coaxing their two front-line platoons up out of their craters to dig connecting lines, and to extend rightward for a connection with Company B and leftward with Company H when a curtain of enemy artillery descended in front of them.

"'[A] big one' exploded within a yard of me blew me about 10 ft.," Lieutenant Church would write home. "God was with me and was not badly hurt." He landed back behind his platoon's trench, unconscious. As the drumfire continued, Church came to, and in actions for which he would be awarded the Distinguished Service Cross, "staggered forward as soon as he regained consciousness and insisted on resuming command, thereby giving a striking example of fortitude to his men." But one of the shards had sliced his forehead, and under the daze of a concussion and with blood dripping into his eye, he too was forced to leave the battlefield.

Steel chunks from another shell blast hit Lieutenant Gahring in his left hip, spun him around, and knocked him to the dirt. Lying dazed and defenseless, six machine-gun bullets tore into his legs before his platoon sergeant could pull him back into a shell crater for safety. Gahring lay bleeding in the dirt, refusing evacuation until nightfall, he too "giving a striking example of fortitude to his men," as his Distinguished Service Cross citation would read. Machine-gun fire lashed the crater lip above him, and he yelled for his platoon—bunched in the holes on either side of him—to fix bayonets and stand prepared to defend against what might be a German counterattack. A bullet from one of the Maxim sweeps pierced the heart of Pvt. William Phillips, a draftee out of West Virginia in just his second day with the company, killing him instantly. Another one zipped in just under Pvt. Edward Joholski's helmet, nicking his skull and embedding in his scalp. Joholski was evacuated to a field hospital, where the bullet was removed, after which he made a full recovery.

Lieutenant Sorensen was down to one able-bodied officer, the leader of 3rd Platoon, Lt. Max Buchanan. The thirty-seven-year-old Brockton, Massachusetts, native had served in the Regular Army since 1899, seeing action in the Philippines and on the Mexican border before he earned his commission and sailed to France with the 1st Division. The nineteen-year-veteran gauged the uptick in enemy fire as an omen of impending counterattack, and he ran back and forth encouraging his soldiers in their second-line trench—now on average three feet deep along its length—to dig deeper and fill sandbags faster.

Lieutenant Sorensen also anticipated a German attack and walked from his command post in the brick ruins on the village edge up to Buchanan's platoon to check on the lines, which he found "in good condition." Over the loudening thunder of shellfire, Sorensen yelled orders "in regards to action to be taken in case of enemy counterattack" to Buchanan, who was standing a few yards away with one of his soldiers, Pvt. Frank Beck. Bunched in their shallow trench, Buchanan's men could hear the sharp whistle of an incoming. "We were digging in when we heard the shell coming," the platoon sergeant would report, "we all dropped down, but the shell hit between Lt. Buchanan and Beck, killing both of them instantly."

The round detonated at head level, and the steel fragments took the heads off both men.

Sorensen, his face covered "with a thick poultice of blood and brains" of his last lieutenant, was correct about a German counterattack. A few minutes earlier, Major Roosevelt's troops with the 26th Infantry Regiment manning the south end of the sector had spotted "about 100 men marching on road" toward the Fontaine Woods. The message was relayed back to General Summerall's headquarters, where word had just arrived from a runner that the German machine guns in Fontaine were "doing us more harm than ever." Orders were phoned to batteries of the 5th Field Artillery to hit the wood line with gas and high-explosive shells.

Company's D's doughboys were driven down into cover as the field-gray shapes of German infantry began emerging from the wood line behind a loosely coordinated covering barrage of artillery and Maxims. "When the Germans started their counterattack, we all took cover in shell holes from the German barrage," Cpl. Ira Huddleston later recounted. With no platoon leaders left, NCOs took charge, and Huddleston noted that his platoon sergeant, John Pooler, was "trying to keep the other men down in holes, when he was struck by a machine-gun bullet killing him instantly."

Another platoon sergeant, James Whalen, led two automatic-riflemen forward fifty yards to a shell hole, where they were able to put down some automatic fire on the attackers. Enemy machine-gun bullets pelted the crater, wounding Sergeant Whalen, who kept firing on the approaching Germans until another sweep of Maxim fire seriously wounded one of his gunners. Whalen picked his wounded man up and "carried him through heavy machine-gun fire to the rear" to safety, but before reaching cover, Whalen was shot again. He made it into the trench with his wounded comrade, where both were evacuated to a field hospital and made full recoveries.

Alone out in a shell crater with his rifle, Pvt. Jerome Angell had been providing covering fire for the company's digging since arriving at the objective. Popping through one five-round clip after another, he sniped approaching Germans until a whiz-bang made "a direct hit," killing him "instantly." In his posthumous Silver Star citation, he was credited with killing "seven of the enemy before he, himself, was killed." And more covering fire came from the German Maxim captured earlier back in the village—three soldiers dragged it up to a shell hole and turned its lethal typewriter racket back on the Germans until running out of ammunition.

Up in the woods, gas shells fired by the 5th Artillery pinged through the treetop canopy, silencing the German Maxims. Only the chatter bursts of Chauchats and popping of Springfields filled the air until 179 high-explosive shells hurled by American 155s tore into the wood line in splashes of orange flame, sending enemy attackers retreating back through the woods. Reportedly, the Germans "dispersed" and "took to the fields to the south at the double time."

The first series of enemy counterattacks, isolated and uncoordinated, had failed, undone by the 1st Division's combined arms. The doughboys, according to German records, were "too combat strong" by the time of the counterstrokes. By noon, with rest and reserve battalions marching toward the front to launch an operation to retake Cantigny, the German 18th Army ordered "concentrated fire" to be placed on their American adversaries, and reported, "A counterattack is under preparation."

For the time being, under a hot noon sun, the doughboys were still holding. The overwhelming blueness of the spring sky was filled with buzzing biplanes and clouded by a tempest of German lead and steel, portending an enemy hell-bent on retaking the high ground of their prized village. Another far stronger counterattack was surely coming, but all along the 1st Division's new front lines, the swift decisions of company commanders, platoon leaders, and NCOs were joining to tighten their grip on a narrow but glaring purchase of enemy territory. Whether covering unexpected open flanks with automatic fire, sending Germans into full flight with the fire of captured Maxims, or employing machine-gun teams to provide temporary cover for infantry advancing through a ravine, improvisation was proving a vital weapon. Among corporals and sergeants thrust by enemy fire into command of platoons or whole companies, or lieutenants finding themselves and their platoons isolated and surrounded only by smoke and confusion, there was no more reliance on the battle plan. As General Pershing had told these young officers six weeks earlier, "[T]he main reliance after all must be upon your own determination, upon the aggressiveness of your men, upon their stamina, upon their character and upon their will to win."

CHAPTER 13

Half Crazy, Temporarily Insane

Down in Division Headquarters, orderlies gulped coffee and puffed cigarettes as they transcribed phone messages from the front. General Summerall's staff officers phoned battery groups with lists of coordinates where German troops were reported gathering, or where barrage flare signals had been observed. Until the noon hour, nearly all battlefield news reaching General Bullard was encouraging, with heartening reports that "[a]ll objectives were taken" and that morning German counterattacks had been repelled, and a late-morning call from George Marshall describing "everything quiet on front."

But still dislodged from the prized centerpiece of the sector, the mood at the headquarters of the German 82nd Reserve Division was decidedly less assured. Since receiving word just before 8:00 a.m. that "Cantigny is occupied by the enemy," all efforts had been directed toward retaking the village. The 2nd, 3rd, and 4th Companies of the 272nd Reserve Infantry Regiment, which had held positions in Cantigny until relieved in the hours after midnight, had just dropped their gear for rest after an eight-mile march back to rest billets when, at 8:20 a.m., word came that the Americans had captured the village and they were to remain awake on standby. By 9:30 a.m., after the failure of the first counterstroke, these exhausted troops were ordered to march back to the front for a counterattack. Ordered separately from rest billets six miles away, four companies of the 271st were also marching toward the front to join the effort. The marshaling of manpower would take a few hours, and coordination with neighboring units and corps artillery would take longer still. So the division commander ordered the counterattack for late afternoon. Until then, the "concentrated fire" ordered by Division would pound away at the Americans.

At the noon hour, George Marshall noted that a "very heavy enemy shelling began on our new first line, together with terrific machine-gun fire."

For the next seventy hours, doughboys hunkered in fresh trenches were to be subjected to what the Division History would later call a "terrific blasting" of enemy fire.

"Along in the afternoon the enemy began to shell us pretty heavily," Lt. Richard Newhall noted. Sprawled helpless and bleeding in shallow wheat chaff under an unforgiving sun, the thin, bespectacled platoon leader's helmet covered his face as he grew ever weaker, "longing for unconsciousness." Earlier, one of his men had tried to evacuate him, but when lifted, Newhall had "fainted with pain." Now as high-explosive shells detonated all around him, he hoped only to be "killed and not merely badly wounded." One round hit the slit trench a few yards away, killing a corporal. Though fate spared Newhall a direct hit, he was "repeatedly showered with loose dirt," and a rock hurled out by one detonation struck him with such force it broke his collarbone. "Another time a tiny splinter hit me in the head," he later recounted, "but it was spent and merely dazed me for a minute."

A couple hundred yards away, privates Jesse Gillespie and Willie Drager lay weak and wounded in their wrecked outpost, whimpering for water and praying the German guns would not shift back to the blackened, blood-spattered dirt of their lonely shell crater. "Every once in a while I would loosen the tourniquet a short time to allow some circulation," Gillespie noted, "and then tighten it again not to lose more blood."

Behind them in the company's trenches, amid the bodies of their captain, two lieutenants, and more than a dozen other fallen comrades, the surviving platoon leaders worked to keep their sweating, exhausted, thirsty troops alert to guard their lines. "Heavy shelling commenced at this time," Lt. John Mays noted. "Large sections of the trench were continually blown in and connections broken." The smoke was too thick for flare signals, but near Mays was the battalion's famed "ragtime bugler," Pvt. Joe Mayuiers, who was serving at the front as a company runner. Mays sent Mayuiers running back with a barrage message to pass on to the artillery, but he made it only a few strides before a sniper's bullet pierced his heart. "He called out 'Oh-la-la' and fell over dead," a nearby private would report.

Up in the orchard, members of the four Hotchkiss teams under Lieutenant Waltz stood in the strongpoint they had spent the morning hours constructing. Engineers had hauled rolls of barbed wire forward and surrounded the position, and each of the four ends of the cross-shaped slit trench was covered by a machine gun. The strongpoint was fortified for enemy attack from any side except above.

Through the creeping moments of the afternoon, each time long-range German artillery fired—sounding like a heavy door slamming—Lieutenant Waltz would watch the sky for shells. "We could look up out of our holes and see them flopping lazily in the air," he noted, adding they were "whistling a very unwelcome tune." The 8.3-inch wide, 250-pound mortar shells were filled with a high-explosive charge and lead shrapnel. The men called them "Ashcans." "They came over so slowly that one, in looking up at them in an endeavor to gauge their line of drift, had too much time for reflection and this condition made their presence very undesirable," Waltz later recalled. "One of these bombs dropped exceedingly close to my hole and the concussion seemed to create a vacuum within the hole," he noted. "It also pulled all the air out of my lungs and I had to stand up, lean over and gasp for my breath. My heart ached for some time after that. The terrific concussion had almost finished me."

Even more unnerving were German biplanes, and at least a half dozen cut figure eights above the orchard strongpoint. Waltz figured they "stood out like a lighthouse in a storm" from above, and periodically a lone plane would swoop down, tilt its nose forward, and strafe the shallow slit trench with fire from its forward machine guns. At one point, Waltz saw the plane dip so low "it looked as though he was going to bury himself in the first fox hole on our left flank." Soldiers stood defiantly and fired their rifles at the plane's metal undercarriage, making "sparks fly," but doing little damage.

Back in the cemetery strongpoint, marble chunks of shattered headstones danced to the enemy artillery's "unwelcome tune" as 77mm whiz-bangs struck at Hotchkiss teams while they fired torrents of bullets into the distant wood lines. One of these machine gunners was big, husky Pvt. Gaspare Ventimiglia, an Italian immigrant and the only man in the company strong enough to carry two full boxes of ammunition to the front. "I remember when he joined up," his buddy Pvt. Webb LaPointe recalled, "he could ride the mules in [the] company anyone else in the company could not ride." But at his Hotchkiss, a German shell hit, and Ventimiglia "disappeared." Private LaPointe would report that the "shell exploded and buried him." Another crew member, nineteen-year-old Pvt. George Hutchins, took over the gun and resumed firing, but the dialed-in German gunners sent another well-aimed shell into the same blast hole, killing Hutchins instantly. His right arm and left leg were blown off, and his jaw and lower face were "completely shot away," but his remains were recovered and eventually shipped home for burial in Hickman, Kentucky. Although the men dug to unearth Private Ventimiglia, no trace could be found, and he is honored on the tablets of the missing.

South of the village, the shellfire was equally relentless and even more accurate, zeroed in on the American lines with adjustments transmitted from enemy planes circling above. The regimental machine-gun company commander, Capt. Adelbert Stewart, found a shell hole where he could establish a small command post with his runner, whom he sent to check the ammunition status of one of his machine-gun squads. "Shortly after entering shell-crater the enemy airplanes were so active that I thought it not advisable to do digging," he noted, "so [I] laid quiet, the shelling being extremely heavy around there." Having not eaten since the night before, Stewart reached into his pack and opened one of his two meat rations, regaining strength and hoping a German shell would not find him.

Still digging deeper in trenches down in the ravine just out of the shade of the Cantigny Woods were two of Lieutenant Anderson's Company A platoons. Pvt. Billie McCombs of New Castle, Pennsylvania, who had most feared "losing our nerve" back at Zero Hour, found holding his low-ground position under shellfire to be the hardest part of the fight. "Going over the top is not so bad as sitting in a dug-out while the enemy is bombarding," he noted. "It racks a fellow's nerve to know that the enemy is on the offensive and you have to sit still and take it." Beside him, Pvt. James Smith of Sargent, Georgia, was thrown clear out of the trench by a mortar blast, but was still alive. With blood trickling from steel puncture wounds to his back and shoulder, Smith was evacuated to a field hospital, where he would die the next day. "I'll be damned if I see any fun in lying in a ditch watching your friends going higher than a kite [and] never know a second ahead but it's your turn next," Private McCombs wrote home. "Going over the top is play compared with this."

Back in Colonel Ely's bunker, a morning filled with triumphant reports of success was replaced by an afternoon of alarming casualty numbers and urgent calls from the front lines for water and ammunition. A runner from 1st Battalion arrived with a message reporting 30 percent casualties to both Companies B and D, who "will have to be reinforced or relieved." A few minutes later, Captain Huebner reported that 2nd Battalion "has had three officers killed and 2 wounded about 80 killed, wounded, or missing." And after a few more minutes, from 3rd Battalion came a message forwarded from Company K: "Capt. Mosher and Lt. Drumm have been killed. The casualties of the company are about 30%. We are digging in, but it would be mighty hard to check a counterattack. Can this company be relieved tonight? If not, strong support."

At 2:17 p.m., Colonel Ely picked up his field phone with a message for Division. He reported one company in his right battalion had lost all its officers and a third of its men, another two officers and a third of its men; that the commanding officer of his center battalion was wounded and eighty men killed or wounded; and in his left battalion the casualties were "not much less." Ely stopped short of asking for relief, but closed with a grim forecast: "Casualties continue from m.g. and shell fire and by morning will be serious." Hearing these reports of "extremely heavy losses in officers and men," George Marshall concluded "that resistance against a strong counterattack was practically impossible."

A strong counterattack was at that moment being planned by the German 82nd Reserve Division. The infantry assault would consist of the rest and support battalions of the 271st and 272nd Reserve Infantry Regiments, along with surviving remnants of the combat companies driven from Cantigny's front lines. To this force, Corps added a company of the 270th Reserve Infantry Regiment to the north and two companies of the 83rd to the south. Each infantry company averaged about fifty men and ten NCOs led by a single officer. All told, the attack force would total just over 1,000 riflemen, half attacking from the l'Alval and Framicourt woods to the northeast and east and half from the Fontaine Woods to the southeast. Supporting this would be artillery from three divisions, the 82nd Reserve Division and the ones to the north and south. These guns would fire a brief preparatory bombardment on the American troops in their new lines as well as a standing barrage on their former lines to prevent reinforcement.

Initially, the infantry attack was scheduled for 5:00 p.m., but with delays in getting the scattered companies of exhausted soldiers into position and coordination issues caused by lack of centralized control, it was delayed to 5:45. Throughout the afternoon, reports reached Colonel Ely's command bunker from neighboring units and observation posts of enemy troops marching or concentrating behind the wood lines, whole companies here and small groups of two or three men there. Coordinates were phoned back to artillery batteries and supporting machine-gun crews, and massed fire was directed on each location, further hampering German efforts at organizing for the assault. Although the twenty infantry companies from four different regiments were not yet in place—most with officers who did not yet even know of the start time of the planned counterattack—the German artillery still commenced its bombardment at 5:00 sharp, having not received word of the forty-five-minute delay.

German batteries that had spent the afternoon hours zeroing their large howitzers on the strongpoints in the cemetery and orchard now united in hurling well-aimed mortar shells into their targets. In their orchard strongpoint, Lieutenant Waltz's men could hear a salvo of ashcans whooshing toward them. "This was the high-angle stuff that the foxhole could not protect one from," Waltz noted. Soldiers dove to the dirt floor, but it did little good. A single shell wiped out Cpl. Bernard Gill and his entire gun crew. The only survivor, Pvt. Sandusky Lynch of Marion, Kentucky, who turned twenty-one the day before, lay breathing but unconscious on the trench floor, blood covering his head. He was evacuated to the field hospital, but shell fragments had cracked his skull, and he would pass quietly from his wounds three days later, having never regained consciousness.

A shell blast left nothing but a pile of dirt where Pvt. Emmett Smith of Montana had been, and it instantly killed PFC Marion Thompson, leaving his comrades crammed in the ditch with his "badly mutilated" remains throughout the bombardment. But grisliest of all was the fate of twenty-four-year-old Pvt. Cyrus Adcox, the third of nine children from a farming family in Rockfish, North Carolina. Mortar fragments ripped off his right shoulder, left arm, left leg below the knee, and shattered his right leg. Without any head wounds, he died hard, screaming in agony and sliding into shock. Stretcher bearers evacuated him, and his remaining limbs were such a mess of blood and shredded khaki that his sergeant presumed "both arms and legs were torn away." Improbably, Private Adcox somehow clung to life long enough to make it to the first-aid station, where his protracted death throes faded and he finally succumbed to his wounds.

The three surviving Company K officers struggled to keep their troops in position under a torrent of steel that plastered nearly every inch of dirt. Privates Arnold Kuester and Teodore Miglas both disappeared in a spray of web gear, khaki twill, and crimson. "The enemy barrage had cut us off and there were only 12 survivors," Lieutenant Mays would report of his platoon. Survivors shriveled in fetal bunches under their helmets, each blast eating at their psyches until a single word became audible up and down the line: "Withdraw." It was a welcome directive for men caught in the killing field all day, many of whom were close to breaking.

The "order" persisted, with growing emphasis in desperate tones, man to man. "Lieutenant says to withdraw." No one asked what lieutenant, and possibly no one wanted to know a name, or what many suspected was the truth: that it was a phantom order, constructed fiction, a product of overstretched nerves and the spreading condition on the battlefield Colonel Ely would later describe as "half crazy, temporarily insane."

"[T]he order was passed down from the right that the company was to retire to the support trench," platoon leader Lt. John Mays later reported. "I had a non-commissioned officer confirm this order and he said that it had been passed down from the right of the sector. He could not tell from whom the order came." Throughout the other front-line platoon led by Lieutenant Si Parker, the rumor spread that a "Lieutenant Ward" had given the order. "Not knowing who Lieut. Ward was or with what authority he gave such an order," Parker later reported, "I ordered my men to stand fast and stand guard for an approach of the enemy." He then ran through the shellfire to the right, finding Lt. Irwin Morris.

Morris had already noticed "some of the troops on my left going back into the original front line" behind him. Parker arrived in a hunched scamper and Morris said they should "hold on" no matter what the rest of the company did. Parker agreed. "I consulted him and we decided to remain in position until something more serious happened or we had the proper authority to withdraw." But then the troops to the right fell back, leaving Morris with "five men, three of whom were wounded." And when Parker returned to his platoon's trench, he "found that someone had led the company to the rear, without calling in the outposts." He ran up to the outposts, each packed with soldiers "discharging their duties faithfully, with some dead and some wounded" in improvised shell craters "in full view of the enemy." Parker explained that the entire company had withdrawn, but he was going "to find it and bring it back into the original position." He ordered the men "to hold out until the wounded were evacuated," and in case of enemy attack, "not to abandon the wounded until it was impossible to save them without all being captured." Then he and Morris and a handful of men ran back three hundred yards to the old front trenches and reported to their battalion commander.

From his strongpoint, Lieutenant Waltz could see the German shells "plow into our line of resistance just to my left front and it wasn't long before a wave of men started back in groups." The momentum of retreat snowballed, and the trickle of men to the rear became a pell-mell rush back across former no-man's-land away from the shellfire. "Those who were able to do so out-ran the barrage and got back to our lines safely," wrote Pvt. Emory Smith, still struggling with a bullet wound to his chest. "Although badly wounded I managed to get to my feet and run with the rest of the men."

Troops ran back to their old trenches, where one lone officer ran forward to try to stem the tide of retreat and turn the men around: Lt. George Redwood. A few minutes prior, the injured intelligence officer had finally made his way to the first-aid station, where he was tagged for transfer to the field hospital. But after hearing the heavy bombardment, he ran back up to the front lines and rushed in against the waves of retreating men even as enemy guns traced their movement, urging them to turn back. He spotted a wounded sergeant and helped him to the rear through what the sergeant described as "intense machine-gun and intense artillery fire." Redwood then turned and "attempted to reach the lines again, in order to lead a retreating company up to their line of resistance," the sergeant noted. "While doing so a high-explosive shell burst near him killing him instantly. You can imagine my sorrow to see the man killed, who a few moments before had saved my life."

For his actions, George Buchanan Redwood was posthumously awarded the Silver Star and a second Distinguished Service Cross. On hearing the news of his death, a French officer reportedly remarked: "I would rather have that man Redwood alive than to have taken Cantigny." After the war, in his hometown of Baltimore, German Street would be renamed Redwood Street in his honor.

Back at the front, even the handful of survivors of Lieutenant Haydock's Company L platoon surrendered their small purchase of enemy trench and joined the withdrawal. The khaki tide flowed back through the wheat and thickened as it was joined by scattered men who had been curled in shell holes or frozen prone in the wheat since morning. The half-conscious Lieutenant Newhall, still flat on his back, sensed the rush of men past his position when his platoon sergeant broke from the pack and crawled over to him: "Lieutenant, the company has fallen back to the old line and the Germans are forming for a counterattack." Newhall replied, "If the company has fallen back, you'd better get back as quickly as you can." The survivors from the slit trench near him "crawled out of their trench and made for the rear on their bellies," but Newhall was still helpless to move. "It was impossible to take me. I couldn't move without pain and couldn't possibly crawl." Newhall again ordered his sergeant to evacuate.

The sergeant kissed Newhall's hand twice, promised him he would return at nightfall, then ran the three-hundred-odd yards back to the old front lines, where the rest of the unglued survivors of Companies L and K huddled, directionless. Attempting to cast the episode in a favorable light, Company L's commander, Captain van Natter, would later claim that a "number of small detachments remained on the assigned objective," but this was untrue. The company had not achieved its objective, and its only soldiers to remain out in no-man's-land were the wounded and dying. And although the battalion commander, Lt. Col. Jesse Cullison, would report that "the two companies withdrew in an orderly manner by echelon," this was also untrue. The troops of half his battalion had returned in haphazard clusters, most without their platoon leaders. "The withdrawal was," one officer noted, "a disorganized retreat."

Still holding their lines up front just past the cemetery strongpoint, Company M's men were enduring what one officer described as "the full force of the German preparation and counterattack." Though waves of their comrades off to the left could be seen receding, Lt. Gerald Tyler, lying bleeding and thirsty, directed his front-line troops to hold under the bombardment. "The way [the enemy] shelled us for two hours was a fright," Tyler later recounted. "I lay in the bottom of the trench and wished for a chance to fight him on an even basis, knowing that I was helpless as a drowning rat in a cage."

Fragments from a shell blast tore into the gut of PFC John Warren of Wisconsin. He was evacuated but would die the next morning, one year to the day after enlisting. Most shells fell in or around the trenches in booming splashes of white and orange flame, but the whistle of one round—an apparent "dud"—fell silent and hit Cpl. Edward Gray, a former pipe fitter from St. Louis, with a muffled thump and knocked him to the trench floor. "I was right alongside of him when an [un]exploded shell took his left arm off," a private wrote. "If it had exploded it would have killed him and about twelve others that were around there." Gray was evacuated to the field hospital, where he would hang on for two painful days before passing.

German soldiers assigned to make the counterattack from the east and northeast of the village had just arrived in the l'Alval and Framicourt woods, where they waited for the bombardment's end—the cue to assault. Many were part of the "rest" battalion and were operating on fumes, having been awake for over twenty-four hours and having marched sixteen miles since midnight. Despite being underneath thick tree cover, they had been spotted, and American artillery hurled heavy fusillades of shells into the woods, smashing trees into splinters and sending the men by the score into full flight. By the time the shelling ceased and German officers managed to regather their troops, it was after 6:00 p.m. When the tired, confused companies of riflemen were ordered from the wood lines, their preparatory bombardment had ended and American troops were manning parapets, ready for action. As the German War Diary would report, they "thrust against an enemy fully prepared for the combat."

Doughboys holding 2nd Battalion trenches in the plateau east of the village spotted the Germans as soon as they drifted from the woods. With pops of Springfields and the chatters of Hotchkiss guns, American soldiers defended their new lines. One of these gunners was thirty-year-old Pvt. Daniel Edwards, the lone survivor of a machine-gun team in a foxhole fifty yards in front of Company F's trenches. He had been bayoneted by an enemy soldier in the morning charge through Cantigny, but he refused evacuation and bandaged the wound himself. Now among the bodies of his three dead comrades, Edwards grabbed handfuls of ammo strips from the open boxes and fed one after another into his Hotchkiss, spraying bullets at the field-gray figures rushing across the open ground. Riflemen standing in the shallow trenches behind him sniped German after German, and the attacking wave was ultimately cut apart and thrown back.

In Company M's trenches to the north, a platoon leader noticed "a number of Germans . . . advancing across no-man's-land" toward the lines abandoned by Companies L and K, and he sent barrage flares hurtling skyward. As field-gray waves of enemy infantry edged into the open plateau, surviving doughboys up in Company K's outposts, entirely isolated but pumping with the adrenaline of kill-or-be-killed, burned into their remaining ammunition and chewed through the attackers. Troops holding Company M's lines and the strongpoints back at the cemetery and orchard did the same, bowling Germans into the weeds wounded, dead, or for cover. "All were beaten off before reaching our line of observation with heavy losses, by our rifle and auto-rifle fire," an officer would report.

Sitting Bull's guns responded quickly to the flare signals, unleashing salvos against the l'Alval and Framicourt wood lines. Shells "smothered" the second and third waves of German infantry, and though the attackers in the first wave had advanced clear of the barrage, most were cut up by small-arms fire while the rest fled north, where many were able to retake their vacated trenches without resistance.

Fighting desolate emotions and sheltered from the hostile battlefield by the helmet over his face, Lieutenant Newhall heard Germans shuffling back into their trenches just a few dozen yards away. "I now expected to be taken prisoner (it never occurred to me that since a battle was going on I was much more likely to be bayoneted where I lay)," he would recount. "But the German attack never got to me." Though still clinging by a thinning tether to life and without water, Newhall was spared capture. But nearest the German lines, Pvt. Carl Fey—jaw-broken, teeth shot out, hole in his cheek, half-conscious and still in shock—was not. Yells in German and boot steps in dry dirt grew nearer and surrounded him, then tugs at his arms and legs lifted and carried him forward, down into the terrifying foreign world of the enemy lines. Like Lt. Judd Kendall, the engineer officer captured three days before, 1st Division reports would soon list Private Fey as missing, and within days, he would be reported "killed in action."

Down along the south edge of Cantigny, in a dark, vaulted cellar below the rubble of a flattened tavern, the commander of 1st Battalion, Maj. George Rozelle, monitored reports of a heavy bombardment on his own troops. The short, red-haired, thirty-nine-year-old West Pointer had advanced with the third wave of his battalion into the village, and when his men discovered this basement, he made it his command post. Wires ran down the concrete steps to a single field phone, which sat on a wood shelf crowded with empty mugs, and cider barrels tapped with spigots lined the far wall. Just as elsewhere, the heavy German bombardment had been thundering down here since 5:00 p.m., rattling the mugs and stirring up dust in Rozelle's underground lair. During a rare moment when phone lines were working, Rozelle had called Colonel Ely to report the bombardment was "increasing steadily" on his troops, and with one frantic runner after another bringing Rozelle grim reports from his front lines, he sent warnings of a probable counterattack from Fontaine to the southeast.

Holding shallow lines facing the Fontaine Woods, the doughboys of Company B had been under sporadic fire all afternoon when the bombardment erupted. Twenty-three-year-old PFC Roman Dzierzak, a Russian immigrant only five years an American citizen, was thrown from the trench, his body so mangled he was identified only by letters found in his pocket.

A shell fragment tore through the face of twenty-five-year-old Pvt. Ira Hawley, killing him instantly. A comrade would write Private Hawley's mother back in Idaho, lamenting that "he was hit by a shell and all that could be found was a tag."

Half the company's front surveillance line was held by the soldiers of 2nd Platoon, leaderless since midmorning when their wounded lieutenant, James Lawrence, was evacuated. For them, the fog of war was proving especially murky. Heavy shelling was replaced by an enemy barrage edging forward from the woods, hitting advance posts and front lines just as panicky, exaggerated rumors burned through the ranks of an impending enemy tank attack. Like Companies L and K up north—but without even a false withdrawal order as a pretext—men began springing from their shell craters and shallow ditches and breaking for the rear. "My line of surveillance withdrew without orders from me," Captain Oliver would report. To his left, Company D's front lines also receded under heavy machine-gun fire, opening a wide gap and spurring more rumors of withdrawal. "[H]earing that everybody had left the sector," Captain Oliver "placed the third platoon in 'D' Company sector," then dispatched a runner back into the village to Major Rozelle's cellar.

An entire platoon fled the front, back across the road and down the slope into the ravine toward the jumping-off trenches. From his shell-hole command post, the regimental MG company commander Capt. Adelbert Stewart spotted "infantrymen retreating and what I took to be a rolling barrage about fifty yards away." He estimated they numbered "about forty men," and they sprinted past him so quickly he could only stop three or four, who told him "they had been ordered to retreat by their sergt., that their officer had been killed and that the whole line was retreating." Stewart chased the horde all the way through the ravine and across the old no-man's-land, stopping them in the jumping-off trenches, where he sent a runner to Colonel Ely's bunker that "the line was reported as retreating."

Back in the village, the bleak—and half-inaccurate—report from Captain Oliver's runner worried Major Rozelle, who immediately sent a message in his hurried cursive to Colonel Ely: "D company has vacated sector . . . Bn sector otherwise intact." Ely sent instructions back to Rozelle to reinforce with Company C, the battalion reserve. But knowing that would take time and worried about a breakthrough, Ely ordered his engineers company forward at once to reinforce 1st Battalion's lines against counterattack.

The day's casualties had cut the engineer company down by a third, and the hundred or so remaining men had been huddled back in the jumping-off trenches since returning from the battlefield around noon. "At 6:00 p.m.," the company commander was, as he would report, "given orders to take his company out and hold a part of the front line." The company's only remaining platoon leader, Lt. Moses Cox, noted the "company was called upon to reinforce the infantry for counter-attacks. This meant a heavy loss to the engineers as they had not been trained that way."

Cpl. Boleslaw Suchocki and Sgt. Carl Thoete—a bandage and dried iodine on his neck still covering shrapnel wounds from the predawn shelling in the quarry—and other veterans of the morning's fighting buckled their gear back on, grabbed rifles, and ran across the shell-scarred plateau toward the front. As Suchocki passed through Cantigny's skeletal remains with the company, he noticed "several dead German bodies" lying outside a smashed house, and other burnt corpses "hanging over the beams pinned down by the falling roof."

The engineers trotted in two columns down a dirt road through the village toward the loudening cackle of pitched battle beyond. Up at the front, thinned ranks of Companies B and D now held a single line of trenches against the enemy assault. With outposts and front lines in both company sectors withdrawn, German machine-gun squads rushed their Maxims forward into the wheat to provide covering fire for the infantry attack. In an all-too-familiar sight of the day, Maxim bullets sliced through the wheat, keeping the doughboys down behind the cover of their parapets. Emerging from the town's rubbled edge behind the American lines into a storm of zipping enemy bullets, the engineers hit the open plateau in a dead sprint for the cover of the trenches.

"[W]e rushed to the trench, and when we got there we found a place to take shelter," one engineer noted. "German machine-guns were sweeping the place and they got seven of our men within a radius of 10 yards around me." Sergeant Thoete stood tall on the rear lip of the trench "directing the men of his section into position" when he was struck in the chest by a machine-gun bullet, a soldier observed. "Sgt. Thoete was unconscious from the time he was hit and died within five minutes." Thirty-four-year-old PFC Daniel Miller of Norristown, Pennsylvania, was cut down just steps from the safety of the trench. "When I saw him he was falling to the ground behind the trench," his platoon sergeant later recounted. "He was killed before he reached the trenches by an enemy bullet." The same fate met thirty-year-old Pvt. William Loftis of San Francisco, who was thrown down as he charged forward. His sergeant saw him "laying on the ground . . . killed before he reached the trench by an enemy bullet."

Corporal Suchocki sprinted up to the trench and found it "very narrow and shallow and also full of men." He jumped in a portion formed from a wide shell hole, packed with his fellow engineers, Company B soldiers, a man getting his shot-up leg bandaged, and Sergeant Thoete's lifeless body. Though bullets sifted through the air and sprayed the dry dirt of the crater's rim, Suchocki stood trying to spot the enemy until a man warned him, "you better get down."

Before a single German rifleman appeared, American shells whizzed over the front-line doughboys and fell in a curtain of explosions on the far edge of the wheat field and enemy-infested wood line beyond. German squads marching by column into the rear of the woods had been spotted and reported to Summerall's gunners by observers in Major Roosevelt's battalion of the 26th, holding the southern half of the Sector. Company A machine gunners opened up heavy fire on their flank from the Cantigny Woods, and the bulk of the attack force and Maxim crews were chewed apart by the hailstorm of 155 shells. The few small clusters of German fighters who managed to squeak through the bombardment were thrown back by the engineers and members of Companies B and D, who stood in shallow trench lines, aimed their Springfields, and picked off targets one by one. Major Rozelle would proudly report: "An enemy counter-attack at this time broke under automatic, rifle, and artillery fire." German reports would admit that "the attack came to a standstill at 250–300 meters east of the road," and "great losses" at the hands of American defenders made further progress impossible.

This first concerted German attempt to recapture Cantigny had failed. It is likely that more than 50 percent of the soldiers making the afternoon counterattack became casualties. At least two commanders were killed at the head of their companies, and some companies could now not muster even a dozen men. Regimental commander Major von Grothe would blame defeat on "the exhausted state of the troops and the heavy losses of officers and leaders." But the Americans had also been reduced by debilitating casualties through the day and had been awake by this point for well over twenty-four hours, and they fought for their ground with unshaken courage, at times even with fervent defiance. German battalion commanders would more accurately attribute their failure to a splintered effort, lack of coordination between their infantry and artillery, and "entirely too insufficient time for the preparation of a united command."

Von Hutier's 18th Army had hurled what it could at the doughboys, but the day's disjointed counterattacks by a makeshift force of exhausted, disoriented soldiers resulted only in heavy losses and near-total failure. Though a handful of German troops had recaptured a short 200- to 300-yard stretch of trenches north of the village, the prize of Cantigny remained unmistakably in the 1st Division's grip. The lacerating sum of pinpricks all along the American lines was a tragic toll of human loss and an escalating mix of fatigue, thirst, hunger, and shell-shock—all proving insufficient to break Bullard's soldiers. The initiative was swinging back to the doughboys holding the high ground, and their afternoon was best captured by a 7:55 p.m. phone call from an observer to Brigade: "Situation fine—enemy beaten off."

General John J. Pershing addresses the officers of the 1st Division on April 16, 1918, the day before their move to the front lines. Standing behind him are (*left to right*) Brigadier General George Duncan, Lieutenant Colonel George Marshall (partially obscured), and Major General Robert Bullard (in fur coat).

Major General Robert Lee Bullard, 1st Division commander, in late April 1918. Unlike Pershing, who was one class behind him at West Point, the folksy Southerner was both informal and personable with his soldiers. While Bullard drove the division through the distinctly American "open warfare" training so urged by his boss, he deftly employed established Allied trench warfare tactics in the successful attack on Cantigny.

Brigadier General Charles P. Summerall, handpicked by Bullard, chose to lead the division's field artillery brigade. Dubbed "Sitting Bull" by his men, the career artilleryman's innovations, which bridged the wide gap between his gun crews and front-line infantry, proved essential in victory at Cantigny and provided a combined-arms model for the rest of the AEF.

Lieutenant Colonel George C. Marshall, Jr., photographed near the time of the Cantigny attack as 1st Division Operations Officer. The man whose name would be forever linked to a mammoth plan to rebuild Europe first showed his organizational genius in May 1918, as he gathered detailed intelligence from nightly patrols—and conducted a few himself—to devise the successful plan of attack on Cantigny. GEORGE C. MARSHALL FOUNDATION, LEXINGTON, VA

Samuel Iredell "Si" Parker, as a student at UNC, circa 1916. When word of America's declaration of war reached campus, he and his classmate, Sam Ervin—though both only a month from graduation— left school and entered Army officer training at Ft. Oglethorpe, Georgia. By war's end, Parker would see action in four separate battles, and—more decorated than the famous Sergeant Alvin York—he would become one of America's most decorated soldiers of the World War. PARKER/MOSS PRIVATE COLLECTION

Sam Ervin, Jr., during training at Ft. Oglethorpe, Georgia, Summer 1917. The future U.S. senator (and chairman of the famed Watergate Committee) would be twice wounded in action and earn two Silver Stars and the Distinguished Service Cross before returning to his hometown of Morganton, North Carolina, for a long career in the law and public service.

Richard Newhall in training at Plattsburgh Camp, New York. WILLIAMS COLLEGE ARCHIVES AND SPECIAL COLLECTIONS, WILLIAMSTOWN, MA

Doughboys training in "Washington Center" trenches in Gondrecourt, Fall 1917.

Left to right: Lt. Samuel I. "Si" Parker, Lt. George Haydock, and Lt. John Mays, Seicheprey Sector, Winter 1918. PARKER/MOSS PRIVATE COLLECTION

Officers of the 1st Battalion, 28th Infantry, April 1918. Selected individuals are, by corresponding number, as follows: **(1)** Lt. Robert B. Anderson; **(2)** Maj. George Rozelle; **(3)** Cpt. Clarence Oliver; **(4)** Cpt. Charles Senay; **(5)** Lt. Soren Sorensen; **(6)** Lt. George Butler; **(7)** Lt. John Church; **(8)** Lt. Neilson "Net" Poe.

Officers of the 3rd Battalion, 28th Infantry, April 1918. Selected individuals are, by corresponding number, as follows: **(1)** Lt. John Scott; **(2)** Cpt. Van Natter; **(3)** Lt. L. Irwin Morris; **(4)** Lt. Daniel Birmingham; **(5)** Cpt. Willis Tack; **(6)** Lt. Gerald Tyler; **(7)** Lt. Charles McKnolly; **(8)** Cpt. Henry Mosher; **(9)** Lt. Howard Hawkinson; **(10)** Lt. George Haydock; **(11)** Lt. Richard Newhall; **(12)** Lt. George Redwood.

Pvt. Carl Fey of Company L. HESSER FAMILY COLLECTION

Clarence Huebner, photographed after the war as lieutenant colonel. He would command the 1st Division himself in World War II, leading it in the assault on Omaha Beach on D-Day.

Battle rehearsal with French Schneider Tanks, May 25, 1918. Note the line of soldiers observing in the distance to the left.

75mm and crew.

Aerial photo of Cantigny taken just after zero hour by a French airplane observer from a height of approximately 500 meters looking westward in the face of the attack. The absolute destruction caused by the hour-long preparatory bombardment is clear, as smoke still rises from the village ruins. NATIONAL ARCHIVES

Soldiers in the third wave carry bangalores, screw picks (for barbwire), machine-gun parts, and ammunition boxes through the wheat behind the tanks and the second wave.

French flamethrower crew "mopping up" in Cantigny's ruins. Note the dead Germans in the rubble.

Hotchkiss machine-gun crew firing up at German planes during the battle.

German prisoners captured in Cantigny marched to the rear of the sector, May 28, 1918.

CHAPTER 14

The World Is Watching

It had been hours since General Pershing had left Bullard's headquarters, but as the division staff monitored reports on the counterattack still coming in from the front, a courier arrived around eight p.m. with a note in Pershing's handwriting imploring Bullard that Cantigny must be held. Though Pershing would tell his diary that this was simply "a letter of congratulations," its words "astonished" Bullard "beyond measure," revealing an anxiety the Big Chief had earlier kept concealed beneath his confident mask. "I need not suggest that you give this your personal attention which I know you will do," Pershing's words urged, "but am writing this note to show you that I am rather anxious about it."

An even sharper anxiety tinted the mood in Colonel Ely's headquarters. Though the afternoon counterattack had been thrown back, calls and runners from the front lines continued flooding the cramped dugout in a tenor of growing desperation: "Our Bn. needs relief"; "My company is practically wiped out"; and "Account shortage of officers and men this Battalion should be relieved at once." All battlefield news reaching Ely suggested that his shattered regiment was exhausted and its position indefensible.

Concerned that the deteriorating welfare of his men compounded the threat of a breakthrough, Ely had been pleading for hours for relief of his unit in a voice pinched with panic and mounting anger. Five forty-five p.m.: "Unless heavy artillery can give us support it will be necessary to withdraw from entire front line"; 6:40 p.m.: "Recommend 18th Inf. relieve entire line or it be brought back to old lines"; 7:23 p.m.: "losses are heavy . . . if they continue to counterattack it may be necessary to draw back or be relieved"; 8:40 p.m.: "Rozelle reports his Bn. has suffered such losses it should be relieved at once." Thus far, Ely had ordered the engineers to the front to reinforce, followed by Company C, then convinced the brigade commander to give him two battalions of the 18th Infantry in addition to the two reserve companies he was already allotted.

Three miles away, General Bullard worried that sending fresh troops into the breach merely to relieve existing units would only cause unnecessary casualties. To keep Ely from throwing new blood on Cantigny's altar—and fueled by the anxiety in Pershing's note—Bullard sent instructions to the front: "Inform Ely as follows: Try tonight if practicable to adhere to original plans by withdrawing some units for counterattack thus thinning lines and reducing losses. The position must be held. The C of C expects it. Bullard." By the time the message reached Ely's bunker, it effectively snatched both 18th Infantry reserve battalions from his control: "Troops sent to you are not to be used to thicken your line but will be used for counter attacks only. The use of either Bn. for counter attack must be authorized by Brigade Commander."

And to pass along General Pershing's resolution to hold the line, Bullard picked up his field phone and called Colonel Ely directly, bridging the three miles and broad temperamental gulf between them: "Ely, you must hold your position and not give any ground at all," Bullard voiced with as much gravity as his folksy, Southern tongue could muster. "The whole world is watching the 28th Infantry and we must continue to hold Cantigny at all costs."

Up at the front, on the dirt floor of Company M's trench, the blood-soaked bandage tied around Lt. Gerald Tyler's leg was still not stopping the flow of blood from his bullet wound. "I was weak from loss of blood and lack of water," he would recall, and though he needed to evacuate to a field hospital soon, that would require a three-hundred-yard trek to the nearest communication trench leading to the rear, and he could not risk a long, slow hobble back across no-man's-land with the late-afternoon sun still up. "I would have given twenty years of my life to be in that trench which was 300 yards away," he later wrote. He had stayed with the men of his two-platoon front through the afternoon counterattack, but when the enemy fire let up a bit, he turned his men over to a sergeant and took advantage of the "short lull" to go for broke.

Lieutenant Tyler peered behind his trench over the open ground he would have to cover: "between it and myself several shells were at that instant exploding and the machine-gun bullets were flicking up the dust everywhere." He thought twice, but then mustered all his reserves of strength and jumped: "I got right up and beat it through that hell, for the communication trench. I shall never know how I made it but I remember running from one shell hole to another as best I could with my lame leg, hearing shell fragments, shrapnel and bullets whizz about my ears. I saw those vile pieces of steel knock the dust up from my very feet." In a limping sprint, he "passed horribly mangled Germans and Americans, some not altogether dead," then spotted his refuge, the edge of the communication trench, and thought to himself, "All hell can't keep me from making it!" He reached it, fell in, "nearly fainted from exhaustion," and made it with help to the first-aid station and then on to a hospital, where he would recover from his wound.

The ground over which Lieutenant Tyler had run spanned the space between Company M's trenches up front and the old front line, a half-mile-wide gap of undefended terrain caused by the "disorganized retreat" of Companies L and K. It was this open flank—presently the left wing of the regiment's forward elements—that now concerned Colonel Ely most, and he sent word to 3rd Battalion's commander, Lt. Col. Jesse Cullison, to close the gap.

Unlike the other two battalion commanders, Cullison had yet to enter the battlefield. Presently, he remained tucked in a small dirt dugout—the same one that had frustrated Company E's Capt. Edward Johnston during the previous morning's raid for being so far from the front lines. Back around six p.m., a flood of Company K soldiers had flowed down the slope toward his command post, where he "headed off" the men and ordered them forward. Lt. Si Parker reported to him soon after, and Cullison ordered him "to round up all the stragglers and report to Capt. Tack," the commander of Company I, the battalion's reserve company occupying the old front-line trenches. Parker searched the maze of serpentine ditches and rounded up small clutches of troops, some of whom he recognized from his company and some he had never seen. He ordered each scattered group to grab their rifles and follow him forward. "I found about 25 men from various organizations, supplied them with ammunition and reported," Parker noted.

Capt. Willis Tack and three of his Company I platoons had been manning the old front-line trenches since just after Zero Hour (one of his platoons held the cemetery strongpoint with attached machine-gun teams). When Parker and his patchwork of collected stragglers reported, Tack ordered them to man the lines on his left. In the jumping-off trenches behind them, Captain van Natter gathered a handful of Company L doughboys who had returned from the killing field uninjured, then began sending runners back to Cullison's command bunker with panicky messages: "My company is practically wiped out," and "I feel I should not ask it, but I believe I owe it to the men . . . What I should like to is to have them relieved." Van Natter's company had in fact suffered the highest casualties in the battalion, but he was relying on reports from men who had returned from the fighting, as he was the only company commander to not move out with his company in the morning advance. There is, in fact, no record he ever personally entered the battlefield. And though he received word that one of his officers, Lieutenant Newhall, was wounded and helpless out in no-man's-land, there is no record that van Natter ever reported this or organized any attempt at evacuation, even after nightfall.

Swamped with messages that his lines had broken and orders from Ely to close the gap, Lieutenant Colonel Cullison finally rushed up toward the front, where he faced the disheartening sight of squads and platoons in scattered bunches packed in the old front lines and jumping-off trenches. In the waning twilight, bursts from enemy machine guns searched the parapets of what had again become the battalion's front lines, making it apparent to Cullison that Germans had reoccupied the trenches across no-man's-land. Along this stretch of front, American and enemy lines had reverted back to where they were prior to Zero Hour.

Cullison wanted to redeem the day, but the only forces at his disposal were Captain Tack's partial company and the shot-up remnants of Companies L and K. To retake the objective—or at least to plug the gap—he asked Colonel Ely for a fresh reserve company. Without any approval from Brigade or Division, Ely phoned the commander of the 18th Infantry's 2nd Battalion at 11 p.m. with an order: "One of your companies will report to Cullison." So Company G of the 18th—one of eight rifle companies in two battalions that had earlier been ordered forward by Ely then pulled back by Bullard—became the first of five that would be sent into the front lines as fresh reinforcements through the next twenty-four hours.

"Word came from the Front that the Colonel of the 28th had asked the Colonel of the 18th for a company to reinforce his men," Pvt. Frank Last of the relief company told his diary. "We hiked about under shellfire . . . passing through very dangerous places." German observers spotted the columns moving toward the front lines and notified their batteries. High-explosive and gas shells began falling and the doughboys had to don masks and sprint forward in small groups through the bombardment. "We were double timing with our gas masks on and ready to drop at any instant," Last noted. "We passed a number of dead and wounded men, some of whom begged us for help, but we couldn't stop as our orders were to keep moving." By the time the company's soldiers filed up the slope through the communication trench to report to Captain Tack in the front lines, they had "lost some men," but, as Private Last would recount, "none at all compared to the Company whose sector we had taken. There were just three men left there."

Cullison ordered the relief company forward to capture Company L's original objective and Company I to the lines Company K had abandoned. But as he would report, "when the attempt was made it was found that the enemy had occupied the vacated position with machine-guns," and the enemy fire made it "impracticable," even in the approaching darkness, without artillery support. The attempt was halfhearted at best, and without requesting artillery support for a stronger effort, Cullison settled for filling the gap, sending Company I forward to dig a half-mile-long trench connecting with Company M.

"I was ordered with my company to connect M company's left with the rt. of Co. G, 18th Inf," Captain Tack noted. He sent a platoon under Lt. Dick Dacus over the top into the pitch-black of no-man's-land, hoping German machine gunners would not spot them. "[W]e were given the rather unusual command to 'Go forward until you meet enemy fire, then stop and dig in!'" Dacus later recounted. When the Maxim's rattle started, Dacus and his platoon dropped and started digging for cover. "My platoon sergeant was a former miner from Pittsburgh, so he and I made the dirt fly," he noted. Though enemy machine guns searched the open ground for targets through the night, improbably none found Dacus and his soldiers while they dug the new line. "[B]y morning," Captain Tack would report, "a fairly good trench connecting shell holes had been dug," and the gap was closed.

Over the battlefield, dusk's final traces disappeared and a thick murkiness descended. Out in 2nd Battalion's trenches east of the village, Captain Huebner took advantage of the darkness to evacuate his wounded and try to resupply his troops with ammunition and food. But German artillery kept Death Valley and the old front lines under such sustained fire that no food, water, or ammo could be reached. All across the front lines, occasional enemy flares and the blasts of single shells broke the silence and lit the scene. The night grew surprisingly cold, and without blankets in their packs, men in sweat-stiffened tunics were left to hug the cold earth. Up in his orchard strongpoint, Lieutenant Waltz described it as "extremely cold," adding, "while up in front of that town . . . it seemed as though one was frozen stiff."

In his lamplit cellar under the rubble on Cantigny's south end, Major Rozelle and his handful of runners and staff officers, sipping on mugs of lukewarm cider, worried that the 1st Battalion's lines, even with the engineers thrown in, would not hold under the weight of another counterattack. "[R]eports led me to believe that my center had broken, so Company C . . . was ordered in as reinforcement to fill the gap," Rozelle would report. Just before dark, General Bullard had reluctantly agreed to send Colonel Ely authorization for Rozelle to "relieve the remainder of Co. that suffered so" with his reserve company, meaning that C should replace D. But as with the 3rd Battalion north of the village, Bullard's orders regarding relief were twisted in relay, resulting in Company C's soldiers entering the line alongside D's, rather than replacing them. Thus Bullard's expressed goal—"thinning lines and reducing losses"—was further frustrated.

"At 10:30 p.m. the company was ordered to thicken the firing line," Company C's commander, Capt. Charles Senay, noted. One of his platoons had moved forward at Zero Hour to help construct a strongpoint in the wooded southeast edge of the village, and his three remaining platoons were left occupying the old jumping-off trenches as battalion reserve. Senay suspected they might get thrown into the fight when Company B's platoon had fled back across no-man's-land during the afternoon counterattack, and when the order finally came, he and his men buckled up, grabbed their rifles, and scurried forward into the dark plateau.

"We moved forward in platoon column," Senay would report, and under the cover of night, "[t]his move was accomplished without incident." After climbing up from the ravine and crossing the road, Senay's doughboys crammed into the half-dug shallow ditches and shell craters on the far side of Company D's thinned ranks just after midnight. But their movement attracted enemy fire, and machine-gun bullets swept the parapet as shells began falling into the khaki-packed trench.

The blast of a mortar shell buried two men under a pile of heavy earth, and their comrades rushed to dig them out. Lit only by the flashes of shell blasts, soldiers flailed at loose dirt as they called out their buried buddies' names. Twenty-three-year-old Pvt. Cabe Keen of Mississippi attempted to give them covering fire with his Springfield at Maxim muzzle flashes in the distant wood line, but his shooting attracted more enemy fire and a sweep of machine-gun bullets knocked him down to the trench floor. Another high-explosive shell whistled in and struck at the feet of seventeen-year-old Pvt. Tom West of Tennessee, the company's youngest, hurling his body from the trench. Ignoring the maelstrom on all sides, soldiers dug until they succeeded in unearthing the buried men, who emerged shaken but un-injured. When the shelling finally subsided, soldiers dressed Private Keen's bullet wound and carried him to a field hospital, but he died two mornings later. They pulled young Private West's lifeless body back into the trench, wrapped him in a blanket, and buried him in a nearby shell hole before dawn.

Private West's older brother, George, who had followed young Tom into enlistment the week America entered the war, was a private in the 1st Di-vision's 16th Infantry, a member of the very company that would take over these lines in two days' time. George carried the sorrow of his brother's pass-ing for six more weeks, until he met his own death by shellfire at Soissons on July 18 at the age of twenty. After the Armistice, in what is one of the saddest letters received by the Graves Registration Service in the course of the war, their father, E. A. West, a drugstore manager, wrote: "If possible, will you please ship the bodies of my two sons, Tom R. and George E. West, at the same time." Today, the brothers lie in peace, side by side, in the West family plot in Oliver Springs, Tennessee.

Of growing concern to Major Rozelle was the wide-open gulf in his battal-ion's lines caused by the ravine. Lt. Robert Anderson's troops of Company A had been unable to span the length of its low ground under the morning's buzz-saw of enemy machine-gun fire. Heavy shelling of the afternoon counterattack had again caused heavy losses in his company's already-thinned ranks, mortally wounding yet another of his platoon leaders and driving his surviving men back over into the cover of the wood line.

Anderson was down to two officers, his ranks had been cut by a third, and his company's position was becoming untenable. And though he kept a stoic face before his men, he was sick nearly to death. He was feverish, his head throbbed with a migraine, he coughed uncontrollably and was grow-ing weak and feeling faint—all symptoms of the same Spanish influenza that had forced his company commander and two other company officers into the hospital before the battle. Still, Anderson did not ask for relief, and the only messages he sent Major Rozelle were requests for water for his men and more ammunition for Lt. Jim Hartney, who by dark was in his sixteenth straight hour directing the fire of his machine-gun teams toward the Fontaine Woods.

Major Rozelle sent a request up for another reserve company to give

Company A some relief, and Colonel Ely's counterpart, the 26th Infantry commander Col. Hamilton Smith, agreed to send a company. Through the battle, the four companies of 1st Battalion of the 26th, commanded by Maj. Theodore Roosevelt Jr., had held the trenches to the south of the Cantigny Woods, providing flank protection to Rozelle's 1st Battalion. Just before ten p.m., Colonel Smith ordered Roosevelt to "Send Co. D to relieve Co A/1 (the Co. of the 28th adjoining you to the left)" to act under Major Rozelle's orders. "In the meantime the orders are to hold the line at all costs."

Like the other members of Company D of the 26th Infantry, twenty-four-year-old Pvt. Frank Goseling of Woodland, California, had been listening to the sounds of the day's fighting carrying from the battlefield north of his position. Now in the dark of night, his platoon leader announced they were headed into the battle to relieve one of the 28th Infantry's companies that had suffered heavy losses. Goseling and the others geared up, grabbed rifles, and quietly snaked out of their trench up into the undergrowth of the Cantigny Woods. "The path lay through the woods," Goseling recalled. "It was narrow and we filed along, one by one. We had advanced but a short distance when the Germans got our range and opened fire. Shells dropped among us like rain."

Ashcans whistled over the treetops and sliced through the foliage. The detonations smashed tree trunks to splinters and sent men diving into the undergrowth. One shell landed in the middle of the column, hitting three men with one blast: privates Theodore Kraakmo, Joseph Carlson, and Wilbur Ward. Ward was "struck almost directly" and died instantly. Kraakmo was slammed against a tree and fell motionless, also dead. Carlson was thrown down but still conscious, and in the midst of the clamor, two of his comrades carried him back to a first-aid station, where he would later die. Private Goseling described the scene: "Men fell across the path and on either side. We stepped over the dead and wounded and advanced, for orders were orders. It was a terrible experience. When we finally arrived at the front line, we had fewer men than the company we were sent to reinforce."

The shellfire followed the relieving company right into Company A's positions, falling on Lieutenant Anderson and his men. "The Company was relieved about 2:30 a.m.," Lieutenant Hartney, one of Anderson's two remaining company officers, noted. Still weak and feverish, Anderson yelled above the din of the bombardment for his surviving men to file out the wood line through the communication trench—"just a little path through a thicket," Pvt. Billie McCombs observed—back toward the old front lines. But German guns traced the soldiers down the exit trench, as Private Mc-Combs would recount: "A shell-shrapnel struck in front of me—the pieces flew in all directions. It tore a huge hole and I was buried. I dug my way out and saw I was wounded in the arm." McCombs clenched his forearm—which "had been ripped open by pieces of shell"—to stop the bleeding, and walked under his own power through the woods to the first-aid station. In a few days, he would write his mother back in New Castle, Pennsylvania: "I do not know what kind of an arm I will have when I get out of the sling, but I'm afraid my days as a soldier are numbered." Doctors operated on Mc-Combs, removing a hunk of steel one and a half inches long from his arm, and he would recover and return home early. But with torn tendons, he never gained back the use of his right hand.

The men of Company D of the 26th who had somehow survived the path through the vortex of fire and shrapnel took over the foxholes and trenches in the Cantigny Woods. Under unceasing German shelling, they tried to steal glances out over the dark ravine at the silhouette of village ruins. Twenty-year-old Pvt. Emil Vanker of Detroit was "[k]illed instantly by artillery fire" just after settling in the trench, making his wife, Mildred, a widow at nineteen. The platoon sergeant, Edward Nesterowicz, had earlier been knocked down by a shell blast while trooping through the woods, only to shake it off and rejoin his men here. Now another detonation knocked him on his back unconscious and killed the man beside him, Pvt. Samuel Buchalter, "instantly." A nearby corporal would recount that Buchalter, a twenty-four-year-old Russian immigrant from Connecticut, had told him "he thought he would be killed that day," but after making it into position unscathed, hoped it was a false omen. Sergeant Nesterowicz would survive this blast "only a few minutes" before breathing his last, having never regained consciousness. The bodies of Nesterowicz, Buchalter, and Vanker were rolled together into a shell hole and dirt packed over them. After the war, all three were shipped home for burial at their families' requests.

And so yet another company of soldiers—uninjured and eager for action just two hours before—was sent into the meat grinder of the front lines, adding three dozen wounded and a dozen dead to the battle's growing tally. Down in his headquarters, General Bullard had no idea all these fresh companies had been thrown into the front trenches as reinforcement, or that so many casualties were resulting—as he predicted they would—by the thickening of the lines. Although the toughest phase of the operation was just beginning, the reports Bullard had so far received left him confident enough of his lines holding to dictate a telegram for dispatch to General Pershing's headquarters: "Operation against Cantigny executed as planned this morning . . . Movement executed with dash and precision. About two hundred prisoners coming to rear now. Our losses now estimated at thirty killed and one hundred wounded. Enemy losses reported heavy."

Word of the Americans' successful capture of Cantigny, however premature, hit the Allied command like a breath of fresh air after weeks of demoralizing defeat under the pressing force of the German offensive. That night, after getting the news, French officers reportedly "Danced upon the table tops," and in Parliament, Prime Minister David Lloyd George called the victory "a most encouraging thing in a day everywhere else sad and depressing for the Allies."

Bullard's doughboys were still holding—many in scanty trenches, some in isolated outposts, others lying in blast craters wounded or shaking from "shell-shock," and all exhausted. On his back out in the dark loneliness of no-man's-land, Lt. Richard Newhall pulled the helmet off his face to see a black sky full of stars. "By night everything was quiet except an occasional burst from a machine-gun fired into the dark at random," he would later write. His arm was numb, the bleeding had somehow stopped, and his sharpest pains were now hunger and thirst. He had no reserve rations, had drunk the last from his canteens by early afternoon, and now clung to the hope that his men would use the cover of darkness to evacuate him. "I lay still, afraid to move for fear the searchers would miss me." But the temperature dropped, his thirst sharpened, and minutes and hours passed. "Nobody ever came."

A couple hundred yards away, privates Jesse Gillespie and Willie Drager kept silent vigil in their abandoned outpost, attended only by the stiff bodies of their dead comrades. As a hometown reporter would later paint the scene, the two nineteen-year-olds spent the long night "listening to the music of warfare as it spent itself in the air above No Man's Land." Shot in the back and with both legs broken by shellfire, Drager lay helpless, unable to move. Gillespie's leg was still cinched in a boot-lace tourniquet and his shot-up arm bandaged. Like Newhall, they had exhausted their water supply hours earlier, so Gillespie crawled to retrieve canteens from the cold bodies surrounding them. As the night's descending chill slowed the passing minutes, the two rationed their water and hoped for rescue.

CHAPTER 15

Novelty of Silence

Lt. Daniel Sargent would lament that Wednesday, May 29, began "long before I thought it should have." He had been ordered back from his observation post after the German afternoon counterattack, and after regaling the members of his artillery battery with stories of what he had seen at the front, he curled up on the same cold turf where he had spent the previous night. But after only a couple of hours—which seemed to him like "but a minute or two after I had closed my eyes"—there was a flashlight in his face and a soldier's voice: "Wake up. You must go into Cantigny." It was just after midnight. With heavy eyes, Sargent buckled on his gear, filled his canteens, and dragged himself forward, where a guide led him through Death Valley and back toward the front.

After a tired shuffle through dark, gray fields, Sargent arrived at the first-aid station in the chalk cliff near Colonel Ely's bunker. "I was astonished to see a couple of French wagons half demolished by shellfire with their drivers face down on the earth beside them, dead, but seeming to be asleep," Sargent noted. "And there were dead horses with them that were so recently dead, that their bellies were not yet swollen." He looked around at the "confusion of things"—medics toiling by lamplight in their cramped earthen dugout, dead bodies stacked under blankets, and men heaving wooden boxes filled with ammunition or shouldering ropes strung with dozens of newly filled canteens back into the dark battlefield for their comrades at the front. A few Ford ambulances had made it to the first-aid station and "[t]heir motors were still chugging" as "[t]he wounded, on stretchers were being loaded into them."

Sargent's guide led him over to a dark entrance of a "cave" lit only by "several lanterns, which revealed Colonel Ely seated on what seemed to be a horse saddle." A handful of eager runners and orderlies lined the walls of the bunker, and in the middle of the dirt floor was a dead artillery officer, a manifest reminder of mortality "staring up at the ceiling glassy-eyed."

Unjarred by the conspicuous presence of death lying beside him, Ely "wore a sleepless look," Sargent observed, "but he had a most calming presence and calming look, and he addressed me by name, which was a calming thing to do."

"Lieutenant Sargent," Ely said gruffly, "[y]ou are succeeding the artillery officer that you are looking at. You are to go to the command post of the [1st] battalion of the 28th Infantry in Cantigny, which is not far from here. The battalion commander is Major Rozelle, who may not be expecting you for the telephone wire between him and me has been momentarily cut, so that I can't announce your arrival. A runner will guide you to Major Rozelle's command post and you can tell him that I have sent you. Once in the dug-out, you will have the task of relaying requests for barrages from the infantry to the artillery. You will do this by the telephone which will begin to function again shortly." Ely nodded at Sargent and sent him on his way.

Ely's present aim was stationing more artillery liaisons like Sargent up in the regiment's new front lines to calculate ranges on German batteries, which had, in the small, dark hours of the morning, been maneuvered into new gun emplacements before thundering again. Around two a.m., the scattered single blasts merged into another escalating fusillade, putting the 1st Division's rear command posts and supply points under heavy fire and gassing artillery batteries. American gun crews on the hilltop near Coullemelle reported that gas shells were hitting every twelve seconds, and within minutes, fifty mustard shells fell around Battery C of the 7th Field Artillery, forcing gunners to work at their 75s blindly in fogged masks. High-explosive shells were mixed in, severing phone lines and disrupting communication among scattered gun groups. Pvt. Barnard Farley was sent by his sergeant to find a break in his battery's phone line and reconnect it, but "that was the last he was seen or heard of." Back in one of the gun pits, a gas shell whistled down from the darkness and hit gunner Pvt. Leon Campbell directly, tossing him to the ground dead and hissing out a mustard cloud from his mangled torso.

Down in Division Headquarters, General Summerall's artillery staff was swamped with reports of German barrages to the north of Cantigny, to the south, and on the field hospital with "patients there who cannot be moved" and a doctor who was "very worried." Orderlies and staff officers were personally shaken just after three a.m. when the brick cellar shook under the detonation of a 250-pound enemy shell that hit "right alongside the chateau" above, one major noted. By a few minutes past four a.m., the barrage returned to a familiar intensity, provoking anxieties of another enemy counterattack. An artillery liaison from the front lines phoned division to report the "Infantry believe the Boche are preparing to attack," and up in Colonel Ely's command post, word came from a front-line commander that the German bombardment was "probably for enemy counterattack." Ely relayed orders to his battalions to stand ready and dispatched a runner to Company A, which was back in reserve and still under command of the feverish Lieutenant Anderson, to "hold itself in readiness to reinforce front line."

The previous night's counterattack was just one of many the German 82nd Reserve Division Headquarters would organize, each with the objective of retaking the village. Until the next assault was announced, the regiments displaced from Cantigny were left with standing orders to continue pressing the Americans. The "rest" battalions of the 271st and 272nd Reserve Infantry Regiments were holding the front of their new, pushed-back German lines east and south of Cantigny, loosely manning wooded foxholes, where they had retrenched after being thrown back the previous night. American artillery kept the supply routes behind the woods under heavy shellfire, preventing soldiers there—just as their doughboy counterparts a few hundred yards away—from getting water or food.

Most of these Germans had not slept for thirty-six hours, and in that they time had marched sixteen miles; been ordered into an uphill, near-suicidal frontal attack across open ground; then held exposed lines through the night under heavy machine-gun and artillery fire. Many companies no longer had a single surviving officer in their ranks, and one—the 11th Company of the 272nd—could only muster seventeen men. Now, before dawn, their battalion commanders were about to order them forward against the Americans again.

The present gas and high-explosive bombardment on American rear positions was the German artillery's attempt at a preparatory bombardment supporting another infantry assault. Between two and four a.m., German Corps Artillery and guns of the 82nd Reserve Division sent more than 1,000 high-explosive and gas shells on Summerall's battery crews, augmented by more than 600 mustard shells hurled by the 25th Reserve Division supporting from the south (they avoided gassing Cantigny itself because they planned on recapturing it). Then at 4:00 a.m., more than 100 German guns from two divisions unleashed a bombardment along the entire American front.

A half mile from the German lines, in Company E's position just east of the village, Capt. Edward Johnston had lost all his lieutenants and was the only remaining officer. His four platoons—all under the charge of sergeants—had spent most of their night digging and resting in alternating shifts. Abruptly, thunder carried from German gun pits, blasts and screams broke the silence, sheets and splashes of orange and white flame lit the darkness, and lead and steel again invaded the shallow foxholes and trenches crammed with doughboys. Johnston sent signal flares fizzing skyward, and his soldiers with heavy eyes and blistered hands grabbed rifles, threw on helmets, and peeked flinchingly over their earthworks to defend their line for the third straight morning.

Whistles pitched louder and lower through the darkness, and doughboys froze in place, yielding to the bleak embrace of fate. Pvt. Robert Darr was blown to bits, leaving only a helmet and rifle in the trench where he had been standing. The same blast killed Pvt. Herbert Dobson beside him, leaving his body unscratched, killed by the concussion alone. Another whiz-bang hit the parapet in front of twenty-six-year-old Pvt. James Burns, blowing his helmet away with the top of his skull and killing him instantly. Burns had left his pregnant young wife, Mary Catherine, back home in Wisconsin when he enlisted the previous fall, and he had spent the past few weeks bragging about the apple of his eye, his daughter, Elaine, born in December, whom he now would never meet. His brother, John, a member of Company L, had survived the previous day's carnage in no-man's-land and was currently back holding the old jumping-off trenches with the few survivors of Lieutenant Newhall's platoon. John would carry the grief of his brother's loss until mid-July, when he would himself be killed by artillery fire at Soissons.

Shell fragments tore through the living and defiled the dead. Without officers to keep them in place, soldiers' hold on the front lines threatened to last only as long as their grip on their own sanity, eroded more and more by each blast. Were it not for the effective leadership of the two front-line platoon sergeants, Henry Johnson and Stephen Palaschak, Company E's front lines might have folded and withdrawn. But in actions for which they would each be awarded the Silver Star, both men—as with the fallen Lieutenant Curry and injured Lieutenant Avery in whose place they now stood—ran up and down their lines, redistributed ammunition, and kept their troops "in position under extremely heavy fire."

Enemy machine-gun fire began strafing the parapet, and one bullet hit Cpl. Anthony Dicello in the head, killing him instantly. In a shell-crater outpost a few dozen yards in front of the company lines, three automatic-riflemen—PFC Edward Pitt, PFC Clarence Fields, and Pvt. Fred Marshall—spotted the Maxim's distant muzzle flashes and directed their Chauchat fire at it. The three burned through ammo, silencing the Maxim and killing its six-man crew. But their own muzzle flashes made their isolated position a target, and a German 77 shifted its fire and dumped shells into the crater, killing Pitt and Fields and wounding Marshall.

Back in the company line, Pvt. Jay Antes and PFC Emory Mahafey, two medics who were "repeatedly pass[ing] up and down the front trenches rendering first-aid under heavy machine-gun fire," noticed the shell blast in the outpost. Private Antes climbed over the parapet and "left the security of the trenches in order to render first-aid" to the wounded Private Marshall. But as well aimed as the first, another enemy shell whistled into the crater, killing Private Antes. His fellow medic, PFC Mahafey, darted over the top and jumped into the hole to give Antes first aid, but like clockwork, another shell struck and killed Mahafey. Improbably, Private Marshall was still alive, and he fired all his remaining Chauchat ammo before finally being evacuated.

To their left, Company F's soldiers were enduring the same pounding. The only remaining officer, twenty-six-year-old Lt. Foster Brown, a congressman's son and VMI graduate from Tennessee, became the third to command the company in just the past eighteen hours. Like Captain Johnston to his right, Brown shot up a flare signal and struggled to keep his men in position under the cannonading. Twenty-three-year-old PFC William Wear of Rome, Georgia, and thirty-nine-year-old PFC Ernest Many of Newburg, New York, were killed side-by-side by a single shell. The rattle of a German machine gun sounded, and a sweep of bullets struck nineteen-year-old PFC Joseph Rountree of Kinston, North Carolina, who "died instantly." Cpl. Joseph Jindra climbed out of the trench and ran forward to man a Hotchkiss that had been abandoned under the previous evening's counterattack, but "while advancing was killed by shellfire." Lieutenant Brown jumped from his trench and ran up and down the lines, between the zipping Maxim fire and flying dirt, yelling to the men at his feet to keep a watch across the dark plateau for an enemy attack. With flat understatement, Brown would later report he was "fortunate enough to escape injury."

Summoned by Johnston's and Brown's flares, Sitting Bull's artillery opened up with a reassuring rumble, sending shells humming over the hunkered doughboys and falling in splashes of flame in the German-held woods. More landed farther off, hitting enemy artillery positions in orange explosions silhouetted behind hilltops and splintered tree trunks, until all German artillery fell silent except for the typewriter tapping of a few Maxims and the lonely door-slam of a solitary 77mm.

A few hundred yards away, German soldiers—as exhausted and hungry as their American counterparts—were ordered to fix bayonets on their Mausers. At 4:10 a.m., they pulled themselves from their foxholes and edged forward across the dark plateau. Lt. Rudolph Koubsky, the sole remaining officer in Company M's bent-back lines hugging the north of the village, noticed the "heavy bombardment of artillery" that had been pummeling Company F's and E's positions to his front-right, followed by an infantry attack. "As the smoke cleared away 3 waves could be seen advancing to our front and left front, attempting to envelop our left flank." All along this stretch of the American front lines, officers and NCOs ordered their troops to open fire over open sights at the waves of gray figures scarcely discernible in the faint predawn light.

With the popping of Springfields and chatter of automatic rifles, doughboys mowed through the front line of German attackers even as enemy Maxims lashed the American parapet with covering fire. Company F's Cpl. Joseph Cely emptied his rifle and while crawling to a nearby shell hole to secure a fallen soldier's ammunition, he was pelted by machine-gun bullets, one blowing his kneecap off. Although pulled back into the trench by comrades who dressed his wounds, Cely could not be evacuated and would eventually lose consciousness, dying of blood loss within a few hours. In Company M's front lines, Sgt. Maniphe Stonecipher "showed remarkable coolness and disregard of danger" while directing his platoon's fire at the attacking Germans "although his casualties were great and his ammunition exhausted." When two of his men, twenty-one-year-old Pvt. Alex Morley of New York and twenty-three-year-old PFC Emory Cohron of Kentucky, were both struck down to the trench floor dead by machine-gun bullets, Stonecipher grabbed five-round clips from their ammo pouches and passed them out to his surviving soldiers as they fired to stop the attackers. The ammo shortage desperate, Stonecipher crawled over the top to collect the clips from the pouches and bandoliers of the fallen, returning to the trench to redistribute them, somehow unharmed, actions that inspired his platoon into ever more defiant action. "I never saw a braver man in all my life," recounted one of his privates admiringly after the war. For his actions, Sergeant Stonecipher was awarded the Distinguished Service Cross and Silver Star, but six weeks later at Soissons, in actions exhibiting equal courage, he would be killed in action.

As for the German attackers, "They were beaten off with heavy losses again," Lieutenant Koubsky noted. The predawn counterattack—the fourth attempt by von Hutier's soldiers to retake their high-ground prize—had failed. German records would reveal that most rifle companies were not notified to organize for the attack until five minutes before jumping off, and regimental command would again blame failure on a lack of coordination with artillery and a "weakness in the organization." But woven through the reports of both attacking regiments is a common refrain: that troop progress was impossible because of the "powerful fire opposition" of not just American artillery, but machine guns and rifles. The 1st Division Journal would credit "the combined fire of our artillery and infantry." And in Colonel Ely's bunker, this success against yet another enemy attack was phoned up the chain of command: "Enemy infantry started across but never reached our lines neither did they return. All quiet now."

The sun broke above the horizon on the dawn of another clear, gorgeous spring day, and for the first time, these doughboys did not awake in the cast shadow of Cantigny. For Lt. Richard Newhall, still flat on his back out in the dry, wheat-stubbled dirt of no-man's-land, dawn shattered any fading hopes of rescue. "When it began to get light I managed slowly to edge myself over to the little trench and to slip into it," he later recounted. He shuffled with his heels and hips and one good arm across the hard dirt, dragging his shredded, bloodied arm until he poured himself into the corner of the small ditch. "I couldn't lie flat because of the dead corporal in the other end," which he added was "fortunate because I never could have got to my feet from a prone position." So Newhall sat, thirsty, hungry, but seated awkwardly upright behind some cover, blood finally flowing through his numb back and stiff muscles once again and "slowly thinking about how I would get myself back that night."

In the blackened and churned-up outpost where privates Gillespie and Drager lay the entire night fighting thirst and hunger and shooting pain, the morning sun warmed the cold dirt beneath them. Drager's shattered legs were numb, the pulpy mass of muscles gashed through with splintered bones concealed by blood-wilted pants. Any attempt he made to reposition his torso sent sharp reminders of the bullet in his back. Gillespie continued loosening and retightening the tourniquet on his leg, and at first light he reached into his tunic pocket and pulled out his soldier notebook and stubby pencil to follow his morning habit of crossing off another day at the front. "I shall always remember checking off May 29, because I had good reason to believe the final entry was being made."

Up in Cantigny, Lieutenant Sargent crunched through the charred cinders coating the village walkways among dew-glossed ruins following his guide toward Major Rozelle's bunker. "I found Cantigny all ashes as I had expected," he observed, "but the ashes had a more sulphorous stench than I had foreseen." He passed houses that were now only the "fragments of four walls" sheltering clutches of wounded soldiers waiting for stretcher bearers. Sargent followed the runner down into "a black hole that stared out of the ashes," and as he got halfway down the steps, a rasping voice yelled up from inside: "What fool is it that is coming down here in broad daylight . . . and showing where we are to the Germans?" Sargent hustled down the last few steps into the dimly lit, vaulted stone cellar and saw a handful of French officers and battalion staff seated on benches against the walls. Seated in the corner was the short, hatless, red-haired Major Rozelle, waiting for an answer to his question.

Lieutenant Sargent quickly dropped Colonel Ely's name and explained he was sent as an artillery liaison, to which Major Rozelle responded: "Come in, Mr. Artilleryman"—stretching the syllables out with no small amount of scorn—"and sit down." Enemy shells were again pounding the village above, shaking the brick ceiling and filling the space with clouds of dust. Rozelle calmly filled a cup of cider from the spigot of a hogshead and passed it to Sargent, who learned his assignment would be passing messages from infantry to artillery and listening to calculate the angle and direction of German batteries by rough acoustic ranging. This would occupy the rest of Sargent's day, and with "duties to perform," time passed faster than the dragging hours of the previous day spent in his observation post hoping to survive. But sipping his cider and monitoring the phone, he could not ignore the "incessant bombardment" continuing above: "Being in it all was like being in the crater of an active volcano."

On the surface up above, the "active volcano" of German artillery fire continued throughout the day, and any doughboys moving over open ground were targets. Twenty-two-year-old Pvt. Wiley Croswell, the youngest of five children to a farming family back in Felicity, Ohio, was lugging Marmite cans of food toward the front lines when a shell blast killed him. His body was never found. Outside Colonel Ely's bunker, Cpl. John Baumgarten and Pvt. Mirko Ivosevich of the 7th Field Artillery had come nearly a mile from their artillery battery to reconnect phone lines. "We were fixing one of F Battery's lines when a 5 inch shell fell about three yards from us and instantly killed Pvt. Ivosevich," Corporal Baumgarten reported. "When my pal was hit we called for a first-aid and a doctor came to his rescue but it was too late as he was taking his last breath."

Across the uneven, cratered open fields around Cantigny, single soldiers darted and sprinted up into the village and back again with messages, regularly attracting German machine-gun fire that followed them in trails of soil bursts at their feet, or whiz-bangs that exploded on all sides in dirt showers. Given the high casualty rates especially during daylight hours, front line commanders would often send two runners with the same message to the same rear command post to ensure at least one would get through safely. Pvt. Dozier Wren was running a folded field message back to Colonel Ely's bunker when a shell detonated alongside him, knocking him unconscious into the wheat. Fellow soldiers carried him back to the first-aid station, but he would die by the next morning.

Because of the lack of phone lines in the new positions and likelihood that artillery would slice up any wire that was laid, extra runners had been marshaled for the battle, mostly drawn from volunteers. "I felt I was helping to win the war by being a runner," twenty-one-year-old Pvt. Frank Groves of Oregon later noted with pride. "I felt I was saving more people and helping to end it sooner. Carrying the messages made me feel effective and important. I moved all the time and saw a lot. I picked up lots of watches from dead Germans and gave them all away to other soldiers."

Most messages carried by winded runners back and forth across no-man's-land contained pleas from front-line officers for food, water, and most pressingly, ammunition. Capt. Clarence Huebner, never one to request relief or reveal any hint of anxiety, scribbled a message on a slip of paper to be run back to Colonel Ely: "We are in pretty bad shape, the men are worn out from continual fighting and no water. Our losses in front line have been very heavy." Rifle companies in all three battalions were so desperately short of Springfield, Chauchat, and Hotchkiss ammunition that they would be unable to fend off another German counterattack.

Spotting the front-line ammunition shortage as dire, one of Captain Huebner's officers, Lt. Vinton Dearing, a twenty-two-year-old son of Baptist missionaries and a graduate of Colgate University, wasted no time taking action. He climbed out of Huebner's command-post cellar and ran back through the village, from one strongpoint to another, recruiting two dozen men to join him for a sprint back to the regimental ammo dump. Using the compass his little sister, Peggy, had sent him—which served as a talisman as much as a directional aid—he led the "carrying party of inexperienced men through heavy shell fire to the regimental dump," to be followed by a four-hundred-yard sprint hauling boxes back across no-man's-land.

Predictably, German artillery observers had spotted them, and as Dearing led his column of men back into the open, the shells began to fall. In the rear of the column were three men, twenty-three-year-old PFC Oscar Bolinger, nineteen-year-old PFC Raymond Pichotta, and twenty-six-year-old Pvt. Leo Monien, shuffling close together. Like the rest of the detail, their forward progress was slowed by their loads, with arms pulled groundward by the heavy ammo boxes they were lugging. Private Monien, missing two fingers on one hand from a saw-mill accident back home in Wisconsin, had difficulty lugging even one. Ignoring the enemy shells dropping in their pathway, a "shell struck directly in front of [Bolinger], blowing him into pieces." Monien and Pichotta, likewise, were each "killed instantly" by the same blast. Dearing and others ran back to check on them, but the three were dead. After hauling the ammunition up to companies in the front line and strongpoints, Dearing led a few men back to retrieve the dropped boxes. After darkness that night, soldiers in the orchard strongpoint came and retrieved the three cold bodies—or pieces—and buried them by the nearby hawthorn hedge.

By early afternoon, from his foxhole behind the barbed-wired slit trench in the middle of the orchard, Lt. Welcome Waltz was shocked at the number of German shells falling on the strongpoint. "I fully decided that our position was going to be pulverized and all of us churned up with it," he would report. "Such a deluge of shells, I never thought possible." Two German long-range howitzers had pinpointed the strongpoint's position with a sniper's accuracy, hurling pairs of ashcans with unrelenting frequency. "We'd hear its report & watch that molasses-can-size bomb as it howled upward, end over end, then head down," one corporal later recounted. "We became very proficient in our footwork." Lieutenant Waltz timed the shots with his Ingersol wristwatch, shots that sounded like "a great roar in the air . . . like a mountain was on the point of smashing us"—hitting every four minutes. Each pair of shells totaled 500 pounds of high explosives, and the resulting "concussion and shock was terrific."

One pair of detonations caved in an entire length of the trench, and PFC Leslie Venters and Pvt. David Wright disappeared. As the smoke cleared, soldiers flailed at the charred dirt to unearth their comrades, but when they pulled the two out, both were dead. "Their faces had turned black," the platoon sergeant noted. After each double blast, the cringing, shaking, and sobbing men cowering in the cross-trench then had four minutes to evacuate the wounded or dig buddies out from under caved-in trench walls before the "great roar" sounded again. "This type of stuff is what makes men go insane," Waltz observed.

The insanity must have possessed the platoon leader in the foxhole beside him, Lt. Thomas Watson, who, Waltz observed, "thought it was his duty to be constantly running over to his men." Driven by a "hopped-up battle condition," Watson was "even taking his pistol and shooting at our runners, from the front line, that were coming back to the strongpoint." Waltz worried that Watson's frantic movements were attracting enemy attention and "bringing a large amount of additional fire on us." "I tried to keep him down," Waltz noted, "but it was no use." As more shells hit the strongpoint, Watson again "ran forward to see something or somebody and one of the big fellows ranged alongside of him and that was the end of a very brave officer." From near a village command post on the orchard's edge another battalion officer, Lt. Jim Quinn, saw Watson get blown to the ground and sprinted to his side. "[A]pparently the burst of the shell was over Lieutenant Watson, and he was killed simply from concussion," Quinn observed. "There were no marks on his body that we found, except the thin skin directly under each eye was broken, and the blood was gushing from each one of these wounds as if it were being forced out with pressure . . . the Medical Corp[s] men could not revive him." That evening after midnight, Quinn and a burial detail buried Lieutenant Watson in a shallow grave near the hawthorn hedge with the bodies of two other lieutenants now over a day gone, John Curry and Wilmer Bodenstab.

The ranks of 1st Battalion troops holding the trenches southeast of the village were still thickened with the battalion reserve company and the engineers, and a rifle company from Major Roosevelt's 26th Infantry battalion still held the southern anchor in the Cantigny Woods. At 5:00 p.m., German artillery fire—uncomfortably steady all afternoon—picked up into another sustained bombardment, and the Cantigny Woods' canopy of foliage-thinned treetops and splintered trunks gave Roosevelt's doughboys no cover from the rain of shrapnel and high explosives. Pvt. Gustave Tack's chest was caved in by an explosion, killing him instantly. Shell fragments from another blast struck Pvt. Elmo Ridges in the face and Pvt. Torgei Roysland in the back. As a nearby corporal would report, Roysland was killed "instantly," and Ridges "only lived a minute or two afterward."

This bore all the unmistakable earmarks of a preparatory bombardment for yet another German counterattack. Down in Major Rozelle's cider cellar, Lieutenant Sargent noticed the bombardment above was getting "unusually intense," and the "aloof and in command" Rozelle sifted through panicky reports from his front lines of another enemy infantry attack, of contact being lost with 2nd Battalion to the left, and even more false rumors of German tanks. He sent a runner darting through the village ruins over to Captain Huebner's command post to reconnect and determine 2nd Battalion's status, but the runner was wounded by shellfire on the way. And although Rozelle deemed the reliability of these reports "unsatisfactory," he again worried his line might break. To be certain, he sent orders to Company A back in the old jumping-off trenches to move forward and "reinforce center and right" of the battalion.

This would push Lieutenant Anderson and his men right back into the deadly crossfire of the ravine, where they had already suffered casualties to a third of their company. Weak and feverish and caught in the tightening grip of the Spanish flu, Anderson shuffled through his company trenches, platoon to platoon, directing his men to gear up, fix bayonets, and prepare to head over the top. He then drew his pistol, climbed up on the parapet, and ordered the remains of his company to follow him forward across no-man's-land. His only two remaining officers, lieutenants Jim Hartney and Martin Williams, each led their platoons—only numbering about thirty men each—forward in columns. "We had to traverse the ground over which the attack had passed the morning before," Lieutenant Hartney noted, "an advance of more than a kilometer through a section which had been swept almost clear of cover." As they entered the ravine, into the line of sight of German machine gunners in the wood line to the front-right, bullets tore through their ranks. "The 3rd and 4th platoons encountered heavy enemy machine-gun fire from right front shortly after moving out into open," Lieutenant Hartney would report.

A few paces out in front of his company, Lieutenant Anderson was hit. "He was shot through the calf of the leg and the groin," Cpl. Gust Behike of the lead platoon would report. Anderson fell, grabbing himself in a futile attempt to stop the excruciating pain. "He spoke only a few words," Behike noted, "saying 'That he knew that he was done for, but I did it for Old Glory.'" With machine-gun fire still sweeping the dirt all around, Behike picked Anderson up, and in actions for which he would be awarded the Silver Star, "displayed courage and fearlessness under machine-gun fire while carrying his company commander to a place of cover." It is likely Anderson lost consciousness in his journey back across the plateau, and though his corporal got him safely to the field hospital, Anderson died an hour later. For "leading his command forward in spite of artillery and machine-gun fire," Lt. Robert Banks Anderson was posthumously awarded the Distinguished Service Cross and the Silver Star.

Back up at the front, Maxim fire and confusion continued tearing through Company A's ranks. Pvt. George Austin, thrust into the role of squad leader by the previous day's casualties, spotted some defilade in the open ground up ahead, and while leading his squad toward it, he was hit. "His death was almost instantaneous," his platoon sergeant would report. Lieutenant Williams led his platoon forward toward a line of shell craters for cover, and when turning to urge his men toward him, enemy fire pelted him in the back. He was still conscious, and two of his men carried him back to the field hospital, where he would linger for two weeks before dying. For "attempting to get his men under cover" in the face of such heavy enemy fire, Williams was posthumously awarded the Silver Star.

The company's only surviving officer, Lieutenant Hartney, and his 1st Platoon soldiers had reached the high ground on the ravine's left, where he led his column forward to cross the road toward Company B's lines. To his right, Hartney could see the other two lead platoons—being led only by a corporal and a sergeant—trapped in the ravine's low ground. He sent a runner, Pvt. Stanley Mullins of Detroit, sprinting across the gun-swept, open ground with orders for them to work their way through the heavy fire over toward the cover of the Cantigny Woods to their right. "[A]bout 15 other casualties occurred before the platoons got under cover," Hartney noted. But as Mullins ran back, an enemy Maxim followed him until it found its mark. He managed to stumble forward up to Hartney's platoon, and with the resignation of a man accepting his fate, said only, "Tell my sister I was not afraid."

Hartney led his platoon in two waves across the road and up toward the American trenches they were to reinforce, but German machine guns traced their movements and they dropped and hugged the dirt, grouping behind patches of tall grass. "The first wave crawled the remainder of the way to the trench and as it was crowded with men the second wave was disposed in shell holes about fifty yds. in rear," Hartney noted. One of his automatic-riflemen, twenty-three-year-old Pvt. Joe Graham of Mississippi, set up in one of the shell craters to fire on the German machine-gun positions, but "was struck thru the neck by a machine-gun bullet and died a few minutes later," his corporal would report.

A heavy German bombardment continued punishing the American defenders up in their crowded trenches, and every doughboy expected another infantry attack to follow. At 5:45 p.m., out to the front-left of 2nd Battalion's trenches northeast of the village, German riflemen could be seen pushing out from the l'Alval and Framicourt woods. "[S]everal of the infantrymen, two or three at a time," were observed exiting the woods and attacking the American lines "very doggedly." Captain Huebner's doughboys again cut the attackers down with small-arms fire, and flare signals brought shells from Summerall's 75s down in a curtain of fire, forcing the rest back into their wood lines. "Never at any time did any [enemy] troops reach our wire," Huebner would proudly report.

In the wood line facing 1st Battalion down south, a few enemy Maxim teams could be seen moving out and setting up, but no attack ever formed. "We reached our objective but did not have to fight," Lieutenant Hartney noted. "It was simply a matter of enduring the shelling and keeping out of the way of the machine-gun bullets after that." Capt. Clarence Oliver later reported that his Company B troops were shelled "heavily" but "[n]o infantry formation for counterattack was seen." Lieutenant Sorensen had his Company D troops prepared to defend against a counterattack, especially after a runner from 2nd Battalion reported an enemy tank attack forming. But as he would dryly report: "none seen."

The afternoon's only significant German infantry attack, fought off by 2nd Battalion troops northeast of Cantigny, had been launched by the surviving remnants of the 272nd Reserve Infantry Regiment. The assault force was beefed up with a few companies from the reserve battalion, but even these soldiers were by no means rested or fresh, having spent most of the day back in low ground under a heavy gas attack at the hands of Summerall's batteries. As with previous attempts to retake the village, this one had been hastily thrown together, rifle companies were notified and assembled late, and failure was owed as much to the attackers' exhausted state as to American fire.

By 6:30 p.m., word of success against yet another enemy counterattack made its way back to General Bullard's headquarters: "Everything O.K. counterattack completely checked." By 6:50 p.m., the artillery officer in Colonel Ely's bunker reported, "All is quiet along our lines." Even the German artillery was at last taking a momentary break, its gun crews gradually accepting a new reality now muscling its way through the consciousness of von Hutier's 18th Army: American soldiers would not be dislodged from the high ground of victory.

For Lieutenant Sargent, the damp darkness of Major Rozelle's small wine cellar had been a small pocket of sanity in the midst of all the madness, but for the constant ringing in his ears left by the counterattack's unrelenting shelling, he almost missed the rare quiet outside. "I did notice that about sundown the German guns ceased," he would later write. "I couldn't help noticing it; it was so remarkable to have a silence."

Down the wooden steps came another artillery officer and a runner, giving Sargent the news he was finally relieved. As he said his farewells to Rozelle and his battalion staff, Sargent walked up the stairs and through the rubble into the night's "novelty of silence" and thought of the admiration he had quickly developed for "the rasping and honest voice" of Major Rozelle: "It was good to have someone in command, enthroned beside the cedar barrels, who was always the same." Barely lit by the failing light of dusk, Sargent walked out of Cantigny's ashen ruins and down the slope of what was once no-man's-land. "It was good to feel the grass under my feet instead of the ashes," he would later recall. "And how good was the silence!"

CHAPTER 16

Final Determined Effort

By nightfall on May 29, the cost of taking and holding Cantigny was more than 1,100 men wounded and 250 killed. The heaviest casualties had been suffered holding the ground gained, just as George Marshall predicted. Seated in Bullard's headquarters and still hobbled with a wrapped ankle, Marshall estimated the division's total casualties so far at 600—half of the actual total. Down in that cellar, the few reliable casualty numbers and imprecise positional reports from the front could only piece together a blurred battlefield map. Even up in his bunker nearer the front, Colonel Ely, whose unheeded calls for relief had left him writhing with impotent rage for the past day, still had no handle on his regiment's total losses, or the reality endured by his soldiers at the battle's edge.

Eager for a firsthand feel, Ely sought and gained approval for "a personal reconnaissance in front of Cantigny." After a starlit walk through the village ruins and a small part of the ragged, crowded front lines beyond—packed with wounded and lined with stacked dead—Ely returned to his bunker in a red fury. His jaw muscles pulsating, he picked up his field phone to relay a message to General Bullard: "Front line pounded to Hell and gone, and entire front line must be relieved tomorrow," he erupted, adding he "would not be responsible"—presumptively for a German breakthrough. And he dispatched his intelligence officer, Lt. Joseph Torrence, back to General Bullard's headquarters to personally push for relief.

A division staff officer who had been observing the battle from Colonel Ely's bunker since Marshall had left the front the first night silently jotted notes in his small notebook, presumably for a later report to General Bullard. When he suggested aloud that the men could hang on longer, Ely exploded: "Let me tell you one thing and you can put it down in your little notebook. These men have been fighting three days and three nights and have been successful, but five of them are not worth what one of them was when he came in." More than merely indulging in a passing rage, Ely calculated that restraint would be incapable of bringing attention to the conditions his men were enduring at the front. "It is an injustice," he concluded, "not to relieve the men who have been fighting so long."

A French plane was sent up in the clear night to check how the front lines were holding, and the pilot tapped out a wireless report: "line is unchanged." Down in the trenches, Captain Huebner managed to get his 2nd Battalion troops some fresh water and food. "At night as soon as it became dark, details were sent back to fill canteens and bring up food," one of his lieutenants noted. "Also the carrying party brought up ammunition and distributed it to the front line companies." Up on the north end, Lieutenant Colonel Cullison remained in his command bunker a few hundred yards behind his 3rd Battalion troops, most reduced to defending their old pre-battle front lines.

Not far from the reoccupied German trenches, Lieutenant Newhall still lay half-upright, sunburned and dehydrated, cooped up in a ditch with the cold body of his dead corporal. With no rations or water left, he would die if he stayed put, and though he had no idea exactly how far back his company had withdrawn, he spent the first hours of darkness tapping his reserves of strength to make a break for the rear. "By midnight it was dark enough to move," he later wrote. "I removed all my equipment and abandoned it, except my gas mask and helmet." He fashioned a sling for his shattered arm out of his flare-pistol carrying case and forced himself upright. "The effort caused me to faint but I fortunately fell against the parapet and so remained upright." Revived by the "cold night wind," he muscled himself up and out of the trench and began shuffling back through the wheat.

In their outpost a couple hundred yards away, after a fruitless search for more canteens on the bodies of dead comrades, privates Gillespie and Drager were arriving at the same conclusion: help was not coming, and they would die if they stayed. With crushed legs and a gunshot wound in his back, Drager—possibly paralyzed—was helpless to move. But Gillespie, like Lieutenant Newhall, dug deep within and muscled his way out of the foxhole. "I put all my strength into the effort and found that I could move a little," he noted. "Knowing that the old German second line trenches from whence I had come out were about seventy-five yards, I started in that direction, with the thought in mind that water could be found there." As he began his shuffle back through the wheat stubble, Gillespie yelled back to his buddy Drager, "I'll send back for you if I reach our men." With lonely resignation, Drager exhaled, "There's no need now, it's too late."

———

Over a mile away, Colonel Ely's intelligence officer, Lieutenant Torrence, worked his way back to General Bullard's headquarters on his mission to push for relief. The motorcycle messenger dispatched to meet him was killed by shellfire, forcing Torrence to walk through Death Valley back to Villers-Tournelle, where another motorcycle driver carried him the rest of the way to Division Headquarters in Mesnil-Saint-Firmin. He descended the stairs into the "old wine cellar underneath a chateau," and found George Marshall on duty, with a handful of orderlies answering the phones. On hearing that Lieutenant Torrence had come directly from Ely's command bunker with a personal request for relief, Marshall sent an orderly up to retrieve General Bullard.

Bullard entered, and as Torrence would later recount the scene, "asked Colonel Marshall if this officer had been fed." The general's thoughtfulness disarmed the keyed-up lieutenant, who noted, "It had been some three days since I had eaten anything except the reserve ration that I carried with me." Bullard sent for the cook, who "prepared a wonderful breakfast" complete with "a bottle of wine." Torrence delivered Ely's clear message requesting—or if delivered equal to Ely's tone, demanding—relief. Though Bullard's reaction is not recorded, he must have left Torrence with the impression that this exchange spurred him to finally order relief. As Torrence would estimate in a letter to Bullard years later: "As a result of this contact with you my regiment was relieved the next night, which, I believe, saved a great many lives."

But General Bullard had ordered the wheels of relief set in motion hours earlier, just after word of the late-afternoon counterattack had reached his headquarters. Even as Torrence was eating his midnight breakfast, reconnaissance teams from the 3rd Battalion of the 16th Infantry were trucking toward the front to prepare for relief, scheduled to occur the next night. To ensure the trenches would be thinned back down to reduce casualties in holding the new lines, Bullard ordered only two battalions—eight companies—to relieve the sixteen companies currently packed into the front lines.

These fresh soldiers had spent the battle in rest billets in villages miles behind the lines, and they moved toward the battlefront as wide-eyed and anxious as Colonel Ely's doughboys had been at Zero Hour two mornings prior. Capt. Stuart Wilder, one of the officers leading a reconnaissance team, later described the scene as they crept through Death Valley, closer to the sights and sounds of war: "The valley was full of gas and bore the marks of heavy shelling . . . around [Ely's bunker] many dead were piled; an aid station had been located in one of the entrances and wounded, who had died, and dead had accumulated there. The quarry was full of dead. All about was the wreckage of battle and the valley floor was well churned up by shellfire except close under the steep reverse slope."

Captain Wilder and his battalion commander reached Colonel Ely's bunker, where "It was immediately apparent that the situation in the front lines was obscure." They made their way up the edge of the Saint-Éloi Woods, which "had been so heavily shelled that the woods were much thinned out," and passed exhausted machine-gun teams, occupying "badly shot up" foxholes in the wood line. In his tiny, lantern-lit dugout, they found Lieutenant Colonel Cullison, who pointed out vague locations on his unfolded map, as if guessing his battalion's lines. As Wilder would recount, Cullison "indicated the positions of the units on a map but it developed that he had never been over his battalion sector since the attack and was very uncertain of the location of his troops."

Captain Wilder and a few members of his reconnaissance team ventured up the slope to find the jumping-off trenches and old front lines "overcrowded with men"—the thin remains of Companies L and K—"scattered without any apparent order." And the doughboys there were as confused as their commander about their battalion's lines. When another officer with the reconnaissance team saw what appeared to be movement out in no-man's-land, he suggested the soldiers open fire. But they declined, admitting they were not sure if it might be one of their own. Their caution was wise—the movement came from a trench filled with the men of Company M covering the regiment's open left flank.

A keen eye might have also picked out two other moving figures beyond the chewed-up barbed wire in the darkness of no-man's-land. One was Lieutenant Newhall, expending his last reserves of strength to stagger nearer the division's lines. His few-hundred-yard journey had so far passed in a blur, as he was driven to the ground every few steps by fainting spells or the tapping bursts of German Maxims. He had blacked out twice and lost his helmet at some point. "The only way I could move was upright which was dangerous because of the random machine-gun fire, but couldn't be helped," he noted; "Movement was slow and I had to crouch frequently for rest when I got dizzy."

Newhall ran into ragged strands of barbed wire, a sign that he had finally reached the homestretch. "When I began to make my way through our wire, fortunately not very thick, I was challenged from our trench. They were suspicious of me for fear it was some German ruse, but finally allowed me to come in, and as soon as I could tell who I was [they] jumped out and helped me into the trench." Newhall recognized them as members of Lieutenant Haydock's platoon. "My first query was 'had we taken Cantigny?' My second was for a friend. . . ." He wanted to know where Haydock was, but the answer was written on their faces. "When I was told that he had been killed I went to pieces, and the sense of despair, which I can recall, I now recognize as grief. It has never been repeated by any other experience." Newhall was taken back to the field hospital, then a Paris hospital, where he would spend the next few months deep in surgery, rehab, and grief for his best friend.

The other shadowy figure out in no-man's-land was Pvt. Jesse Gillespie, crawling back toward the old German front lines, the ones Company K had captured and, for all he knew, still held. "Moving on my stomach caused such pain to my battered leg that I turned on my back, making use of both elbows and my left leg." He found the trench and rolled in, finding it occupied only by the lifeless bodies of Captain Mosher and Lieutenant Drumm. His despair at finding the line abandoned was relieved only by water he was able to find in a few canteens. Panting and exhausted, Gillespie sipped some water and rested to regain his strength. At the first hazy signs of the coming dawn, he pulled out his pocket calendar, and crossed off May 30.

After getting word that his regiment would be relieved the following night, Colonel Ely decided the shot-up survivors of Company F—still under the leadership of their only surviving lieutenant—needed immediate relief, and he sent Company F of the 18th Infantry forward to replace them. He also moved another company of the 18th up to stand ready as regimental reserve in the old jumping-off trenches of 1st Battalion's sector, empty since Company A had left them during the afternoon counterattack. When he phoned his decision up the chain—more as a pronouncement than a request for permission—he was told to "wait on Division."

But Ely did not wait. Although earlier ordered to employ reserve companies only for counterattack and not for thickening the line, he unilaterally decided that replacement of an exhausted, decimated company with one fresh and full-strength was actually good preparation for counterattack and not, in fact, thickening. Ely would not have to lean on such nuanced interpretation long, as General Bullard reluctantly agreed within the hour to release two reserve companies to Ely, absolving him retroactively.

By the hour leading to dawn, the surviving, shell-shocked remains of Company F filed back through the orchard and across the former no-man's-land for well-earned rest. They were replaced in the front lines by Company F of the 18th Infantry, whose captain and first sergeant immediately noticed unburied dead stacked behind the trenches. The captain organized a small detail to bury the dead "so that the sight of the bodies would not lower the morale of our men who were new to such conditions."

The company's four fresh platoons were still squeezing into the shallow trenches when enemy artillery opened up, giving the combat rookies immediate baptism by fire in the new reality of "such conditions" at the division's crowded edge. Detonations crept closer and closer until a single, direct hit killed three privates, Patrick Barthelotte, Forest Johns, and Thomas Zangara, and wounded fourteen others. Their corporal, twenty-three-year-old Elmer Dommel of Lancaster, Pennsylvania, checked on them, but another shell struck the same spot, killing him instantly. That morning, all four were buried in the same shell hole, but after the war, none of their remains could be found.

Dawn was again greeted by German guns pounding the full length of the American lines. Up in Company M's trenches north of Cantigny, shrapnel from a single mortar shell killed four men in a flash. Two of them, twenty-one-year-old Pvt. Conrad Malzahn and nineteen-year-old Pvt. Bernard Davidoff, both from Chicago, left no discernible remains. Down in Company C's lines fencing the village's southeastern edge, twenty-four-year-old Cpl. Sam Schmidt held his rifle over the parapet beside a member of his squad, Pvt. George Murphy. A whiz-bang struck in front of Schmidt, flinging him to the trench floor dead. Private Murphy ducked, and though showered with dirt, he was left unscratched. As their commander, Capt. Charles Senay, would later observe: "Battle, like baseball, becomes a matter of inches."

The bombardment intensified, and the field telephone in Ely's bunker began ringing as breathless runners started appearing at the entrance. Reports announced more shelling and urgently requested artillery support. At 3:30 a.m.: "enemy barrage came down on 1st and 2nd battalion sectors." At 3:40: "Report of 3-star rocket from 1st and 2nd battalion." At 4:25: "Shelling front line positions pretty heavily." At 4:35: "Heavy corps artillery counter battery requested."

Then the enemy shelling stopped all at once, the cue for German infantry to assault. Up in the front lines, doughboys could see two waves of gray-clad, rifle-wielding figures emerging from the woods. It was yet another counterattack, and as soon as flares shot up from the division's front, Summerall's artillery threw down a barrage. "[T]he first wave got through before our barrage was put down but was soon put out of action by infantry and machine-gun fire," a captain in Ely's bunker would record in the regimental journal. "The second wave was caught in our barrage and put out of action. Our losses slight. Enemy losses: a great many. No part of their line reached our first line."

Again the Germans had counterattacked the Americans, and again the Americans beat them back. The 1st Division History would call it the enemy's "final determined effort to retake the town"—an effort that was halfhearted at best. No fresh or additional troops were provided to strengthen the attack force; no protective artillery barrage was prepared to screen the infantry; and German records would refer to it only as "a feint attack." After the now-familiar sight of a tide of field gray receding back into the woods, the guns fell finally quiet for a few hours.

By midmorning, a full-strength battalion of rested troops from the German 270th Reserve Infantry Regiment relieved the 271st and 272nd, which, after two full days of being ordered into suicidal frontal attacks on the new, thickly held American lines, were only skeletal units, with many rifle companies unable to muster even ten survivors. And with more and more manpower getting pulled into the German offensive at Chemin des Dames, General von Hutier's forces could not afford to endeavor any more counterattacks against the stubborn Americans. No more attempts to recapture the prize of Cantigny would be launched.

For General Bullard's 1st Division, the fight for Cantigny was over, the battle won. After that point, as one officer would later boast, "no German set foot in Cantigny except as a prisoner of war." But for exhausted, parched, hungry, edgy, heavy-eyed men up in the trenches, the fight for survival continued. With no way of knowing the Germans had given up the quest for the village, the doughboys could only wait on another bombardment, or still another attack, knowing that up in these lines, with enemy artillery zeroed in on each new trench, death could still claim them at any moment.

Artillery on both sides pounded on through the overcast, gloomy day. The 1st Division Journal would note "heavy concentrations of 77, 88, 105, 150, and 210 caliber on Cantigny" in the afternoon alone, with more than 4,000 shells falling on American positions through the day, resulting in over a dozen more dead and twice as many injured. Summerall's guns—which had collectively fired more than 30,000 shells the day before—continued firing 75s against enemy lines and hurling 155 shells into enemy battery emplacements, their task aided by the capture of a map from a German pilot shot down midafternoon near Villers-Tournelle.

By nightfall, as soldiers in the front lines chewed on their last bits of hardtack rations and took turns catnapping and keeping watch, word that they were about to be relieved swept through their ranks with lightning speed. In his strongpoint, Lt. Welcome Waltz "very quickly, ran from one gun position to another" sharing the news with his Hotchkiss teams. "I had some difficulty in awakening them," he noted, "for everybody was down and out, having been without sleep for three days." Like most doughboys stuck for sixty straight hours in the same dirt, these men had reached the end of their physical tether, no longer capable of effective defense. "I doubt whether an enemy break-through at this time would have been seriously combated," Waltz would admit, "for I don't think the men would have awakened."

In the old German lines conquered and abandoned two days earlier by Company K, Pvt. Jesse Gillespie had spent the warm day resting between slithering trips up and down the trench gathering water from the canteens of the dead. After darkness fell, the cool night air energized him, and he plotted a way back to the American lines. "[T]he thought came to me that I might use two rifles as crutches and be able to make better progress, advancing at night with such protection as the dark would give. I tried this scheme in the trench, but it did not work. My right foot dragged the ground in spite of all I could do, causing unbearable pain." Desperate and running out of resources to sustain him for another long day trapped in the trench, he thought of cutting off his wounded leg. "I had with me a pocket knife with a blade about six inches long. I took it from my pocket and looked it over carefully. It was so dull from cutting tips, though, that I knew it would not do the job."

As the hours crept closer to dawn, Gillespie grabbed a Colt .45 from the body of a dead officer, chambered a round and turned the barrel to his head. But he couldn't pull the trigger. When asked years later why he didn't, he responded that "the end of that pistol barrel pressed against my temple was as cold as a lump of ice. It cleared my brain and gave me the realization that maybe, after all, the time was not quite ripe for such a step." As he

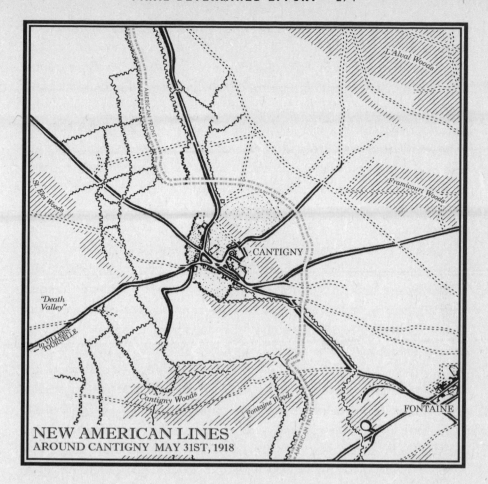

NEW AMERICAN LINES
AROUND CANTIGNY MAY 31ST, 1918

dropped the pistol, his thoughts turned to his buddy, Willie Drager, whom he had left up in the outpost twenty-four hours earlier. Gillespie wondered if he was still hanging on, and whether help for either of them would ever come.

By midnight, help arrived for the platoons in the front lines as soldiers of the 16th Infantry shuffled across open ground, squad by squad, allowing Colonel Ely's men to gear up, grab their rifles, and break for the rear in columns. In his strongpoint, Lieutenant Waltz was told to move his men back immediately and not to wait for relief. "I got them on the surface with their guns and equipment," he noted of his machine-gun teams, who broke down their guns and heaved them back across the former no-man's-land. They filed past the jumping-off trenches and old front lines and rested for a few moments before continuing the haul for three miles past Villers-Tournelle to Rocquencourt. "How we ever got our equipment back, I know not, but we did," Waltz noted.

Wearied doughboys from front-line rifle companies filed back across the dark plateau, stepping carefully through shell craters and tall grass, occasionally tripping over scattered bodies. In one shell hole, troops encountered Pvt. Harry Heath, still hanging on after being shot through his hips and foot two mornings earlier just after Zero Hour. "I only went about 400 yards when I got bumped," he noted. Since then, as with many other wounded soldiers, he had "laid in a shellhole two days and nearly two nights," immobile, rationing his water and waiting for help. Now he was saved. Two men carried him back to the first-aid station, where he was patched up, then trucked to a Paris hospital, where he underwent surgery, leaving him "minus an inch or two of leg." He would recover, but would forever walk with a limp.

War-weary, heavy-eyed soldiers, some with undressed wounds and all with strained nerves, dragged themselves from the battlefield and back toward Death Valley. "They could only stagger back, hollow-eyed with sunken cheeks, and if one stopped for a moment he would fall asleep," Colonel Ely noted. Many who filed past the first-aid station were awakened to a scale of carnage they had not known in their small, closed-in worlds at the front. Bodies of the dead were stacked like cordwood, with streams of bandages hanging from stiff arms and legs—bloodied testaments to round-the-clock life-saving efforts by tireless medics. One private walking past later confided to his diary: "[T]here we found a great many dead Americans—piles of them—who had gotten back for first aid and after receiving it had died before they could be gotten to a hospital. In several cases more shells from the Germans had come over and blown them and the litters they were in into little bits."

From there the battle's survivors trooped back through Death Valley and a gauntlet of still more scattered blasts of German shells. But the men, having spent the past two and a half days backed up against their human limits, walked through without flinching. These few soldiers were the tried and tested, America's first veteran warriors of a world at war. Back at billets they gulped down fresh water and a warm breakfast—"the first meal we've had in three days," Cpl. Boleslaw Suchocki noted—then peeled off uniforms stiff with sweat and dirt, and collapsed like heaps into cots where they could finally find rest, quiet, and sleep. There was no flag-raising or operatic finale, just relief, which had come, in the words of one company commander, "[j]ust in time."

Back at his headquarters, General Bullard typed out an official congratulatory statement he would send to Col. Hanson Ely: "The Division Commander takes great pleasure and feels it his duty to recognize, as much as in him lies, the gallant and efficient action and bravery of your regiment in the taking and holding of Cantigny for three days, May 28th, 29th, and 30th, under the most determined resistance and repeated counter-attacks of the enemy. Your losses in officers and men were large and the strain upon you very great, but you won." In a triumphant message to War Secretary Baker, General Pershing reduced nearly three days of fighting to four words: "Well planned, splendidly executed."

Up in the front lines, the doughboys of the 16th Infantry Regiment not tasked with improving the ragged trenches were assigned the grim job of burying the dead. Over the past two days of heavy fighting, the remains of the fallen, as one sergeant would report, had been "rolled in the nearest shell hole and covered up to keep down the odor from their bodies." But many bodies remained out on the surface, stiff and bloated. Sgt. John Wallace "helped bury a number of bodies there that were in such condition as to make it impossible to identify them." He reported burying a few the first night, then when he and his team ran out of darkness, burying "another bunch in the same hole." A captain noted that because burials were "under heavy artillery and machine-gun fire, as conditions were, it was impossible to place markers on graves in any way . . . No identification tags were taken from the bodies." As Sergeant Wallace would recount years after the war, "There are shell holes in Cantigny that I know had four layers of bodies buried in them and no markers were put up to show who or how many were buried there."

The remains of the few fallen who had been carried back from the battlefield—and the wounded who had made it back alive but then died of their injuries—were added to the division's makeshift cemetery near Villers-Tournelle. Just this fraction of the total losses in the two-and-a-half day battle doubled the temporary cemetery's tragic ranks, providing a disheartening glimpse of the battle's total cost.

Two days later, Colonel Ely submitted a regimental report based on the best information he then had, totaling the killed at 199 and wounded at 638. But his report accounts only for the 28th Infantry Regiment and does not include the total losses of the attached machine-gun companies, engineers, artillery, signal corps, medics, or any of the half-dozen reserve companies from the 18th and 26th thrown into the fight. And considering last-minute replacements, inaccurate morning reports prepared under the stress of battle, and many in the field hospitals who would still die from their wounds in the days and weeks following, an accurate total casualty count for the battle remains imprecise.

A search of all best available records, however, reveals the total cost of capturing and holding Cantigny at just over 300 men—either killed in action or later dying of wounds received in the battle—and approximately 1,300 wounded. And the French supporting the attack suffered their own casualties: a lieutenant with the tank battalion was killed by a sniper bullet to the head, and two members of the flamethrower section were killed. When considered beside the incomprehensible losses Allies had suffered in the mammoth engagements up to that point, the battle's casualty total inappropriately seems small. But as Maj. Raymond Austin would write home, "Casualty lists of an attack like this don't look very large beside those of a German 50 mile front drive, but when you see fine, young American boys lying dead in heaps of 6 or 8 or 12 here and there it's more than enough."

Even more elusive is a count of German losses. Swollen bodies of dead Germans filled Cantigny and the battlefield surrounding it. There were 275 bodies recovered from the village, and the number of dead that lay beyond the American trenches could only be estimated. Colonel Ely would report approximately 800 Germans killed, 500 wounded in action, and 255—including five officers—captured as prisoners of war. German records revealed a slightly higher number, reporting a total of more than 1,700 casualties, which left the entire 82nd Reserve Division with a "combat strength" only about 2,500 infantry.

On June 2, the same day as Colonel Ely's report, after improbably hanging on to cross off two more days in his notebook, Pvt. Jesse Gillespie finally mustered enough strength to slither back toward the old American lines. "I prodded myself into action," he noted of his inch-by-inch journey through the dirt. "Two hundred and fifty yards to go! Could I hold out?" He paused every few yards to catch his breath and find fleeting relief in the coolness he felt chewing on ripening wheat stalks. "With renewed strength and hope I hauled myself along until only thirty-five or forty yards separated me from my goal." Through his dry, strained throat, Gillespie called for help, and ahead he spotted movement—a soup-bowl helmet, khaki—to his relief, "a fellow Yankee" from the 16th Infantry, who approached in caution clutching a pistol in one hand and two grenades in the other. Recognizing Gillespie's uniform the soldier asked, "Can you stand for me to drag you in?" Gillespie whimpered, "I suppose I can, I've been dragging myself for several days." After being carried to the first-aid station and getting a shot for lockjaw at the field hospital, Gillespie spent the next eighteen months in hospitals in Paris and Fort McPherson, Georgia.

That same night, when companies of the 16th Infantry moved forward under orders to straighten the "big jagged dent in the line" left by Lieutenant Colonel Cullison's 3rd Battalion, a platoon found Pvt. Willie Drager lying in the same outpost Captain Mosher had ordered him and Private Gillespie and four others to hold five days earlier. Drager was dead, and likely had let go two days earlier, shortly after Gillespie had gone for help. The soldiers buried his body with the others in the foxhole, and after the war, at his mother Maude's request, his remains were shipped back for burial in South Kaukauna, Wisconsin.

For the men holding on to the division's new, exposed lines, life grew no easier, and over the next five weeks, battalion after battalion would take their turn riding out artillery bombardments and getting deadly reminders of enemy snipers and machine gunners that kept close watch on the sandbagged rim of the American trenches. As before the battle, patrols went out nightly to feel out the contours of a new no-man's-land; a few companies launched raids on enemy lines; and casualties continued to mount at a daunting pace—more than 500 more men would be killed in action before the 1st Division was finally relieved from the sector on July 8.

Along the length of the Western Front, the war continued, though at a quickened pace. Kaiserschlacht rolled on full-steam gaining ground, and French defenses strained near collapse as the German Army approached the Marne River in a thrust toward Paris. With the question of American aptitude in battle answered loudly at Cantigny, General Foch again took up General Pershing's offer for help. The very day Colonel Ely's fighters were relieved from the front, the US 2nd and 3rd Divisions were sent into battle. The 3rd would support the French in a stalwart defense of the Marne bridges at Château Thierry, and at Belleau Wood two regiments of Marines from the 2nd Division would not only hold the line against wave after wave of violent enemy attacks, but would counterattack, purging German fighters from the thick woods with such ferocity, they would earn the nickname "Devil Dogs."

By early July, with four corps formed, the AEF machine was finally operating near a capacity commensurate with Pershing's vision. In mid-July, General Foch ordered a counteroffensive launched against the large German salient still pointed toward Paris, and when General Ludendorff launched the fourth stage of Kaiserschlacht in the same place, in Pershing's estimation, it "played into the hands of the Allies." Twenty-four French divisions and eight US divisions—including the "Fighting First" led by General Summerall after Bullard had been elevated to corps command— were in position and not only repelled the German attack, they pushed enemy lines back nearly to their pre-Kaiserschlacht positions in a victory Pershing would say "marked the turning of the tide." It was here, German Field Marshal von Hindenburg would later admit, that his armies "lost the initiative to the enemy."

In growing numbers and strengthened more and more by a tidal flood of fresh American troops landing in France at the rate of 250,000 per month, the Allies kept the pressure on the German Army, forcing Ludendorff to cancel the planned final stage of Kaiserschlacht. From that point forward, the kaiser's forces would gain no more ground, able only to retrench between backpedaling retreats.

In early August, British forces in the north would attack the Germans at Amiens, pushing the enemy lines back over seven miles in a single day, one that General Ludendorff would call "the black day of the German Army." By mid-August, General Pershing had enough divisions in place to form the First Army, a force of a half million troops—to include the 1st Division— which he employed in a successful assault on the enemy salient around Saint-Mihiel mid-September. So complete was victory there that General Summerall would note that the Germans "set fire to all of the villages in [their] retreat" and "saw that the war must be lost."

Allied leaders joined to plan a knockout blow, a grand offensive in which British forces to the north and French and American to the south would advance "as nearly simultaneous as possible all along the Western Front," with "each army driving forward as rapidly as possible." The attack was launched on September 26, and again the American First Army played a pivotal role, grinding through strongly fortified enemy trenches from the Argonne Forest to the Meuse River. By the first week of October, German losses were so devastating that Field Marshall von Hindenburg cabled the German chancellor that "[t]here is now no longer any possible hope of forcing peace on the enemy," and urging him to extend "an offer of peace to our enemies."

While a flurry of diplomatic cables darted back and forth across western Europe, the Atlantic, and the English Channel, Allied forces continued forcing the Germans back on their heels with overwhelming speed. In what would become the largest battle in American history—and that Col. George Marshall would call "a wonderful and inspiring feat of arms"—doughboys helped purge the Argonne Forest and west bank of the Meuse of German defenders and kept advancing. By mid-October, Pershing had enough divisions in France to form a Second Army, the command of which he handed to General Bullard. By November, the First Army's khaki legions had pushed the kaiser's armies back more than thirty-two miles.

On the morning of November 11, Allied troops were still pushing forward when word of an Armistice reached front-line commanders: "Hostilities will be stopped on the entire front beginning at 11 o'clock." Word of the end spread like wildfire among soldiers who, per their orders, kept pressing their advance until the second hands on watches and timepieces all along the Western Front clicked onto the eleventh hour. The moment caught the 1st Division waiting on open ground in corps reserve for an Allied advance toward Sedan across the Meuse River, and for them, news of war's end "brought a confusion of incredulity and wonder." Pvt. Frank Groves, who had served as a runner at Cantigny and subsequently survived fighting at Soissons, Saint-Mihiel, and in the Meuse-Argonne, later recounted the moment the guns fell silent: "On Nov. 11 at 11:00 a.m. those sounds and vibrations abruptly stopped. The quietness that followed was awesome; you could feel it—almost smell and taste it. There was no singing, no shouting, no laughter; we just stood around and looked and listened."

Thus ended what was, to that point, the bloodiest war in human history: 8.5 million troops had been killed in action, more than 5 million on the Allied side. The United States, with more than 2 million military personnel in Europe by the Armistice, had suffered 116,516 killed, nearly all in the last five and a half months of the war. Of that total, the 1st Division had not only suffered the first casualties, but the most, with nearly 5,000 killed in action—more than 1,200 in the Meuse-Argonne offensive alone.

Though the doughboys of the Fighting First had fought in nearly every major Allied engagement in the final march to victory, they would be known not for their biggest success but for their loudest: Cantigny. Colonel Ely's 28th Infantry Regiment would be forever named "The Black Lions" after the region's coat of arms, and as a French Corps commander would declare in his commendation of the division: "[Y]ou, Sons of America, we are happy to call 'The Men of Cantigny.'"

For the soldiers who survived the battle and then lived to fight the rest of the war, their experience served as a psychological battlement against whatever the enemy could throw at them. "I saw more hell in two days at Cantigny than in all the rest of the war combined," Lt. Gerald Tyler would later write. The shellfire alone, George Marshall noted, "exceeded any experience they were to have later on in the great battles of the war." And it was the division's success in such a crucible that, in Marshall's view, "demonstrated conclusively the fighting qualities of the American soldier."

To be sure, benefits from the capture of the village were entirely local, and the strategic effect of the straightening of the small salient was almost inconsequential. But beyond battlefield consequences, victory at Cantigny had what General Pershing would call "an electrical effect," as it revealed the AEF's "fighting qualities under extreme battle conditions." The win finally muted the voice of skeptics and gave Allied leaders confidence in the ability of the American soldier in combat. "Had it not been for Cantigny," a 1st Division intelligence officer estimated, "the French would certainly not have entrusted a portion of the defense of the Marne to two other American divisions a week later." It was a confidence revealed in the words of the *London Evening News* just as word of the American victory broke: "[T]he short story of Cantigny is going to expand into a full length novel which will write the doom of the Kaiser and Kaiserism."

For the Germans, the loss of the village touched core anxieties about their American adversaries, especially after months of propaganda bent on coloring them in a contemptible light. The Americans had outsmarted them and outfought them, proving themselves a formidable enemy. A captured German officer would tell his captors: "The artillery and infantry work of your 1st division is worthy of the best armies in the world." Years later, after retiring as a major general, Hanson Ely—who despite his later, larger victories would be known as "Ely of Cantigny"—assessed that his regiment's victory "place[d] a scare" in the enemy: "To my mind the engagement at Cantigny was a cloud upon the German's horizon that later meant defeat to their cause."

Decades after the Armistice, on the verge of becoming the US Army chief of staff just as the world steered unwittingly toward an even larger clash of humanity, George Marshall rendered his own judgment on Cantigny's place in history: "This little village marks a cycle in the history of America. Quitting the soil of Europe to escape oppression and the loss of personal liberties, the early settlers in America laid the foundations of a government based on equality, personal liberty, and justice. Three hundred years later their descendants returned to Europe and on May 28, 1918, launched their first attack on the remaining forces of autocracy to secure these same principles for the peoples of the Old World."

A weighty verdict from the man destined to shape the battle lines of freedom in mankind's two largest wars. Like Marshall's words, the small battle inscribed on the narrative of the World War, in characters too bold to overlook, America's place among the Allied nations. Now nearly a century gone, beyond the turmoil of a world at war, the fullness of time has enshrined the victory at Cantigny as an indispensable link in the chain of American destiny, and one small step, a mile over the high ground of a small French village, toward an end of the madness of total war.

EPILOGUE
Until We Meet Again

On the evening of June 20, 1918, while the 1st Division was still holding its new lines around Cantigny, Mrs. Lottie Trout, the mother of Pvt. Carl Fey, was delivered a telegram while visiting her parents just down the road from her Schuylkill Haven, Pennsylvania, home. It was from the War Department, the return address every mother of a deployed soldier dreaded. As the hometown newspaper would report, "Tenderly she tore open the envelope and then burst into tears." Lottie's eyes absorbed the awful words between uncontrollable sobs: "Deeply regret to inform you that Private Carl Fey, infantry, is officially reported as killed in action, May 29th." It would be several minutes before she could tell her watching parents the news.

The following Sunday most of the town attended a memorial service for Carl, but in the days and weeks that followed, friends and neighbors returned to normal life, and for Lottie, time passed in a gloomy blur. More letters from the War Department came, promising "full particulars of the sad event," but breaking the news that his body could not be returned "before the end of the war." Her boy—her only child—was only seventeen when she had accompanied him to Pottsville and signed permission for him to enlist just three weeks after America declared war. The next day she had sent him off on the train to Hoboken and said good-bye. Since then, she had clung to his letters from France—like his first one from last July 4, or the one from May 6 telling her he was "going into the trenches again for the sixth time," or the last one, written on Mother's Day, which she had received just three weeks before the telegram.

Then came the mail one Friday in August, and the print on one envelope caught Lottie's eye: "Kriegsgefangenenlager, Darmstadt, 5th June, 1918." She ripped it open, and inside was a letter in Carl's unmistakable handwriting. "Dear Mother, I thought I write you a few lines to let you know I was wounded and got shot . . . also got captured . . ." He was alive. A prisoner of the Germans, but alive. It was, in the words of the local newspaper, "Like word from the dead." With relief but lingering worry, Lottie corresponded with Carl—he could send one postcard per week and two letters per month, and she sent him what he requested: cigarettes and candy. As the war wore on and the German lines kept getting pushed farther and farther back, Carl's prison-camp address moved from Darmstadt to Worms to just outside Berlin.

At the hour of the Armistice, Private Fey was released, and finally made his way back home to Lottie and his stepdad. He was honorably discharged, worked as a brakeman on the Reading Railroad, married, and had six children, though only three lived to adulthood. Refusing further surgery for his cheek and jaw, he forever bore the scar of the German bullet, but as his daughter would later recount, "he never talked about the wound or about being a POW." Carl raised his family in his mother's house after her death in 1944, and one bitterly cold morning in January 1952, his four-year-old grandson found him lying on the living room floor, dead at fifty-one of a heart attack after returning home from work.

Most loved ones back home who received the dreaded War Department telegrams knew the end had come, even if it would take some time to accept it. But those who received word that their son or brother or husband had been "wounded in action" were left in a horrible emotional limbo of uncertainty, fearing the worst until they heard further. There was no telephone number to call, only a mailbox to watch and wait. Lt. Charles Avery's mother learned her son was alive from her Emporia, Kansas, neighbors, whose son, Lt. Harry Martin, had written home from his own hospital bed: "I forgot to say that Charley Avery was slightly wounded and received a shell-shock, but not serious, so tell his mother not to worry." In Edgerton, Wisconsin, Pvt. Harry McCann's father received a letter in unfamiliar writing from a Paris hospital. It was written by a Pvt. A. L. Strong, who explained that Harry was injured on May 28 and could not write so he was writing for him: "I saw your son, Harry, today . . . He was feeling quite well today and there is no need for you to worry." Private Strong added that Pvt. Edison Ogden of nearby Janesville "asks you to give the news of him to his sister."

Linnie May Kendall, the widowed mother of Lt. Judd Kendall, the engineer who went missing three nights before the battle, was forced to wait much longer for news of her son's fate. She knew only what the War Department knew, that he was "reported missing in action" on May 25, 1918.

It was not until months after the Armistice, in the spring of 1919, that his body was discovered behind the former German lines in a shallow grave under a cross labeled "Lieutenant Kendall—American Officer." His remains were moved for reburial in the Somme American Cemetery, and "when the body was disinterred," a soldier with the Graves Registration Service reported, "there were no marks upon it with the exception of a gash in the throat." That, together with the uniform "heavily stained with blood just below the throat," and nine missing teeth, all attest to a violent, painful death at the hands of the enemy. Eighty years to the day after his final assignment, on May 25, 1998, Lieutenant Kendall was posthumously awarded the Silver Star and Purple Heart, presented in a ceremony at the Memorial Day parade in his native Naperville, Illinois, to his nephew and namesake, Oliver J. Kendall II.

In the summer of 1919, the doughboys who survived the war finally sailed back across the Atlantic, welcomed home as victorious heroes. The troops of the 1st Division arrived at Hoboken the first week of September, and were selected to lead a victory parade through downtown Manhattan and Washington, DC, led by General Pershing himself. As in Paris two July 4s before, the mood was exultant, but this time they marched with the sureness of veterans. Many in the khaki ranks had suffered physical wounds— vision permanently blurred by mustard gas, severe hearing loss from concussive shell blasts, or deep scars from shrapnel gashes. Pvt. William Evans, who was scarred by a machine-gun bullet at Cantigny, a bayonet at Soissons, and shrapnel at Saint-Mihiel, quipped proudly: "I was born lucky." Pvt. Jimmy Ross, whose dark-brown hair had been salted gray by the war, could only watch as his comrades marched the parade: he had been hurled from his feet in Cantigny's orchard by a shell and now could walk only with a cane.

A good number had made it through without a single physical scar, but for all they had witnessed and endured, no man returned unwounded. After the war, Russell Goodwin, who had earned a Silver Star for running back through heavy fire down into the ravine to retrieve the gun tripod from his friend Private McCracken's dead arms, transitioned from Army private to delivery driver. But over the next few years he would juggle jobs from his home state of Kentucky to Ohio until one cold Wednesday in January 1926, when he bought some strychnine from the local pharmacy, took it home, and swallowed it, killing himself at the age of thirty-two. Hometown papers would blame financial problems, but it is difficult to rule out post-traumatic stress disorder, a condition the medical field was still decades away from recognizing or understanding.

Families of the fallen, forced to move forward without their son, brother, or husband—and often without remains to bury—would also suffer deep emotional scars. Francis Redwood, the younger brother of Lt. George Redwood, had been only one when his father passed and was only thirteen when his father figure, George, was killed at Cantigny. Young Francis tried to continue life as a teenager, attending prep school with plans to attend Harvard like his hero brother. But while home on spring break in 1923, he killed himself with a friend's pistol at just eighteen years old.

Every survivor of the battle was forced to find his own separate peace. Sam Ervin had still not fully recovered from the bullet to his foot when he rejoined his 28th Infantry in time to fight at Soissons. There he and his buddy Lt. Si Parker, coordinated an attack on two German machine-gun nests, actions for which Ervin—who used a rifle as a crutch throughout the battle—would be awarded the Distinguished Service Cross and a second Purple Heart. Ervin returned after the war to study law at Harvard, then set up a law practice back in his hometown of Morganton, North Carolina, where he would marry and raise three children. He was elected a state legislator, state Supreme Court Justice, then US senator, a seat in which he would serve for twenty years, culminating in his famed role as chairman of the Senate Watergate Committee in 1973–1974, the year before his retirement. Senator Ervin corresponded often with his comrades from the 1st Division about Cantigny and time in the trenches, and he strongly supported veterans' causes, but with his friends and family he only rarely mentioned his war experience. Ever humble about his heroism, he never requested his Silver Star or his two Purple Hearts from the War Department, and he kept his Distinguished Service Cross locked away in a safety deposit box. The man who desired only to be known as an "old country lawyer"—and who was known throughout North Carolina and much of the country simply as "Senator Sam"—passed away in 1985 at the age of eighty-eight.

Ervin's good friend and UNC classmate, Lt. Si Parker, would earn the Medal of Honor for his own actions in taking the German machine-gun nest with Ervin at Soissons. After the war, Parker returned home to Monroe, North Carolina, where he married, raised a daughter, and worked in textiles while keeping a captain's rank in the Army Reserves. In World

War II, Parker was recalled to active duty and taught military leadership as a lieutenant colonel in the Infantry School at Fort Benning, Georgia. He continued working in textiles, retiring as vice president of sales in 1956, after which he remained active in his local Rotary, the American Legion, and served as director of Concord National Bank and as an elected officer in the Congressional Medal of Honor Society. In addition to the nation's highest award for bravery, Parker's decorations include the Distinguished Service Cross, two Silver Stars, two Purple Hearts, the Legion of Merit, and the French Fourragère, making him more decorated than the famous Sergeant York and one of the most decorated soldiers of the First World War. On the first day of December 1975, Samuel Iredell Parker passed away at age eighty-three. For all his accomplishments, it was his experience leading his platoon at Cantigny that he cherished most: "As a point of personal pride, I want remembered that I was in the First Wave of the First Attack that the United States Army made against Germany, and that the operation was entirely successful."

Artillery officer Robert McCormick returned from the war to his job as *Chicago Tribune* editor and publisher, but the battle of Cantigny forever colored his legacy. Although he had, in the days leading up to the attack, contracted the Spanish flu, he refused evacuation and insisted on being present to lead his battalion of 155s in the opening hours of battle. But the lingering effects of recent mustard gas attacks combined to aggravate his deathly condition, and he finally allowed himself to be taken to a field hospital. Major McCormick recovered, was awarded the Distinguished Service Medal, was promoted twice more, and finished the war as a colonel, a title he favored for his remaining life. After the war, he continued to run the *Tribune*, expanded into radio (naming the station "WGN" modestly for "World's Greatest Newspaper"), and annually hosted 1st Division veterans' reunions on his estate, which he renamed "Cantigny" for the battle. Colonel Mc-Cormick passed in 1955 at the age of seventy-four, establishing through his will a charitable foundation and leaving his five hundred-acre estate and property as a park for "the people of the state of Illinois." To this day, at Cantigny Park in Wheaton, Illinois, the First Division Museum and the McCormick Research Center preserves and shares the history of the colonel's storied 1st Division.

For Lt. Richard Newhall, life after the war began the day he was carried off the battlefield at Cantigny. The doctors and surgeons at the field hospital and Paris Army hospitals were able to save his arm, but it was mostly useless, and he would spend the rest of his life wearing a sling. He returned to Massachusetts, married, and began the career he most desired, professor of history, first at Harvard, then at Yale, then finally at Williams College in Williamstown, Massachusetts, where he would settle. There he would teach history for more than thirty years, with students that included future CIA director Richard Helms, and future Pulitzer Prize–winning historian James MacGregor Burns, who, until he passed in 2014, remembered Professor Newhall—who taught him freshman year history and "bore his injury conspicuously with his sling"—as "perfectly pleasant," but "very strict and very impersonal."

In 1924, Newhall published his first book, *The English Conquest of Normandy, 1416–1424: A Study in Fifteenth Century Warfare*, which he dedicated "To the Memory of George Guest Haydock, First Lieutenant, Twenty-eighth Infantry, A.E.F." As time passed, Newhall thought more and more of George and their wartime friendship. He corresponded and visited with George's family often, and each May 28—what he and the Haydock family would perpetually call "Cantigny Day"—he would send George's mother roses (after her death in 1948, he would send them annually to George's sister, Louisa). But of his own experience in the trenches and at Cantigny, Newhall would speak only rarely and with his customary cold, scholarly detachment. Although awarded the Silver Star for leading "his platoon in an attack on an enemy strongpoint" and retaining "command until he lost consciousness"—a citation he described as "quite inaccurate"— Newhall would never apply to the War Department to receive either this or his Purple Heart, explaining: "I have no desire to fly any false colors even of an 'official' sort." And when asked at a dinner party why his arm was in a sling, he responded frostily: "There was a war, you know."

Dr. Richard Newhall retired from teaching in 1955 but remained in Williamstown. In the years that followed, he spent much of his time reading, keeping current on world events, and corresponding with friends. In the privacy of his diary or in correspondence with close friends, he would write more and more about the battle, about getting shot, about his long vigil in no-man's-land, and about George Haydock, with whom he had shared a "most perfect" friendship. In June 1973, Richard Newhall passed away, six days after his eighty-fifth birthday and two weeks after sending George's sister, Louisa, her last set of Cantigny Day roses. He is buried in Williams College Cemetery.

Death, as it must to all, came to John Joseph Pershing at the age of eighty-seven on July 15, 1948 at Walter Reed Army Medical Center, his home the last four years of his life. He spent the years after his 1924 retirement writing his memoirs, *My Experiences in the World War*, which won the Pulitzer Prize for History in 1932. He maintained a public profile, promoting US involvement in World War II in support of England and taking pride in the service of his son, Warren, who served in the ranks as an enlisted soldier, and the advancement of his favorite former staff officer, George C. Marshall. Pershing's promotion to "General of the Armies of the United States" by President Wilson after the war leaves him senior to all subsequent five-star generals and second only to George Washington in American military history. He rests forever in the manner he wished, under a humble, unadorned soldier's headstone in Arlington National Cemetery.

As the only man to command a division, a corps, and an army in France, Robert Lee Bullard returned from the war with his own palpable taste of fame. Newspapers had dubbed him "No Retreat Bullard" after his 1st Division held on for victory at Cantigny. Between the Armistice and 1922, the Army shrunk from nearly 3 million troops down to fewer than 140,000, during which time Bullard was placed in command of 2nd Corps. His wife, Rose, died of cancer, and when he reached the Army's age limit of sixty-four, Bullard retired from service in January 1925. He made his home in New York City and took a job as president of the National Security League, promoting military preparedness and civilian training camps.

Although Bullard kept constant contact with his daughter and three sons and remained intellectually active—writing or co-writing three books about the war—his world continued to shrink. As his biographer tells us, by the 1940s, Bullard worked alone in a "dilapidated, walk-up office on Forty-fifth Street" and was "[t]hin, weak-looking, indifferently dressed in a rumpled suit that was too big for his shrinking body." He received the occasional letter from his former soldiers, and touched by their sentiment, he saved them all. One former lieutenant wrote, "It seems only yesterday that I saw that great bear coat of yours moving from place to place in the division sector to cheer and hearten those wearied by hardship and worn by the long nights' vigil . . . You were made of that stronger stuff that makes real men." Another effused, "I am frank to state that in my opinion you are not only one of the greatest leaders and tacticians that this country had ever produced, but that you are a real human being, which, after all, is perhaps the greatest compliment."

When World War II broke out, Robert Bullard followed its progress mostly in the newspapers. A print reporter stopped by to interview him—a war relic of another generation—and Bullard's blue eyes lit up recalling his glory days, his words as straightforward as ever: "My job as an officer was to make my men fight." On an icy day in February 1947, his thin, frail figure slipped on the steps of the Wall Street subway station and broke his leg. Shortly after, still in the hospital, he suffered a cerebral hemorrhage. Bedridden, he lived six more months, passing quietly on September 11, 1947, at age eighty-six. He was buried as he wished, in the West Point Cemetery.

Appropriately, on Robert Bullard's retirement in 1925, his successor as 2nd Corps commander was old "Sitting Bull" himself, Charles Summerall. Just one year later, Summerall was promoted to full general and appointed Army chief of staff, a position he would hold for five years, succeeded by Douglas MacArthur. Unwilling to lapse into quiet retirement, he moved to Charleston, South Carolina, and took the job as president of the Citadel, in which capacity he would work tirelessly for twenty-two years. At the age of eighty-six, he finally retired, and less than two years later, in May 1955, he died at Walter Reed—in the very room where John Pershing had died seven years before—at eighty-eight years old. To this day, the Citadel finds ceremonial pride in the perfectly drilled Summerall Guards, and its cadets worship in the Summerall Chapel.

Most of the 1st Division's junior officers at Cantigny returned home and to their former civilian professions, but a handful stayed in the Army, and a few squeezed through decades of downsized ranks to fill large roles in the next world war. Company M platoon leader Gerald Tyler, who stayed in the Army Reserves while he practiced as an architect in New York City and Philadelphia through the 1920s and '30s, was recalled to active service at the outbreak of World War II in the Corps of Engineers. As a colonel he would serve as post commander at Los Alamos, where he was one of a very small handful of individuals involved at the highest levels in the Manhattan Project. Tyler retired from the service in 1955 to Arlington, Virginia, and passed away in 1983. Company D platoon leader John Church served as an assistant division commander in World War II; and in the earliest fighting in Korea, as major general, he took command of the 24th Infantry Division when its commander was captured, leading it in brave fighting at the Naktong Bulge of the Pusan Perimeter until reinforcements finally arrived. Church retired in 1952 and died the next year, at sixty-one. In World

War II, Clarence Huebner commanded the 1st Division at Omaha Beach, through Saint-Lô and the Hürtgen Forest, and after getting his third star, he led V Corps across the Rhine and into Germany. After serving as military governor of the American Zone in Germany and then director of New York State's Civil Defense Commission, Huebner—the only man to have fought in America's first victory in Europe, at Cantigny; its largest, the Meuse-Argonne; and its greatest, at Normandy—passed away in 1972 at age eighty-three.

But of all the military careers launched in the Battle of Cantigny, none would shine brighter than the taciturn and expertly capable staff officer who planned the attack, George C. Marshall. After Cantigny, Marshall was promoted to colonel and continued logistical and battle planning in the Operations section of General Headquarters, and after the Armistice, he served as General Pershing's aide-de-camp. He became an instructor at the Army War College, supervised the publication of *Infantry in Battle*—which would become the Army's handbook for infantry tactics for a half-century—and headed up the northwest section of President Franklin Roosevelt's Civilian Conservation Corps. By 1936, Marshall was promoted to general officer, and on September 1, 1939—the very day Germany invaded Poland—he was sworn in as Army chief of staff.

At the outset of World War II, General Marshall coordinated the largest military expansion in American history, and was personally responsible for the promotion and selection of many whose names would become revered martial demigods, including Dwight Eisenhower, Omar Bradley, and George Patton. After the war, British prime minister Winston Churchill called Marshall the "true architect of victory" in Europe. In 1947, Marshall was drafted by President Truman to become secretary of state and head the European Recovery Program, which became known as the "Marshall Plan"—and for which Marshall would be awarded the Nobel Peace Prize. After serving as president of the American Red Cross and as secretary of defense, Marshall finally retired from public life for good in 1951. He spent his remaining years with his wife, Katherine, in their homes in Pinehurst, North Carolina, and Leesburg, Virginia, where he filled his days with gardening and avoided the spotlight as his mind and memory sadly deteriorated. On October 16, 1959, George C. Marshall Jr., the architect of American victory from the village of Cantigny to the shores of Normandy, passed away at Walter Reed at the age of seventy-eight.

As time marched on and the United States passed through new eras of warfare, from Vietnam to Grenada to Panama to Kuwait, living World War I veterans became a rarer and rarer sight, and the ranks of those who fought at Cantigny dwindled to just a small handful. Through the 1980s and early '90s, Herman "Dick" Dacus, the former lieutenant who served as a platoon leader in Company I throughought the battle, remained active in the local American Legion and 1st Division Society, often hosting meetings in his Brentwood, Missouri, home. When he passed at ninety-six on August 18, 1992, he was the last surviving Cantigny officer.

Through the mid-1990s, Frank W. Groves, the former private who acted as a 2nd Battalion runner throughout the battle, could still sharply describe Lieutenant Colonel Maxey's death ("He got hit, and I raised him up a little on the back the neck or head was a shell shrapnel," he recounted in the summer of 1996), and could remember carrying messages between Captain Huebner and Colonel Ely. Groves traveled to 1st Division veterans' gatherings, gave interviews describing his memories of the war and the Western Front, and marched in the annual Veterans' Day parade in his hometown of Lebanon, Oregon, wearing his old doughboy uniform. On September 22, 1996, he passed quietly in his sleep at age ninety-nine, sealing forever the memory, in living color, of a few thousand young men in khaki marching through the dew of French wheat fields into the rising sun of a new day.

The final words of this great American triumph cannot be my own, as any epitaph worthy of their sacrifice cannot be scripted a century later from the high ground of history. Only the voice of the silenced fallen offer words that bear the weight of the battle's personal cost—more than 300 soldiers, aged seventeen to forty-six, who breathed their last in their own corners of the bloodstained swatch of French soil that inch-by-inch measured their country's first step forward to victory on the Western Front.

Ruffus A. Shelton grew up one of nine siblings on a farm in Honey Grove, Texas. When he was six, his father, Benjamin, died suddenly, and it was left to young Ruffus, his five brothers, and three sisters to help his mother, Ruth Ann, maintain the family farm. He volunteered at nineteen the month after America entered the war, shipping off to France with that first summer convoy of the 1st Division and leaving his mother with daily worry for the safety of her youngest son. On the eve of the battle, shaped by the experience of eleven months in the training fields and trenches of northern

France, twenty-year-old Ruffus took a moment and wrote his mother a letter—an in-case-I-don't-make-it-through message.

Corporal Shelton went over the top loaded down in his gear with his letter in his pocket, advancing with Lieutenant Newhall's platoon in the first wave of Company L on the left flank. When Newhall was shot, the platoon pushed forward until overwhelmed by machine-gun fire, and Shelton and a handful of others fell back and dug a slit trench within sight of their wounded platoon leader. As the morning wore on and German artillery began ranging on their position, Shelton's thin five-foot-nine-inch khaki figure disappeared into the fire and thrown dirt of a shell blast.

Unlike so many young men whose bodies were blasted into crimson clouds of unrecognizable remains, young Shelton's body remained intact, but his brown eyes and dark brown hair framed a grisly repose: his jaw was blown off, his skull was fractured, and his pelvis and legs were shattered—another American son broken head to toe by the hot steel of a cold enemy. When the company evacuated midafternoon, Shelton's mangled body was left in the slit trench—where the wounded Lieutenant Newhall would take refuge after dark that night. It was Corporal Shelton's remains that Newhall shared the small space with for two days until finally crawling out for help.

A few nights later, Ruffus Shelton's lifeless body was found by soldiers of the 16th Infantry as they moved up to retake the position. His identification tag, watch, helmet, and equipment were removed, and in his pocket, the folded note to his mother was found. In his words, written at the precipice of mortality, are blended the hope, pride, and fear of a young boy willingly trading his future for the cause of country. There can be no better tribute to him and all who fell with him:

> Dear Mother: I am writing these few lines that in case I do not return you may know how I feel about the war. Mamma, we are about to enter into the first drive that the United States has made in the war and I am sure it will be a great success—In fact, I know it will. There are some of us that will not live through it, but mamma, the reason I am writing you these few lines is to let you know that I am willing to give my life gladly and I think very little of the man who would not. For me to fall on the field of honor I know would hurt you, but not like it would if you knew I was not giving my life freely for my country and that I am leading a better life—a life that when the Lord calls me I am ready to go.

Mother, we may not meet on earth again, but some day we will meet and there will be no sorrows there. And if I go, mother, in my last minutes on earth my thoughts will be of the dear little mother who has fought the battles of life for the last fourteen years—long years—to raise me to where I am now.

I have gone through many hardships since I have been over here that I did not look like I could go through, but I went through all okay and I am glad I have. I have always tried to do my duty and be as cheerful as I could. It does not matter what hardships I have gone through I could not compare them with yours or what you have suffered for me, but if I had lived to come back and show the world that I could be somebody, and most of all to show my mother how much I love her.

With love to mother, I remain your son. God keep and bless you until we meet again.

ACKNOWLEDGMENTS

My singular aim in this book has been to accurately tell the story of the men who fought the Battle of Cantigny, a daunting challenge in a time where death has forever placed each participant beyond my reach. The story is not mine to tell; it is theirs, and I have sought to build the narrative around their words. Reconstructing what happened on a battlefield ninety-six years ago has only been possible with the help of countless researchers, archivists, caretakers of regional or ancestral histories, and family members of the soldiers themselves.

I must begin with Joseph Persico, the best-selling military historian, who took time out of the research and writing of his final book to review the manuscript and give this first-time author incalculable guidance and wisdom. Right up until his passing in the late summer of 2014, Mr. Persico was never too busy to offer his advice and encouragement, and this book—impossible without his help—serves as one of many monuments to his legacy.

Col. Paul Herbert (US Army, retired) went above and beyond his calling as the executive director of the First Division Museum at Cantigny Park, Illinois, and gave me his indispensable advice and discerning eye in reviewing the manuscript. Andrew Woods, the research historian at the First Division Museum's Col. Robert R. McCormick Research Center, plumbed the depths of the museum's archives to provide me with unit muster rolls, soldiers' diaries and letters, oral histories, and photographs. Both he and Eric Gillespie, the museum's research center director, were extremely gracious with their time and made my visits there productive and enjoyable.

James Carl Nelson graciously shared stacks of primary source material he uncovered in his indefatigable research for his own wonderful books on the First World War, *The Remains of Company D* and *Five Lieutenants*. He provided a knowing ear for factual issues that arose, and his review of the manuscript and continued encouragement were most helpful.

Dr. John Milton Cooper, Professor Emeritus at University of Wisconsin–Madison, a studied historian on the causes and diplomatic aftermath of the First World War and biographer of President Woodrow Wilson, was kind enough to review the manuscript with a professor's eye. His feedback was invaluable, and I remain indebted to him for his time.

My researcher in Washington, DC, Kevin Morrow, a master of navigating all branches and wings of the National Archives and Library of Congress, provided timely assistance in tracking down volumes of archival records in both DC and Maryland. And Norm Richards, my researcher back in my hometown of St. Louis, Missouri, unstintingly answered my continued calls for hundreds of burial files, enlistment records, and unit morning reports from the National Personnel Records Center.

At the US Army Heritage and Education Center in Carlisle Barracks, Pennsylvania, Paul Kurzawa compiled for me countless World War I veterans' surveys, diaries, and letters from the archives. At the United States Military Academy at West Point, Marilee Meyer, the memorial/archives administrator, was always available to answer questions and uncover biographical facts about former cadets. Russell Horton, the reference and outreach archivist at the Wisconsin Veterans Museum in Madison, was very helpful in providing a transcribed copy of Ruben J. Nelson's diary. And down at the Donovan Research Library at Ft. Benning, Georgia, Genoa Stanford provided yeoman's work in digging up Infantry School student monographs from the 1920s and '30s.

Patricia Poland, librarian for the Local History Room in the Union County Library in Monroe, North Carolina, was extremely helpful in gathering all the local papers compiled on Samuel I. Parker, and she made my visit very pleasant and productive. Also in Monroe, all three of the sweet ladies in the Heritage Room at the Union County Courthouse were most informative and helped me immensely, and I am ashamed I did not get their names.

I also extend my deep gratitude to the following: Sara Keckeisen, librarian at the Kansas Historical Society; Linda Hall, archives assistant at Williams College; Elena Versenyi, undergraduate assistant at the Wilson Library at UNC; Nancy Daniel, assistant curator at the Senator Sam J. Ervin Jr. Library and Museum; and at the George C. Marshall Foundation, the archivist, Jeffrey Kozak, and the director, Paul Barron.

Although there is no substitute for archival research, as a finding aid, the Internet is unmatched. A few specific Web sites have been most helpful in tracking down true digital copies of documents and periodicals not otherwise preserved in physical storage, among them www.newspaperarchive.com, www.fold3.com, and www.newspapers.com. The Web site www.ancestry .com has proved essential in finding relatives and family members, as well as century-old census and birth records. I found www.findagrave.com to be a great help in tracking down burial locations as well as connected family histories, and for locating graves in US national cemeteries, the searchable databases of http://gravelocator.cem.va.gov (for those buried stateside) and www.abmc.gov (for those buried overseas) are unparalleled.

Through the course of my research, by far the most enjoyable and rewarding times were connecting with descendants and family members of Cantigny soldiers.

John Curry's great-nephew, Jim Nolan, was kind enough to provide me with the letters his grandmother—Curry's sister—received from Company E officers, as well as family history and photographs. Additionally, Jim's continued interest and encouragement in the project have been most uplifting.

Charles Avery's great-granddaughter, Annette Jensen, was kind enough to put me in touch with her grandmother—Avery's daughter—Corinne Avery Smith, who corresponded with me and spoke with me by telephone, giving me great insight into her father's active life, sense of humor, and colorful personality.

Sen. Sam Ervin's grandson, the Hon. Sam Ervin IV, a justice on the North Carolina Supreme Court (and whom I, as an attorney, address as "Your Honor"), was very giving of his time to correspond and meet with me to give me personal insight into the larger-than-life man he knew simply as "Granddad."

Sam Parker Moss very graciously shared wartime photographs, family history, and detailed biographical information of his grandfather, Samuel I. Parker. Michael Fey Hesser shared the letters of his grandfather, Carl Fey, from before and after his time as a German prisoner of war, as well as family and wartime photographs, War Department paperwork, and his mother's personal memories. And Tom Hartney, grandson of James Leo Hartney, was kind enough to share the wartime correspondence between his grandfather and grandmother—"dearest" Margaret herself—letters that could stand on their own as a fascinating love story of the First World War.

Additionally, I am deeply indebted to each of the following for opening their family treasure chests and sharing letters, journals, wartime photographs, and extensive family history related to their relatives: William

Morris, grandson of L. Irwin Morris; Charles Tyler, great-nephew of Gerald R. Tyler; Sam Morris, great-nephew of Richard S. Conover II; Stephen Smith, great-nephew of Robert Banks Anderson; Tim Senay, grandson of Charles Senay; Brenda McKenzie, great-niece of Paul Eskew; Christina Goldstein, great-niece of John Eaves; Bob Shelton, great-nephew of Ruffus Shelton; and Tricia Pearlswig, whose great-grandfather, Jack Jacobs, was General Bullard's wartime chauffeur.

Cameron Jones has done great work to transform my pencil scratches into professional maps that clearly illustrate the flow of battle. My friend and colleague Jeff Foster has proven his own talent for a second profession in photography with his wonderful shots capturing the battlefield and memorials in and around Cantigny.

Rob Kirkpatrick, my editor at St. Martin's Press/Thomas Dunne Books, not only edited and nurtured the manuscript but also propelled the story into a fitting vehicle and drove it onto a bright stage. He and his assistant editor, Jennifer Letwack, have both been ever-present and responsive to this first-time writer's questions and concerns, and have steered the course of the book's publication with energy and skill.

My agent, Sam Fleishman of Literary Artists Representatives in New York, has embraced this project from an early stage with enthusiasm and focus. His advice, fanfare, constructive criticism, and genuine friendship have been a source of confidence in the narrative and a reservoir of wisdom.

Many writers, present and past, have served as a personal inspiration to me, and their master strokes of talent continue to serve as a beacon where words match beauty and fill me with energy to keep trying: Anthony Trollope, F. Scott Fitzgerald, Barbara Tuchman, Ron Chernow, Jon Meacham, Richard Norton Smith, and David McCullough.

Many friends and family members have, through long conversations, listening ears, unique perspectives, and large and small acts of kindness, helped shape the project in ways they could not ever know: Lee Allen, Robert Brock, Chris Congleton, Phil Dixon Jr., Bill Drew, Clark Everett, Cliff Everett Jr., Mike Fitzpatrick, Frank Harper, Stephen Home III, Glenn Jonas, Glenn Keefe, Bert Kemp, Katie Motola, Dixie Parrish, Angela Pratt, Jon Randall, Peter Romary, Whitney Stallings, Kevin Sutterfield, and Greg Whelan.

For the deep insight of a career Army officer and West Pointer, I owe my brother-in-law Blair Ross Jr. a huge debt of gratitude. Years of book exchanges and countless hours of conversation over Scotch and cigars, centered on military history and stretching from the Napoleonic Wars to Iraq and Afghanistan, have granted me a perspective and depth of understanding I could not have acquired elsewhere.

To my late uncle John Zimmerman, who was twice wounded in action while serving with the Big Red One in France in World War II, and my late Uncle Ted Bossert, who served as a combat engineer in the same war, I appreciate them taking the time to share their wartime experiences, and I am still fueled by the fire of interest they lit in me as a young boy. And to Uncle Johnny's friend, the late Mr. Dick Dacus, a Cantigny veteran who hosted 1st Division veterans' gatherings at his St. Louis home where I was honored to meet him on a few occasions—and who often proudly stated "I was first of the *First*"—it was the stitched word "Cantigny" on his veterans' cap that left me with a lasting curiosity for the story surrounding a small French village with a name I could not pronounce.

To my late grandfather, who served as an artilleryman in the Army during World War II, I would like to think he would appreciate reading the contribution of his favored "big guns" to victory at Cantigny. And to my father, who served in the Army in Vietnam, I thank him for teaching me not only the obligation of national service but also instilling in me a love of history and reverence for the fallen.

To my sons, Watson and Keegan, I can only hope they will grow to grasp and appreciate the gravity of sacrifice in the cause of country, and I pray their generation will never experience it.

To my wife, Jessica, the star I steer by, I could never have told this story without her constant feedback, support, and encouragement. In the spirit of saving the best for last, of all my acknowledgment listings, she is the best and the last.

To all whom I have specifically mentioned and to the many I have neglected, all that is accurate in this story is a credit to you, and any mistakes are mine alone.

NOTES

ABBREVIATIONS USED

ABMC American Battle Monuments Commission, Arlington, VA
AHEC Army Heritage and Education Center, US Army War College, Carlisle Barracks, PA
CARL Combined Arms Research Library, Ft. Leavenworth, KS
DRL Donovan Research Library, Maneuver Center of Excellence Libraries, Ft. Benning, GA
FDM First Division Museum and the Colonel Robert R. McCormick Research Center, Cantigny, IL
LOC Library of Congress, Washington, DC
NA National Archives, Washington, DC
NPRC National Personnel Records Center, St. Louis, MO
PSA Pennsylvania State Archives, PA Historical & Museum Commission, Harrisburg, PA
WVM Wisconsin Veterans Museum, Madison, WI
WWR *World War Records, First Division A.E.F. Regular*. 25 Vols.

PRELUDE: A Speech

1. "a cold, bleak April day": Thomas F. Farrell, letter to Robert L. Bullard, January 11, 1925, Robert Bullard Papers, LOC, Box 5.
2. "Valley Forge of the War": Charles P. Summerall, *The Way of Duty, Honor, Country*, 114.
2. "ready to do and to bear all . . .": Allan Millett, *The General: Robert L. Bullard and Officership in the United States Army 1881–1925*, 193.
2. "all that we have": John J. Pershing, *My Experiences in the World War*, vol. 1, 365.
2. "speak a few words of confidence . . .": Ibid.
3. "the heart and arteries of a man . . .": Donald Smythe, *Pershing: General of the Armies*, 242–43.
3. "slender as a sub-lieutenant": Rheta Dorr, *A Soldier's Mother in France*, 79.
3. "tall, powerful of frame . . .": Ibid., 76.
3. "tailor-made for monuments": S.L.A. Marshall, *World War 1*, 279; Smythe, *Pershing*, 243.
4. "Robert Lee": Millett, *The General*, 22.
4. "couldn't pronounce the 'g' . . .": Ibid., 23.
4. "respected [his] poise, aggressiveness . . .": Ibid., 149.
4. "too impersonal": Robert Lee Bullard, *Personalities and Reminiscences of the War*, 42.
4. "He spoke of the soldiers as . . .": Dorr, *A Soldier's Mother*, 5–6.
5. "formed a rare group . . .": Pershing, *Experiences*, vol. 1, 392.
6. "personal connection with the general": Richard Newhall, "With the First Division— Winter 1917–1918," *The Historical Outlook*, 10 no. 7, October 1919.
6. "makes me shiver": Smythe, *Pershing*, 241.

6. "Lafayette, we are here": Pershing, *Experiences*, vol. 1, 393.

6. "found no difficulty": Ibid, 392.

6. "spoken under the inspiration . . .": Ibid., 393.

6. "I did not want you to enter . . .": Ibid.; "Speeches 1918–1920", Folder: "Speeches—1918 (and previous)," John J. Pershing Papers, LOC.

6. "upon their stamina . . .": Ibid.

7. "a few simple words": Charles Dawes, *A Journal of the Great War*, vol. 1, 92.

7. "personality and his lofty sentiments . . .": W. Gary Nichols, *American Leader in War and Peace—The Life and Times of World War 1 Soldier Charles Pelot Summerall*, 198.

7. "Pershing's Farewell to the First": Shipley Thomas, *History of the A.E.F.*, 69; *History of the Seventh Field Artillery, First Division, A.E.F.*, 43.

7. "solemn, determined look": Thomas Farrell letter to Bullard, January 11, 1925.

7. "it was not oratory": Bullard, *Personalities*, 181.

7. "[h]is manner and his expression . . .": George C. Marshall, *Memoirs of My Services in the World War*, 79.

7. "very stirring talk": James Harbord, *Leaves from a War Diary*, 265.

7. "earnestness impressed all hearers": Stuart G. Wilder, "Operations of Co. M, 16th Infantry (Personal Experience)," Infantry School Advanced Course 1929–1930 Monograph, DRL, 10.

8. "a certain lack of Napoleonic . . .": Edward S. Johnston, *Americans vs. Germans*, 40.

8. "I did not come here to make . . .": Pershing, *Experiences*, vol. 1, 394; "Speeches," Pershing Papers.

8. "Centuries of military and civil . . .": Ibid.

8. "Could there be a more . . .": Ibid.

8. "Our people today are hanging . . .": Ibid.

8. "said a few words": Dawes, *Journal*, 93.

8. "There was no effort on the part . . .": Ibid.

9. "made a profound impression on all . . .": Marshall, *Memoirs*, 78.

9. "a weak speech saying we were . . .": Richard Norton Smith, *The Colonel: The Life and Legend of Robert R. McCormick*, 201.

9. "[W]hat did you think of the . . .": *History of the Seventh Field Artillery*, 43–44. Note: for clarity, the ending quote from the same source was changed from the original ". . . but did you get the boots?" to "but did you [notice] the boots?"

9. "We began to think when our . . .": Experience Report of Lt. Anton W. Schneider, 1st Engineers, December 20, 1918, NA, Record Group 92, Entry 1241, Box 70.

9. "with a rather creepy feeling . . .": Experience Report of Lt. Thomas F. Farrell, 1st Engineers, December 1918, NA, Record Group 92, Entry 1241, Box 70.

9. "A picture that vividly comes . . ." Thomas Farrell letter to Bullard, January 11, 1925.

9. "one of the outstanding incidents . . .": Nichols, *Summerall*, 198.

9. "solemn": Dawes, *Journal*, 93.

9. "supreme sacrifice": Pershing, *Experiences*, vol. 1, 394; "Speeches," Pershing Papers.

11. 116,516 envelopes . . . Department of Veterans Affairs, "America's Wars Fact Sheet," May 2013.

12. "this great battle": Pershing, *Experiences*, vol. 1, 394; "Speeches," Pershing Papers.

12. "Americans Take Town Alone": May 29, 1918, issue of *Lima Daily News* (OH).

12. "Sammies Shout 'We're on . . .": May 29, 1918, issue of *Clearfield Progress* (PA).

12. "Yankees Yell As They . . .": May 29, 1918, issue of *Decatur Daily Democrat* (IN).

13. "The world must be made safe . . .": John Milton Cooper, *Woodrow Wilson: A Biography*, 387; *Source Records of the Great War*, vol. 5, A.D. 1917, 116.

14. "great battle of the greatest war . . .": Pershing, *Experiences*, vol. 1, 394; "Speeches," Pershing Papers.

1. Let 'em Come

16. "battle rehearsal": Lt. Col. George C. Marshall, Memorandum on Infantry training for Operation Against Cantigny, May 19, 1918, NA, RG 120, Entry1241, Box 18.

16. "great battle of the greatest war . . .": Pershing, *Experiences,* vol. 1, 394; "Speeches," Pershing Papers.

17. "the most terrible and disastrous . . .": *Source Records of the Great War,* vol. 5, 116–17.

17. "J-Day": 'Very Secret' Memorandum on J-Day and H-Hour, Col. Campbell King, May 27, 1918, NA, RG 120, Entry 1241, Box 18.

18. "the fun maker": Lt. Irving Wood, Letter to sister of Lt. John V. Curry, January 8, 1919, Private Collection.

18. "No such thing as a dugout . . .": Gerald R. Tyler, letter to mother, June 3, 1918, "Aiken Co. Boy Goes Over the Top," July 10, 1918, issue of *Aiken Journal and Review* (SC).

18. "nothing can be done but wait . . .": Cpt. Edward S. Johnston, Infantry School Monograph, "The Day Before Cantigny," DRL, 30.

18. "wrapped in smoke and fire": Ibid.

18. "when the scattered mist . . .": Ibid.

19. "Ollie": Report of Pvt. Franklin Berry, April 1920, Burial File of Fred E. Turner, NPRC.

19. "killed instantly by piece of shell . . .": Report of Pvt. Franklin Berry, Burial File of Charles T. Shepard, NPRC.

19. "instantly": Report of Pvt. Charles Morrison, Burial File of Homer H. Blevins, NPRC.

19. "It was more concussion than . . .": Report of Pvt. Franklin Berry, Burial File of Fred E. Turner, NPRC.

19. "Captain, I don't want to wake . . .": Johnston, Monograph, 16.

19. "somewhat concerned": Ibid.

19. "Lieutenant Desmond here": Johnston, *Americans,* 52.

19. "Desperate": Report of Pvt. Mitchell Crowell, Burial File of Lt. Thomas W. Desmond, NPRC.

20. "liaison officer": Field Order No. 19, Relief in Northern Subsector, 26 May 1918, NA, RG 120, Entry 1241, Box 15.

20. "[I]t's hard to tell; the old . . .": Johnston, Monograph, 16.

20. "too far from the platoons": Ibid., 15.

20. "stood still in the hush . . .": Ibid., 16.

20. "hard winter": Johnston, *Americans,* 12

21. "a warm and living symbol . . .": Ibid., 32.

21. "soul-searching experience": Ibid., 34.

21. "If this man can be slain . . .": Ibid.

21. "[W]e were particularly blessed . . .": Irving Wood letter to sister of Curry, December 8, 1919.

21. "a happy family, bound together . . .": Ibid.

21. "the confidence born of unity . . .": Johnston, *Americans,* 35.

21. "was certainly the best in . . .": Capt. Edward S. Johnston, Letter to sister of Lt. John V. Curry, November 20, 1918, PSA.

21. "Daylight had come": Ibid.

22. "[t]he bombardment on the plateau . . .": Ibid.

22. "plump and placid": Johnston, *Americans,* 53.

22. "The Boches are going to attack . . .": Johnston, Monograph, 18.

22. "keep in frequent touch by runner . . .": Ibid.

22. "instantly": Reports of Pvt. Franklin Berry, Burial Files of Mike Dummit and James W. Adams, NPRC.

22. "shell wound penetrating left leg . . .": Report of Field Hospital No. 12, Daily Report of Casualties and Changes, May 27, 1918, NPRC.

22. "movement there . . . unquestionably something . . .": Johnston, *Monograph*, 31.

23. "There was a tumultuous thudding . . .": Ibid.

23. "Go to the captain. Tell him . . .": Ibid.

23. "lengthen the range": Annex 9 to Field Order No. 18, May 22, 1918, NA, RG 120, Entry 1241, Box 18.

23. "The trench had become a scene of horror": Ibid.

23. "exploded at his feet": Grave Location Data Form, Burial File for William Cameron, NPRC.

24. "exhibited unusual courage in . . .": *WWR*, vol. 23.

25. "Dickie": Lt. Jeremiah Evarts, *Cantigny: A Corner of the War*, 56.

25. "By God, I'll bet they are as scared . . .": Johnston, *Monograph*, 32.

25. "bit of sleep": Ibid., 18.

25. "Gray with dirt, and somewhat . . .": Ibid., 19.

26. "attacking": Ibid., 31.

26. "I'm going up to look at things": Johnston, *Americans*, 54.

26. "[T]he courteous calm of our distant . . .": Ibid., 54–55.

26. "Lieutenant says Boches are attacking": Ibid., 55.

26. "Notify battalion.": Ibid.

27. "steady, even popping": Johnston, *Monograph*, 32.

28. "the thin crackle of rifles": Ibid., 31.

28. "the rear line of attack went down . . .": Ibid., 32–33.

28. "Whatever it was, it meant a lot to them": Johnston, *Americans*, 59.

28. "All six of them went down": Ibid.

28. "new replacement": Ibid.

28. "deserter, traitor, spy": Johnston, *Monograph*, 35.

29. "[W]e all started to pick off the Germans . . .": *St. Paul's School in the Great War*, 58.

29. "cool, enthusiastic, and was doing good work": Ibid.

29. "I'm through, take my rifle": Ibid.

29. "had a smile on his face . . .": Ibid.

29. "in spite of all the turmoil and death . . .": Ibid., 59.

30. "over blocks of earth and debris": Johnston, *Monograph*, 21.

30. "only three or four": Ibid., 36.

30. "not a trench, but a twisted conglomeration . . .": Ibid., 33.

30. "[H]e was immediately over me . . .": Charles D. Avery, Letter to sister of Lt. John V. Curry, April 28, 1919, PSA.

31. "almost suffocated, and in pitiful physical condition": Johnston, *Monograph*, 34.

31. "Ten minutes more and I know I should have suffocated": Avery letter, April 28, 1919.

31. "tender way": Ibid.

31. "a proud mental state": Johnston, *Monograph*, 34.

31. "I think we both cried a little": Avery letter, April 28, 1919.

31. "sat down suddenly, this steady, brave . . .": Johnston, *Americans*, 60.

31. "that prisoners must be taken at all costs": Col. Frank Parker, "Report on German Raid and Prisoners Taken This Date," HQ, 18th Infantry, May 27, 1918, FDM.

32. "had told them everything they would have to do": Ibid. 66.

32. "with courage and with dogged endurance": Ibid.

32. "safe for democracy": Cooper, *Woodrow Wilson*, 387; *Source Records of the Great War*, vol. 5, A.D. 1917, 116.

2. The Advance Guard

33. "lack of belligerence": Cooper, *Woodrow Wilson*, 285.

33. "[t]he United States must be neutral . . .": Ibid.

33. "put a curb on our sentiments": Ibid.

34. "Plattsburg Movement": J. Garry Clifford, *The Citizen Soldiers: The Plattsburg Training Camp Movement, 1913–1920.*

34. "call to duty": Richard Newhall, *Newhall and Williams College—the Selected Papers of a History Teacher at a New England College*, 53.

34. "He kept us out of war": Cooper, *Woodrow Wilson*, 359.

34. "Zimmermann Telegram": Barbara Tuchman, *The Zimmermann Telegram.*

35. "never saw a fight he didn't . . .": Smith, *The Colonel*, 180.

35. "Wilson Confirms Fact of German Plot Against U.S.": March 1, 1917, issue of the *New Castle News* (PA).

35. "Three Musketeers": June 5, 1918, June 28, 1918, August 14, 1918, September 24, 1918, and October 3, 1918 issues of the *Denton Record-Chronicle* (TX).

35. "distressing and oppressive duty": *Source Records of the Great War, Vol. V, A.D. 1917*, 116–17.

36. "to employ the entire naval and military . . .": Ibid.

36. "immediate addition to the armed forces": Ibid.

36. "Citizens of Janesville: The National . . .": April 7, 1917, issue of the *Janesville Daily-Gazette* (WI).

37. "[f]rom town and country, salon and factory . . .": James Mead, *The Doughboys*, 73.

37. "I made such good progress in running . . .": September 24, 1918, issue of the *Denton Record-Chronicle* (TX).

37. "We were at war, I was single . . .": Herman Dacus, World War I Veterans Survey, September 1982, AHEC.

37. "wished to volunteer . . .": Frank William Groves, World War I Veterans Survey, December 1980, AHEC.

38. "[A]pplied for enlistment on April 10, 1917 . . .": Ruben J. Nelson diary, WVM.

38. "None of the new weapons developed . . .": Dacus, WWI Veterans Survey.

38. "the training did nothing to equip us . . .": Groves, WWI Veterans Survey.

38. "in active mutiny or sullen noncooperation": Millett, *The General*, 302.

39. "Wilson was": Cooper, *Woodrow Wilson*, 396.

39. "plainly the estate of man . . .": Bullard, *Personalities*, 42.

39. "Nigger Jack": John Perry, *Pershing, Commander of the Great War*, 34.

39. "cool as a bowl of cracked ice": Ibid., 34.

40. "four infantry regiments and . . .": Pershing, *Experiences*, vol. 1, 2.

41. "Find Co. of 70 men and one officer . . .": Nelson diary.

41. "was not on the list of those to be transferred": September 24, 1918, issue of the *Denton Record-Chronicle* (TX).

41. "Every man stepped forward": March 18, 1919, issue of the *Denton Record-Chronicle* (TX).

41. "These volunteers . . .": Clifford, *Citizen Soldiers*, 260.

42. "Like cadets at the U.S. Military Academy . . .": Bullard, *Personalities*, 17.

42. "He knows how to handle men . . .": Richard Newhall, letter to mother, May 19, 1917, *Selected Papers*, 57.

42. "learned quickly to obey acting non-coms": Dacus, WWI Veterans Survey.

42. "Commander-in-Chief": *The History of the First Division During the World War*, 40.

42. "depressed": Ibid., 18.

43. "impressed with his poise and his air . . .": Ibid., 37.

43. "General, we are giving you some . . .": Ibid.

43. "complete freedom in conducting operations": Cooper, *Woodrow Wilson*, 402.

43. "cooperate as a component of whatever army . . .": Pershing, *Experiences*, vol. 1, 38–39.

44. "in a most depressed frame of mind over being left behind": Marshall, *Memoirs*, 3.

44. "First Expeditionary Division": *History of the First*, 1.

44. "the best one received and the only complete one": Forrest Pogue, *George C. Marshall: Education of a General, 1880–1939*, 89; Leonard Moseley, *Marshall: Hero for Our Time*, 32.

44. "Once an army is involved in war . . .": Pogue, *George C. Marshall*, 29.

45. "fate": Marshall, *Memoirs*, 5.

45. "for extended foreign service": Millett, *The General*, 309.

45. "the next train": Bullard, *Personalities*, 19.

45. "watching the endless column of infantry . . .": Marshall, *Memoirs*, 6.

46. "Set sail for France . . .": Nelson diary.

46. "About 1 p.m., June 14th, we put to sea . . .": Bullard, *Personalities*, 32.

46. "Everyone was ill": Groves, WW1 Veterans Survey.

46. "Everyone was new to everything": Marshall, *Memoirs*, 6–7.

46. "On 19th day we run into school of porpoise . . .": Nelson diary; Note: "porpose" in original corrected to "porpoise."

46. "On the 24th we run into a sub zone . . .": Ibid.

46. "We were soon zig-zagging . . .": Bullard, *Personalities*, 32.

46. "Immediately all the ships changed their course . . .": Marshall, *Memoirs*, 9.

47. "slept little until 1 a.m., and then with all . . .": Bullard, *Personalities*, 35.

47. "June 28th 1917 . . .": Nelson diary; Note: the misspelled "battle cruise" in the original corrected to "Battle Cruiser."

47. "the thing that impressed these unaccustomed eyes . . .": Bullard, *Personalities*, 37–38.

47. "the green hill slopes and little cottages . . .": Marshall, *Memoirs*, 11.

47. "There was not a cheer": Ibid.

47. "There was an air of grimness and sadness . . .": Charles Senay, "From Shavetail to Captain," Unpublished Memoir, Private Collection, 15.

48. "the advance guard of America's fighting men": Pershing, foreword to *History of the First*, xv.

3. Must Not Fail

49. "The towns in which the division was billeted . . .": Newhall, "With the First Division."

49. "often dilapidated, always dark, and invariably cold": Ibid.

49. "The nearest open ground . . ." Marshall, *Memoirs*, 15.

50. "untrained, awkward appearance": Pershing, *Experiences*, vol. 1, 91.

50. "It was a fine, fine sight": Bullard, *Personalities*, 51.

50. "The men of the newly arrived division . . .": Theodore Roosevelt, *Average Americans*, 25–26.

50. "They call us the foreign legion": Dorr, *A Soldier's Mother*, 65.

50. "The Division was truly representative of America": *History of the First*, 13.

51. "Harlem Hellfighters": Stephen L. Harris, *Harlem's Hellfighters*.

51. "troops lived daily and hourly . . .": *History of the First*, 18.

51. "There was a constant rumbling of guns . . .": Senay, "Shavetail to Captain," 22.

51. "In the midst of war, we had to prepare for war . . .": Bullard, *Personalities*, 60.

51. "There was nothing but drill every day . . .": Nelson diary.

52. "First call about 6 o'clock . . .": Roosevelt, *Americans*, 55.

51. "[T]here was no one with the command . . .": Ibid., 59.

52. "devil-may-care": *History of the First*, 20.

52. "They had a magnificent fighting record": Marshall, *Memoirs*, 18.

52. "friendly rivalry": *History of the First*, 21.

52. "Washington Center": Ibid.

53. "Yeah, they tell you it is timed for 5 seconds": July 4, 1918, issue of *Emporia Gazette*.

53. "not too good—first military funeral I attended . . .": Dacus, WWI Veterans Survey.

53. "jammed frequently": Ibid.

53. "French instructors were greatly surprised . . .": *History of the First*, 22.

54. "must be won by driving the enemy out . . .": Pershing, *Experiences*, vol. 1, 152.

54. "[t]he infantry is the principal and most important . . .": *Field Service Regulations—U.S. Army 1914 (Corrected to 1917)*, 74.

54. "the essential weapons of the infantry": Pershing, *Experiences*, vol. 1, 154.

54. "emergency weapons": *Field Service Regulations*, 79; Mark Grotelueschen, *The AEF Way of War*, 15–16.

54. "the ultimate act": Grotelueschen, *The AEF Way*, 23; Douglas Johnson and Rolphe Hillman, *Soissons 1918*, 153.

54. "as obsolete as the crossbow": Grotelueschen, *The AEF Way*, 13.

54. "the benefit of our dearly bought experience": John F. Votaw, *The American Expeditionary Forces in World War I*, 64.

55. "utter discouragement and spiritlessness": Bullard, *Personalities*, 98.

55. "very tactfully": Ibid., 103.

55. "Not only did no one know how to teach . . .": Wilder, "Operations of Co. M," 4.

55. "Both tactics and equipment were tried on the dog . . .": Ibid.

56. "acclimatization and instruction in small units": *History of the First*, 18.

56. "serve with French battalions in trenches . . .": Ibid.

56. "The enthusiasm of the infantrymen reached . . .": Marshall, *Memoirs*, 42.

56. "rolling and attractive country": *History of the First*, 27.

56. "relatively quiet": Ibid.

56. "Serious operations in this section of France": Marshall, *Memoirs*, 45.

56. "were all very green and very earnest": Roosevelt, *Americans*, 86.

56. "The first thrill of service in the trenches soon passed": Marshall, *Memoirs*, 45.

56. "knew no bounds": John S. D. Eisenhower and Joanne Thompson Eisenhower, *Yanks*, 83.

56. "During the ten days we spent in the sector": Roosevelt, *Americans*, 86.

57. "The artillery on both sides contented itself . . .": Marshall, *Memoirs*, 45.

57. "It is quite true": Newhall, letter to mother, December 6, 1917, *Selected Papers*, 69.

57. "My own experience in the trenches . . .": Ibid.

58. "rapid progress": Historical Sketches of Subsidiary Units, Charles P. Summerall Papers, LOC, RG 291, Box 23.

58. "generally reinforce the French Artillery behind trenches . . .": 1st Division Résumé of Operations, October 21, 1917–November 7, 1918, Summerall Papers, LOC, RG 291, Box 14.

58. "The enthusiasm of the French was tremendous . . .": "History of the First Division from April 6, 1917 to Sept. 26, 1919," NA, RG 120, Entry 1241, Box 7.

58. "[t]he enthusiastic activity of the newly-arrived American . . .": Marshall, *Memoirs*, 45.

58. "going over with a long, slow swishy sort of sound": James L. Hartney, letter to Margaret, November 8, 1917, Private Collection.

58. "on having the honor to be the first American officer . . .": Roosevelt, *Americans*, 86.

59. "tense with the novelty and the sense of danger": *History of the First*, 30.

59. "blinding flash and a crash and a roar": Ibid.

59. "Nothing but the boom of big guns and explosion . . .": Nelson diary.

59. "about 300 Germans making our lines . . .": Ibid.

59. "Our men were some nervous when it was over": Ibid.

60. "Men! These graves, the first to be dug in our national soil . . .": Mosley, *Marshall*, 54.

60. "We will inscribe on their tombs: 'Here lie the first . . .'": Ibid.

61. "Our losses were slight during the remaining days . . .": Nelson diary.

61. "Must say [we] were glad to get out": Ibid.

61. "At the end of the ten days we were relieved": Roosevelt, *Americans*, 87.

61. "The men thought that now they were veterans . . .": Newhall, "With the First Division."

61. "The Division Commander wishes to congratulate . . .": General Order No. 67, November 23, 1917, *History of the First*, 342–43.

62. "training of the combined division in the tactics of open warfare": *History of the First*, 18.

62. "depend on every individual soldier to meet the situation . . .": General Order No. 67, 35.

62. "highly essential": Millett, *The General*, 321.

62. "He is without much training since cadet days": Harbord, *Leaves from a War Diary*, 202.

62. "note of deep pessimism": Pershing, *Experiences*, vol. 1, 199.

62. "institution is the lengthened shadow of one man": Ralph Waldo Emerson, "Self-Reliance," *Essays: First Series*, 17.

62. "If we cannot do the job, we will be replaced": Millett, *The General*, 332.

63. "Under rattling fire from the enemy": Bullard, *Personalities*, 110.

63. "saw rendered by any officer or man": Ibid., 111.

64. "marked changes": Summerall, *Way of Duty*, 23.

64. "the infantry would pay in losses for lack of artillery": Ibid., 107.

65. "influence of a master artilleryman and commander was felt": Bullard, *Personalities*, 114.

65. "the severest reprimand in the quietest words": Ibid, 112.

65. "the hand of destiny": Summerall, *Way of Duty*, 113.

65. "We have been enjoying a large quantity of snow recently": Samuel Ervin, letter to mother, December 30, 1917, Senator Samuel J. Ervin Jr. Papers—Southern History Collection of the Wilson Library, UNC–Chapel Hill Subgroup 17.2, Box 288.

65. "When we were not cursed with mud . . .": Marshall, *Memoirs*, 52.

65. "inured the men to withstand the worst exposure . . .": Wilder, "Operations of Company M," 5.

65. "[T]he Father of his country and Valley Forge . . .": *The Twenty-Sixth Infantry in France*, 12.

65. "There were many Poles and Russians . . .": Wilder, "Operations of Company M," 8.

65. "A large percentage had never shot any firearms . . .": Roosevelt, *Americans*, 93.

66. "staying power": Millett, *The General*, 338.

66. "in handling men by the thousands . . .": Newhall, "With the First Division."

66. "very bad, unusually cold and exceedingly wet": Ibid.

66. "long hikes on slippery roads": *Memoirs of the Harvard Dead in the War Against Germany*, vol. 3, 120–21.

67. "Seemingly in an instant the cause of the Allies . . .": Pershing, *Experiences*, vol. 1, 207.

67. "a present total of 150 divisions": October 17, 1917, cable to Washington, Ibid., 198; November 15, 1917, cable to Secretary Baker, Ibid., 235.

67. "rushed to Italy . . .": Ibid., 235.

67. "fit for open warfare": *History of the First*, 67.

67. "I think we came too late": Bullard, *Personalities*, 83.

68. "They must not fail.": Ibid., 108.

4. Adventure of War

69. "Your letter of Nov. 12 arrived this week . . .": James L. Hartney, letter to Margaret, December 31, 1917. Private Collection.

69. "dearest beloved": Letters from Margaret to James L. Hartney, 1917. Private Collection.

69. "nine months had now passed since . . .": Bullard, *Personalities*, 125.

70. "half-trained American companies . . .": Pershing, *Experiences*, vol. 1, 255.

70. "identity of our forces": Cooper, *Woodrow Wilson*, 402.

70. "full authority to use the forces . . .": Ibid.

70. "any critical situation": Ibid.

70. "Everyone was relieved that the period . . .": Marshall, *Memoirs*, 57.

70. "terrific blizzard": Ibid., 59.

70. "roads heavily glazed with smooth ice": Ibid.

70. "The roads are full of ice and snow . . .": Nelson diary.

71. "bitter cold": Summerall, *Way of Duty*, 114.

71. "progress was slow": Ibid.

71. "worst day he had seen troops out . . .": Wilder, "Operations of Co. M," 7.

71. "penetrated the thickest clothing": Marshall, *Memoirs*, 59.

71. "The weather is much better now . . .": *Memoirs of the Harvard Dead*, vol. 3, 154–55.

71. "spring weather" . . . Letter, Sam Ervin to Grandfather, January 24, 1918, Ervin Papers.

71. "[W]ith the prospect of spring": Newhall, "With the First Division."

71. "the front lines lay in low, marshy valley . . .": Thomas, *History of the A.E.F.*, 57.

71. "men and officers were in the mud . . .": Bullard, *Personalities*, 160.

71. "neither quiet nor restful": *History of the First*, 49.

71. "This was a real fighting front": Newhall, "With the First Division."

71. "a very lively sector with raids . . .": Irving Wood letter, January 8, 1919, Private Collection.

71. "our first real taste of war": Roosevelt, *Americans*, 108.

72. "hideous phase of warfare": Bullard, *Personalities*, 193.

72. "I couldn't speak for about a month . . .": January 25, 1919 issue of *Ironwood News Record* (MI).

72. "water from a shell hole which happened . . .": Maj. Raymond Austin, letter to his mother, March 27, 1918, AHEC.

72. "burned from sitting in the grass . . .": Ibid.

72. "As soon as the shells hit the ground . . .": August 5, 1918, issue of *Waterloo Evening Courier* (Iowa).

73. "SBR": *1st Division at Cantigny*, US Chemical Corps, 1958, DRL, 23.

73. "were not the easiest things to fight in": Jesse O. Evans diary, FDM.

73. "painfully oppressive": *1st Division at Cantigny*, US Chemical Corps, DRL, 19.

73. "It seemed to me in all my trials . . .": Bullard, *Personalities*, 159.

73. "I put on the French because it is more . . .": Jesse Evans diary.

73. "Put on your mask, you damn fool . . .": Summerall, *Way of Duty*, 117.

73. "I was never able to find this young man . . .": Bullard, *Personalities*, 161.

73. "[T]here were vermin and rats . . .": Roosevelt, *Americans*, 76.

73. "picking out cooties and their eggs": Evarts, *Cantigny*, 50.

73. "I carry a blanket with me and . . .": Vinton Dearing, letter to mother, June 12, 1918, *My Galahad of the Trenches Being a Collection of Intimate Letters of Lieut. Vinton A. Dearing*, 73.

74. "soaked with rain till they are . . .": Newhall, letter to father, March 20, 1918, *Selected Papers*, 70.

74. "we even had to go so far as to . . .": *Memoirs of the Harvard Dead,* vol. 3, 129.

74. "The men either huddled against the side . . .": Roosevelt, *Americans,* 84.

74. "It is pretty hard to ask a man to be . . .": *Memoirs of the Harvard Dead,* vol. 3, 128.

74. "The most disagreeable part about the trenches . . .": "First Alumnus Killed in France," *Trinity Alumni Register,* vol. 4, July 1918, 102.

74. "We had only two canteens of water each . . .": Dacus, WWI Veterans Survey.

74. "The only thing we lack is something to eat": Nelson diary.

74. "soaked and muddy hardtack": Evarts, *Cantigny,* 10.

74. "corned willie": Ibid.

74. "They just couldn't get that meat to us": January 19, 1919, issue of *Boston Daily Globe* (MA).

74. "slumgullion": Paul Clancy, *Just a Country Lawyer: A Biography of Senator Sam Ervin,* 66.

74. "a favorite method of preparing the meal": Marshall, *Memoirs,* 91.

75. "Food and coffee were always cold . . .": Bullard/Reeves, *American Soldiers Also Fought,* 30.

75. "a head, a hand, any sign of a human body . . .": Bullard, *Personalities,* 117.

75. "I guess the worst thing is to sit in the bottom . . .": Newhall, letter to mother, May 26, 1918, *Selected Papers,* 80.

75. "are indeed very noisy things and make you move . . .": *Memoirs of the Harvard Dead,* vol. 3, 128.

75. "Jack Johnsons": Paul Strong and Sanders Marble, *Artillery in the Great War,* xxi.

75. "nothing left to bury": Report of Pvt. Austin Bradley, Burial File of Lt. Norborne R. Gray, NPRC.

75. "There's a bunch of scrap iron . . .": *Emporia Gazette,* July 4, 1918.

75. "Perhaps it is good luck": James L. Hartney, letter to Margaret, March 28, 1918, Private Collection.

76. "A 3" shell will temporarily scare or deter a man . . .": Marshall, *Memoirs,* 96.

76. "Be active all over no man's land . . .": Millett, *The General,* 343.

76. "I remembered the tradition of the loss of heart . . .": Bullard, *Personalities,* 141.

76. "extremely dangerous but very necessary work": Ibid., 147.

76. "If you kept your head down there was no firing . . .": March 2, 1919, issue of *La Crosse Tribune and Leader Press* (WI).

77. "We got into their trench and started the slaughter . . .": December 31, 1918, *Reno Evening Gazette* (NV).

77. "Our artillery fire was so intense . . .": Major Austin letter, March 27, 1918.

77. "[I]ts suddenness, its hand-to-hand deadly . . .": Bullard, *Personalities,* 148.

77. "vigorously replied": Summerall, *Way of Duty,* 115.

77. "Sitting Bull": Ibid., and Millett, *The General,* 334.

78. "The support from our artillery came the moment . . .": Nelson diary.

78. "Sausage Machine": Edmond Taylor, *The Fall of the Dynasties: The Collapse of the Old Order, 1905–1922,* 237.

78. "shook the entire battle front": *History of the First,* 64.

79. "a surf of ten thousand breakers . . .": Frederick Palmer, *Newton D. Baker: America at War,* vol. 2, 104.

79. "Owing to the breakdown of Russia": Erich Ludendorff, *My War Memories 1914–1918,* vol. 2, 537.

79. "This was only possible on the Western Front": Ibid., 543.

79. "Von Hutier method": A. W. Page, *Our 110 Days Fighting,* 15.

79. "The Germans had beaten Pershing to open warfare": Nelson, *The Remains of Company D*, 74.

80. "the battle won. The English utterly defeated": Martin Gilbert, *The First World War—A Complete History*, 407.

80. "last awarded to Blücher . . .": John Keegan, *The First World War*, 403.

80. "The last man may count": Gilbert, *First World War*, 410.

80. "threatened to bring the war to a sudden conclusion . . .": Marshall, *Memoirs*, 62.

80. "The whole Allied world, especially America . . .": Bullard, *Personalities*, 173.

80. "The big drive is on now in the west": James L. Hartney, letter to Margaret, March 28, 1918, Private Collection.

80. "Fighting had to be done at once": Bullard, *Personalities*, 173.

81. "[O]ur General Pershing is not a fighter . . .": Ibid., 91–92.

81. "an extremely dark picture of disaster": Pershing, *Experiences*, vol. 1, 356.

81. "any of our divisions that could be of service": Ibid., 357.

81. "be held in readiness for any eventuality": Ibid.

81. "I have come to tell you that the American people . . .": Ibid., 365; Smythe, *Pershing*, 101.

82. "very much touched": Pershing, *Experiences*, vol. 1, 364.

82. "rose to greatness": Marshall, *Memoirs*, 79.

82. "At Pétain's request . . .": Pershing, *Experiences*, vol. 1, 359.

82. "Never a commander received an order . . .": Bullard, *Personalities*, 177.

82. "was a matter of great elation": Newhall, "With the First Division."

82. "were delighted": Roosevelt, *Americans*, 122.

82. "a test of administrative ability": *The Twenty-Sixth Infantry in France*, 12.

83. "With straw in the bottom, we had . . .": Dearing, letter to mother, May 22, 1918, *My Galahad*, 57.

83. "corn-willie": Ibid.

83. "To go to the toilet": Senay, "Shavetail," 19.

83. "no scars and no desolation of war": *History of the First*, 67.

83. "a beautiful peaceful country, the most lovely . . .": Roosevelt, *Americans*, 126.

83. "Every position must be held to the last man . . .": Keegan, *First World War*, 405.

83. "Where would we be put?": Bullard, *Personalities*, 179.

84. "constant sound of heavy cannonading": *History of the First*, 66.

84. "Both officers and men were in splendid condition . . .": Pershing, *Experiences*, vol.1, 392.

84. "[O]ne could not help thinking": Ibid.

84. "[W]e started on a long march . . .": Nelson diary.

84. "Spring was on the land . . .": Roosevelt, *Americans*, 126.

84. "some wonderful old houses and gardens . . .": *Memoirs of the Harvard Dead*, vol. 3, 133.

84. "Our move has been to quite an extent . . .": James L. Hartney, letter to Margaret, April 5, 1918, Private Collection.

84. "I wouldn't change places with anyone . . .": Dearing, letter to mother, April 7, 1918, *My Galahad*, 46.

84. "more like a pleasure jaunt than a march into battle": Irving Wood letter, January 8, 1919, Private Collection.

85. "where the rumble of guns, like distant thunder . . .": Dorr, *A Soldier's Mother*, 88.

85. "This was what we had crossed the Atlantic to do": Newhall, "With the First Division."

85. "They knew the discomforts of trench life": Ibid.

85. "the war was still an adventure": Ibid.

85. "an eagerness to go 'over the top' . . .": Ibid.

85. "did not know what they were going to . . .": Ibid.

5. Life and Death

88. "sound of guns in the line warned . . .": Summerall, *Way of Duty*, 121.

88. "Silver, linen, clothing . . .": Marshall, *Memoirs*, 83.

88. "nearer the enemy than ever before": Bullard, *Personalities*, 186.

89. "[Y]ou hardly ever see anybody . . .": Anderson, "First Alumnus Killed," 103.

89. "The guns could be heard from this billet . . .": October 20, 1918, issue of *La Crosse Tribune & Leader Press* (WI).

89. "On the evening of the 23rd . . .": Nelson diary.

89. "All Allied eyes were cast upon . . .": September 20, 1919, issue of *Portland Commercial Review* (IN).

89. "He said we were going into a place . . .": Nelson diary.

89. "Not far after we split the Co. . . .": Ibid.

89. "burst at the roadside": October 20, 1918, issue of *La Crosse Tribune & Leader Press* (WI).

89. "to hold its position": Wilder, "Operations of Company M," 11.

90. "To say that we took over a line rather overstates the case": Bullard/Reeves, *American Soldiers*, 29.

90. "a position consisting of practically nothing . . .": Lt. George E. Butler, "Battle of Cantigny," Personal Experience Monograph, DRL, 2–3.

90. "Dead Colonials still lay in the fields": Newhall, "With the First Division."

90. "large numbers of large black buzzards eating . . .": March 2, 1919, issue of *La Crosse Tribune & Leader Press* (WI).

90. "Trenches were shallow and scanty": Roosevelt, *Americans*, 128.

90. "newly thrown-up earth": "History of the First Division," NA, RG 120, RG 1241, Box 6, 22.

90. "In front of Cantigny, in woods on hill . . .": Cpl. Tom Carroll diary, FDM.

90. "would peer through an opening in the clods . . .": "History of the First Division," NA, RG 120, RG 1241, Box 6, 22.

91. "It's not a sector . . .": Wilder, "Operations of Company M," 13; Johnston, Monograph, 7.

91. "sector-holding troops": Wilder, "Operations of Company M," 13.

91. "by no means inferior": Ibid., 13–14.

91. "The Germans were good . . .": Dacus, WWI Veterans Survey.

92. "typewriter": Dorr, *Soldier's Mother*, 94.

92. "The engineers were called on to do all this work": Experience Report of Lieutenant Moses E. Cox, 1st Engineers, December 21, 1918, NA, RG 92, Entry 1241, Box 70.

92. "They simply rained shells everywhere": Farrell, Experience Report.

93. "light from 4 a.m. until 10 p.m.": Dearing, letter to mother, June 12, 1918, *My Galahad*, 72–73.

93. "because of enemy fire and the shortness of . . .": Wilder, "Operations of Company M," 16.

93. "I know of no duty which new troops dislike . . .": Bullard, *Personalities*, 158.

93. "Here we worked for more than a month . . .": Irving Wood letter, January 8, 1919, Private Collection.

93. "remarkable achievement": "History of the First Division," NA, RG 120, Entry 1241, Box 6, 22.

93. "permitted deep and dry dugouts . . .": Welcome P. Waltz, "Operations of Company C, 3d Machine Gun Battalion at Cantigny (Personal Experience)," Infantry School Monograph, Advanced Course 1928–1929, Ft. Benning, GA, DRL, 4.

93. "all the trenches in the sector had . . .": Butler, Monograph, 3.

93. "showed badly on aerial photographs . . .": Wilder, "Operations of Company M," 12.

93. "pitch black nights": Dearing, letter to sister Louise, May 15, 1918, *My Galahad*, 54.

94. "I averaged more narrow escapes per day . . .": Farrell, Experience Report.

94. "Men lived in that sector under the most . . .": Evarts, *Cantigny*, 2.

94. "We kept shovels and tools in small piles . . .": Lt. Jason L. Bronston, letter to ABMC, May 29, 1926, NA, RG 117, Entry 31, Box 184.

94. "Guns and machine-guns on both sides . . .": Nelson diary.

94. "the Germans shelling us almost every 15 minutes . . .": Bronston letter.

94. "First a few flashes can be seen . . .": Roosevelt, *Americans*, 110–11.

94. "[S]hells come over so big . . .": June 5, 1918, issue of *Denton Record-Chronicle* (TX).

95. "In a very heavy bombardment when . . .": Evarts, *Cantigny*, 72.

95. "They gave off different sounds": Senay, "Shavetail," 35.

95. "largely imitated the lonesome night howl . . .": March 2, 1919, issue of *La Crosse Tribune & Leader Press* (WI).

95. "[W]e soon learned the different noises . . .": Haydock, *Memoirs of the Harvard Dead*, 138.

95. "were hurled daily against our poorly . . .": "The 5th Field Artillery in the Last War: Its Accomplishments and the Accomplishments of Its Commanding Officers," Summerall Papers, LOC, RG 291, Box 23, 6.

95. "Death Valley": Johnston, Monograph, 9; Pvt. Bert Carl Tippman, letter to friend, October 20, 1918, issue of *La Crosse Tribune & Leader Press* (WI); *The Story of the 16th Infantry in France*.

95. "[I]t certainly earned its name": October 20, 1918, issue of *La Crosse Tribune & Leader Press* (WI).

95. "the knowledge that one would always run . . .": Waltz, "Operations of Company C," 10.

96. "the valley was one big shell hole . . .": February 24, 1919, issue of *Logansport Pharos Reporter* (IN).

96. "At night every road was swept with a fire . . .": Thomas, *History of the A.E.F.*, 70.

96. "badly torn up by the intense artillery fire": Butler, Monograph, 3.

96. "City of Suicides": June 28, 1919, issue of *Clinton Daily Clintonian* (IN).

96. "Shells were bursting frequently": Summerall, *Way of Duty*, 121.

96. "The Germans evidently spotted the kitchen coming . . .": Memoir of Earl D. Seaton, *American Voices of World War I*, 71.

96. "whomp": Ibid., 71–72.

97. "constantly subjected to a fierce fire": *History of the 7th Field Artillery (First Division, A.E.F.)*, 47.

97. "[O]ne of our Captains was buried by a shell . . .": Smith, *The Colonel*, 203.

97. "a molelike existence": Ibid., 202.

97. "While in this sector I wouldn't . . .": January 22, 1919, issue of *Clinton Daily Clintonian* (IN).

98. "grass-cutters": Bullard, *Personalities*, 188.

98. "There is almost a continuous hum of airplanes . . .": Dearing, letter to mother, March 11, 1918, *My Galahad*, 41. Note: "aeroplanes" in original corrected to "airplanes."

98. "almost feel the whiff of [their] wings": Bullard, *Personalities*, 188. Note: Bullard originally wrote "whiff of his wings" even though speaking collectively of German planes.

98. "became sometimes almost hysterical in the feeling . . .": Ibid., 189–90.

98. "Our ammunition supply": *History of the 7th Field Artillery*, 48.

99. "paralyz[ed] the enemy's movements": "The 5th Field Artillery in the Last War," 6.

99. "demoralizing losses": Marshall, *Memoirs*, 83.

99. "the whole German sky lit up . . .": Evarts, *Cantigny*, 34–36.

99. "the blazing, crashing wall of steel . . .": Ibid.

99. "[S]o prompt and rapid was the response . . .": "The 5th Field Artillery in the Last War," 4.

99. "I relieved Red Kelly of the 18th Infantry . . .": Senay, "Shavetail," 35.

100. "It was terrible to realize that there . . .": January 25, 1919, issue of *Ironwood News Record* (MI).

100. "[f]or a quarter mile outside of the little village . . .": Marshall, *Memoirs*, 85.

100. "holding the position": Message from Bullard to Pershing, 5 p.m., May 28, 1918, NA, RG 120, Entry 1241, Box 27.

101. "mechanical limit": Bullard/Reeves, *American Soldiers*, 26.

101. "capture the plateau north of Mesnil St. Georges": Memorandum, May 12, 1918, 28th Infantry, NA, RG 120, Entry 1241, Box 54.

101. "The days passed without a hostile advance": Marshall, *Memoirs*, 89.

101. "The Boche could look down our throats": Senay, "Shavetail," 46.

101. "to improve its position": Pershing, *Experiences*, vol. 2, 54–55.

102. "[A]t this moment the morale of the Allies . . .": Ibid.

102. "Before we came Cantigny had been twice taken . . .": Bullard, *Personalities*, 196.

102. "the best equipped, best officered . . .": Ibid., 164.

102. "new and distinctly American operation": Marshall, *Memoirs*, 89.

6. Marshall's First Plan

103. "out of a clear sky": Marshall, *Memoirs*, 89.

103. "No battle plan survives contact with the enemy": *Moltke on the Art of War: Selected Writings*, 45–47.

103. "By direction, this was to be an operation . . .": Marshall, *Memoirs*, 90.

104. "We have taken no prisoners since . . .": Col. Hamilton Smith, Memorandum, May 23, 1918, 26th Infantry Regiment, NA, RG 120, Entry 1241, Box 50.

104. "One or more prisoners": Ibid.

104. "I've had a patrol out every night": Tom Carroll diary.

105. "enemy working parties, enemy strongpoints . . .": Lt. Samuel Smith, Memorandum, February 18, 1918, George Redwood Papers, Maryland Historical Society Library, Baltimore, MD.

105. "A machine-gun fired on us from a point . . .": Lt. L. Irwin Morris, patrol report, May 17–18, 1918, NA, RG 120, Entry 1241, Box 55.

105. "moved towards enemy's trenches . . .": Cpt. Henry Mosher, patrol report, May 18–19, 1918, NA, RG 120, Entry 1241, Box 55.

105. "MG active and flash seen near . . .": Lt. George Redwood, patrol report, May 20–21, 1918, NA, RG 120, Entry 1241, Box 55.

106. "like a Hun": Pvt. "Paddy" Davis, interview in August 25, 1918, issue of *Washington* (DC) *Post*.

106. "extraordinary heroism": *WWR*, vol. 23.

106. "our little adventure": *Memoirs of the Harvard Dead*, vol. 3, 158.

106. "did not know what fear was": Ibid., 151.

106. "took prisoners he would read us . . .": Ibid., 157–58.

106. "The joke of it": August 25, 1918, issue of *The Washington Post*.

106. "the best reputation I ever heard a man get": *Memoirs of the Harvard Dead*, vol. 3, 152.

106. "brought something back that could walk": James Carl Nelson, *The Remains of Company D*, 73.

106. "scout officer": Lt. George Redwood, patrol report, May 18–19, 1918, NA, RG 120, Entry 1241, Box 55.

107. "During the night we could check up [on] most . . .": Marshall, *Memoirs*, 84.

107. "we studied the lay of the ground until shortly . . .": Ibid., 90.

107. "having for its object the capture of Cantigny": Field Order No. 18, May 20, 1918, with Annexes May 22 and Amendments to May 24, Lt. Col. George C. Marshall, NA, RG 120, Entry 1241, Boxes 16 & 18.

108. "creeping barrage": Ibid.

109. "mopping up the caves and the underground": Ibid.

110. "follow the barrage as closely as possible": Ibid.

110. "to absolutely *prevent firing at the wrong range*": 1st Field Artillery Brigade Records, NA, RG 120, Entry 1241, Box 66.

111. "the counter battery artillery must be extremely . . .": Field Order No. 18.

111. "work independently of the quality of the hand . . .": Bullard, *Personalities*, 95.

112. "optional with the regimental commander . . .": Capt. Paul Parker, "The Battle of Cantigny," Infantry School Monograph, DRL, 339.

112. "giant of a man": Bullard, *Fighting Generals*, 45.

112. "[F]ew officers of any army were as well prepared . . .": Ibid.

112. "steam-roller": Ibid.

113. "was chosen, because of its splendid discipline . . .": "First American Attack Remembered," May 29, 1938, issue of *San Antonio Light* (TX).

113. "about the size of a piano box": Pvt. Earl D. Seaton, memoir published in *American Voices of World War I: Primary Source Documents, 1917–1920*, 78.

113. "special instruction": Memorandum re. F.O. #18, Col. King, Chief of Staff, 1st Div. May 18, 1918. NA, RG 120, Entry 1241, Box 18.

113. "a long, hard, all-night pull": *Memoirs of the Harvard Dead*, vol. 3, 139.

113. "Ground was selected as near the actual terrain . . .": "First American Attack Remembered," May 29, 1938, issue of *San Antonio Light* (TX).

114. "In addition": Butler, Monograph, 8.

114. "represented by men carrying tree branches": Col. Hanson Ely, Report for 28th Infantry Regiment on Capture & Consolidation of Position, June 2, 1918, NA, RG 120, Entry 1241, Box 55.

114. "During next two days the entire Regiment . . .": Ibid.

114. "[W]e practiced for the attack for three days": Wood letter, January 8, 1919.

114. "One French General gave a long critique . . .": Dacus, WWI Veterans Survey.

114. "This demonstration was quite impressive": Waltz, "Operations of Company C," 7.

115. "French machine gunners played the role of Germans": July 23, 1918, issue of *La Crosse Tribune & Leader Press* (WI).

115. "They were kept at it until they were letter perfect . . .": December 22, 1918, issue of *Boston Globe* (MA).

115. "They knew where they were to jump off . . .": Ibid.

115. "In the last day's practice the entire Regiment . . .": Ely, Report on 28th Infantry Regt.

115. "General Pershing said that 'no inch was to be given up' . . .": Smythe, *Pershing*, 125.

115. "a few rough edges could have been better smoothed off": Ely, Report on 28th Infantry Regt.

115. "In his characteristic, forceful way . . .": Waltz, "Operations of Company C," 8.

116. "a big batch of mail": *Memoirs of the Harvard Dead*, vol. 3, 139.

116. "This isn't the eve of battle but it is so close . . .": Newhall, letter to mother, May 26, 1918, *Selected Papers*, 78.

116. "Mother I will stay with you if I ever get back": Carl Fey, letter to mother, May 26, 1918, Private Collection.

116. "Watch the papers and magazines for the efforts of . . .": Lt. Dan Birmingham, letter to mother, May 1918, FDM.

116. "Things are very different this time": *Memoirs of the Harvard Dead*, vol. 3, 137.

116. 265 men from two companies . . . 18th Infantry Regiment Daily Report, May 26, 1918, NA, RG 120, Entry 1241, Box 46.

117. "to help out on some rush trench digging . . .": McClure, Experience Report.

117. "deeply concerned": *History of the First*, 38–39.

117. "would disclose to the enemy our intentions . . .": Marshall, *Memoirs*, 93.

117. "considered suspending the operation": *History of the First*, 38–39.

117. "J day will be May 28": Campbell King, Very Secret Memorandum on J-Day and H-Hour, May 27, 1918, NA, RG 120, Entry 1241, Box 18.

118. "This was the subject of careful consideration beforehand": Ely, Report on 28th Infantry Regt.

118. "This was wrong because it is the same as bringing . . .": Waltz, "Operations of Company C," 32.

118. "the dim white roads to the front": Johnston, Monograph, 12.

118. "[T]heir minds": Ibid.

118. "*bon chance!*": Millett, *The General*, 363.

118. "All the French peasants in the nearby villages . . .": Waltz, "Operations of Company C," 8.

118. "All nights near the front lines were very dark . . .": Ibid., 9.

119. "to avoid all possibility of error . . .": Annex 1 to Field Order No. 18, May 22, 1918, NA, RG 120, Entry 1241, Box 16.

119. "in the dark": Newhall, letter to mother, June 28, 1918, *Selected Papers*, 83.

119. "There was no moon at all at this late hour . . .": Johnston, Monograph, 13.

119. "narrow trails winding through the wheat": Ibid.

119. "The moon was veiled and the stars were hidden": Ibid., 29.

119. "with a view to getting a little sleep": Newhall, letter to mother, June 28, 1918, *Selected Papers*, 83.

120. "quite fatigued": Waltz, "Operations of Company C," 10.

120. "a real drum fire barrage . . .": Ibid.

120. "At five fifteen, the Germans opened bombardment . . .": Newhall, letter to mother, June 28, 1918, *Selected Papers*, 83.

120. "I got a little scratch on my left arm": Lt. Samuel Parker, letter to brother John Parker, June 2, 1918, published in July 15, 1918, issue of *Monroe Enquirer* (NC); July 16, 1918, issue of *Monroe Journal* (NC).

120. "H-1": Field Order No. 18.

121. "a 105 hit the place we had just left . . .": Tyler, letter to mother, June 3, 1918.

121. "huddled . . . in the bottom of the trench": Ibid.

121. "[o]ver an hour had gone by and still . . .": Waltz, "Operations of Company C," 11.

121. "Retreat, they have broken through!": Ibid., 12.

121. "took one look at those huge geysers of dirt . . .": Ibid., 13.

121. "It made quite a show . . .": Ibid.

121. "We were": Herman Dacus, letter, August 15, 1984, Private Collection, provided to the author by James Carl Nelson.

121. "scurrying to escape the grenade fragments . . .": Johnston, Monograph, 57.

122. "buried and shell shocked": Morning Report, May 27, 1818, NPRC.

122. Pvt. Clifford Ledford . . . Burial File of Pvt. Clifford Ledford, NPRC.

122. "Tarnopol": War Diary, German 26th Reserve Corps, 39.

123. "Raid was repulsed with heavy casualties": Johnston, letter to American Battle Monuments Commission, December 19, 1925, NA, RG 117, Entry 31, Box 184.

123. "I do not believe that the Second Battalion, 28th Infantry . . .": Capt. Charles Senay, letter to American Battle Monuments Commission, April 21, 1926, NA, RG 117, Entry 31, Box 184.

123. "Their efforts failed . . .": Parker, letter to brother, June 2, 1918.

7. A Hellish Clamor

125. "beautiful dug-outs": Daniel Sargent, "Cantigny," unpublished personal account, January 28, 1976, AHEC, 2.

125. "an unfamiliar sight . . .": Ibid., 3.

125. "a grandiose nineteenth century chateau . . .": Ibid., 4.

126. "a little bit": Ibid.

126. "making dangerous headway": Pershing, *Experiences,* vol. 2, 60.

126. "feint attacks": War Diary, German 26th Reserve Corps, 39.

126. "Once more it proved a brilliant success": Ludendorff, *My War Memories,* vol. 2, 629.

126. "This was a heavy blow": Marshall, *Memoirs,* 94.

127. "As we left the trucks we heard . . .": Pvt. John Johnston, March 2, 1919, issue of *La Crosse Tribune and Leader Press* (WI).

127. "That night everything seemed quiet": Thomas, *History of the A.E.F.,* 75.

127. "as black as hell itself": Lt. M.P. "Doc" Bedsole, Letter to sister, dated August 17, 1918., Alabama Textual Materials Collection, Alabama Department of Archives and History, Box #SG017101, Folder #1 "World War 1, 1917–1918—Soldiers' Letters."

127. "Very secret. H hour will be 6:45 a.m. . . .": "Very Secret" Memorandum on J-Day and H-Hour, Col. Campbell King, May 27, 1918, NA, RG 120, Entry 1241, Box 18.

127. "prepared schedules for each gun": Major Austin, letter to mother, June 1, 1918, AHEC.

127. "in person": Colonel King Memorandum, May 27, 1918.

127. "reliable watches": "Very Secret" Memorandum on Synchronization of Watches, May 27, 1918, NA, RG 120, Entry 1241, Box 18.

128. "came a wait of perhaps an hour before . . .": Newhall, letter to mother, June 8, 1918, *Selected Papers,* 83.

128. "[I] tried my best to take a little snooze . . .": Sgt. Cesar Santini, November 1, 1919, issue of *Middlesboro Pinnacle News* (KY).

129. "5440": Ely, Report on 28th Infantry Regt.

129. "Don't be late": Sargent, "Cantigny," 6.

129. "I could see the stars . . .": Ibid., 10.

129. "still a chance of being late": Ibid.

129. "seemed to be luminous . . .": Ibid.

130. "could hear a fly buzzing in the air": Cpl. Boleslaw Suchocki, first account, NA, RG 117, Entry 31, Box 184, 1.

130. "Suchocki, why don't you rest . . .": Ibid.

130. "but after one had slept . . .": Experience Report of Lt. John McClure, 1st Engineers, 12/21/1918, NA, RG 92, Entry 1241, Box 70.

130. "I was colder than I had been . . .": Ibid.

130. "all awake, half sitting up.": Ibid.

130. "carrying on a very interesting conversation": Suchocki, second account, NA, RG 92, Entry 1241, Box 70, 1.

130. "I remarked to Jones . . .": McClure, Experience Report.

131. "It burst with a thunderous roar.": Suchocki, first account, 1.

131. "go way up in the air . . .": Ibid.

131. "is no need to run around . . .": Ibid.

131. "an impossibility for a shell . . .": McClure, Experience Report.

131. "We heard another one coming . . .": Ibid.
131. "At once a tremendous explosion . . .": Suchocki, second account, 2.
131. "I had a random thought . . .": McClure, Experience Report.
132. "as soon as I put my arms . . .": Suchocki, second account, 3.
132. "as soft as a pillow": Ibid.
132. "Jones never knew what hit him": Report of Lt. Moses E. Cox, Burial File of Lt. Hamlet P. Jones, NPRC.
132. "a small hole and . . .": Suchocki, second account, 2.
132. "sitting on a stone pile . . .": Report of 1st Sgt. Thomas M. Kelly, Burial File of PFC Albert V. MacDougall, NPRC.
132. "was hot as fire and . . .": Suchocki, second account, 2.
132. "That was a busy bunch in there": McClure, Experience Report.
133. "caused an immediate change . . .": Experience Report of Capt. Horace Smith, 1st Engineers, 12/22/1918, NA, RG 92, Entry 1241, Box 70.
133. "made the work very hard . . .": Cox, Experience Report.
133. "which glinted in the starlight": Sargent, "Cantigny," 11.
133. "how small the village was": Ibid., 8.
133. "blanched white": Ibid., 11.
134. "seriously subdued": Newhall, "With the First Division."
134. "the first moment the light would permit . . .": Marshall, *Memoirs*, 94.
134. "quite clear. More so than usual": "Journal of Cantigny Operations"—First Field Artillery Brigade, NA, RG 92, entry 1241, Box 61; also "First Field Artillery Brigade, January 1918—November 1918, Memos and Notes," Summerall Papers, LOC, RG 291, Box 14.
134. "there was plenty to occupy . . .": Newhall, "With the First Division."
135. "at the first shots the Boches' . . .": Major Austin letter, June 1, 1918.
135. "[t]hree enemy balloons up": "Journal of Cantigny Operations," NA, and Summerall Papers, LOC.
135. "*Tout le artillerie est comme ça* . . .": Millett, *The General*, 363.
135. "How many guns there were . . .": Bedsole letter, August 17, 1918.
135. "Mother of God!": Ibid.
135. "at 5:45 all batteries began a heavy . . .": Major Austin letter, June 1, 1918.
136. "you cannot see Cantigny on account . . .": "Journal of Cantigny Operations," NA, and Summerall Papers, LOC.
136. "The ground was pounded . . .": Major Austin letter, June 1, 1918.
136. "[A]t 5:45 a.m., the world turned . . .": Sargent, "Cantigny," 12.
136. "statistics can give no idea . . .": Ibid.
136. "If the men felt confident before . . .": Newhall, "With the First Division."
136. "Every one of us came to life . . .": Waltz, "Operations of Company C," 15.
136. "All of us, at once, sensed . . .": Ibid.
136. "practically melt down.": Clancy, *Just a Country Lawyer*, 67.
136. "Cantigny itself took on the appearance . . .": Marshall, *Memoirs*, 95.
137. "to destroy the enemy's trenches . . .": Ibid.
137. "The shells kept on going overhead . . .": Recollections of Capt. Daniel R. Edwards, in *Doughboy War*, edited by James Hallas, 80.
137. "One could see half a building rise . . .": Tyler, letter to mother, June 3, 1918.
137. "a sight never to be forgotten.": Capt. Stuart D. Campbell, "Positions Occupied, Situation and Events that took place before, during and after the Battle of Cantigny by 'E' Co. 2nd Bn., 18th Infty." 7/4/1918, NA, RG 92, Entry 1241, Box 47.
137. "could not hear any response": Sargent, "Cantigny," 13.
137. "Our artillery was pounding the German lines . . .": Newhall, letter to mother, June 8, 1918, *Selected Papers*, 83.

137. "brought the awaiting troops to their feet": Waltz, "Operations of Company C," 15.

138. "still in the act of installing themselves . . .": War Diary of 26th German Reserve Corps, 58, CARL; NA, RG 165, Box 15.

138. "had not yet become fully acquainted . . .": Ibid.

139. "Enemy preparing attack against 82nd . . .": Ibid., 56.

139. "special understanding": Corps HQ Report, June 2, 1918, in Ibid., 82.

140. "cannot be justified": Ibid.

140. "Enemy artillery very quiet": "Journal of Cantigny Operations," NA, and Summerall Papers, LOC.

140. "lengthen the range": "Journal of Cantigny Operations—Headquarters, 1st Field Artillery Brigade," NA, RG 120, Entry 1241, Box 61.

140. "[a]nother report that 75's . . .": Ibid.

140. "in action": Ibid.

140. "any Germans who were not in deep . . .": Major Austin letter, June 1, 1918.

141. "a million dollar barrage": March 2, 1919, issue of *La Crosse Tribune & Leader Press* (WI).

141. "I can truthfully say . . .": Ibid.

8. Zero Hour

143. "It is a queer sensation when you climb . . .": December 31, 1918, issue of *Reno Evening Gazette* (NV).

144. "not fear, but a sort of excitement": May 29, 1918, issue of *Marion Daily Star* (OH).

144. "I honestly was nervous and rather excited": July 4, 1918, issue of *Emporia Weekly Gazette* (Kansas).

144. "I can only tell of my feeling . . .": November 12, 1918, issue of *New Castle News* (PA).

144. "We had practiced it until each man . . .": Newhall, letter to mother, June 8, 1918, *Selected Papers*, 84.

145. "One by one the batteries dropped their fire . . .": Major Austin letter, June 1, 1918.

145. "a wall of heavy smoke within which . . .": James Hopper, "Our First Victory, Part II—Over the Top and Beyond," *Collier's, The National Weekly,* New York, September 7, 1918.

145. "Our guns made so much racket . . .": May 29, 1918, issue of *Marion Daily Star* (OH).

145. "I would look at my watch and when . . .": July 4, 1918, issue of *Emporia Weekly Gazette* (Kansas).

145. "While waiting for H hour the men never . . .": Capt. Adelbert B. Stewart, Report of Reg. M.G. Co, June 1, 1918, NA, RG 120, Entry 1241, Box 55.

145. "This was our first real attack and naturally . . .": Parker, letter to brother, June 2, 1918.

146. "Everybody seemed to be more or less excited . . .": Pvt. Frank J. Last diary, FDM.

147. "[A]t 6:45, as though by the command of a single . . .": Major Austin letter, June 1, 1918.

147. "At the same time as the barrage left the line . . .": Ibid.

147. "The jump-off at dawn": "First American Attack Remembered," article in May 29, 1938, issue of *San Antonio Light* (TX).

147. "started up from the earth and began . . .": Maj. Frederick Palmer, *Source Records of the Great War,* vol. 6, A.D. 1918, 191.

148. "walked steadily along behind our barrage": Major Austin letter, June 1, 1918.

148. "beautiful plateau . . .": James Hopper, "Our First Victory," *Collier's.*

148. "It was a wonderful sight . . .": July 4, 1918, issue of *Emporia Weekly Gazette* (Kansas).

148. "I will never forget it as long as I live": August 11, 1918, issue of *Ft. Wayne Journal-Gazette* (IN).

148. "It was a wonderful picture when we went over . . .": June 26, 1918 issue of *Lima Daily News* (OH).

148. "Zero hour itself consists merely of blowing . . .": Newhall, letter to mother, June 8, 1918, *Selected Papers*, 84–85.

148. "to act as a sort of pivoting unit . . .": Letter from Capt. Francis M. van Natter to ABMC, April 24, 1926, NA, RG 117, Entry 31, Box 184.

149. "to reach the German trenches and hold them, . . .": Newhall, letter to mother, June 8, 1918, *Selected Papers*, 84.

149. "a plain ordinary frontal attack to make": Ibid.

149. "the whole 1st line down toward the right . . .": Ibid., 84–85.

149. "as far as the eyes can reach": Newhall, "With the First Division."

149. "It is impossible to imagine a sight more . . .": Ibid.

149. "Everyone was on his toes . . .": Parker, letter to brother, June 2, 1918.

149. "Attack formation was quickly taken up . . .": Ibid.

149. "[W]e went over the top cheering . . .": September 24, 1918, issue of *Denton Record-Chronicle* (TX).

150. "after that—well, I thought a little more . . .": January 21, 1919, issue of *Janesville Daily Gazette* (WI).

150. "They went over into the fighting singing . . .": Wood letter, January 8, 1919.

150. "I took my men, for the first time . . .": July 4, 1918, issue of *Emporia Weekly Gazette* (KS).

150. "The tanks looked like haycarts (horseless)": Sargent, "Cantigny," 13.

150. "followed the tanks over, and ran ahead . . .": Fred S. Ferguson, United Press Correspondent, "America Holds Power Balance," July 23, 1918, issue of *La Crosse Tribune and Leader Press* (WI).

150. "The formations were the same as those . . .": Major Palmer, *Source Records*, vol. 6, 191.

151. "Their line was perfect and they looked as if . . .": Capt. Stuart Campbell, report, "Positions Occupied," July 5, 1918, NA, RG 92, Entry 1241, Box 47.

151. "The barrage proceeded as we went ahead in waves": December 31, 1918, issue of *Reno Evening Gazette* (NV).

151. "All the men were walking with a firm step, . . .": July 4, 1918, issue of *Emporia Weekly Gazette* (KS).

151. "trampling with high steps . . .": Hopper, "Our First Victory," *Collier's*.

151. "The rolling barrage was extremely accurate": Ely, Report on 28th Infantry Regt.

152. "[T]he commanders, as well as the men . . .": War Diary, 26th German Reserve Corps, 58.

152. "[a] defense could not be undertaken . . .": Ibid., 70.

152. "destroyed": War Diary, German 26th Reserve Corps, 86.

152. "a heavy barrage": War Diary, German 18th Army, 9.

152. "At the same moment": War Diary, German 272nd Reserve Infantry Regiment, 69.

153. "an utter absence of confusion": Lt. Col. Jesse M. Cullison, Report of 3rd Battalion, 28th Infantry, June 2, 1918; NA, RG 120, Entry 1241, Box 55.

153. "No battle plan survives contact with the enemy": *Moltke on the Art of War: Selected Writings*, 45–47.

153. "heavy infantry and machine gun fire": Ibid.

153. "saw flame come out of his back when he fell": Burial Case File of Sgt. Harry Klein, NPRC.

154. "very feeble": Waltz, "Operations of Company C," 17.

154. "enhanced by tanks . . .": War Diary, German 18th Army, 17.

154. "one big howitzer shell after another": Waltz, "Operations of Company C," 17.

155. "a complete surprise to the Huns": September 5, 1918, issue of *Altoona Mirror* (PA).

155. "surrendered immediately": Report of French Tank Detachment, translated by Maj. P. L. Ransom, NA, RG 120, Entry 1241, Box 55.

155. "We captured about all of them . . .": September 5, 1918, issue of *Altoona Mirror* (PA).

155. "had erased them from the terrain,": Waltz, "Operations of Company C," 17.

155. "The force of the blow knocked me over": Newhall, letter to mother, August 1, 1918, *Selected Papers*, 89.

155. "My first reaction was astonishment that it hit . . .": Ibid., 96.

155. "jumped up and resumed the advance": Ibid., 89.

156. "[W]hat went on after that I only know . . .": Ibid., 84–85.

156. "I got shot in the right jaw": Letter from Pvt. Carl L. Fey to his mother, June 5, 1918; Private Collection.

156. "I got a hole through my right cheek": Postcard from Pvt. Carl L. Fey to his mother, June 12, 1918; Private Collection.

157. "a part ran back to the trenches . . .": Lt. von Vegesack, 10th Company Report; War Diary, 272nd Reserve Infantry Regiment.

157. "lost one or two men wounded by the advance . . .": Lt. Samuel I. Parker, Report on 1st Platoon, Company K, 28th Infantry, June 2, 1918, NA, RG 120, Entry 1241, Box 55.

157. "began jumping out of shell holes and beating it . . .": Parker, letter to brother, June 2, 1918.

157. "I saw your infantry coming . . .": Recollection of a German Lieutenant, Summerall Papers, LOC, RG 291, Box 40.

158. "The French tanks were right along with us": Tyler, letter to mother, June 3, 1918.

158. "moved forward encountering little resistance": Gerald R. Tyler, unpublished account, "The Cantigny Operation," enclosed in letter to ABMC, October 23, 1929; NA, RG 117, Entry 31, Box 184.

158. "I went over there and could see no connecting . . .": Ibid.

159. "suffered heavy losses": War Diary, German 26th Reserve Corps, 69.

159. "died instantly": Report of Sgt. Louis Abend, Brooklyn, NY; Burial File of Harvey W. Fahnenstalk, NPRC.

159. "instantly": Report of Sgt. Louis Abend, Brooklyn, NY; Burial Record of Thomas Larsen; NPRC.

160. "drill movement": Capt. Stuart Campbell Report.

160. "everyone was enthusiastic and delighted": Marshall, *Memoirs*, 95.

160. "the infantry has gone over the top . . .": Phone message received at 6:46 a.m., "Journal of Cantigny Operations—HQ First Field Artillery Brigade," NA, RG 120, Entry 1241, Box 61.

160. "very little enemy fire": Phone message received at 6:47 a.m., Ibid.

161. "First line went over led by tanks . . .": Phone message sent from 2nd Brigade to Division at 6:50 a.m., Field Messages of 2nd Brigade, NA, RG 120, Entry 1241, Box 41. Note: "lead" in original corrected to "led."

9. Second Wave

163. "The worst part was the minutes approaching . . .": May 29, 1918, issue of *Marion Daily Star* (OH).

163. "We were": Ibid.

163. "As the line reached the crest . . .": Major Austin letter, June 1, 1918.

164. "advance was swift and unchecked": Lt. L. Irwin Morris, Report for 2nd Platoon, Company K, 28th Infantry, June 2, 1918, NA, RG 120, Entry 1241, Box 55.

164. "The Germans just threw up their hands and ran . . .": September 24, 1918, issue of *Denton Record-Chronicle* (TX).

164. "I was between the first and second waves . . .": Ibid.

164. "[I]t was our duty to clean out . . .": Lt. John Mays, letter to mother, published in article

"Atlantan Writes of Terrific Fight At Cantigny Town," July 7, 1918 issue of *Atlanta Constitution*.

164. "Two squads of automatic riflemen ran . . .": Morris, Report for 2nd Platoon, Company K.

164. "I myself killed two Boches . . .": Mays letter, *Atlanta Constitution*.

165. "covered with growing crops . . .": Wilder, "Operations of Company M," 20.

165. "The 2nd lines rapidly closed on the 1st . . .": Ely, Report on 28th Infantry Regt.

165. "[t]he Lieutenant walked from one end . . .": *Memoirs of the Harvard Dead*, Vol. III, 141.

166. "Lieutenant you keep low": Ibid.

166. "They can't kill me": Ibid.

166. "He was hit by a machine-gun bullet . . .": Ibid.

166. "he won the highest respect of every man . . .": *Memoirs of the Harvard Dead*, vol. 3, 141.

166. "displayed qualities of coolness and gallantry . . .": *WWR*, vol. 23.

166. "rudderless": James Carl Nelson, *Five Lieutenants*, 266.

166. "gallantry in action . . .": *WWR*, vol. 23.

166. "[m]any machine-gun positions": Cullison, Report of 3rd Battalion.

167. "advanced 20 yards when he was seen to fall": Burial file of PFC Edward Lutz, NPRC.

167. "Mechanic Lockwood ran over to him . . .": Ibid.

168. "the company reached its assigned objective . . .": van Natter letter, April 24, 1926.

169. "The advance was made at schedule rate . . .": Lt. Jim Quinn, report of Company G, 28th Infantry, June 2, 1918, NA, RG 120, Entry 1241, Box 55.

169. "skeleton squads": Johnston, Monograph, 40.

169. "a football rush, only less rough": Irving Wood, *Rushville Daily Republican* (IN), June 26, 1918.

169. "From the time we left our jumping off . . .": Capt. James V. Ware, report of Company H, 28th Infantry, June 4, 1918, NA, RG 120, Entry 1241, Box 55.

169. "were given the complete plan and full liberty . . .": Marshall, *Memoirs*, 94.

169. "should not precede the first infantry wave . . .": Ibid.

170. "The sun, which had risen above the barrage . . .": James Hopper, "Our First Victory, Part II—Over the Top and Beyond," *Collier's, The National Weekly*, New York, September 7, 1918.

170. "Nobody was running,": Sargent, "Cantigny," 13.

170. "climbing equally steadily up the slope": Ibid., 14.

170. "And our soldiers were entering Cantigny": Ibid.

170. "Cantigny had not a wall left standing when . . .": Jesse Evans diary.

171. "Cantigny is completely wrecked": Fred Ferguson, UPI, June 6, 1918 issue of *Ackley World Journal* (IA).

171. "I tell you, you can't tell when you are . . .": Lt. Harry Martin, July 4, 1918, issue of *Emporia Weekly Gazette* (KS).

171. "I raised my pistol on him . . .": Ibid.

171. "The town was hit at the correct places": Ware, report of Company H.

171. "strutting among them and displaying . . .": Waltz, "Operations of Company C," 17.

171. "charged in a straight rhinoceros line . . .": Hopper, Ibid.

172. "these tanks got in some good work . . .": Waltz, "Operations of Company C," 17–18.

172. "They seemed to be off to themselves . . .": Ibid., 18.

172. "Tell Ruth Uncle Levy killed her a big fat one . . .": Levy Wilson, letter home, May 31, 1918, *Denton Record-Chronicle* (TX), June 28, 1918.

172. "falling down": Boleslaw Suchocki, "The Battle of Cantigny—As Seen by One Who Was There," *The Military Engineer*, 13, no. 71, September–October 1921, 393.

172. "[A] shell burst about ten feet in front . . .": Ibid.

173. "I could not see farther than 100 feet . . .": Ibid.

173. "[T]he shell exploded directly in front of him . . .": Report of Cpl. Jesse Allen, Burial File of PFC Wilford Wethington, NPRC.

173. "Forward!": Suchocki, "The Battle of Cantigny," 393.

173. "violent machine-gun fire": Pvt. Earl Simons, September 5, 1918, issue of *Altoona Mirror* (PA).

174. "there stop us some kind [of] unknown . . .": Suchocki, "The Battle of Cantigny," 395.

174. "lay down": Ibid.

174. "the first man in Co. F that was killed": Report of Pvt. Bernard E. Kavanaugh, Burial File of Pvt. Joseph Leiter, NPRC.

174. "only six of us left, the rest killed or wounded": Suchocki, "The Battle of Cantigny," 395.

175. "to watch closely the compass reading . . .": Lt. Gerald Tyler, "The Cantigny Operation," narrative of the battle enclosed in letter to American Battle Monuments Commission, October 23, 1929, NA, RG 117, Entry 31, Box 184.

175. "had been killed by shell fire": Ibid.

175. "a fan shaped forward movement": Ibid.

175. "Our men have entered Cantigny": 6:56 a.m. entry, May 28, 1918, 1st Field Artillery HQ Journal, NA, RG 120, Entry 1241, Box 61.

10. We Took the Hill

177. "Nothing was seen any more of the other platoons . . .": War Diary, German 26th Reserve Corps, 72.

178. "in dense masses": Ibid.

178. "*No* artillery fire followed these signals": Ibid.

179. "Tomorrow we are going to attack": Lt. Robert B. Anderson, letter to mother, May 27, 1918, Private Collection.

179. "prevent the right flank being turned": Maj. George Rozelle, report of 1st Battalion, June 3, 1918, NA, RG 120, Entry 1241, Box 55.

179. "The digging in woods was very difficult": Lt. James L. Hartney, report of Company A, 28th Infantry, June 2, 1918, NA, RG 120, Entry 1241, Box 55.

180. "about 50 yards of trench . . .": Ibid.

180. "down the field under the kick-off . . .": Lt. Nielson Poe letter, June 5, 1918, "Was in Cantigny Fight," July 21, 1918, issue of *The Baltimore Sun* (MD).

180. "The artillery laid a beautiful barrage . . .": Ibid.

180. "We were to take a hill to the right . . .": Pvt. William McCombs, November 18, 1918, issue of *New Castle News* (PA).

180. "Sometimes you would hear shells . . .": Poe letter, June 5, 1918.

180. "When we reached Cantigny it was only . . .": Lt. George Butler, May 29, 1918, issue of *Muskogee Times Democrat* (OK).

181. "It was the finest example of teamwork . . .": Ibid.

181. "Our fellows threw grenades like baseballs . . .": Lt. George Butler, May 29, 1918, issue of *Marion Daily Star* (OH).

181. "Huns were called upon to come out": Lt. Samuel Smith, Intelligence Officer, 1st Battalion, 28th Infantry, "Report on Conditions and Material in Captured Area of Cantigny," June 2, 1918, NA, RG 120, Entry 1241, Box 55.

181. "[A] general clean up took place . . .": Ibid.

181. "The enemy ran out of caves . . .": Lt. George Butler, May 29, 1918, issue of *Marion Daily Star* (OH).

181. "Map of enemy's positions of rear . . .": Smith report, June 2, 1918.

181. "The men were rolling cigarettes as . . .": Pvt. John Johnston, March 2, 1919, issue of *La Crosse Tribune and Leader Press* (WI).

182. "It was a great sight to see . . .": Pvt. Ralph E. Loucks letter, June 27, 1918, *Fort Wayne Journal-Gazette* (IN), August 11, 1918.

182. "The platoon I was in was nearly up . . .": Ibid.

182. "I crawled into a shell hole and just . . .": Ibid.

183. "He was hit several times, . . .": Report of First Sgt. Joseph L. Olbrych, Burial File of Pvt. Jacob Ciezielczyk, NPRC.

183. "I am going to die": Report of Sgt. Walter Christenson, Burial File of PFC Frank Caralunas, NPRC.

184. ""Tell my mother I died like a man": Report of Pvt. Joseph Lukaschonski, Burial File of PFC Clifton B. Eby, NPRC.

184. "the bark could be seen peeling off . . .": Pvt. John Johnston, March 2, 1919, issue of *La Crosse Tribune and Leader Press* (WI).

184. "On reaching the objective": Parker, Report of 1st Platoon, Company K.

185. "The enemy saw me rush-in": Parker, letter to brother, June 2, 1918.

185. "Yes, a Hell of a Kamerad": Ibid.

185. "The gun was then slewed around and . . .": Morris, Report for 2nd Platoon, Company K.

186. "directed me to the exact location . . .": Samuel Ervin Jr., letter to mother of George Redwood, May 2, 1920, FDM.

186. "I remarked to him that he was somewhat . . .": Ibid.

186. "Instead of doing what is ordinarily . . .": Ibid.

186. "I told him I thought it inadvisable . . .": Tyler, "The Cantigny Operation."

186. "decided to follow his advice": Ibid.

186. "I gave him what information I could": Ibid.

187. "I had nearly reached it when things . . .": Lt. James J. Lawrence, July 13, 1918, issue of *Atlanta Constitution* (GA).

187. "Then I saw red": Hamilton Holt, "The Black Snakes: A Visit to Bullard's Boys at Cantigny," *The Independent*, August 3, 1918, issue, 184.

187. "These men were also killed": Capt. Clarence Oliver, Report of Company B, 28th Infantry, June 1, 1918, NA, RG 120, Entry 1241, Box 55.

188. "I was a pretty good baseball pitcher . . .": Cpl. Lewis L. Kowaski, December 12, 1918, issue of *Des Moines Daily News* (IA).

188. "banged away": Ibid.

188. "We took Cantigny on schedule time . . .": Wood letter, January 8, 1919.

189. "And now our men were walking through . . .": Sargent, "Cantigny," 14.

189. "Objective reached": Message, 7:24 a.m., May 28, 1918, Field Messages of 2nd Brigade, NA, RG 120, Entry 1241, Box 41.

189. "The success of this phase of the operation . . .": Marshall, *Memoirs*, 95.

189. "Over 100 prisoners from two different regiments . . .": Colonel Ely phone message, 8:00 a.m., May 28, 1918, Field Messages of 2nd Brigade.

189. "most successful": General Pershing diary entry, May 28, 1918, Pershing Papers, Box 2, Folder 13, Manuscript Division, LOC, 449.

189. "with the wonder of the performance": Bullard, *Personalities*, 197.

189. 140 German prisoners brought in . . . Pershing diary entry, May 28, 1918.

190. "We took the hill—and held it": Pvt. William McCombs, November 12, 1918, issue of *New Castle News* (PA).

190. "losing our nerve": Ibid.

11. A Pack of Bumblebees

191. "The pick or the shovel . . .": Poe letter, June 5, 1918.

191. "Just as the digging began . . .": Parker, report of 1st Platoon, Company K.

191. "dodging from one shell hole to another": Pvt. Emory Smith, September 24, 1918, issue of *Denton Record-Chronicle* (TX).

192. "taking an entrenching tool from comrade's pack . . .": Report of Cpl. Clayton O. Waite, Burial File of Pvt. Amelet Gialanella, NPRC.

192. "a quiet fellow": Report of Pvt. Ernest Drake, Burial File of PFC Charles H. Harsch, NPRC.

192. "made a step for a shell hole to start . . .": Report of Pvt. Harry C. Langley, Burial File of Pvt. Eugene Griepentrog, NPRC.

192. "As soon as he was injured he became . . .": Report of Pvt. Harry C. Langley, Burial File of Cpl. Harry McCredie, NPRC.

192. "was struck in the left temple with a machine-gun bullet . . .": Report of Pvt. Ernest Drake, Burial File of Cpl. Jethers Schoemaker, NPRC.

193. "I'm shot": Report of Pvt. Richardson Peters, Burial File of Pvt. Matthew B. Juan (aka Matthew Rivers), NPRC.

193. Matthew Juan . . . Correspondence between Mary B. Juan with War Department, Burial File of Matthew B. Juan (aka Rivers), NPRC; also July 1, 1927, issue of *Casa Grande Dispatch* (AZ).

193. "encouraged his men by his example . . .": *WWR,* vol. 23.

194. "We dug while the sun was coming up": Pvt. John Johnston, March 2, 1919, issue of *La Crosse Tribune and Leader Press* (WI).

194. "As soon as we reached the objective . . .": Poe letter, June 5, 1918.

195. Pvt. Harry Gums was still lying . . . December 27, 1918, issue of *Janesville Daily Gazette* (WI).

195. "chewed": Lt. James J. Lawrence, August 3, 1918, issue of *Indiana Evening Gazette* (PA).

195. Lt. Soren Sorensen . . . Nelson, *Remains of Company D,* 49–54.

195. "most casualties were on reaching . . .": Lt. Soren Sorensen, Report of Company D, 28th Infantry, June 1, 1918, NA, RG 120, Entry 1241, Box 55.

195. "between the shoulder blades": Report of Sgt. Ira Huddleston, Burial File of PFC Walter Daw, NPRC.

195. "When they began digging in . . .": George Butler, May 29, 1918, issue of *Marion Daily Star* (OH).

196. "The bullet hit him in the forehead . . .": Report of Cpl. Oscar Roulo, Burial File of Pvt. William Fishette, NPRC.

196. "[d]ropped his head a little": Report of Sgt. Willard Storms, Burial File of Cpl. George Anslow, NPRC.

196. "It was like a pack of bumblebees": George Butler, May 29, 1918, issue of *Marion Daily Star* (OH).

196. "He was hit by at least five bullets . . .": Report of Cpl. Walter B Rice, Burial File of Sgt. Roy N. Hockenberry, NPRC.

196. "Now I could see into its ruined . . .": James Hopper, "Our First Victory, Part II," *Collier's.*

197. "a bushy black beard": Cpl. Daniel Edwards, *Doughboy War,* James Hallas, editor, 81–82.

197. "So many young boys . . .": James Hopper, "Our First Victory, Part II," *Collier's.*

197. "some running but few looking back . . .": Cpt. Stuart Campbell, "Positions Occupied," July 5, 1918, NA, RG 120, Entry 1241, Box 47.

197. "They were so thin it looked impossible . . .": Cpl. George Ross, June 28, 1919, issue of *Clinton Daily Clintonian* (IN).

197. "seemed quite young and all . . .": Major Austin letter, June 1, 1918.

198. "just as I had seen rabbits in Kansas . . .": Edward Coffman, *The War to End All Wars*, 156–57.

198. "We didn't have money in those days": Capt. Clarence Huebner, March 10, 1971, issue of *The Holyrood Gazette* (KS).

198. "I took good aim right through . . .": Suchocki, second account, 4.

199. "I saw that a Dutchman stick . . .": Ibid.

199. "alone killing four enemy snipers . . .": *WWR*, vol. 23.

199. "During this time the counter-battery . . .": Brig. Gen. H. W. Butner, "Report on Operation Against Cantigny, May 28, 1918," NA, RG 120, Entry 1241, Box 61.

199. "Orders for the withdrawal of more . . .": Marshall, *Memoirs*, 95.

199. "neutralization of enemy batteries . . .": Field Order No. 18, May 20, 1918, with amendments to May 24 and Annex 1, 3, 4 (May 22), NA, RG 120, Entry 1241, Boxes 16 and 18.

199. "The German guns, unsuppressed . . .": Marshall, *Memoirs*, 95.

200. "everything changed. Our artillery . . .": Sargent, "Cantigny," 14.

200. "made a direct hit and mangle[d] . . .": Report of Cpl. Leon C. Kohmann, Burial File of PFC Marion Thompson, NPRC.

200. "had started to dig in": Report of Sgt. James Whalen, Burial File of Pvt. Paul Davis, NPRC.

200. "instantly killed": Ibid.

200. "so I can buy a nice stone to put . . .": Eliza Davis, letter to War Department, Burial File of Pvt. Paul Davis, NPRC; Note: "semetery" in original corrected to "cemetery."

200. "PAUL DAVIS CO D 28 INF": Burial File of Pvt. Paul Davis, NPRC.

200. "I had been hit three times more . . .": Newhall, letter to Paul Birdsall, April 29, 1963, *Selected Papers*, 96.

201. "drew hostile artillery and machine-gun fire": Wilder, "Operations of Company M," 28.

201. "Within the first five minutes . . .": Morris, Report for 2nd Platoon, Company K.

201. "Just as he got on the parapet . . .": Report of PFC James Chastain, Burial File of Pvt. Joseph Zboran, NPRC.

201. "The trench being too crowded . . .": Report of Pvt. Charlie Havens, Burial File of Cpl. August Schmidt, NPRC.

202. "Morris come over here and fix me up": Report of Lt. Irwin Morris, Burial File of Lt. Paul Waples Derrickson, NPRC.

202. "Fearlessly walking up and down . . .": *WWR*, vol. 23.

202. "lived only a moment or two": Report of Lt. Irwin Morris, Burial File of Lt. Clarence Milton Drumm, NPRC.

202. "he was captured or is in a hospital . . .": Letter from Linnie Booth to Lt. Irwin Morris, June 28, 1918, Private Collection.

202. "I opened my 1st aid packet . . .": Report of PFC Thomas Fursh, Burial File of Pvt. Virgil Varnado, NPRC.

203. "very well-liked by the boys": Report of Pvt. Edward Derrick, Burial File of Pvt. Raymond Branshaw, NPRC.

203. "Here's my watch . . .": Report of Lt. Samuel Parker, Burial File of Pvt. Raymond Branshaw, NPRC.

203. "immediately began to dig in . . .": Capt. Clarence Huebner, Report of 2nd Battalion, 28th Infantry, June 2, 1918.

203. "When I reached the colonel I found . . .": Report of Capt. Clarence Huebner, Burial File of Lt. Col. Robert Jayne Maxey, NPRC.

204. "Maxey seriously wounded . . .": Capt. Clarence Huebner, phone message, 9:07 a.m.,

May 28, 1918, Report of Capt. William Livesay, Adjutant, 28th Infantry, NA, RG 120, Entry 1241, Box 55.

205. "28th Inf. reports everything fine here . . .": Marshall, phone message, 9:22 a.m., May 28, 1918, Field Messages of 2nd Brigade, NA, RG 120, Entry 1241, Box 41.

12. Ignore the Bullets

207. "laughing at the photographer who . . .": Nelson, *Five Lieutenants*, 259.

207. "It was nature to ignore the bullets": Wood letter, December 8, 1919.

208. "queer sense of unreality": Ibid.

208. "I saw his body jerk and then . . .": Johnston letter, November 20, 1918.

208. "He was in an exhausted position . . .": Capt. William G. Livesay, report of Adjutant, 28th Infantry, NA, RG 120, Entry 1241, Box 55.

208. "lengthen barrage 200 yards": Message received at 28th Infantry P.C., 9:15 a.m., May 28, 1918, "Report on operations Against Cantigny," Livesay, report of Adjutant, 28th IR.

208. "The slope of the plateau was . . .": Butler, Monograph, 11.

209. "in order to shelter ourselves . . .": Report of Pvt. Edward White, Burial File of Cpl. Arthur J. Wood, NPRC.

209. "I heard the shell coming and knew . . .": Pvt. Earl Simons, September 5, 1918, issue of *Altoona Mirror* (PA).

209. "The large number of wounded . . .": Ely, Report on 28th Infantry Regt.

209. "I had never imagined that carrying a man . . .": James Hopper, "Our First Victory, Part II," *Collier's*.

209. "Sure was an awful day": PFC Vernon L. Scobie diary, FDM.

210. "went to the spot where the wounded . . .": Report of Pvt. George Spitler, Burial Files of Pvt. Martin L. Shelton and Pvt. George Ratzlaff, NPRC.

210. "There was": Report of Pvt. Austin Bradley, Burial File of Lt. Norborne R. Gray, NPRC.

210. "[I]n the face of the heavy fire . . .": September 5, 1918, issue of *Altoona Mirror* (PA).

210. "I was taken on a two-wheeled dinky . . .": Pvt. Earl Simons, September 5, 1918, issue of *Altoona Mirror* (PA).

211. "certainly wasn't a pleasant place . . .": Pvt. William McCombs, July 15, 1918, issue of *New Castle News* (PA).

211. "[D]octors work to the noise of bursting shells . . .": Dorr, *A Soldier's Mother*, 111.

211. "a series of more or less painful . . .": Ibid., 116.

211. "evacuating patients on litters . . .": Report of Pvt. Claude Medley, Burial File of Pvt. Harry H. Eschbach, NPRC.

211. "as close to the ground as possible": Sargent, "Cantigny," 15.

211. "A splinter of it tore into . . .": Ibid., 18.

211. "flank protection": Annex No. 6 to Field Order No. 18, May 22, 1918, NA, RG 120, Entry 1241, Box 18.

212. "probable enemy strong points": Ibid.

212. "well worthwhile if only for the moral . . .": Huebner, Report of 2nd Battalion.

212. "kept together and travelled in a . . .": Waltz, "Operations of Company C," 22.

212. "very active": Ware, Report of Company H.

212. "struck by a shell splinter . . .": Report of Sgt. Vincenzo Farchi, Burial File of Cpl. Herman Evans, NPRC.

212. "He was holding his watch timing . . .": Report of Sgt. Fred Benning, Burial File of PFC Ivan Stringer, NPRC.

213. "to God that whatever occasion . . .": George Stein, letter to father, January 14, 1918, Private Collection.

213. "until so severely wounded as to be unable . . .": *WWR*, vol. 23.

213. "until severely wounded": *WWR*, vol. 23.

213. "We went forward about seventy-five . . .": Gillespie, "Pickens Man in No Man's Land 5 Days," August 29, 1928, issue of *Aiken Journal and Review* (SC).

214. "under heavy fire, back to a place of safety": Mays letter, *Atlanta Constitution*.

214. "walking from one place to another . . .": *WWR*, vol. 23.

214. "I am glad I was there to have my old friend . . .": Mays letter, *Atlanta Constitution*.

214. "with great efficiency and coolness . . .": John Mays, letter to John J. Parker, March 29, 1920, Samuel I. Parker File, Heritage Room, Union County Courthouse, Monroe, North Carolina.

214. "marked gallantry under the most difficult conditions": Ibid.

214. "I fell where I lay and was bleeding . . .": Pvt. Emory Smith, September 21, 1918, issue of *Denton Record-Chronicle* (TX).

214. "hit in the neck by a sniper's bullet": Report of Bugler William Turner, Burial File of Sgt. Thomas E. Peden, NPRC.

214. "He was conscious about thirty seconds": Report of PFC William Mervyn, Burial File of Cpl. Nathan Korngold, NPRC.

215. "A good sized piece of the metal . . .": Gillespie, "Pickens Man in No Man's Land."

215. "that Captain Anderson and all other officers . . .": Tyler, "The Cantigny Operation."

215. "By this time machine-gun bullets . . .": Tyler, letter to mother, June 3, 1918.

215. "It was the sniper's bullet": Ibid.

215. "hit by a sniper": Report of Cpl. Louis Abend, Burial File of Pvt. Archie Lackshire, NPRC.

216. "slim, very quiet . . .": Report of Cpl. Louis Abend, Burial File of Pvt. Emery Dean, NPRC.

216. "The work of this carrying party . . .": Capt. Willis Tack, Report of Company I, 28th Infantry, June 2, 1918, NA, RG 120, Entry 1241, Box 55.

216. "And so I got down and took . . .": Clancy, *Just a Country Lawyer*, 67.

216. "He refused to believe they were Americans . . .": Ibid., 68.

216. "*Wir sind verdammte Schweine*": Ibid.

216. "exceptional courage and perseverance": *WWR*, vol. 23.

217. "action had quieted down considerably . . .": Lieutenant Sorensen, Report of Company D.

217. "'[A] big one' exploded within a yard . . .": Nelson, *Remains of Company D*, 100.

217. "staggered forward as soon as he regained . . .": *WWR*, vol. 23.

218. "giving a striking example of . . .": *WWR*, vol. 23.

218. "in good condition": Sorensen, Report of Company D.

218. "We were digging in when we heard . . .": Report of Sgt. Barley Larkin, Burial File of Lt. Max Buchanan, NPRC.

219. "with a thick poultice of blood and brains": Nelson, *Remains of Company D*, 102.

219. "about 100 men marching on road": Report at 1st Field Artillery Brigade HQ, 9:46 a.m., May 28, 1918, "Journal of Cantigny Operations," NA, RG 120, Entry 1241, Box 61.

219. "doing us more harm than ever": Ibid.

219. "When the Germans started their counterattack . . .": Report of Sgt. Barley Larkin, Burial File of Pvt. Frank Beck, NPRC.

219. "trying to keep the other men down . . .": Report of Cpl. Ira Huddleston, Burial File of Sgt. John R. Pooler, NPRC.

219. "carried him through heavy machine-gun fire . . .": *WWR*, vol. 23.

219. "a direct hit": Report of Cpl. John Rusinowecz, Burial File of Pvt. Jerome Angell, NPRC.

219. "seven of the enemy before he . . .": *WWR*, vol. 23.

220. "dispersed": Report at 1st Field Artillery Brigade HQ, 10:40 a.m., May 28, 1918.

220. "too combat strong": Major P. L. Ransom, "The Capture of Cantigny—An Account Based Upon the Official German Records," FDM.

220. "concentrated fire": War Diary, German 18th Army, 8.

220. "[T]he main reliance must be upon . . .": Pershing, *Experiences,* vol. 1, 393; April 16, 1917, speech, Pershing Papers.

13. Half Crazy, Temporarily Insane

221. "[a]ll objectives were taken": Operations Report, 10:00 a.m. May 27 to 10:00 a.m. May 28, 1918, NA, RG 120, Entry 1241, Box 27.

221. "everything quiet on front": 11:30 a.m., May 28, 1918, Field Messages of 2nd Brigade.

221. "Cantigny is occupied by the enemy": War Diary, German 18th Army, 17.

221. "concentrated fire": War Diary, German 18th Army, 8.

221. "very heavy enemy shelling began . . .": Lt. Col. George Marshall, Memorandum: Report of Incidents Immediately Prior to and During the Operation Against Cantigny carried out on May 28, 1918, May 29, 1918, NA, RG 120, Entry 1241, Box 42.

222. "terrific blasting": "The History of the First Division," NA, RG 120, Entry 1241, Box 6, 25.

222. "Along in the afternoon the enemy . . .": Newhall, letter to mother, August 1, 1918, *Selected Papers,* 88–89.

222. "fainted with pain": Ibid., 90.

222. "killed and not merely badly wounded": Ibid., 89.

222. "Every once in a while I would loosen . . .": Gillespie, "Pickens Man in No Man's Land."

222. "Heavy shelling commenced . . .": Lt. John Mays, Report of 4th Platoon, Company K, 28th Infantry, June 2, 1918, NA, RG 120, Entry 1241, Box 55.

222. "ragtime bugler": August 22, 1918, issue of *New Oxford Item* (PA).

222. "He called out 'Oh-la-la' . . .": Report of Pvt. Emmet Shipp, Burial File of Bugler Joe Mayuiers, NPRC.

223. "We could look up out of our holes . . .": Waltz, "Operations of Company C," 26.

223. "Ashcans": Ibid.

223. "They came over so slowly . . .": Ibid., 27.

223. "stood out like a lighthouse in a storm . . .": Ibid., 23.

223. "I remember when he joined up": Report of Pvt. Webb LaPointe, Burial File of Pvt. Gaspare Ventimiglia, NPRC.

223. "shell exploded and buried him": Ibid.

223. "completely shot away": Report of grave searcher, Burial file of Pvt. George Hutchins, NPRC.

224. "Shortly after entering shell-crater . . .": Stewart, report of Reg. M.G. Co.

224. "losing our nerve": Pvt. William McCombs, November 12, 1918, issue of *New Castle News* (PA).

224. "Going over the top is not so bad . . .": Ibid.

224. "I'll be damned if I see any fun . . .": Ibid.

224. "will have to be reinforced or relieved": Message from Rozelle to Ely, May 28, 1918, Report on Operations Against Cantigny, HQ, 28th Infantry, NA, RG 120, Entry 1241, Box 54.

224. "has had three officers killed . . .": Message from Huebner to Ely, 1:00 p.m., May 28, 1918.

224. "Capt. Mosher and Lt. Drumm have . . .": Message from Cullison to Ely, 1:08 p.m., May 28, 1918.

225. "not much less": Phone call from Ely to 2nd Brigade, 2:17 p.m., May 28, 1918, Field Messages of 2nd Brigade.

225. "Casualties continue from m.g. . . .": Ibid.

225. "extremely heavy losses in officers . . .": Marshall, Memorandum, May 29, 1918.

226. "This was the high-angle stuff that . . .": Waltz, "Operations of Company C," 26-27.

226. "badly mutilated": Report of Cpl. Leon Kohmann, Burial File of PFC Marion Thompson, NPRC.

226. "both arms and legs were torn away": Report of Sgt. Harry Hildebrand, Burial File of Pvt. Cyrus P. Adcox, NPRC.

226. "The enemy barrage had cut us off . . .": Mays, Report of 4th Platoon, Company K.

226. "Withdraw": Parker, Report of 1st Platoon, Company K.

227. "half crazy, temporarily insane": Smythe, *Pershing*, 128.

227. "[T]he order was passed down from the right . . .": Mays, Report of 4th Platoon, Company K.

227. "Lieutenant Ward": Parker, Report of 1st Platoon, Company K.

227. "some of the troops on my left . . .": Morris, Report for 2nd Platoon, Company K.

227. "to hold out until the wounded were evacuated": Parker, Report of 1st Platoon, Company K.

227. "plow into our line of resistance . . .": Waltz, "Operations of Company C," 25.

228. "Those who were able to do so . . .": Pvt. Emory Smith, September 24, 1918, issue of *Denton Record-Chronicle* (TX).

228. "intense machine-gun and intense artillery fire": Nelson, *Remains of Company D*, 108-109.

228. "attempted to reach the lines again . . .": Ibid.

228. "I would rather have that man Redwood . . .": *Memoirs of the Harvard Dead*, Vol. III, 161.

228. "Lieutenant, the company has fallen . . .": Newhall, letter to mother, August 1, 1918, *Selected Papers*, 89.

228. "It was impossible to take me . . .": Ibid., 90.

229. "number of small detachments . . .": van Natter letter, April 24, 1926.

229. "the two companies withdrew . . .": Cullison, Report of 3rd Battalion.

229. "The withdrawal was": Wilder, "Operations of Company M," 20.

229. "the full force of the German preparation . . .": Ibid., 21.

229. "The way [the enemy] shelled us . . .": Tyler, letter to mother, June 3, 1918.

229. "I was right alongside of him . . .": Report of Pvt. Otto Bjorkman, March 15, 1919, Burial File of Cpl. Edward W. Gray, NPRC.

230. "thrust against an enemy fully prepared . . .": War Diary, German 26th Reserve Corps, 48.

230. "a number of Germans . . .": Lt. Rudolph Koubsky, Report of Company M, 28th Infantry, June 2, 1918, NA, RG 120, Entry 1241, Box 55.

230. "All were beaten off before reaching . . .": Ibid.

230. "smothered": Gen. Robert Bullard, Special Situation Report, Noon, May 29, 1918, NA, RG 120, Entry 1241, Box 27.

231. "I now expected to be taken prisoner . . .": Newhall, letter to mother, August 1, 1918, *Selected Papers*, 90.

231. "killed in action": Letter from Adjutant General's Office of the War Department re: Private Carl Fey, June 22, 1918, Private Collection.

231. "increasing steadily": Message from Rozelle to Ely, 4:55 p.m., May 28, 1918, Report on Operations Against Cantigny, HQ, 28th Infantry.

232. "he was hit by a shell and all that could . . .": Mary Hawley, letter to Adjutant General, November 15, 1920, Burial File of Pvt. Ira A. Hawley, NPRC.

232. "My line of surveillance withdrew . . .": Oliver, Report of Company B.

232. "infantrymen retreating and what I took . . .": Stewart, Report of Reg. M.G. Co.

232. "the line was reported as retreating": Ibid.

232. "D company has vacated sector . . .": Message from Rozelle to Ely, 5:45 p.m., May 28, 1918, Report on Operations Against Cantigny, HQ, 28th Infantry.

233. "At 6:00 p.m.": Capt. Horace D. Smith, Experience Report, December 22, 1918.

233. "company was called upon to reinforce . . .": Cox, Experience Report.

233. "several dead German bodies": Suchocki, second account, 6.

233. "[W]e rushed to the trench . . .": Report of Pvt. John Dowd, Burial File of PFC Daniel S. Miller, NPRC.

233. "directing the men of his section . . .": Report of First Sgt. Thomas Kelly, Burial File of SFC Carl G. Thoete, NPRC.

233. "Sgt. Thoete was unconscious . . .": Ibid.

233. "When I saw him he was falling . . .": Report of Sgt. William Riehl, Burial File of PFC Daniel S. Miller, NPRC.

234. "laying on the ground . . .": Report of Sgt. Ray Deane, Burial File of Pvt. William R. Loftis, NPRC.

234. "very narrow and shallow and . . .": Suchocki, second account, 6.

234. "you better get down": Ibid.

234. "An enemy counter-attack . . .": Rozelle, Report of 1st Battalion, 28th Infantry, June 3, 1918, NA, RG 120, Entry 1341, Box 55.

234. "the exhausted state of the troops . . .": War Diary, German 272nd Reserve Infantry Regiment, 59.

235. "entirely too insufficient time . . .": War Diary, German 26th Reserve Corps, 77.

235. "Situation fine—enemy beaten off": Phone message from 18th Infantry HQ to 2nd Brigade, 7:55 p.m., May 28, 1918, Field Messages of 2nd Brigade.

14. The World Is Watching

237. "a letter of congratulations": Pershing diary, entry for May 28, 1918.

237. "astonished": Bullard, *Personalities*, 197–98.

237. "I need not suggest that you give . . .": Millett, *The General*, 365.

237. "Our Bn. needs relief": Message from Rozelle to Ely, 6:20 p.m., May 28, 1918, Field Messages of 28th Infantry P.C., NA, RG 120, Entry 1241, Box 53.

237. "My company is practically . . .": Message from van Natter to Ely, 7:00 p.m., May 28, 1918, Report on Operations Against Cantigny, 28th Infantry.

237. "Account shortage of officers . . .": Message from Rozelle to Ely, 8:30 p.m., May 28, 1918, Ibid.

237. "Unless heavy artillery can give . . .": Message from Ely to 2nd Brigade, 5:45 p.m., May 28, 1918, Field Messages of 28th Infantry P.C.

237. "Recommend 18th Inf. relieve . . .": Message from Ely to 2nd Brigade, 6:40 p.m., May 28, 1918, Field Messages of 2nd Brigade.

237. "losses are heavy . . .": Message from Ely to 2nd Brigade, 7:23 p.m., May 28, 1918, Ibid.

237. "Rozelle reports his Bn. has suffered . . .": Message from Ely to 2nd Brigade, 8:40 p.m., May 28, 1918, Ibid.

238. "Inform Ely as follows . . .": Message from Bullard to 2nd Brigade, 7:35 p.m., May 28, 1918, Ibid.

238. "Troops sent to you are not to be used . . .": Message from 2nd Brigade to Ely, 8:25 p.m., May 28, 1918, Ibid.

238. "Ely, you must hold your position . . .": Millett, *The General*, 366.

238. "I was weak from loss of blood . . .": Tyler, letter to mother, June 3, 1918.

238. "I would have given twenty years . . .": Ibid.

238. "short lull": Tyler, "The Cantigny Operation."

238. "between it and myself several shells . . .": Tyler, letter to mother, June 3, 1918.

239. "disorganized retreat": Wilder, "Operations of Company M," 20.

239. "headed off": Message from Cullison to Ely, 6:40 p.m., May 28, 1918, Field Messages of 28th Infantry P.C.

239. "to round up all the stragglers . . .": Parker, Report of 1st Platoon, Company K.

239. "I found about 25 men from various . . .": Ibid.

239. "My company is practically wiped out": Message from van Natter to Ely, 7:00 p.m., May 28, 1918, Report on operation against Cantigny, 28th Infantry.

240. "One of your companies will report . . .": Message from Ely to Hunt, 11:00 p.m., May 28, 1918, Field Messages of 28th Infantry.

240. "Word came from the Front . . .": Pvt. Frank J. Last diary, FDM.

241. "when the attempt was made it was found . . .": Cullison, Report of 3rd Battalion.

241. "I was ordered with my company to connect . . .": Tack, Report of Company I.

241. "[W]e were given the rather unusual command . . .": Lt. Herman Dacus, letter to Ed Burke, August 15, 1984, private collection.

241. "My platoon sergeant was a former miner . . .": Nelson, *Remains of Company D*, 108.

241. "[B]y morning": Tack, Report of Company I.

241. "extremely cold": Waltz, "Operations of Company C," 30.

242. "[R]eports led me to believe . . .": Rozelle, Report of 1st Battalion.

242. "relieve the remainder of Co. . . .": Message from Col. Campbell King (for Gen. Robert Bullard) to 2nd Brigade, 8:40 p.m., May 28, 1918, Field Messages of 2nd Brigade.

242. "thinning lines and reducing losses": Message from Bullard to 2nd Brigade, 8:27 p.m., May 28, 1918, Field Messages of 2nd Brigade.

242. "At 10:30 p.m. the company was . . .": Capt. Charles Senay, Report of Company C, 28th Infantry, June 1, 1918, NA, RG 120, Entry 1241, Box 55.

242. "We moved forward in platoon column": Ibid.

243. "If possible, will you please ship . . .": E. A. West, letter to War Department, Burial File of Pvt. Tom West, NPRC.

244. "Send Co. D to relieve Co A/1 . . .": Message from Colonel Smith to Major Roosevelt, 9:45 p.m., May 28, 1918, Field Messages of 26th Infantry, NA, RG 120, Entry 1241, Box 49.

244. "The path lay through the woods": Pvt. Frank Goseling, March 13, 1919, issue of *Woodland Daily Democrat* (CA).

244. "struck almost directly": Report of 1st Sgt. John E. Francis, Burial File of Pvt. Wilbur Ward, NPRC.

244. "Men fell across the path . . .": Pvt. Frank Goseling, March 13, 1919, issue of *Woodland Daily Democrat* (CA).

244. "The Company was relieved about 2:30 . . .": Hartney, Report of Company A.

244. "just a little path through a thicket": Pvt. William McCombs, July 15, 1918, issue of *New Castle News* (PA).

245. "A shell-shrapnel struck in front . . .": Pvt. William McCombs, November 12, 1918, issue of *New Castle News* (PA).

245. "[k]illed instantly by artillery fire": Report of Sgt. James Rause, Burial File of Pvt. Emil Vanker, NPRC.

245. "instantly": Report of Cpl. John Johnson, Burial File of Pvt. Samuel Buchalter, NPRC.

245. "he thought he would be killed . . .": Ibid.

245. "only a few minutes": Report of Sgt. James Rause, Burial File of Sgt. Edward Nesterowicz, NPRC.

246. "Operation against Cantigny executed . . .": Telegram from Gen. Bullard to GHQ, 9:38 p.m., May 28, 1918, NA, RG 120, Entry 1241, Box 27.

246. "Danced upon the table tops": Bullard/Reeves, *American Soldiers*, 32.

246. "a most encouraging thing in a day . . .": Ibid.

246. "shell-shock": Morning Reports, May 28–30, 1918, NPRC.

246. "By night everything was quiet except . . .": Newhall, letter to mother, August 1, 1918, *Selected Papers*, 90.

246. "I lay still, afraid to move . . .": Ibid.

246. "Nobody ever came": Ibid.

246. "listening to the music of warfare . . .": Nelson, *Five Lieutenants*, 263.

15. Novelty of Silence

247. "long before I thought it should have": Sargent, "Cantigny," 22.

247. "I was astonished to see a couple . . .": Ibid., 23.

247. "cave": Ibid.

248. "Lieutenant Sargent": Ibid., 24. Note: In his original memoir, Sargent mistakenly recalled Ely saying, "You are to go to the command post of the 2nd battalion . . ." This is corrected to reflect what Ely would have actually said, "the 1st battalion . . ."

248. "that was the last he was seen or heard of": Pvt. Fred Allen, letter to War Department, May 15, 1926, Burial File of Pvt. Barnard Farley, NPRC.

248. "patients there who cannot be moved": Message, 2:36 a.m., May 29, 1918, Journal of Cantigny Operations, 1st Field Artillery Brigade, NA, RG 120, Entry 1241, Box 61.

249. "right alongside the chateau": Maj. R. H. Lewis, Liaison Report, 9:00 a.m., May 29, 1918, NA, RG 120, Entry 1241, Box 28.

249. "Infantry believe the Boche are . . .": Message, 4:20 a.m., May 28, 1918, Journal of Cantigny Operations, 1st Field Artillery Brigade.

249. "probably for enemy counterattack": Message, 4:00 a.m., May 28, 1918, Journal of Cantigny Operations, 28th Infantry.

249. "hold itself in readiness to reinforce . . .": Ibid.

251. "in position under extremely heavy fire": *WWR*, vol. 23.

251. "repeatedly pass[ing] up and down . . .": Ibid.

251. "left the security of the trenches . . .": Ibid.

251. "died instantly": Report of PFC Carl Powell, Burial File of PFC Joseph Rountree, NPRC.

251. "while advancing was killed by shellfire": *WWR*, vol. 23.

252. "fortunate enough to escape injury": Foster V. Brown Jr., letter to American Battle Monuments Commission, July 9, 1929, NA, RG 117, Entry 31, Box 184.

252. "heavy bombardment of artillery": Koubsky, Report of Company M. Note: original "envelope" corrected to "envelop."

252. "showed remarkable coolness and . . .": *WWR*, vol. 23.

253. "I never saw a braver man in all my life": Pvt. Floyd H. Weeks, handwritten annotations in Division History, FDM.

253. "They were beaten off with heavy losses again": Koubsky, Report of Company M.

253. "weakness in the organization": War Diary, German 272nd Reserve Infantry Regiment, 67.

253. "powerful fire opposition": Ibid.

253. "the combined fire of our artillery . . .": 1st Division Journal, NA, RG 120, Entry 1241, Box 9.

253. "Enemy infantry started across . . .": Message, 8:00 a.m., May 29, 1918, 1st Artillery Brigade Records for Cantigny Operation, NA, RG 120, Entry 1241, Box 66.

253. "When it began to get light I managed . . .": Newhall letter, August 1, 1918, *Select Papers*, 90.

253. "I couldn't lie flat because of the dead . . .": Ibid.

253. "slowly thinking about how I would . . .": Ibid.

254. "I shall always remember checking . . .": Gillespie, "Pickens Man in No Man's Land."

254. "I found Cantigny all ashes . . .": Sargent, "Cantigny," 25.

254. "fragments of four walls": Ibid.

254. "a black hole that stared out . . .": Ibid.

254. "What fool is it that is coming . . .": Ibid.

254. "Come in, Mr. Artilleryman . . .": Ibid., 26.

254. "duties to perform": Ibid., 30.

255. "incessant bombardment": Ibid., 29–30.

255. "Being in it all was like being . . .": Ibid., 29.

255. "We were fixing one of F Battery's lines . . .": Report of Cpl. John Baumgarten, Burial File of Pvt. Mirko Ivosevich, NPRC.

255. "I felt I was helping to win the war . . .": Groves, WWI Veterans Survey.

256. "We are in pretty bad shape . . .": Message from Huebner to Ely, 8:25 a.m., May 29, 1918, Report on Operations Against Cantigny, 28th Infantry.

256. "carrying party of inexperienced men . . .": *WWR,* vol. 23.

256. "shell struck directly in front of . . .": Report of Pvt. Henry Olson, Burial File of PFC Oscar Bolinger, NPRC.

256. "killed instantly": Burial Files of Pvt. Leo Monien and PFC Raymond Pichotta, NPRC.

256. "I fully decided that our position . . .": Waltz, "Operations of Company C," 27.

257. "We'd hear its report & watch . . .": Jefferson D. White letter, August 1, 1962, FDM.

257. "Their faces had turned black": Report of Sgt. Phillip Bilgway, Burial File of PFC Leslie R. Venters, NPRC.

257. "This type of stuff is what makes . . .": Waltz, "Operations of Company C," 28.

257. "thought it was his duty to be . . .":Ibid.

257. "[A]pparently the burst of the shell . . .": Report of Lt. Jim Quinn, Burial File of Lt. Thomas H. Watson, NPRC.

258. "instantly": Burial File of Pvt. Torgei Roysland, NPRC.

258. "only lived a minute or two . . .": Burial File of Pvt. Elmo Ridges, NPRC.

258. "unusually intense": Sargent, "Cantigny," 31.

258. "unsatisfactory": Rozelle, Report of 1st Battalion.

258. "reinforce center and right": Ibid.

258. "We had to traverse the ground . . .": James L. Hartney, letter to father of Lt. Robert B. Anderson, "First Alumnus Killed in France" from the *Trinity Alumni Register*, vol. 4, July 1918, no. 2, 100–101.

259. "He was shot through the calf . . .": Report of Cpl. Gust Behike, Burial File of Lt. Robert B. Anderson, NPRC.

259. "displayed courage and fearlessness . . .": *WWR,* vol. 23.

259. "leading his command forward in . . .": Ibid.

259. "His death was almost instantaneous": Report of Sgt. Robert Doyle, Burial File of Pvt. George W. Austin, NPRC.

259. "attempting to get his men under cover": *WWR,* vol. 23.

260. "[A]bout 15 other casualties occurred . . .": Hartney, Report of Company A.

260. "Tell my sister I was not afraid": Report of Cpl. Jefferson White, Burial File of Pvt. Stanley Mullins, NPRC.

260. "The first wave crawled . . .": Hartney, Report of Company A.

260. "was struck thru the neck by a . . .": Report of Cpl. Jefferson White, Burial File of Pvt. Joe L. Graham, NPRC.

260. "[S]everal of the infantrymen . . .": van Natter letter, April 24, 1926.

260. "Never at any time did any . . .": Huebner, Report of 2nd Battalion.

260. "We reached our objective but did . . .": Hartney letter, "First Alumnus Killed in France."

260. "[n]o infantry formation for counterattack . . .": Oliver, Report of Company B.

260. "none seen": Sorensen, Report of Company D.

261. "Everything O.K. . . .": Message from 18th Infantry to 2nd Brigade, 6:26 p.m., May 29, 1918, Field Messages of 2nd Brigade.

261. "All is quiet along our lines": Entry, 6:50 p.m., May 29, 1918, 1st Field Artillery Brigade HQ Journal, NA, RG 120, Entry 1241, Box 61.

261. "I did notice that about sundown . . .": Sargent, "Cantigny," 38.

261. "novelty of silence": Ibid.

16. Final Determined Effort

263. "a personal reconnaissance . . .": Message from Ely, 8:55 p.m., May 29, 1918, 1st Artillery Brigade Records for Cantigny Operation, NA, RG 120, Entry 1241, Box 66.

263. "Front line pounded to Hell and gone . . .": Ibid.

263. "Let me tell you one thing . . .": Smythe, *Pershing*, 128.

264. "It is an injustice": Ibid.

264. "line is unchanged": Lt. Col. George Marshall, phone call to 2nd Brigade, 9:19 p.m., May 29, 1918, Field Messages of 2nd Brigade, NA, RG 120, Entry 1241, Box 41.

264. "At night as soon as it became dark . . .": Quinn, Report of Company G.

264. "By midnight it was dark enough . . .": Newhall, letter to mother, August 1, 1918, *Selected Papers*, 90–91.

264. "The effort caused me to faint . . .": Ibid.

264. "I put all my strength into the effort . . .": Gillespie, "Pickens Man in No Man's Land."

264. "There's no need now": Ibid.

265. "old wine cellar underneath a chateau": Joseph Torrence, letter to Robert Bullard, April 29, 1936, Bullard Papers, LOC, Box 5.

265. "asked Colonel Marshall if this officer . . .": Ibid.

265. "As a result of this contact with you . . .": Ibid.

265. "The valley was full of gas . . .": Wilder, "Operations of Company M," 25.

266. "It was immediately apparent . . .": Ibid.

266. "overcrowded with men": Ibid., 27.

266. "The only way I could move was upright . . .": Newhall, letter to mother, August 1, 1918, *Selected Papers*, 90–91.

266. "When I began to make my way through . . .": Ibid., 91.

267. "My first query was 'had we taken Cantigny?' . . .": Newhall, letter to Paul Birdsall, April 29, 1963, *Selected Papers*, 97.

267. "Moving on my stomach caused such pain . . .": Gillespie, "Pickens Man in No Man's Land."

267. "wait on Division": Message from 2nd Brigade to Ely, 8:15 p.m., May 29, 1918, Field Messages of 2nd Brigade, NA, RG 120, Entry 1241, Box 41.

268. "so that the sight of the bodies . . .": Report of First Sgt. John Klima, Burial File of Pvt. Forest G. Johns, NPRC. Note: original "moral" corrected to "morale."

268. "Battle, like baseball, . . .": Senay, "Shavetail," 37.

268. "enemy barrage came down on 1st and 2nd . . .": Field message received at 3:30 a.m., May 30, 1918, Cpt. William Livesay, 28th Infantry Regimental Report on Operations Against Cantigny, NA, RG 120, Entry 1241, Box 54.

269. "[T]he first wave got through before . . .": Ibid.

269. "final determined effort to retake the town": "History of the First Division," NA, RG 120, Entry 1241, Box 6, 25.

269. "a feint attack": War Diary, German 272nd Reserve Infantry Regiment, 150.

269. "no German set foot in Cantigny . . .": Beaumont Buck, *Memories in Peace and War*, 176–77.

269. "heavy concentrations of 77 . . .": 1st Division Journal, 6:21–6:45 p.m., May 30, 1918, NA, RG 120, Entry 1241, Box 9.

270. "very quickly, ran from one gun position . . .": Waltz, "Operations of Company C," 31.

270. "[T]he thought came to me that I might . . .": Gillespie, "Pickens Man in No Man's Land."

270. "the end of that pistol barrel pressed . . .": Ibid.

271. "I got them on the surface with their guns . . .": Waltz, "Operations of Company C," 31.

272. "I only went about 400 yards when I . . .": Pvt. Harry Heath, quoted in *Concord Enterprise* (MA), October 30, 1918.

272. "They could only stagger back . . .": Smythe, *Pershing*, 128.

272. "[T]here we found a great many dead . . .": Frank Last diary.

272. "the first meal we've had in three days": Suchocki, first account, NA, RG 117, Entry 31, Box 184, 7.

272. "[j]ust in time": Waltz, "Operations of Company C," 31.

273. "The Division Commander takes great pleasure . . .": Bullard, "Commendation of the 28th Infantry for the Capture and Holding of Cantigny," June 2, 1918, *History of the First*, 87.

273. "Well planned, splendidly executed": Allan R. Millett, *Well Planned, Splendidly Executed: The Battle of Cantigny, May 28–31, 1918*, 53.

273. "rolled in the nearest shell hole . . .": John D. Licklider, letter to War Department, July 30, 1926, Burial File of Pvt. Paul Davis, NPRC.

273. "helped bury a number of bodies there . . .": Report of Sgt. John R. Wallace, Burial File of Pvt. Harold H. Johnson, NPRC.

273. "under heavy artillery and machine-gun fire . . .": Report of Cpt. Ray Harrison, Ibid.

273. "There are shell holes in Cantigny . . .": John D. Licklider letter, July 30, 1926.

274. "Casualty lists of an attack like this . . .": Maj. Raymond Austin letter, June 1, 1918.

274. There were 275 bodies recovered . . . Unpublished "History of the First Division," NA, RG 120, Entry 1241, Box 7, 7.

274. 800 Germans killed . . . Col. Hanson Ely, June 3, 1918 attachment to June 2, 1918 Report on 28th Infantry Regt.

274. "combat strength": War Diary, German 26th Reserve Corps, 86.

274. "I prodded myself into action": Gillespie, "Pickens Man in No Man's Land."

274. "With renewed strength and hope . . .": Ibid.

274. "a fellow Yankee": Ibid.

275. "big jagged dent in the line": *The Story of the 16th Infantry in France*, 24.

276. "played into the hands of the Allies.": Pershing, *Experiences*, vol. 2, 157.

276. "marked the turning of the tide.": Ibid. 161.

276. "lost the initiative to the enemy.": Ibid. 162.

276. "the black day of the German Army": Ludendorff, *My War Memories*, vol. II, 678.

276. "set fire to all of the villages . . .": Summerall, *The Way of Duty*, 136.

276. "as nearly simultaneous as possible . . .": Pershing, *Experiences*, vol. 2, 280.

276. "[t]here is now no longer any possible hope . . .": Ibid. 342.

277. "a wonderful and inspiring feat of arms": Marshall, *Memoirs*, 192.

277. "Hostilities will be stopped on the entire front . . .": *History of the First*, 236.

277. "brought a confusion of incredulity . . . ": Ibid.

277. "On Nov. 11 at 11:00 a.m. those sounds . . .": Groves, WWI Veterans Survey.

277. 5,000 killed in action—more than 1,200 . . . *History of the First,* 337.

278. "[Y]ou, sons of America . . .": Gen. Charles A. Vandenburg, General Order from 10th French Army Corps, NA, RG 120, Entry 1241, Box 46.

278. "I saw more hell in two days at Cantigny . . .": Gerald Tyler, letter to ABMC, July 10, 1929; NA, RG 117, Entry 31, Box 184.

278. "exceeded any experience they were to have . . .": Marshall, *Memoirs,* 97.

278. "an electrical effect": Page, *Our 110 Days Fighting,* 29.

278. "Had it not been for Cantigny": Thomas, *History of the A.E.F.,* 78.

278. "[T]he short story of Cantigny is going to expand . . .": *London Evening News,* article reprinted in *Galveston Daily News* (TX), May 31, 1918.

278. "The artillery and infantry work of . . .": Statements of German prisoner, Summerall Papers, LOC, RG 291, Box 40.

278. "place[d] a scare": *San Antonio Light* (TX) May 29, 1938.

279. "This little village marks a cycle . . .": Marshall, *Memoirs,* 99.

EPILOGUE: Until We Meet Again

281. "Tenderly she tore open the envelope . . .": *The Call* (PA), June 21, 1918.

281. "Deeply regret to inform you that . . .": Telegram from War Department to Lettie Trout, June 20, 1918, Private Collection.

281. "full particulars of the sad event": Letter from War Department to Lettie Troup, June 22, 1918, Private Collection.

281. "going into the trenches again . . .": Carl Fey letter to mother, May 6, 1918, Private Collection.

281. "Kriegsgefangenenlager, Darmstadt . . .": Carl Fey letter to mother, June 5, 1918, Private Collection.

281. "Dear Mother, I thought I write . . .": Ibid.; note: "let you no" in original corrected to "let you know."

281. "Like word from the dead": *The Call* (PA), August 9, 1918.

282. "he never talked about the wound . . .": Michael Fey Hesser, e-mail to author, March 7, 2013.

282. "I forgot to say that Charley Avery . . .": Lt. Harry Martin, *Emporia Weekly Gazette* (KS), July 4, 1918.

282. "I saw your son, Harry, today . . .": Pvt. A. L. Strong, letter to Harry McCann, June 4, 1918, *Janesville Daily Gazette* (WI), August 31, 1918.

282. "asks you to give the news of him . . .": Ibid.

282. "reported missing in action": Letter from War Department to Linnie May Kendall, June 16, 1918, Burial File of Oliver J. Kendall, NPRC.

283. "Lieutenant Kendall—American Officer": Report of Oliver Grosvenor, Graves Registration Service, Burial File of Oliver Kendall.

283. "when the body was disinterred": Ibid.

283. on May 25, 1998 . . . Jeff Coen, "War Hero Finally Honored 80 Years After His Death," *Chicago Tribune* (IL), May 25, 1998.

283. "I was born lucky": Pvt. William N. Evans, *The Oxford Mirror* (IN), July 28, 1921.

284. Francis Redwood, the younger brother . . . Nelson, *Five Lieutenants.* 321–22.

284. kept his Distinguished Service Cross locked away . . . Interview with grandson, Hon. Samuel J. Ervin, IV, June 16, 2013, and June 15, 2014.

284. "old country lawyer": James Dickenson, "Sen. Sam Ervin, Key Figure in Watergate Probe, Dies," April 24, 1985, issue of *The Washington Post.*

285. "As a point of personal pride . . .": Parker, letter to brother, June 2, 1918.

285. "the people of the state of Illinois": Society for Military History, *Headquarters Gazette*, vol. 23, no. 2, Summer 2010, 1.

286. "bore his injury conspicuously . . .": Susan Dunn, writing on behalf of James MacGregor Burns, e-mail to author, September 26, 2013.

286. "To the Memory of George Guest Haydock . . .": Richard Newhall, *The English Conquest of Normandy,1416–1424: A Study in Fifteenth Century Warfare*, New Haven: Yale University Press, 1924, v.

286. "Cantigny Day": Nelson, *Five Lieutenants*. 330.

286. "his platoon in an attack . . .": *WWR*, vol. 23.

286. "quite inaccurate": Newhall, letter to mother, May 18, 1919, *Select Papers*, 86.

286. "I have no desire to fly any . . .": Ibid.

286. "most perfect": Nelson, *Five Lieutenants*, 159.

287. "No Retreat Bullard": Millett, *The General*, 369.

287. "dilapidated, walk-up office . . .": Ibid., 468.

287. "It seems only yesterday that I saw . . .": Farrell letter, January 11, 1925.

287. "I am frank to state that in my opinion . . .": Torrence letter, April 29, 1936.

288. "My job as an officer was to make . . .": Millett, *The General*, 470.

289. his mind and memory sadly deteriorated . . . : Thomas Ricks, *The Generals: American Military Command from World War II to Today*, 189.

290. "He got hit, and I raised him up . . .": Frank Groves, interview with First Division Museum director Tom Votaw, July 11, 1996, FDM.

291. "Dear Mother: I am writing . . .": Pvt. Ruffus Shelton, May 27, 1918, letter to mother Ruth Ann, February 25, 1919, issue of *Galveston Daily News* (TX).

SELECTED BIBLIOGRAPHY

Books and Periodicals

Bailey, J.B.A. *Field Artillery and Firepower*. Oxford: The Military Press, 1989.

Beaver, Daniel R. *Newton D. Baker and the American War Effort*. Lincoln: University of Nebraska Press, 1966.

Berg, A. Scott. *Wilson*. New York: G.P. Putnam's Sons, 2013.

Berry, Henry. *Make the Kaiser Dance: The American Experience in World War I*. New York: Doubleday, 1978.

Blumenson, Martin, and James L Stokesbury. *Masters of the Art of Command*. Boston: Houghton Mifflin, 1975.

Bowman, Stephen L. (Col., ret.). *A Century of Valor—The First One Hundred Years of the Twenty-Eighth United States Infantry Regiment—Black Lions*. Wheaton, IL: Cantigny First Division Foundation, 2004.

Browne, G. Waldo, and Resecrans W. Pillsbury. *The American Army in the World War: A Divisional Record of the American Expeditionary Forces in Europe*. Manchester, NH: Overseas Book Company, 1921.

Bruce, Robert. *Machine Guns of World War I*. London: Windrow and Greene, 1997.

Bull, Dr. Stephen. *World War I Trench Warfare (2) 1916–1918*. Oxford, UK: Osprey Publishing, 2002.

Clancy, Paul R. *Just a Country Lawyer—A Biography of Senator Sam Ervin*. Indianapolis: Indiana University Press, 1974.

Clements, Kendrick A. *Woodrow Wilson—World Statesman*. Chicago: Ivan R. Dee, 1999.

Clifford, John Garry. *Citizen Soldiers: The Plattsburg Training Camp Movement, 1913–1920*. Lexington: University Press of Kentucky, 1972.

Coffman, Edward M. *The Old Army: A Portrait of the American Army in Peacetime, 1784–1898*. New York: Oxford University Press, 1986.

———. *The Regulars: The American Army, 1898–1941*. Cambridge, MA: Belknap Press of Harvard University Press, 2004.

———. *The War to End All Wars—The American Military Experience in World War I*. New York: Oxford University Press, 1968.

Cooke, James J. *Pershing and His Generals: Command and Staff in the AEF*. Westport, CT: Praeger, 1997.

Cooper, John Milton, Jr. *Woodrow Wilson—A Biography*. New York: Vintage Books, 2009.

Cron, Hermann, translated by C. F. Colton, M.A. *Imperial German Army 1914–1918—Organization, Structure, Orders-of-Battle*. United Kingdom: Helion & Company, 2001 (originally published as *Geschichte des Deutschen Heeres im Weltkriege 1914–1918* in Berlin, Germany, 1937).

Cullum, George W. (Brevet Maj. Gen., ret.), ed. *Biographical Register of the Officers and Graduates of the U.S. Military Academy at West Point, New York*. Saginaw, MI: Seemann & Peters, Printers, 1920.

Drury, Ian. *German Stormtrooper 1914–1918*. Oxford, UK: Osprey Publishing, 1995.

Eisenhower, John S. D., and Joanne Thompson Eisenhower. *Yanks—The Epic Story of the American Army in the First World War*. New York: A Touchstone Book, published by Simon & Schuster, 2001.

Ervin, Samuel J. Jr. *Preserving the Constitution: The Autobiography of Senator Sam J. Ervin Jr.* Charlottesville, VA: Michie, 1985.

Farwell, Byron. *Over There—The United States in the Great War, 1917–1918*. New York & London: W. W. Norton, 1999.

Faulkner, Richard S. *The School of Hard Knocks: Combat Leadership in the American Expeditionary Forces*, Texas A&M University Press, 2012.

Ferrell, Robert H. *America's Deadliest Battle: Meuse-Argonne, 1918*. University Press of Kansas, 2007.

Ganoe, William Addleman. *The History of the United States Army*. New York and London: D. Appleton, 1924.

Garey, E. B., O. O. Ellis, and R.V.D. Magoffin. *The American Guidebook to France and Its Battlefields*. New York: Macmillan, 1920.

Gilbert, Martin. *The First World War: A Complete History*. New York: Henry Holt, 1994.

Goerlitz, Walter. *History of the German General Staff 1657–1945*. Translated by Brian Battershaw. New York: Praeger, 1959. (Originally published as *Der Deutsche Generalstab*. Frankfurt am Main: Verlag der Frankfurter Hefte).

Gray, Randal. *Kaiserschlacht 1918—The Final German Offensive*. Oxford, UK: Osprey, 1991.

Griess, Thomas E., ed. *The West Point Atlas for the Great War*. Garden City Park, NY: Square One Publishers, 2003.

Grotelueschen. Mark E. *The AEF Way of War—The American Army and Combat in World War I*. Cambridge University Press, 2007.

———. *Doctrine Under Trial: American Artillery Employment in World War I*. Westport, Connecticut: Greenwood Press, 2000.

Hallas, James H., ed. *Doughboy War—The American Expeditionary Force in WWI*. Mechanicsburg, PA: Stackpole Books, 2000.

Harries, Meirion, and Susie Harries. *The Last Days of Innocence: America at War, 1917–1918*. New York: Vintage Books, 1997.

Harris, Stephen L. *Harlem's Hellfighters*. Washington, DC: Potomac Books, 2003.

Hart, Peter. *The Great War: A Combat History of the First World War*. New York: Oxford University Press, 2013.

———. *The Somme: The Darkest Hour on the Western Front*. New York: Pegasus Books, 2008.

Hatcher, Julian S., Glenn P. Wilhelm, and Harry J. Malony. *Machine Guns*. Menasha, WI: George Banta, 1917.

Herbert, Paul (Col., ret.). "The Battle of Cantigny." *On Point: The Journal of Army History*. Spring 2007.

Herwig, Holger. *The First World War: Germany and Austria-Hungary 1914–1918*. London: Arnold, 1997.

———. *The Marne, 1914*. New York: Random House, 2009.

Hicks, Maj. James E. *German Weapons, Uniforms, Insignia 1841–1918*. La Canada, CA: James E. Hicks & Son, 1937.

Holt, Hamilton. "The Black Snakes: A Visit to Bullard's Boys at Cantigny." *The Independent*. August 3, 1918.

Huelfer, Evan Andrew. *The "Casualty Issue" in American Military Practice: The Impact of World War I.* Westport, CT: Praeger, 2003.

Hughes, Daniel J., ed. *Moltke on the Art of War: Selected Writings.* New York: Presidio Press, 1993.

Jäger, Herbert. *German Artillery of World War I.* Wiltshire, UK: The Crowood Press, 2001.

Johnson, Douglas V., II, and Rolfe L. Hillman Jr. *Soissons 1918.* College Station: Texas A&M University Press, 1999.

Keegan, John. *The Face of Battle.* London: Penguin Group, 1978.

———. *The First World War.* New York: Vintage Books, 2000.

Kennedy, David M. *Over Here: The First World War and American Society.* New York: Oxford University Press, 1982.

Lengel, Edward G. *To Conquer Hell: The Meuse-Argonne, 1918.* New York: Henry Holt, 2008.

Lloyd, Nick. *Hundred Days: The Campaign That Ended World War I.* London: Viking, 2013.

Marshall, S.L.A. *World War I.* Boston: Houghton Mifflin Company, 1964; updated 1987.

Mead, Gary. *The Doughboys: America and the First World War.* New York: Penguin, 2000.

Meyer, G. J. *A World Undone: The Story of the Great War, 1914–1918.* New York: Bantam Dell, 2006.

Millett, Allan R. *The General—Robert L. Bullard and Officership in the United States Army, 1881–1925.* Westport, CT & London, England: Greenwood Press, 1975.

———. *Well Planned, Splendidly Executed: The Battle of Cantigny, May 28–31, 1918.* Wheaton, IL: Cantigny First Division Foundation, 2010.

Mosley, Leonard. *Marshall—Hero for our Times.* New York: Hearst Books, 1982.

Nash, David. *German Artillery 1914–1918.* Middlesex, England: Almark, 1970.

———. *German Infantry 1914–1918.* Middlesex, England: Almark, 1971.

Neiberg, Michael S. *Fighting the Great War: A Global History.* Boston: Harvard University Press, 2006.

———. *The Military Atlas of World War 1.* New York: Chartwell Books, 2014.

———. *The Second Battle of the Marne.* Bloomington and Indianapolis: Indiana University Press, 2008.

———. *The Western Front 1914-1916: From the Schlieffen Plan to Verdun and the Somme.* London: Amber Books, 2011.

Nelson, James Carl. *Five Lieutenants.* New York: St. Martin's Griffin, 2012.

———. *The Remains of Company D.* New York: St. Martin's Griffin, 2009.

Newhall, Richard. *The English Conquest of Normandy, 1416–1424: A Study in Fifteenth Century Warfare.* New Haven: Yale University Press, 1924.

Nichols, W. Gary. *American Leader in War and Peace—The Life and Times of WW1 Soldier, Army Chief of Staff and Citadel President General Charles P. Summerall.* Shippensburg, PA: White Mane Books, 2011.

Page, Arthur. *Our 110 Days Fighting.* Garden City, NY: Doubleday, Page, 1920.

Palmer, Frederick. *America in France.* New York: Dodd, Mead, 1918.

———. *Newton D. Baker: America at War,* 2 Vols. New York: Dodd, Mead, 1931.

———. *Our Greatest Battle (The Meuse-Argonne).* New York: Dodd, Mead, 1919.

Perry, John. *Pershing.* Nashville: Thomas Nelson, 2011.

Pogue, Forrest C. *George C. Marshall: Education of a General, 1880–1939.* New York: Viking Press, 1963.

Pugh, Irving Edwin, and William F. Thayer. *Forgotten Fights of the A.E.F.* Boston: Roxburgh Publishing, 1921.

Ricks, Thomas E. *The Generals: American Military Command from World War II to Today.* New York: Penguin, 2012.

Roberts, Andrew. *Masters and Commanders: How Roosevelt, Churchill, Marshall, and Alanbrooke Won the War in the West, 1941–1945.* New York: Harper Perennial, 2008.

Rubin, Richard. *The Last of the Doughboys: The Forgotten Generation and Their Forgotten World War.* Boston, New York: Houghton Mifflin Harcourt, 2013.

Scott, Emmett J. *Scott's Official History of the American Negro in the World War.* Washington, DC: Privately Published, 1919.

Sheffield, Gary, ed. *War on the Western Front—In the Trenches of World War I.* Oxford, UK: Osprey, 2007.

Smith, Gene. *Until the Last Trumpet Sounds: The Life of General of the Armies John J. Pershing.* New York: John Wiley & Sons, 1998.

Smith, Richard Norton. *The Colonel: The Life and Legend of Robert R. McCormick 1880–1955.* Boston and New York: Houghton Mifflin, 1997.

Smythe, Donald. *Guerilla Warrior: The Early Life of John J. Pershing.* New York: Charles Scribner's Sons, 1973.

———. *Pershing: General of the Armies.* Bloomington & Indianapolis: Indiana University Press, 1986.

Stallings, Laurence. *The Doughboys: The Story of the AEF, 1917–1918.* New York: Popular Library, 1964.

Strachan, Hew. *The First World War.* New York: Viking Penguin, 2004.

———. *The First World War: To Arms.* New York: Oxford University Press, 2001.

Strong, Paul, and Sanders Marble. *Artillery in the Great War.* London: Pen & Sword Books, 2011.

Thomas, Shipley, *The History of the A.E.F.* Nashville: The Battery Press, 1920.

Toland, John. *No Man's Land: 1918, the Last Year of the Great War.* Garden City, NY: Doubleday, 1980.

Tuchman, Barbara W. *The Guns of August.* New York: Random House, 1962,

———. *The Zimmerman Telegram.* New York: Random House, 1958.

Vandiver, Frank Everson. *Black Jack: The Life and Times of John J. Pershing.* 2 Vols. College Station: Texas A&M University Press, 1977.

Venzon, Anne Cipriano, ed. *The United States in the First World War: An Encyclopedia.* New York: 1995.

Votaw, John F. (Lt. Col., ret.), with consultant ed. Dr. Duncan Anderson. *The American Expeditionary Forces in World War I.* Oxford, UK: Osprey, 2005.

Wise, Jennings C. *The Turn of the Tide—American Operations at Cantigny, Chateau Thierry, and the Second Battle of the Marne.* New York: Henry Holt, 1920.

Zaloga, Steven J. *French Tanks of World War I.* Oxford, UK: Osprey, 2010.

Official Histories and Publications

American Armies and Battlefields in Europe. ABMC. Washington, DC: Government Printing Office, 1938.

Armistice Day: North Carolina in the World War. Raleigh, NC: State Superintendent of Public Instruction, 1921.

Brockton's Honor Roll of Her Sons Who Made the Supreme Sacrifice in the World War. Brockton, MA: Brockton World War Victory Association, May 1919.

Congressional Medal of Honor, the Distinguished Service Cross, and the Distinguished Service Medal Issued by the War Department Since April 6, 1917. US Adjutant General's Office. Washington, DC: Government Printing Office, 1920.

Field Service Regulations—United States Army, 1914 (Corrected to April 15, 1917). Washington, DC: Government Printing Office, 1917.

1st Division, Summary of Operations in the World War, ABMC. Washington, DC: Government Printing Office, 1944.

Histories of the Two Hundred and Fifty-One Divisions of the German Army Which Participated in the War (1914–1918). Washington, DC: Government Printing Office, 1920.

The History and Achievements of the Fort Sheridan Officers' Training Camps. Myron E. Adams and Fred Girton, eds. Fort Sheridan, IL: The Association, 1920.

History of the First Division During the World War 1917–1919. Society of the First Division. Philadelphia: John C. Winston, 1922.

A History of the 1st U.S. Engineers 1st Division. American Expeditionary Forces. Coblenz, Germany, 1919.

Infantry Drill Regulations, United States Army, 1911. US War Department. New York: Military Publishing, 1911.

Infantry in Battle. Washington, DC: The Infantry Journal Incorporated, 1939.

Order of Battle of the United States Land Forces in the World War. Washington, DC: Government Printing Office, 1931.

Soldiers in the Great War, Volumes I–III. Compiled by W. M. Haulsee, F. G. Howe, and A. C. Doyle. Washington, DC: Soldiers Record Publishing Association, 1920.

Source Records of the Great War, Volumes I–VII. Charles F. Horne, PhD, editor. Indianapolis: The American Legion, 1931.

The Story of the Sixteenth Infantry in France. American Expeditionary Forces, 1919.

The Story of the Twenty-Eighth Infantry in the Great War. American Expeditionary Forces, 1919.

St. Paul's School in the Great War: 1914–1918. Concord, NH: St. Paul's Alumni Association, 1926.

The Twenty-Sixth Infantry in France. American Expeditionary Forces, July 1919.

United States Army in the World War, 1917–1919. 17 vols. US Department of the Army, Historical Division. Washington, DC: Government Printing Office, 1948.

The War with Germany: A Statistical Summary. Leonard P. Ayers, ed. Washington, DC: Government Printing Office, 1919.

World War Records. U.S. Army, First Division A.E.F. Regular. 25 Volumes. Washington, DC: Government Printing Office, 1928–1930.

Published Letters, Diaries, and Memoirs

Buck, Beaumont B. *Memories in Peace and War*. San Antonio, TX: The Naylor Company, 1925.

Bullard, Robert Lee. *Fighting Generals: Illustrated Biographical Sketches of Seven Major Generals in World War I*. Ann Arbor, MI: J. W. Edwards, 1944.

———. *Personalities and Reminiscences of the War*. Garden City, NY: Doubleday, Page, 1925.

———, in collaboration with Earl Reeves. *American Soldiers Also Fought*. New York: Maurice H. Louis, 1939.

Dawes, Charles Gates. *A Journal of the Great War, Volume I*. Boston and New York: Houghton Mifflin, 1921.

Dearing, Vinton A., *My Galahad of the Trenches: Being a Collection of Intimate Letters of Lieut. Vinton A. Dearing*. Compiled and with introduction by Mary A. Dearing. New York, Chicago, London: Fleming H. Revell, 1918.

Evans, Martin Marix, ed. *American Voices of World War I: Primary Source Documents, 1917–1920*. Chicago: Fitzroy Dearborne, 2001.

Evarts, Jeremiah M. *Cantigny: A Corner of the War*. USA: Privately Printed, 1938.

Harbord, James G. *The American Army in France, 1917–1919*. Boston: Little, Brown, 1936.

———. *Leaves from a War Diary*. New York: Dodd, Mead, 1925.

Howe, M. A. DeWolfe, ed. *Memoirs of the Harvard Dead in the War Against Germany*. 3 Vols. Cambridge: Harvard University Press, 1921.

Johnston, Edward S. "Portrait of a Soldier" and "The Day Before Cantigny." *Americans vs. Germans.* Washington, DC: The Infantry Journal, 1942.

Ludendorff, Erich F. W. *My War Memories 1914–1918, Volumes I & II.* London: Hutchinson, 1919.

Marshall, George C. *Memoirs of My Services in the World War 1917–1918.* Boston: Houghton Mifflin, 1976.

McCormick, Robert R. *The Army of 1918.* New York: Harcourt, Brace, and Howe, 1920.

McLendon, Idus R., "Before Cantigny," article in *Field Artillery Journal* 18, Nov–Dec 1928.

Newhall, Richard. *Newhall and Williams College: Selected Papers of a History Teacher at a New England College 1917–1973.* Edited by Russell H. Bostert. New York: Peter Lang Publishing, 1989.

———. "With the First Division—Winter 1917–1918," article in *The Historical Outlook,* 10, no. 7, October 1919.

Palmer, Frederick. *Our Greatest Battle.* New York: Dodd, Mead, 1919.

Pershing, John J. *My Experiences in the World War.* 2 Vols. New York: Frederick A. Stokes, 1931.

Roosevelt, Theodore Jr. *Average Americans (1919).* New York and London: G. P. Putnam's Sons, the Knickerbocker Press, 1920.

Suchocki, Boleslaw. "The Battle of Cantigny—As Seen by One Who Was There." *The Military Engineer,* 13, no. 71, October 1921.

Summerall, Charles Pelot. *The Way of Duty, Honor, Country—The Memoir of General Charles Pelot Summerall.* Edited and annotated by Timothy K. Nenninger. University Press of Kentucky, 2010.

Archival Records and Oral Histories

Alabama Textual Materials Collection, Alabama Department of Archives & History, Birmingham, AL
Letter from Lt. "Doc" Bedsole, letter to sister, August 17, 1918
Army Heritage and Education Center, US Army War College, Carlisle Barracks, PA
Letters of Maj. Raymond B. Austin, March–June, 1918
Unpublished memoir by Lt. Daniel Sargent, F Battery, 5th Field Artillery
Unpublished memoir by Pvt. Earl D. Seaton, signaler, 16th Infantry
World War I Veterans Surveys
Combined Arms Research Library, Ft. Leavenworth, KS
"The 1st Division at Cantigny, May 1918," by Rexmond C. Cochrane, US Army Chemical Corps
"History of the 7th Field Artillery (First Division A.E.F.)" Privately Published
First Division Museum and the Colonel Robert R. McCormick Research Center, Cantigny, IL
Diary of Cpt. Francis M. van Natter, Co. L, 28th Infantry Regiment
Diary of Cpl. Tom Carroll, Co. F, 16th Infantry Regiment
Diary of Pvt. Frank J. Last, Co. G, 18th Infantry Regiment
Diary of Pvt. Jesse O. Evans, Co. L, 18th Infantry Regiment
Diary of PFC Vernon L. Scobie, 2nd Ambulance Co., 1st Division
Diary of 2nd Lt. Daniel Birmingham
"Foot Soldiers," unpublished memoir by 1st Division soldier Ben H. Bernheisel
"Journal of Operations, December 23, 1917, through October 12, 1918," by Alban B. Butler
Pvt. Frank Groves, interview by Tom Votaw, July 11, 1996

Letters of Lt. Daniel Birmingham, April–June, 1918
Letter from Pvt. Frank Groves to mother, March 3, 1919
Letter from Pvt. Jefferson D. White, August 1, 1962
Muster Rolls, US 1st Division AEF, June, 1917–October, 1918
US Army Signal Corps Photographic Collection, 1917–1923
George C. Marshall Foundation Library
Hanson E. Ely, Speeches 1929 and 1931, Collection No. 45
Mervyn F. Burke Collection, Collection No. 30
Infantry School Monographs, Donovan Research Library, Ft. Benning, GA
Capt. Edward S. Johnston, "The Day Before Cantigny (Personal Experience)."
Capt. George E. Butler, "The Battle of Cantigny (Personal Experience)."
Capt. Paul B. Parker, "The Battle of Cantigny (Personal Experience)".
Capt. Welcome Waltz, "Operations of Co. C, 3rd M.G. Battalion (Personal Experience)."
Maj. Stuart G. Wilder, "Operations of Co. M, 16th Infantry (Personal Experience)."
Library of Congress, Washington, DC
Papers of Charles P. Summerall
Papers of John J. Pershing
Papers of Robert L. Bullard
Papers of Theodore Roosevelt Jr.
Maryland Historical Society Library, Baltimore, MD
Papers of George B. Redwood
National Archives, Washington, DC
Correspondence with former officers of the 1st Division, RG 117, Entry 31
"The Night Before Cantigny," alternate account of the quarry shelling by Sgt. Boleslaw
    Suchocki, RG 117, Entry 31, Box 184
"The Night Before Cantigny," memoir of the battle by Sgt. Boleslaw Suchocki, Co. D, 1st
    Engineers, RG 120, Entry 1241, Box 6
Records of the US Army 1st Division in World War I, RG 120, Entry 1241 (73 Boxes)
Records of the War Department General and Special Staffs, RG 165
National Personnel Records Center, St. Louis, MO
Burial Files of the US Army Adjutant General, Cemeterial Division
Morning Reports, Companies of the US 1st Division, May–June, 1918
Pennsylvania State Archives, PA Historical & Museum Commission, Harrisburg, PA
Letter from Capt. Edward S. Johnston to the sister of Lt. John Curry, November 20, 1918
Letter from Lt. Charles A. Avery to the sister of Lt. John Curry, April 28, 1919
Letter from Lt. Irving W. Wood to the sister of Lt. John Curry, January 8, 1919
Queens Library, New York, NY
Letters of Lt. John H. Church, January, 1918–August, 1919, "The Charles Crispin
Scrapbook of John H. Church during World War I, 1918–1919" (courtesy of James Carl
    Nelson)
Southern Historical Collection, Wilson Library, UNC–Chapel Hill
Papers of Frank Parker
Papers of Samuel J. Ervin Jr.
Union County Library and Union County Heritage Room, Union County Courthouse, Mon-
    roe, NC
The Samuel I. Parker Collection
Williams College, Williamstown, MA
Papers of Richard A. Newhall
Wisconsin Veterans Museum, Madison, WI
Diary of Pvt. Ruben J. Nelson

Private Collections

Letters of Lt. Herman "Dick" Dacus, August 15, 1984 (courtesy of James Carl Nelson)
Letters of Lt. L. Irwin Morris, April–June, 1918
Letters of Lt. James L. Hartney, April 1917–December, 1918 (Courtesy of James Carl Nelson)
Letters of Lt. Robert B. Anderson, April–May, 1918
Letters of Lt. Samuel I. Parker, June–December, 1918
Letters of Pvt. Carl Fey, May–November, 1918
Letters of Pvt. Robert I. Gilliam, June–October, 1918
Letters of Sgt. Carl R. Sohncke, February, 1916–May, 1918
"Shavetail to Captain," unpublished memoir by Capt. Charles T. Senay

German Sources

Reichsarchiv, *Der Weltkrieges 1914 bis 1918,* Berlin: Verlag Mittler & Sohn, 1925–1929.
Reichsarchiv, *Schlachten des Weltkrieges,* Bands 32, 33. Berlin, 1930.
War Diary of the 18th Army, May 27–31 (translation from the original on file in the German Reichsarchive by Major Harm, US Army), National Archives, RG 165.
War Diary of the 26th Reserve Corps, May 27–June 5 (translation from the original on file in the German Reichsarchive by Major Harm), National Archives, RG 165.
War Diary of the 272nd Reserve Infantry Regiment, May 27–June 6 (extracts translated from the original on file in the German Reichsarchive by Major Harm), National Archives, RG 165.

Newspapers and Periodicals

Ackley World Journal (IA)
Acton Concord Enterprise (MA)
Aiken Journal and Review (SC)
Altoona Mirror (PA)
Atlanta Constitution (GA)
The Arkansas City Daily News (KS)
The Baltimore Sun (MD)
Boston Daily Globe (MA)
The Boston Globe (MA)
The Call (PA)
Charlotte Observer (NC)
Chicago Tribune (IL)
Clearfield Progress (PA)
Clinton Daily Clintonian (IN)
Collier's, The National Weekly
Concord Enterprise (MS)
Coshocton Tribune (OH)
Decatur Daily Democrat (IN)
Denton Record-Chronicle (TX)
Des Moines Daily News (IA)
Emporia Gazette (KS)
Emporia Weekly Gazette (KS)
Fort Des Moines Post (IA)
Fort Wayne Journal Gazette (IN)

Galveston Daily News (TX)
Holyrood Gazette (KS)
The Independent
Indiana Evening Gazette (PA)
Ironwood News Record (MI)
Janesville Daily Gazette (WI)
Kansas City Star (KS)
La Crosse Tribune and Leader Press (WI)
Lima Daily News (OH)
Marion Daily Star (OH)
Mexia Weekly Herald (TX)
Middlesboro Pinnacle News (KY)
Monroe Enquirer (NC)
Monroe Enquirer-Journal
Monroe Journal (NC)
Muskogee Times Democrat (OK)
New Castle News (PA)
The New York Times
New-York Tribune
News & Observer (NC)
Portland Commercial Review (IN)
Reno Evening Gazette (NV)
Rushville Daily Democrat (IN)
San Antonio Evening News (TX)
San Antonio Light (TX)
The Stars and Stripes
Steubenville Herald Star (OH)
The Times (London, UK)
The Washington Post (DC)
Waterloo Evening Courier (IA)
The Wilkes-Barre Times (PA)
Woodland Daily Democrat (CA)

INDEX

ML   .7-15